The Calligraphy Book

Lindsey Bugbee

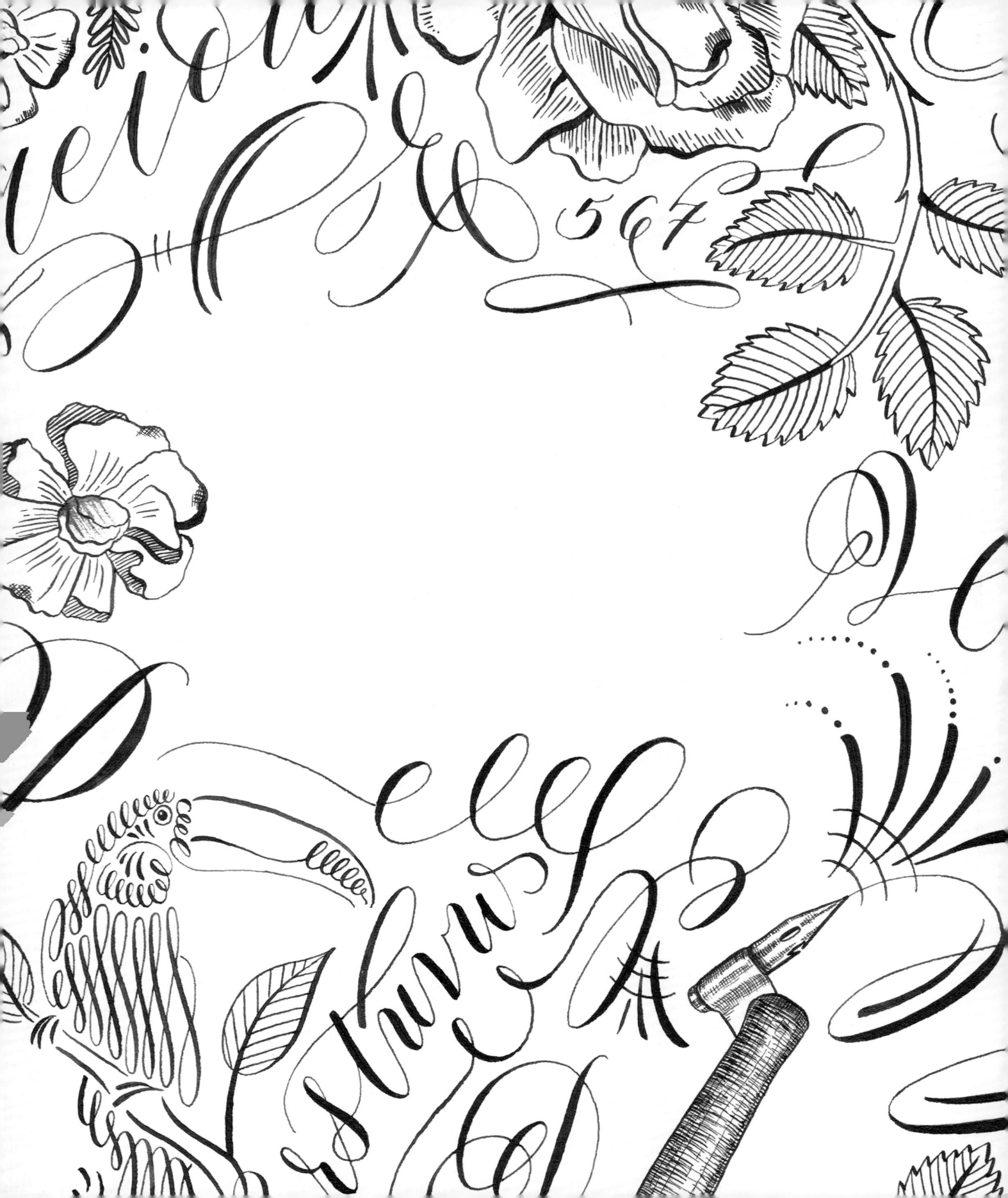

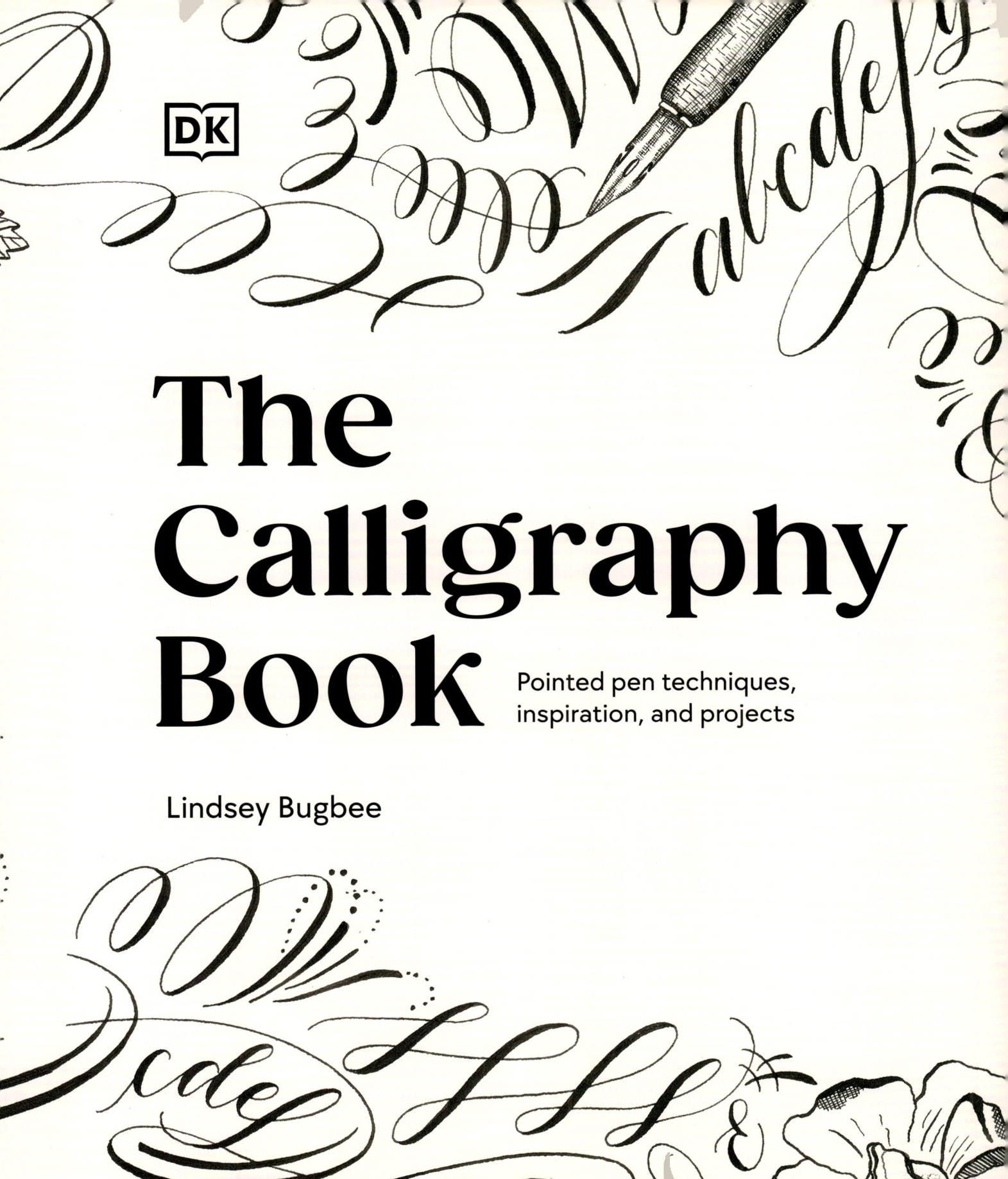

DK

The Calligraphy Book

Pointed pen techniques, inspiration, and projects

Lindsey Bugbee

Contents

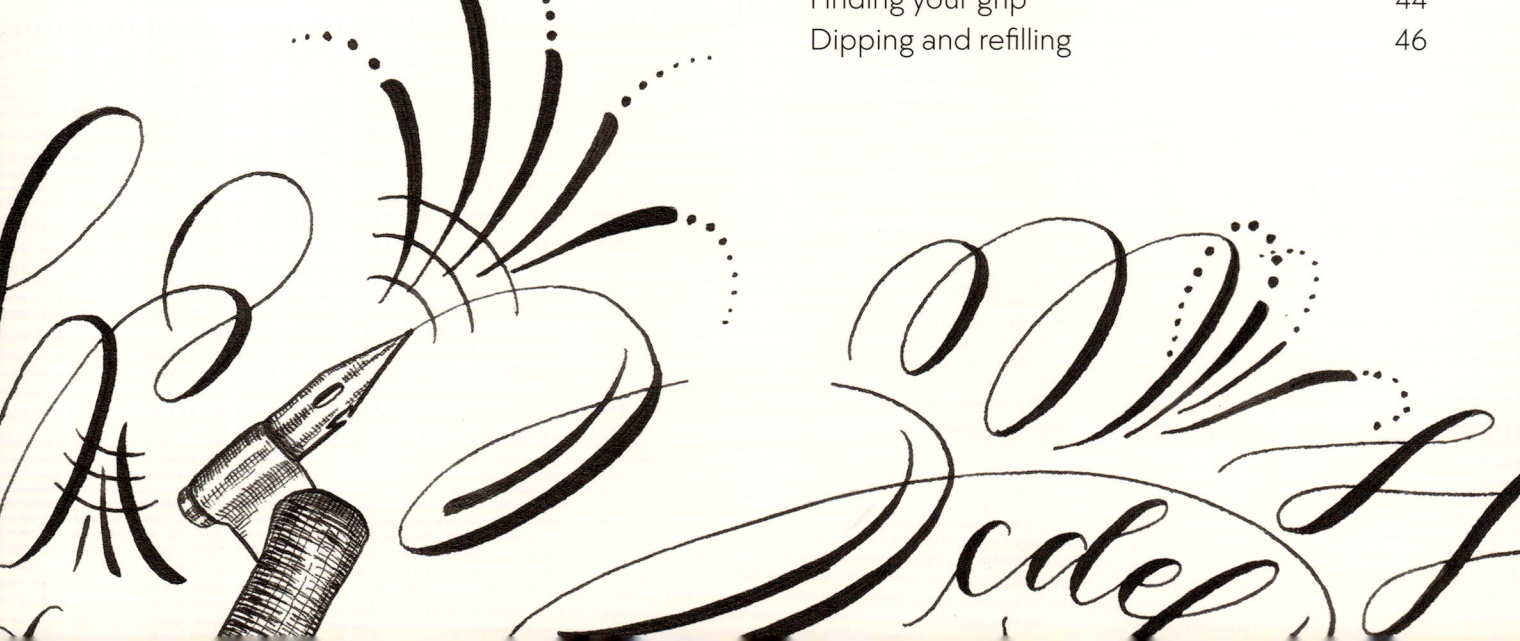

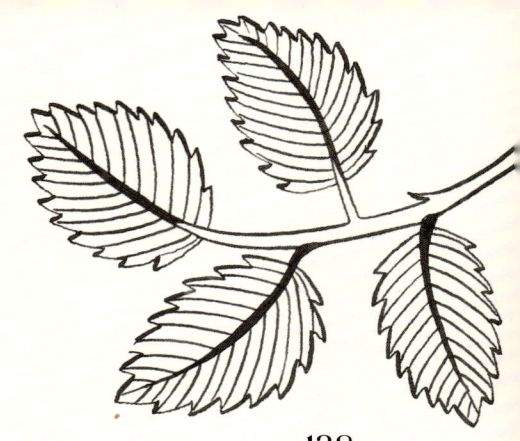

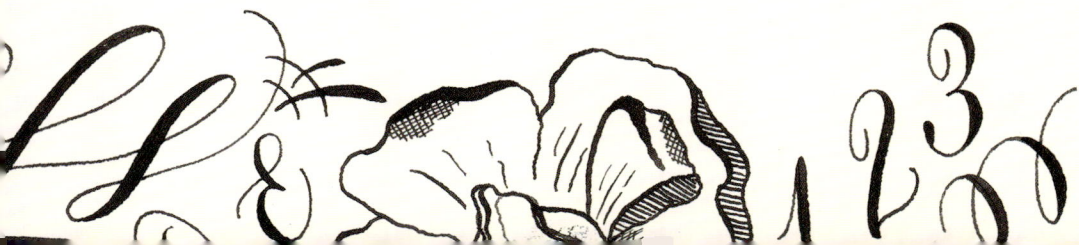

Introduction

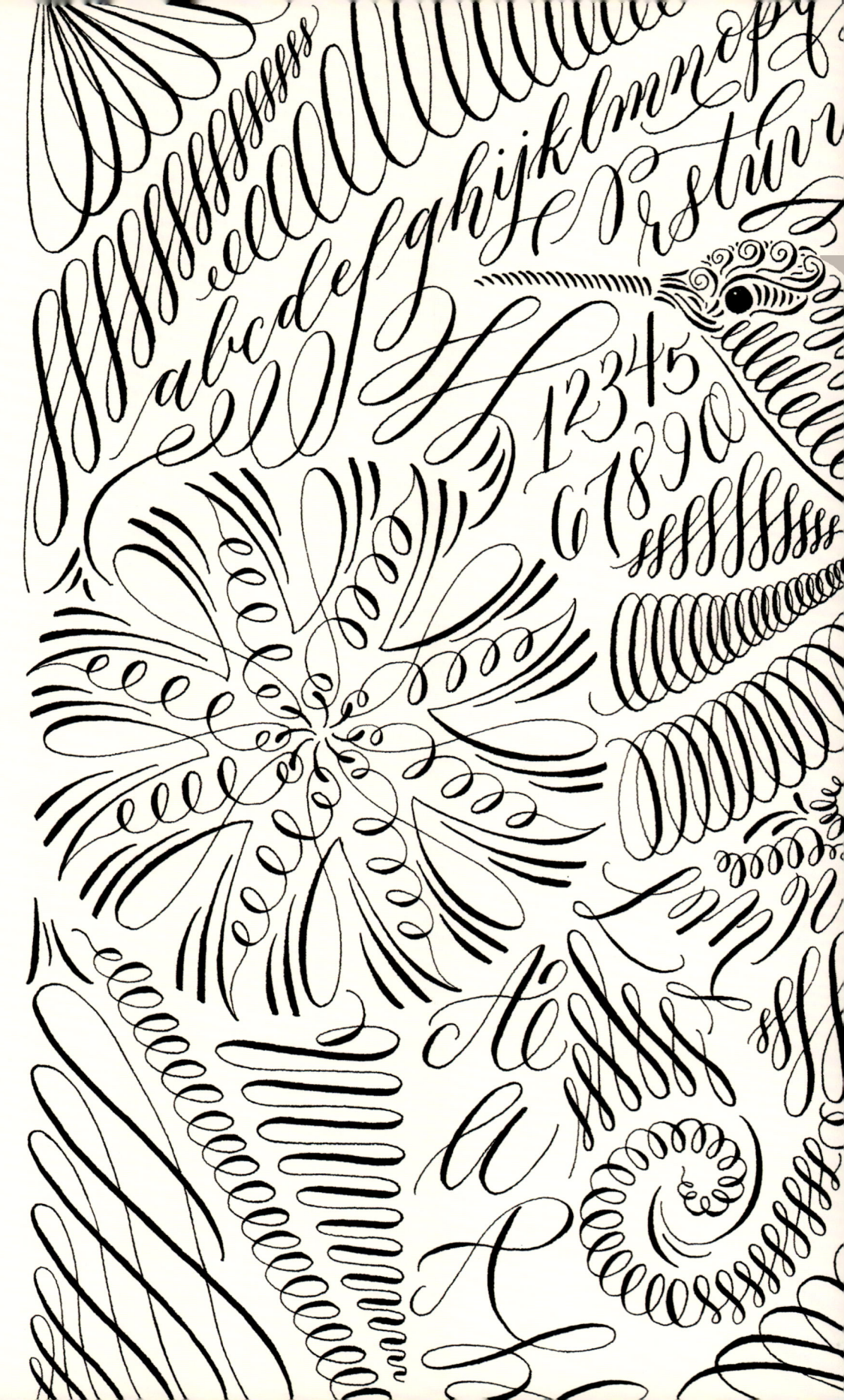

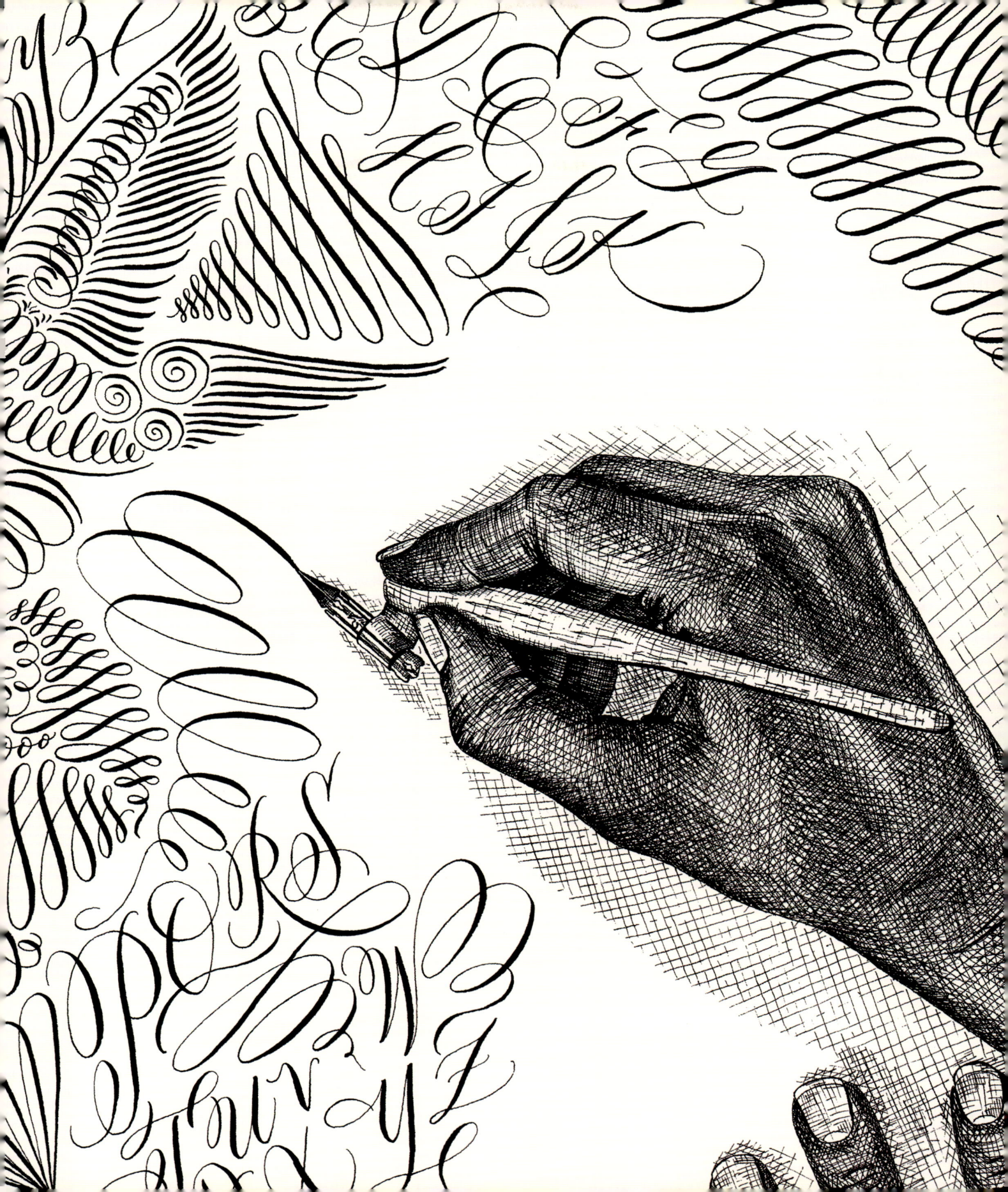

Discovering calligraphy

Calligraphy is an uncommon skill, and something that adds intrigue to even the simplest piece of paper. In an age where digital text reigns supreme, the tactile pleasure of pen and ink connects us with the artistry of the written word and allows for self-expression.

My path to calligraphy

My interest in calligraphy was born out of homesickness. After graduation, my husband and I moved from Kansas to Colorado so he could pursue his PhD. I soon began to miss my friends, so I started writing letters to them. I found comfort and creativity in these stationery endeavors. At that time, I wasn't trying to create calligraphy. I just liked drawing on envelopes.

Later, I began working as an office manager at a software company in Boulder, Colorado. It wasn't the job of my dreams, so I found myself pondering alternative career paths. When a friend at work mentioned that she created wedding envelope calligraphy for extra income, a seed was planted. I found myself looking at examples of calligraphy online, which led me to modern pointed pen calligraphy. I fell in love with this style of writing because it takes words and turns them into expressive works of art.

The Postman's Knock

It wasn't long before I bought a pointed pen calligraphy kit at a craft store. I gave calligraphy a try and failed miserably, which is unsurprising: I had the wrong materials and zero instruction. Undeterred, I started an Etsy shop called The Postman's Knock (TPK) and began taking "faux calligraphy" commissions created with a ballpoint pen. The idea behind the name came from the hope that my clients, and their envelope calligraphy recipients, would be delighted to hear "the postman's knock."

While a ballpoint pen was my comfort zone, I was determined to figure out how to properly wield a pointed pen. As I experimented, I began writing about my

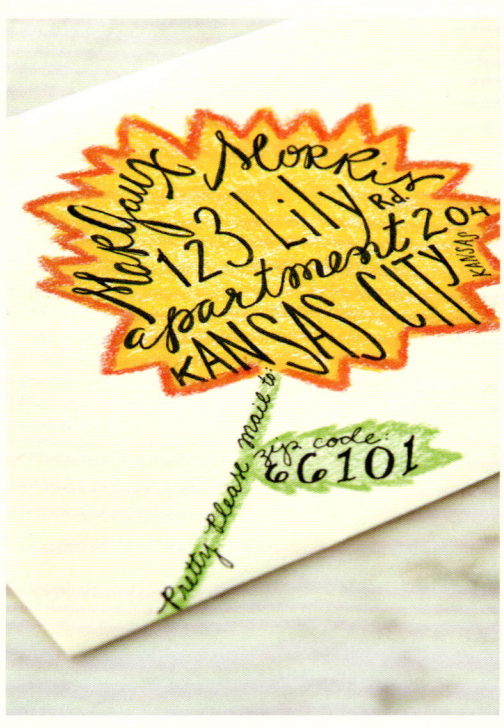

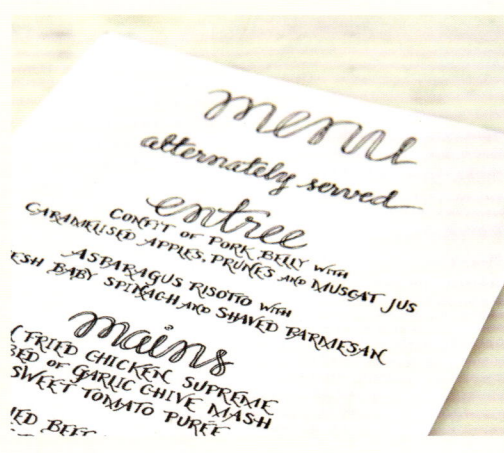

Top: An early example of my calligraphy, showing an undeveloped style.

Above: A faux calligraphy style of writing done with a regular pen.

experiences on my blog. I detailed the calligraphy problems that thwarted me and what I did to solve them, posted tutorials, and developed instructions to create a variety of calligraphy-related projects.

Over the years, I've continued to write blog posts. As a result, The Postman's Knock (TPK) has become the premier source on the web for all things calligraphy. My teaching philosophy is to break things down into simple steps and never assume anything.

Teaching calligraphy

If there's something I love just as much as creating calligraphy, it's teaching calligraphy. This book aims to set you up for success in your pointed pen calligraphy endeavors and ignite your creativity. You'll learn the basics and find inspiration in project tutorials that give you the chance to hone your skills. Beyond a basic knowledge of cursive writing, there are no prerequisites for creating calligraphy. The clearest path to success is keeping your practice fresh with a variety of projects. As you create calligraphy, be gentle with yourself. While it's beneficial to recognize deficiencies in your work and fix them in the future, a focus on the things you did well will keep you motivated. Finally, you've got to know when to call it a day. Calligraphy is a practice, a skill that you build up in small increments over time. Four 20-minute writing sessions in a month will do much more than one three-hour power practice binge in the same period of time.

I wrote this book for anyone who has an interest in calligraphy. Whether you're a beginner or have been practicing for years. No matter where you're at, I invite you to enjoy this inspirational resource and use it to progress with your own calligraphy journey.

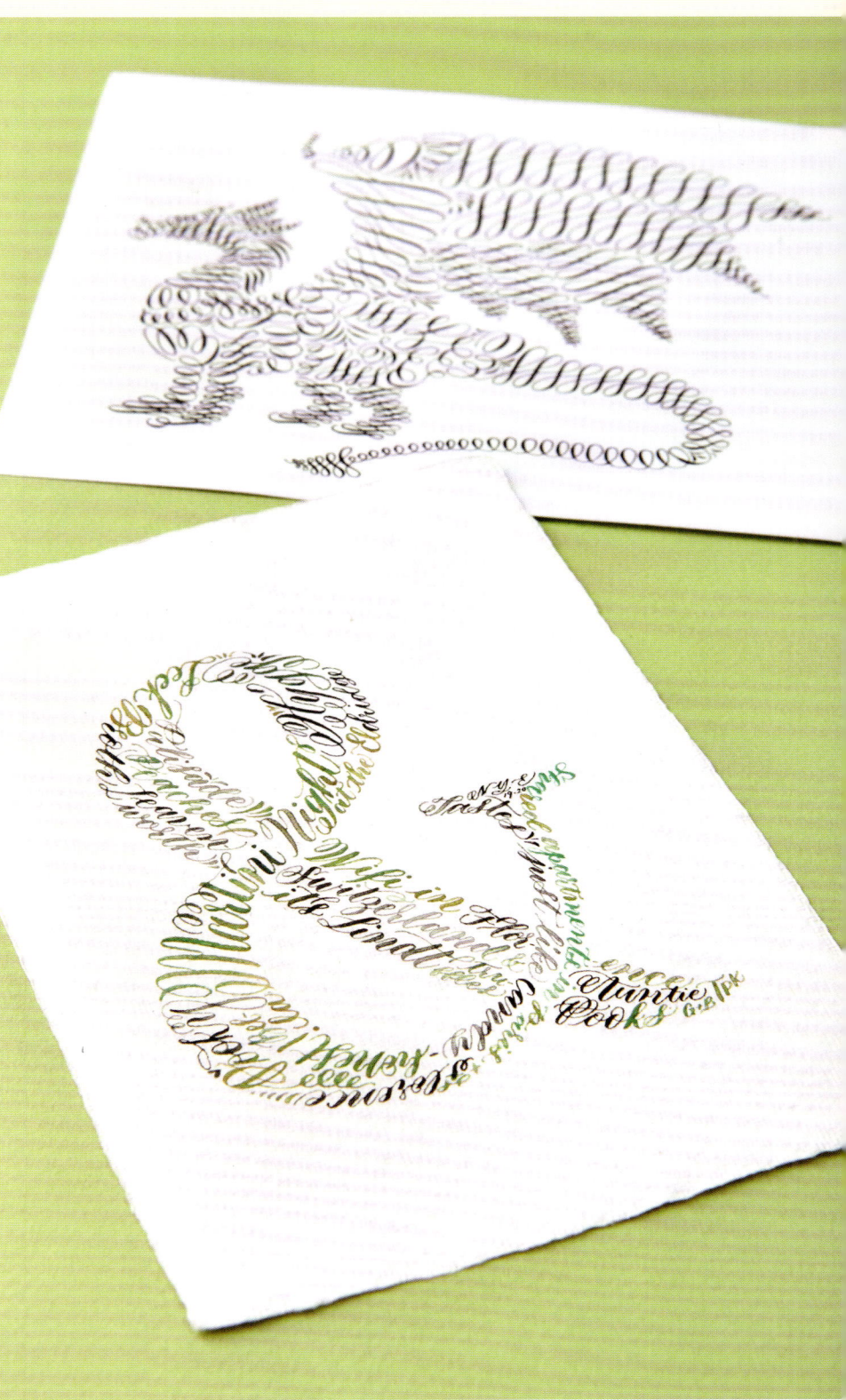

Some more developed pieces made using a pointed pen and regular more precise letter forms.

Discovering calligraphy

Types of calligraphy

"Calligraphy" means different things to different people. There are many different styles to explore and you don't have to choose one form over another. Each type has its own characteristics and charm.

A dictionary definition of "calligraphy" might say "artistic, stylized, or elegant handwriting or lettering." The root of the word is "kalli," from the Greek language, meaning "beautiful." In fact, any piece of visually appealing writing can be considered calligraphy. Here is a brief overview of some of the more common types:

Pointed pen calligraphy

In pointed pen calligraphy, you use a flexible pointed nib to create thin upstrokes and thick downstrokes. This type of calligraphy relies on pressure. When you exert pressure on your pen, the nib splits at the end and creates a thick downstroke. When you let up on pressure, the split closes and you create a thin upstroke.

Broad edge calligraphy

To create broad edge calligraphy, you use nibs that have a flat or angled edge. You navigate the nib's position to control the thickness of your strokes. Where pointed pen calligraphy relies on pressure exertion, broad edge calligraphy is all about the nib's orientation. As a general rule, broad edge calligraphy favors block letterforms.

Brush pen calligraphy

In brush pen calligraphy, you use a tapered marker to create letterforms. Brush pen calligraphy pulls elements from both pointed pen and broad edge calligraphy in that you vary your pressure and your pen position in order to achieve stroke contrast. This calligraphy style largely owes its popularity to its accessibility; you need only a marker to get started, and you can write on any type of paper.

Artistic handwriting or lettering

Several other techniques fall under the umbrella of "artistic, stylized, or elegant handwriting or lettering." The following approaches are also considered calligraphy:

Faux calligraphy is a technique that involves using any pen or pencil to write and then manually filling in the downstrokes.

Good penmanship or pretty handwriting can be referred to as "calligraphy."

Pencil calligraphy can be done using a lead pencil and is often the easiest writing utensil to get started in calligraphy. Vary the pressure that you exert while writing to vary your stroke widths.

Digital calligraphy can be done using digital art apps on a tablet using a specialized stylus.

From traditional to modern

In this book, we will focus on a style known as modern pointed pen calligraphy. In order to understand why we call this type of calligraphy "modern," it's helpful to first take a look at some more traditional pointed pen calligraphy styles.

Traditional calligraphy encompasses styles like copperplate and Spencerian scripts, which you may have spotted on formal event invitations. Traditional calligraphy follows certain rules. In copperplate, for example, each letter has a specific formation, and the vertical strokes in the letters should slant at a consistent 52–55-degree angle. Special attention also needs to be paid to the length of ascenders and descenders to ensure their consistency.

While it can be useful to have some knowledge of traditional styles and to learn a traditional script like copperplate (see pp.82–89) before you move on to creating modern calligraphy styles, it is not absolutely necessary. Even so, it can be fun to try your hand at different styles. You can even combine them together in the same project to create high-impact designs and effects.

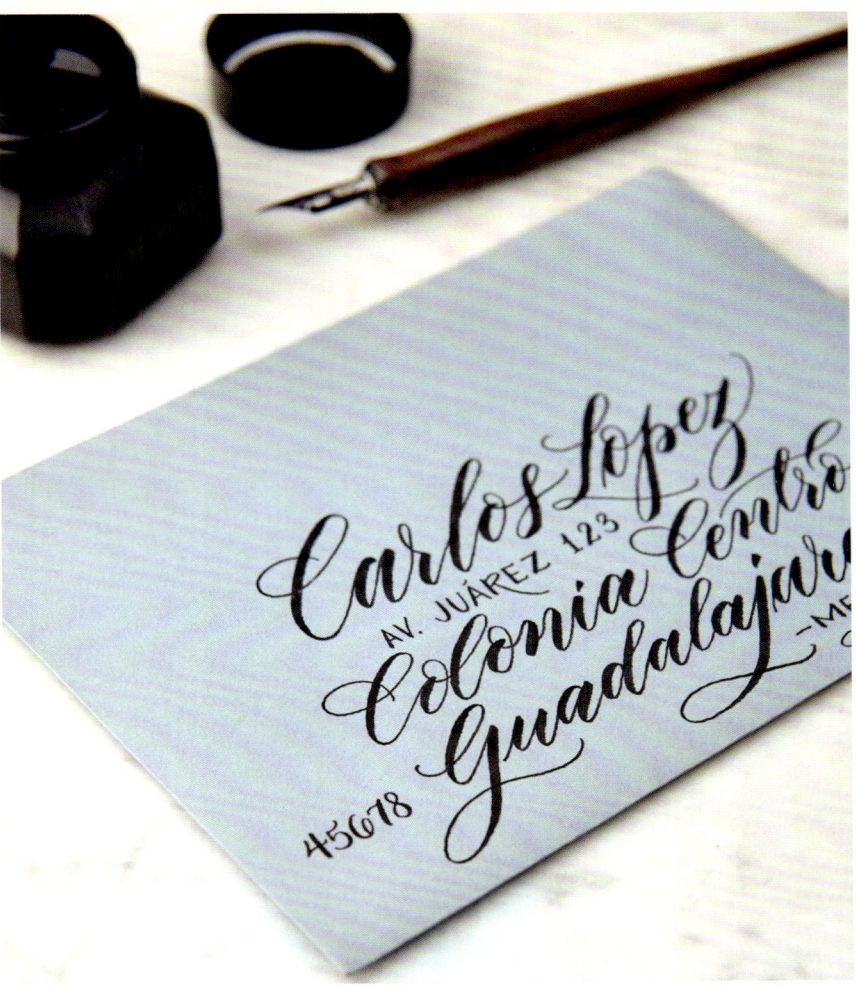

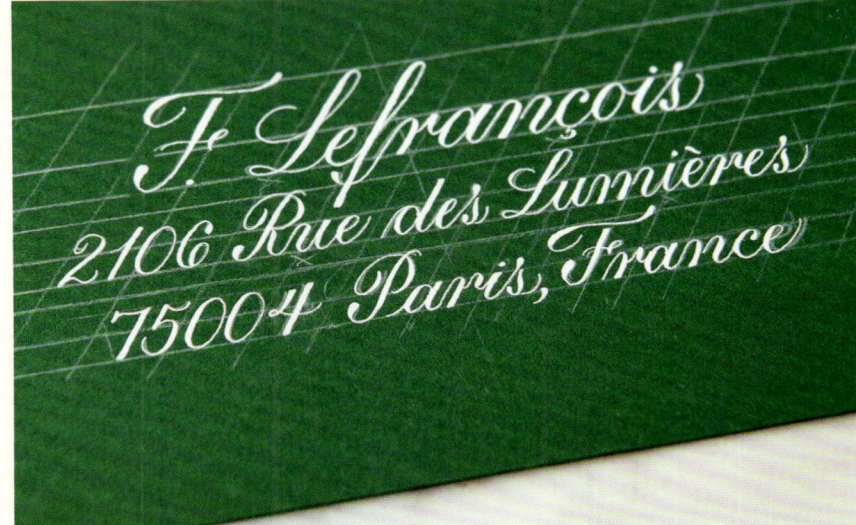

Top right: Brush pen calligraphy relies on using pressure variation to create accessible letterforms with just a marker.

Right: Traditional copperplate calligraphy follows specific rules to result in neat and orderly letterforms.

Modern pointed pen calligraphy

Modern pointed pen calligraphy is a free-flowing, flexible form of writing that can be used to make eye-catching, beautiful projects. It embraces creativity, allowing you to develop your own distinctive styles once you master the basics.

Creating modern styles

You use the same tools and basic concepts to create both modern and traditional pointed pen calligraphy styles. Modern calligraphy, however, sometimes disregards the rules and consistency of traditional calligraphy. It allows for creativity and flexibility. There are a number of ways that you can play with the letters in order to create your own modern pointed pen calligraphy, including:

- Changing the letter slant
- Making "bouncy" calligraphy
- Adding flourishes to letters
- Experimenting with new ways to write letters
- Playing with the sizes of uppercase versus lowercase letters

Keep an eye out for individual letters that you like and can use for future projects. Sometimes, certain letterforms will stick while other styles may come and go. I have several modern calligraphy styles in my repertoire with names like "Amy style" (see pp.66–73) or "Kaitlin style" (see pp.74–81), named after the clients who inspired them. Throughout the years, the styles have evolved to suit my changing tastes. You'll find that your calligraphy styles change over time, as well.

Before you create modern pointed pen calligraphy, you must first master the basics of using the pointed pen. You'll need to develop a good grip (see pp.44–45), understand how to make foundational strokes (see pp.50–53), discover your

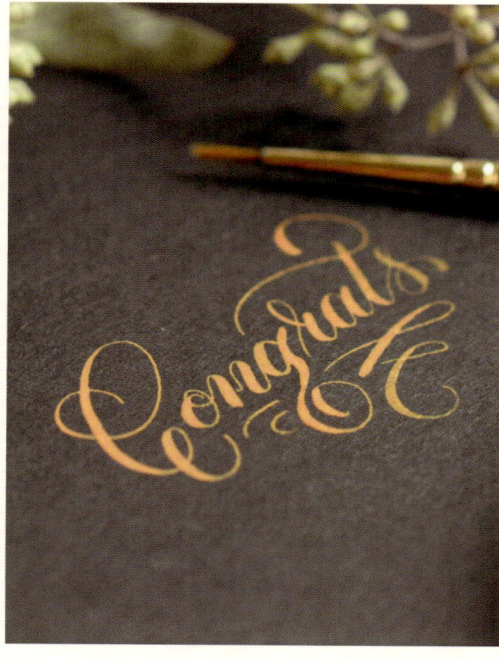
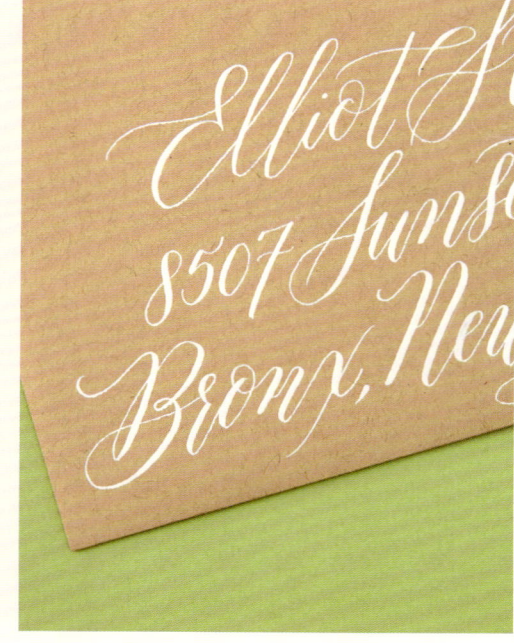

Below: Flourishes give any
calligraphy project an
elegant, regal feel.

Bottom: This flourished
map of Brazil features
embellished hand
lettering and flourishes.

favorite pens and nibs (see pp.20–23), and
find your ideal paper and ink combinations
(see pp.24–27). As you do all of this, try
mastering at least one alphabet that
someone else developed. Practice until you
feel comfortable writing that alphabet.

Finding your style

Once you've become proficient at creating
at least one of the calligraphy styles in this
book, you can start to develop your own
styles (see pp.110–113). Try riffing on an
existing alphabet until you've created
something that is unique to you. The beauty
of modern calligraphy is that you can never
get bored with it. If a style you're working
with starts to feel stale, move on to develop
another one. There is always a new direction
to explore and master.

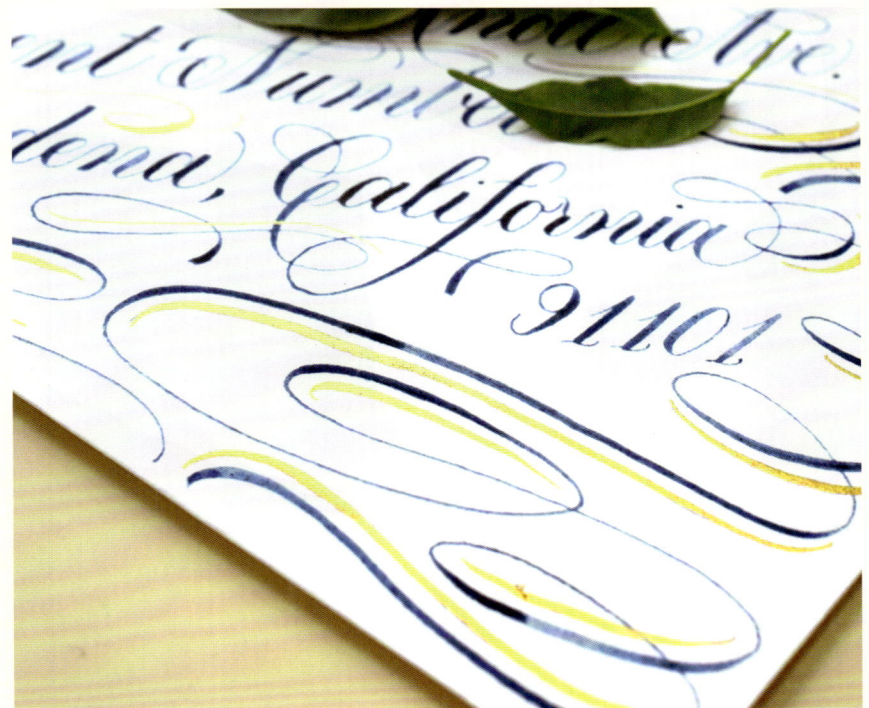

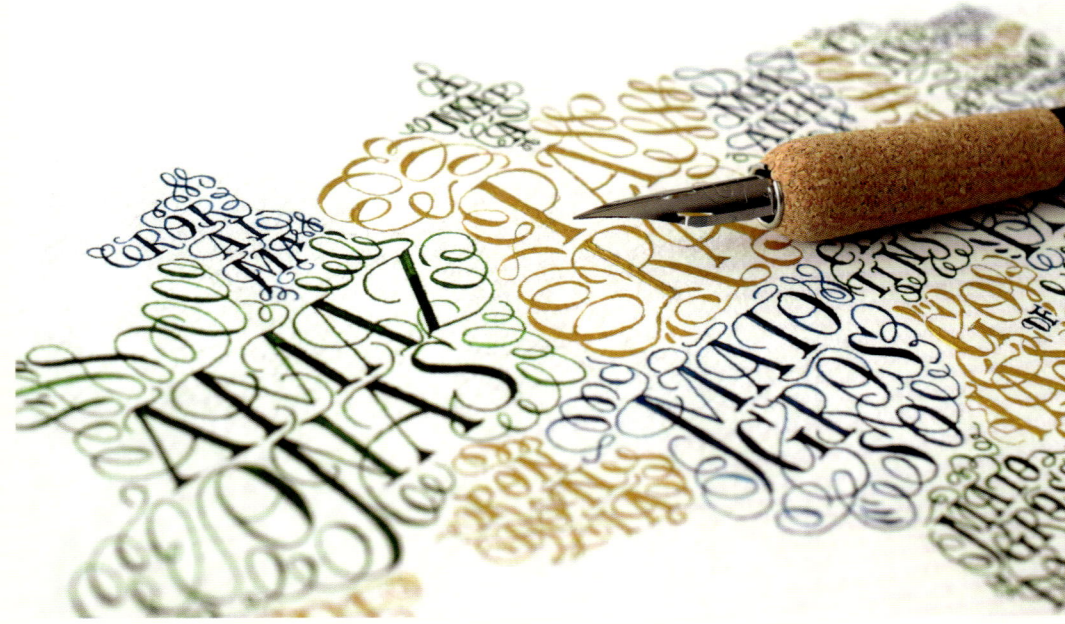

Far left: Modern
calligraphy encourages
experimentation and
innovation.

Left: Try adding bounce
to your calligraphy for a
casual look.

The joy of calligraphy

It's difficult to overstate the meditative and satisfying nature of pointed pen calligraphy. In today's world of constant technological stimulation, taking a break from the digital buzz can be incredibly refreshing.

Creating pointed pen calligraphy forces you to slow down, take a breath, and focus on an inherently relaxing activity. One of the most appealing aspects of calligraphy for many people is its meditative nature.

Getting set up

Although you may appreciate the beauty of the things that you create, it's very often the experience of writing calligraphy that will pull you back to your desk. Put on some comfortable clothing, make a drink, and turn on your favorite audiobook or a podcast. Then, arrange your workspace how you like it: with your paper or an envelope in front of you, a cup of cleaning water on one side, ink on the other, and the pen and nib that best suits the project you're making. Once you get the hang of calligraphy, you'll be happy sitting like this for hours, letting yourself relax more deeply with every stroke.

Enjoy the process

It's fine to compare your work with other people's creations as long as you maintain compassion for yourself and where you are on your personal calligraphy journey. Everyone starts off as a beginner, and the point is to enjoy the process. Try to think positive and praise yourself every step of the way. You may look back later on some of your early projects and see them as juvenile, even if you loved making them at the time. Don't think too much about your skill level; instead, focus on how your projects make you feel. Remember to celebrate small victories like finding the perfect opaque gold ink (see pp.130–133) and understanding how to form delicate upstrokes. You can identify errors and do things better the next time around, but you should also make it a point to find at least one thing that you're proud of in each project that you create.

One of the best parts of calligraphy is the fact that you get to nurture your mental health and make something that adds value to the world at the same time. That's true whether you're writing an inspirational quote, embellishing an envelope to brighten someone's day, or just doodling. Commit to making at least one pointed pen calligraphy project per month—small or big—and you'll be amazed at how you start to crave your creation sessions and the satisfying respite that they provide.

Set yourself up for success by making your workspace clear and efficient with everything you need to get started.

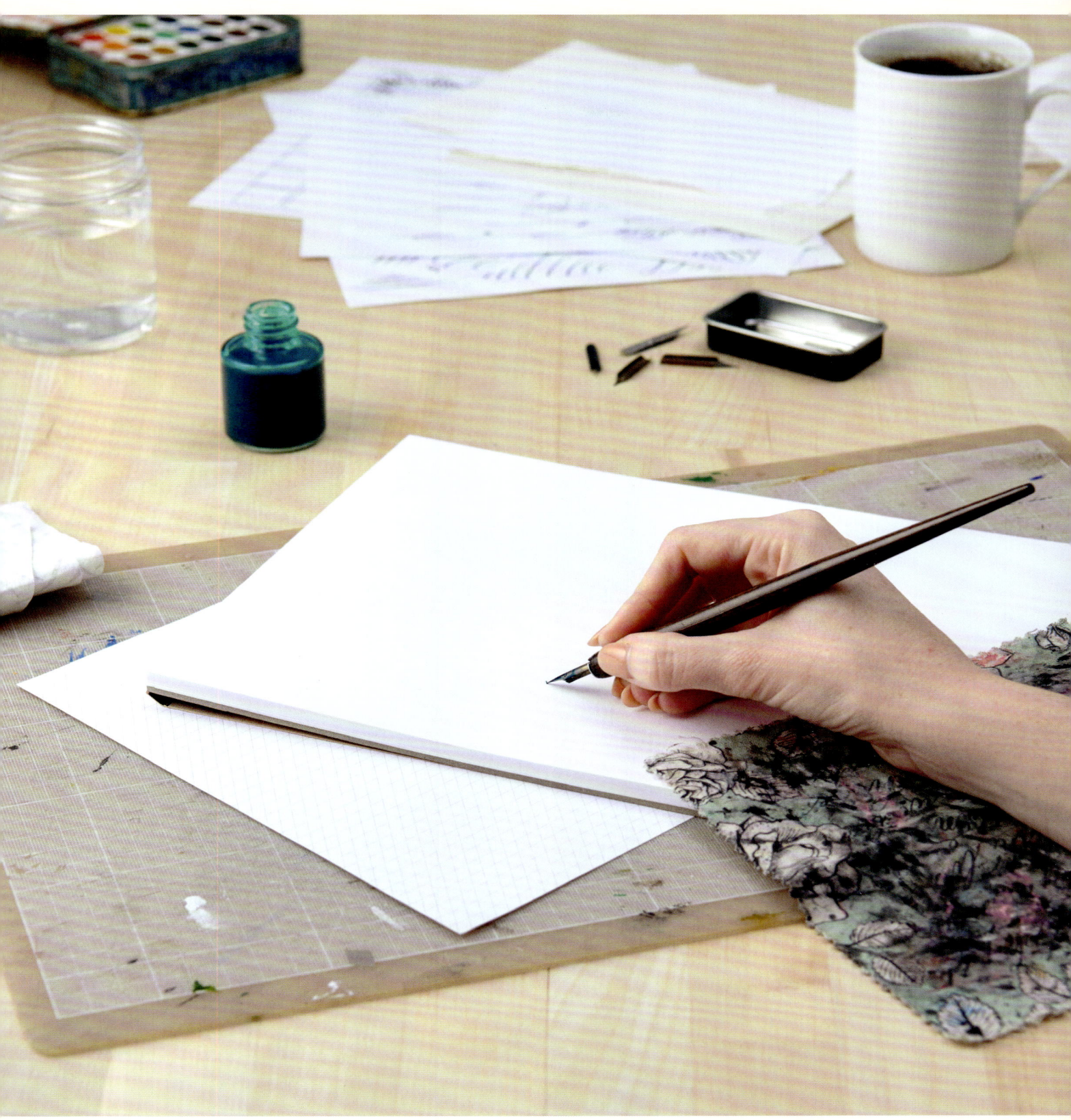

The joy of calligraphy

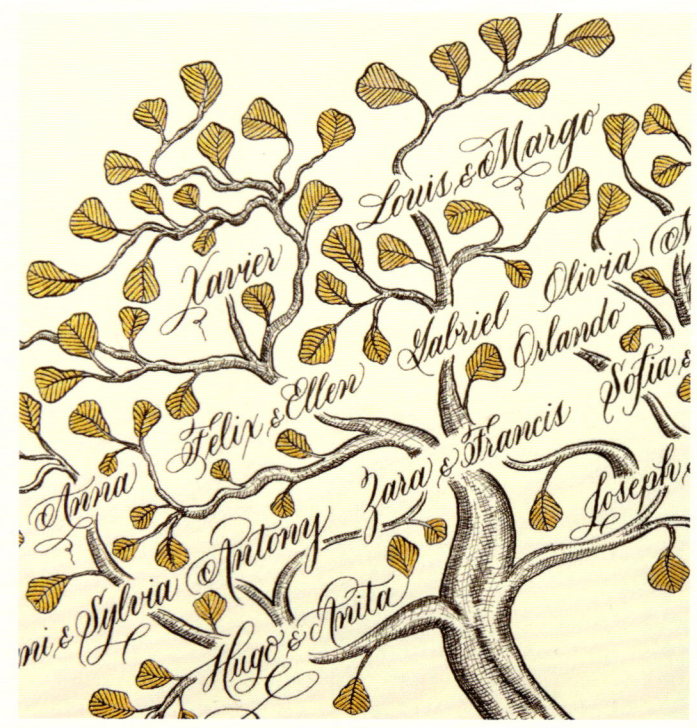

"Pointed pen calligraphy can make your everyday writing more meaningful and memorable."

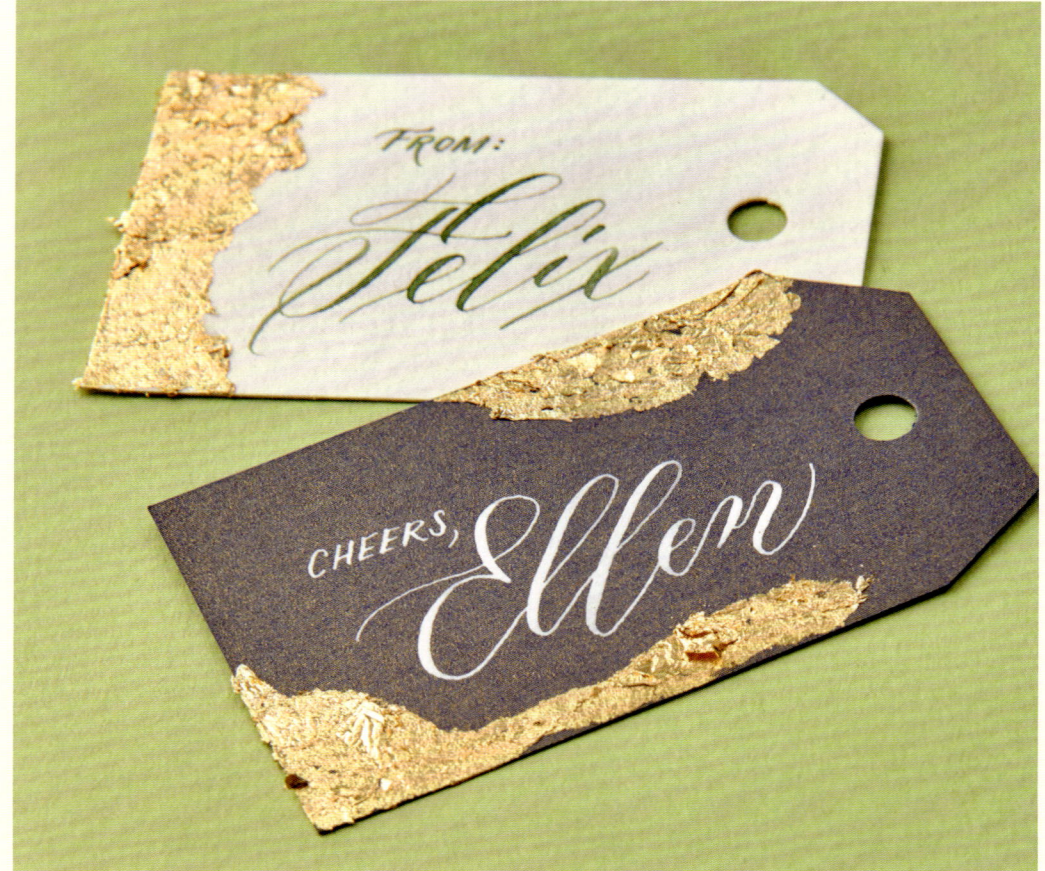

Above right: Creating personalized calligraphy art like a family tree is meaningful and satisfying.

Right: Even small pieces of calligraphy like these gift tags can elevate the everyday.

Why create calligraphy?

There are many reasons to start practicing calligraphy. In general, the motivation behind learning calligraphy can be attributed to one (or more) of six reasons:

Taking on a new hobby

Often the main motivation behind learning calligraphy is having something productive and creative to do. Instead of scrolling through a social media feed, it feels satisfying to dedicate time to making beautiful alphabet characters and strokes.

Finding a challenge

Calligraphy is a stimulating endeavor because of all the challenges you encounter along the way. First, you have to educate yourself about supplies and source them. Then comes writing with the proper form and trying out different types of calligraphy alphabets. After that, you might learn how to work with different inks or watercolors or add flourishes and decorative elements. No matter what skill level you reach, there's always something new to learn.

Handwriting improvement

Pointed pen calligraphy and everyday handwriting are not synonymous. That said, once you write with a dip pen and learn some nice writing styles, your handwriting can improve. You might find yourself incorporating some of your pointed pen deliberateness into the notes you jot.

A knowledge of pointed pen calligraphy can make your everyday writing more meaningful and memorable.

Bonding with loved ones

There's strength in numbers, and learning something with a loved one can be a very fulfilling experience. You might try attending a calligraphy workshop with a parent, child, sibling, or best friend and learn a new skill together. People who are close tend to encourage one other, and the journey is a pleasant one for both sides.

Finding calm in the storm

For some people, calligraphy serves as a welcome distraction when things get tough. The unfortunate fact of life is that it sometimes presents difficult times, including separations, serious illnesses, and the deaths of loved ones. Getting through those hard times can seem impossible, but many people use pursuits like calligraphy as part of their coping strategy. In times of stress and anxiety, it can feel calming to focus your mind on a meditative and tactile activity.

Creating personalized projects

Having the ability to create beautiful things for special people and occasions is another great reason to try calligraphy. From designing your own wedding stationery to making a breathtaking handmade birthday gift for a loved one, you've got the power to create eye-catching paper goods that make a difference in someone's world.

The supplies

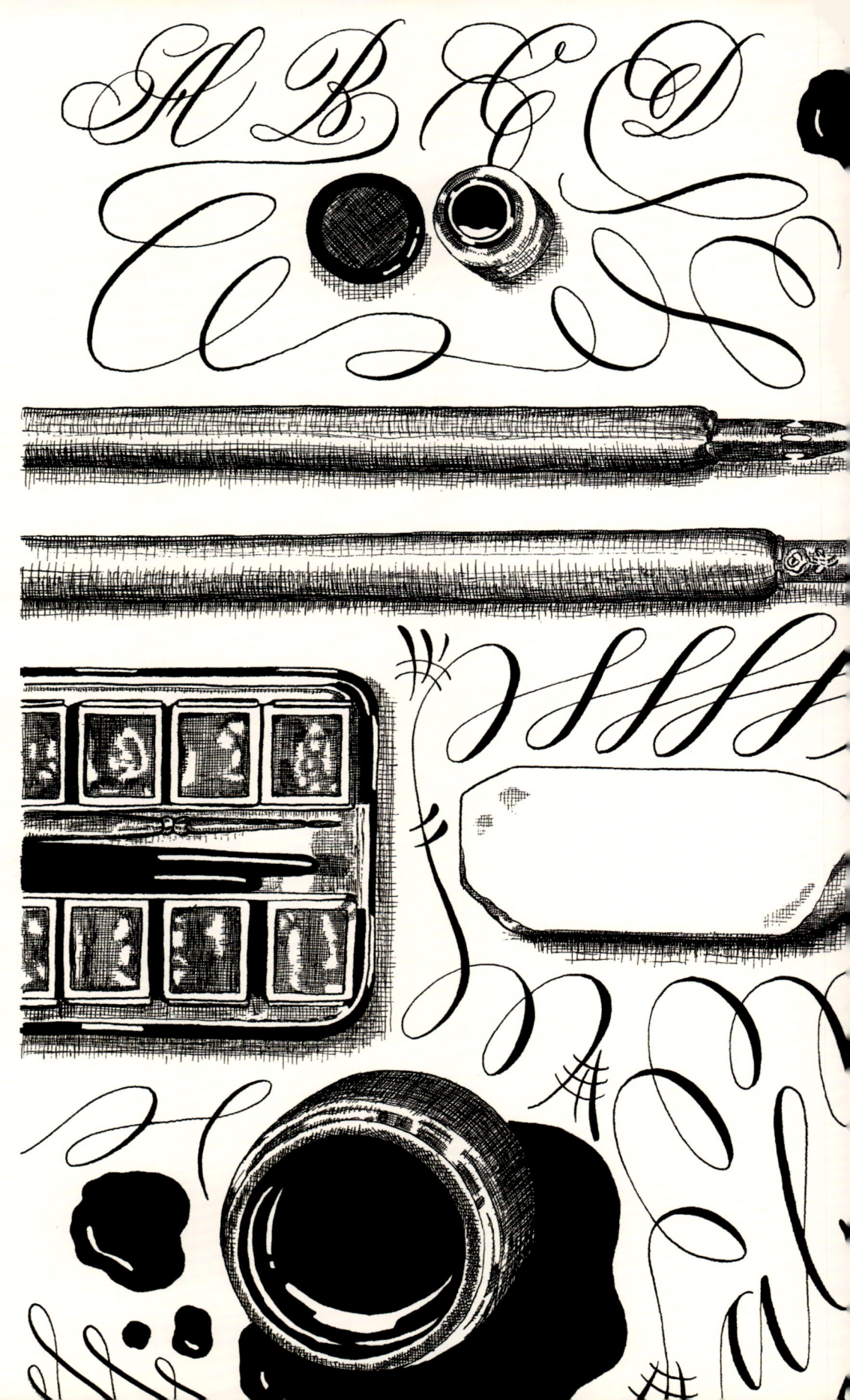

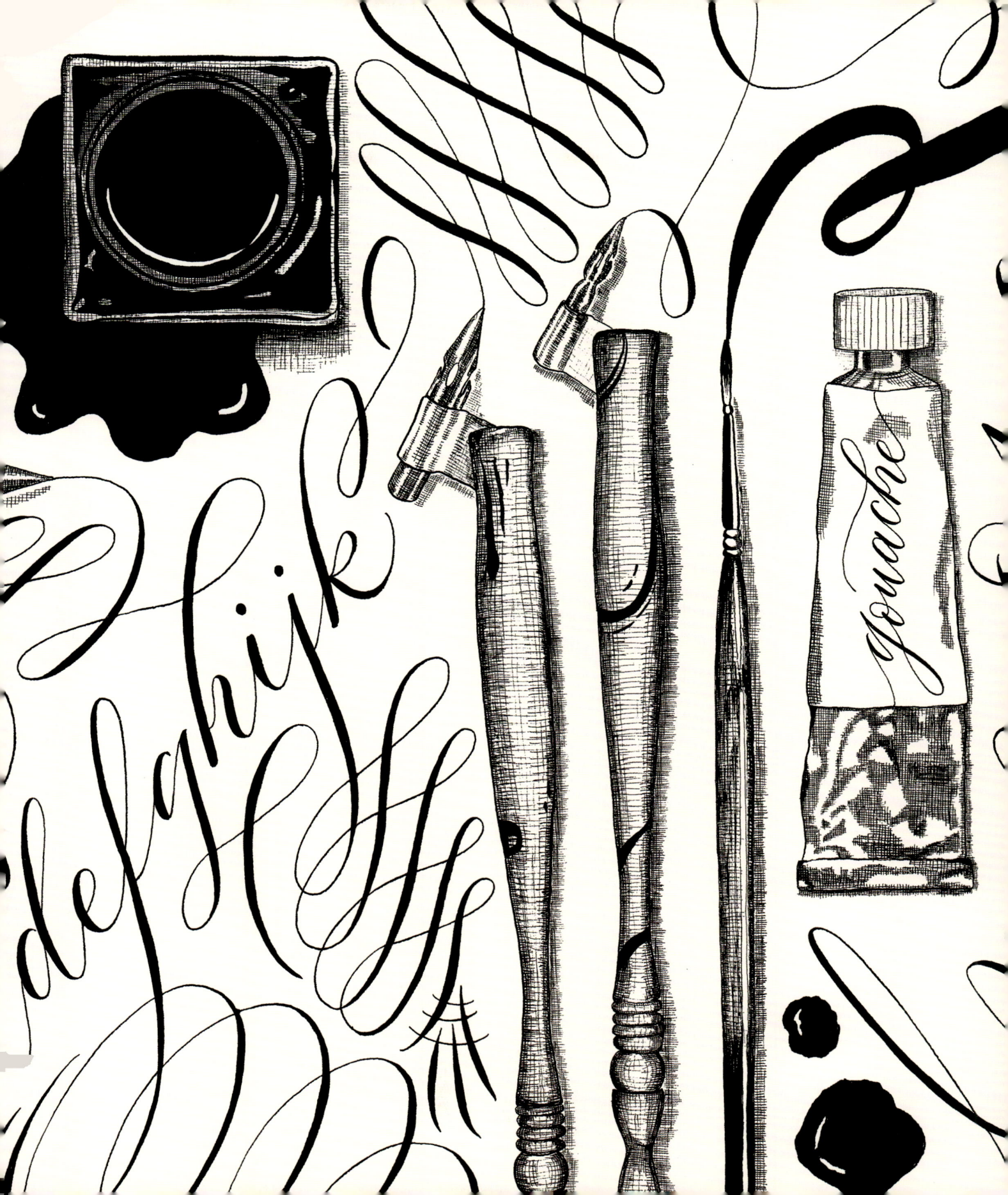

Pen holders

There are several different types of pen holders you can use for calligraphy. One of the most common is a straight pen holder. Another option is an oblique pen holder, which can be very useful for right-handed calligraphers.

Straight pen holder

A standard straight pen holder is designed with a wider base that gradually tapers toward the top. This shape allows for a comfortable and secure grip while providing flexibility for different hand sizes and writing styles. Holders come in various materials, although plastic and wood are the most common. At the wider base, there is a slot to insert the metal nib (see pp.22–23).

Oblique pen holders

To successfully create calligraphy, your nib must remain parallel to the writing slant that you wish to achieve (see p.59). With that in mind, right-handed people may have a difficult time creating calligraphy that slants to the right. When you're right-handed, your arm tends to end up in a left-facing position as you write, so right-leaning calligraphy styles can be a challenge to create with a straight pen holder. Oblique pen holders help right-handed calligraphers achieve a more comfortable and consistent slant in certain pointed pen scripts. They allow for a more natural writing angle and make it easier to produce thick and thin strokes. I always recommend a brass-flanged oblique pen holder because you can adjust it more easily to fit different-sized nibs.

Left-handed calligraphers

Most left-handed calligraphers use a straight pen, though some actually create their best work with a right or left oblique pen. It all depends on individual writing style and preference. If you're a left-handed writer who struggles with a straight pen, try a left oblique pen holder. It's designed in a way that allows you to write at a comfortable angle while keeping your hand above the written ink, reducing the likelihood of smudging.

Materials

Traditionally, calligraphy pen holders were made of wood, which may have been decorated or carved. More modern styles are made of plastic or metal and can be more durable and lightweight. Some pen holders have a grip made of cork or shaped as part of the material itself to make it easier to handle. The choice of pen holder is a personal one and you may find that different holders work best with different nibs. As you gain more experience, you'll find a combination that works for you.

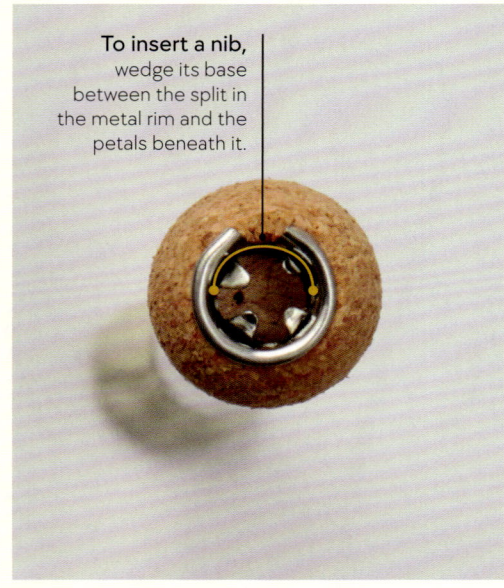

To insert a nib, wedge its base between the split in the metal rim and the petals beneath it.

A "universal insert" is the metal cylindrical piece inside the end of the pen that features four metal "petals" that grip the base of a variety of pointed pen calligraphy nibs.

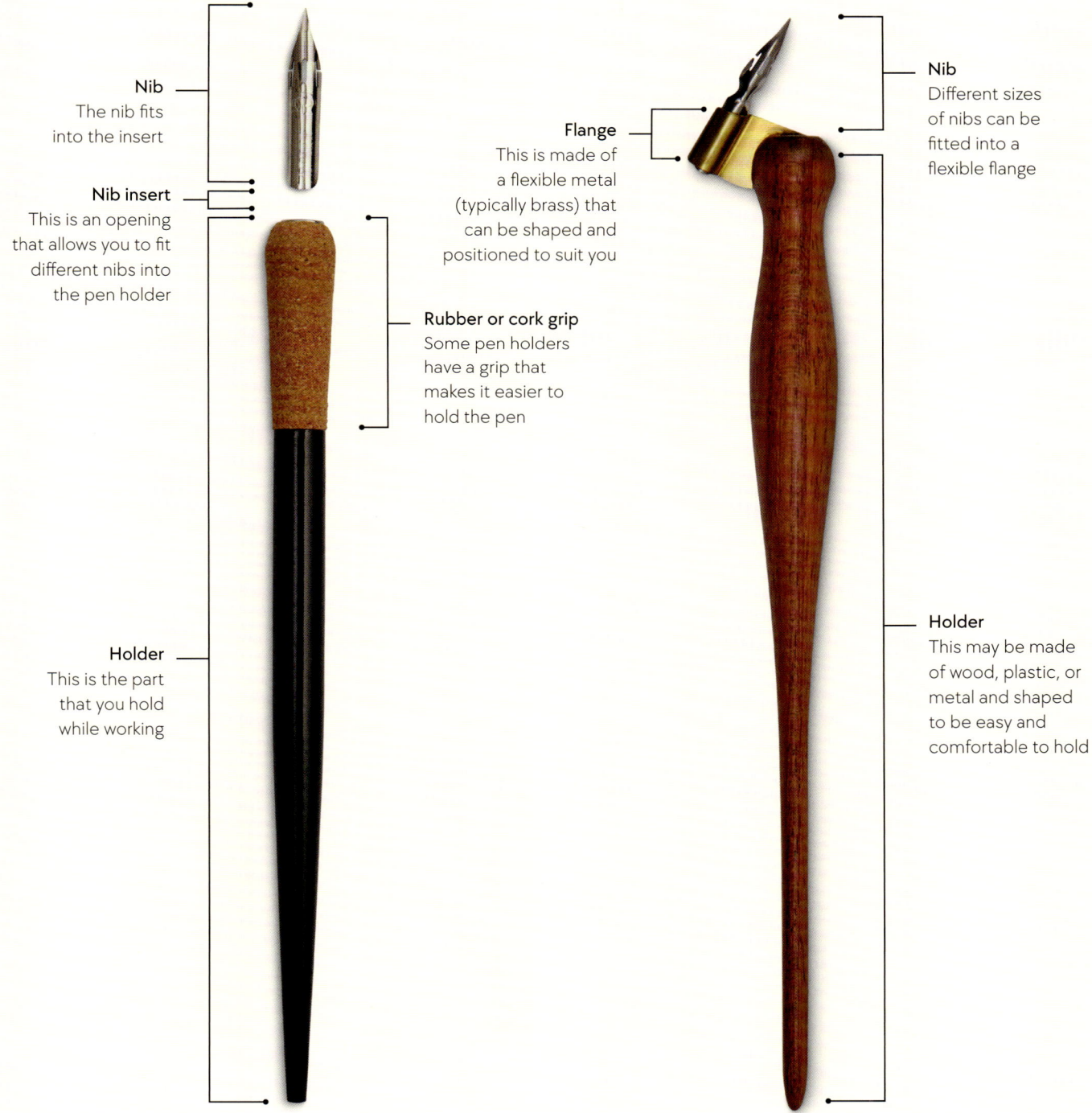

Straight pen holder

The handle that holds the nib in place is known as the holder. This is an essential tool that not only provides stability but also allows you to control the flow of ink and the thickness of your strokes.

Nib
The nib fits into the insert

Nib insert
This is an opening that allows you to fit different nibs into the pen holder

Holder
This is the part that you hold while working

Rubber or cork grip
Some pen holders have a grip that makes it easier to hold the pen

Oblique pen holder

This style of pen holder is especially useful for right-handed calligraphers as it allows you to hold the nib at the correct angle to the paper and write in a consistent style.

Nib
Different sizes of nibs can be fitted into a flexible flange

Flange
This is made of a flexible metal (typically brass) that can be shaped and positioned to suit you

Holder
This may be made of wood, plastic, or metal and shaped to be easy and comfortable to hold

Pointed pen nibs

A pointed pen nib is a curved piece of metal or steel with a reservoir in its center that helps regulate ink flow. The nib is divided into two tines, which form a point that channels the ink down to reach the paper.

If you apply pressure to a pointed pen calligraphy nib, its tines splay apart, creating a gap through which ink flows onto the paper. The width of the resulting stroke corresponds to the size of the gap between the tines. Generally, you need to apply pressure to the nib only when you're making a downward stroke. It's nearly impossible to make an upward motion with the pen if the nib is under pressure and its tines are splayed.

To make a thin stroke, apply minimal pressure to the nib while writing. Calligraphers normally exert minimal pressure on their nibs when they're pushing their pen up or pulling their pen across the page to make a stroke.

Low-flex nibs

These produce stroke widths with minimal stroke contrast regardless of the pressure used. Low-flex nibs are suitable for calligraphers who prefer a uniform and controlled writing style. Examples of popular low-flex nibs include the Tachikawa T-99 Maru crowquill nib and the Gillott 1158.

Medium-flex nibs

Medium-flex nibs are versatile and popular among calligraphers because they provide a good balance between control and variation in stroke width. With medium-flex nibs, you can achieve both thin hairlines and broader strokes with relative ease. Examples of popular medium-flex nibs include the Gillott 303, Nikko G, Leonardt Principal, and Brause Steno.

High-flex nibs

High-flex nibs are often preferred by calligraphers who enjoy creating expressive writing styles and styles with flourishes. They are excellent for producing intricate and ornamental lettering. However, using high-flex nibs requires more skill and control than when using other styles of nibs, as they can be more challenging to handle compared to medium-flex nibs. Examples of popular high-flex nibs include the Hunt 22, Brause EF66, Brause Rose, and Hunt 101 Imperial.

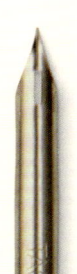

Low-flex nibs have limited flexibility, meaning they do not bend easily when you apply pressure to them.

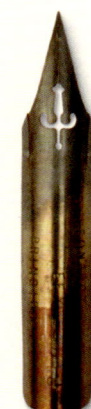

Medium-flex nibs offer moderate flexibility, allowing some bending when pressure is applied during writing.

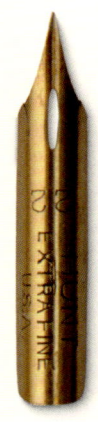

High-flex nibs have greatest flexibility, meaning their tines splay apart easily when pressure is applied.

Anatomy of a nib

In order to understand how calligraphy works, it helps to study a nib up close. While nibs can differ, they usually share these common features.

Tip
This part of the nib makes contact with the paper.

Slit
This cut separates the two tines of the nib

Tines
By applying pressure to the nib, the two tines spring apart, creating thick downstrokes. Let up on pressure and they snap back together, resulting in thin upstrokes and horizontal strokes

Reservoir
This part of the nib ensures that your tines don't split too far apart, adds additional flex to the nib, and helps regulate ink flow

Shoulders
The shoulder marks the transition from tines to shank. Nibs like this one have side slits at the shoulders

Shank
The part between the reservoir and the base

Decoration
Some nibs feature an embossed design between the reservoir and the base

Imprint
The imprint tells you what company made the nib, what type it is, and sometimes where the nib was made.

Base
This is the part of a nib that you insert into the holder.

BRAUSE & CO
NO 76
ISERLOHN

Pointed pen nibs

Inks

The number-one thing that sets calligraphy apart from other writing techniques is the versatility of what you can write with. Virtually any liquid that stains can be used as a calligraphy ink (see pp.130–133).

Some of the most popular calligraphy inks are described here, but there are many other mediums you can use. If you're a beginner, sumi ink is a great ink to start with because it's versatile and easy to use.

Sumi ink

Sumi ink has traditionally been used in Chinese, Japanese, and Korean calligraphy, and it offers an excellent balance between thickness and flow. It is thicker than some other inks, allowing it to sit well on most papers without spreading or feathering. At the same time, it has a smooth flow, making it easier to achieve consistent and controlled strokes.

Sumi ink is typically made from soot mixed with water and a gluelike binder, and it comes in both liquid and solid forms. Get the liquid version; it's ready to use right out of the bottle. One of the advantages of starting with sumi ink is its forgiving nature. It allows you to practice your strokes and letterforms without the frustration of ink flow issues that beginners commonly face (see pp.122–123). People love sumi ink's unique sheen, which is fairly matte. Colored sumi inks are also available and are worth trying out for their vibrancy.

India ink

Another excellent choice is India ink, also known as "Chinese ink" or "Indian ink." It is made by combining carbon black pigment with a binder, typically gum arabic, which acts as a medium to hold the pigment together. The carbon black is derived from burning various materials, such as wood or oil, and the resulting soot is collected and mixed with water to form a paste. Gum arabic, a natural resin extracted from the acacia tree, is then added to the paste to create a smooth and stable ink solution. India ink is valued for its rich black color and water-resistant qualities and is used to create crisp, precise lines.

Colored India inks are made by adding pigments or dyes to the standard ink formulas. These are usually quite vibrant and pleasant to use.

Iron gall ink

A traditional ink made from the growths on oak trees, iron gall ink is now available in modern formulations for convenience and safety. Iron gall ink is known for its rich, dark color and an occasional gradated effect. It is also acidic, so you will need to clean your nibs thoroughly after use to prevent damage. Also note that iron gall ink is not long-lasting. Over time, it will "eat" through paper, which is why there are so many manuscripts in museums with holes in them.

Walnut ink

A brown ink made from the husks of walnuts, walnut ink is a popular choice among calligraphers and artists for its warm and sepia-toned hue, ideal for creating vintage and antique-inspired works. You can experiment with different concentrations to achieve various shades. However, walnut ink is not permanent nor lightfast. Over time, it may fade, especially if exposed to light, and it can also be affected by moisture.

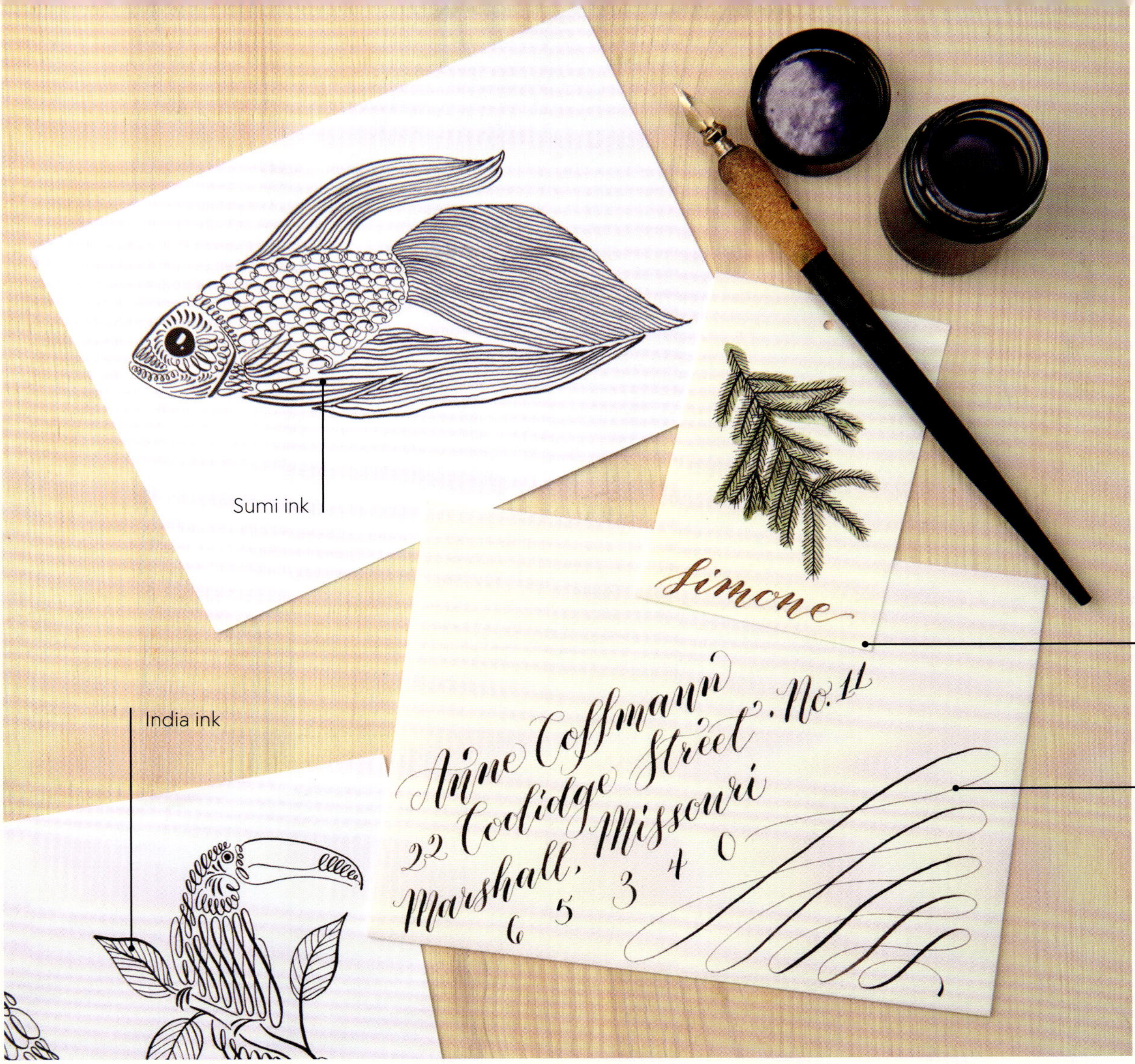

Sumi ink

Walnut ink

India ink

Iron gall ink

Simone

Anne Coßmann
2² Coolidge Street · No. 11
Marshall, Missouri
6   5   3   4   0

Above: Sumi and India inks
tend to be richly colored, with a
balanced viscosity. Walnut and iron
gall inks are thin and so can help
you produce a stunning contrast
between stroke widths.

Left: Ink containers can vary
depending on the manufacturer.
If you can't dip your pen directly
into a bottle, it's a good idea to
permanently relocate the ink to
a clean, pointed pen-friendly jar
(such as a miniature jelly jar or
baby-food jar) for easy dipping.

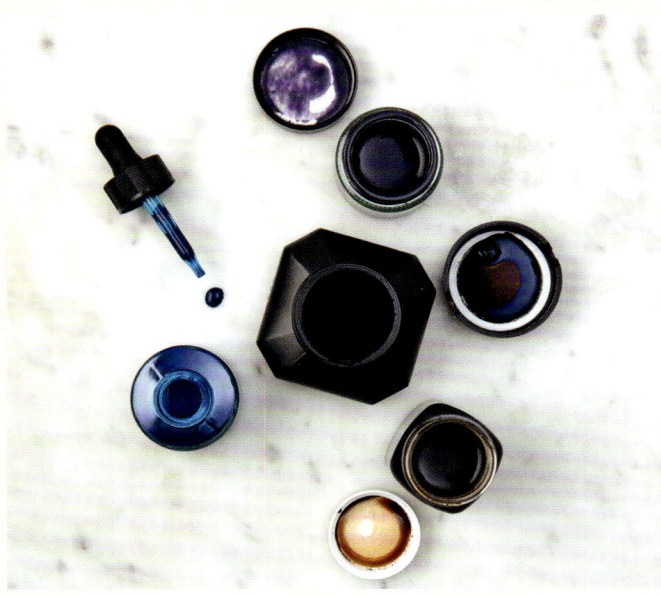

Papers

When I first began learning how to create pointed pen calligraphy, it never occurred to me that specific papers for calligraphy might exist. After watching my ink feather and my nib catch on paper fibers, it clicked for me that paper makes all the difference.

On these pages, you'll find some of the more commonly used papers for calligraphy. Your choice will come down to the project you're working on, the ink you are using, and personal preference.

Laserjet paper

Standard printer paper is too thin and lacks the necessary smoothness for pointed pen calligraphy. However, a slightly heavier 80lb (120gsm) laserjet paper is a great practice paper. It's an obvious choice once you consider the smooth surface, heavy weight, and economical price. The advantage of choosing laserjet paper for calligraphy practice is that you can use it in a printer to print off practice guidelines and worksheets, many of which are available for free online.

Calligraphy practice pads

Some paper brands offer calligraphy practice pads specifically designed for pointed pen calligraphy. These feature smooth surfaces and an appropriate weight, making them ideal for beginner calligraphers. The only disadvantage is that they are often more expensive than other paper. That said, many practice pads contain helpful grids and guidelines that make them worth the splurge, particularly if you're a beginner.

Heavyweight paper

Pointed pen calligraphy requires a sturdy paper that can handle watery inks without bleeding or feathering. Look for drawing or mixed media papers with a weight of around 100–145lb (150–214gsm). You should be able to use any ink on these heavyweight papers with minimal issues. Cardstock isn't suitable for many inks as it allows feathering to occur, although it can sometimes be used with large-particled and paintlike inks such as bleedproof white, metallic watercolors, and gouache.

High-quality cotton paper

Cotton papers are a favorite among experienced calligraphers for their smooth

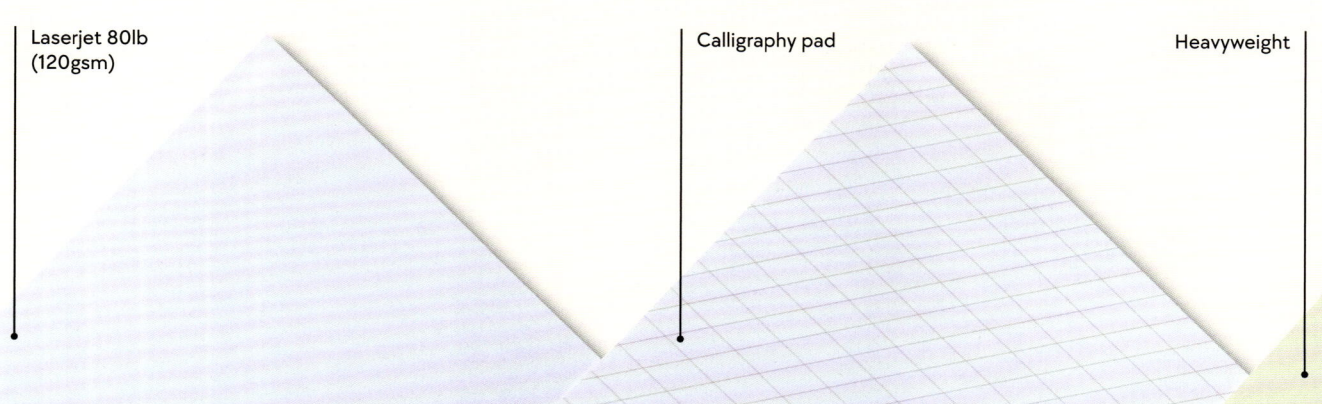

Laserjet 80lb (120gsm)

Calligraphy pad

Heavyweight

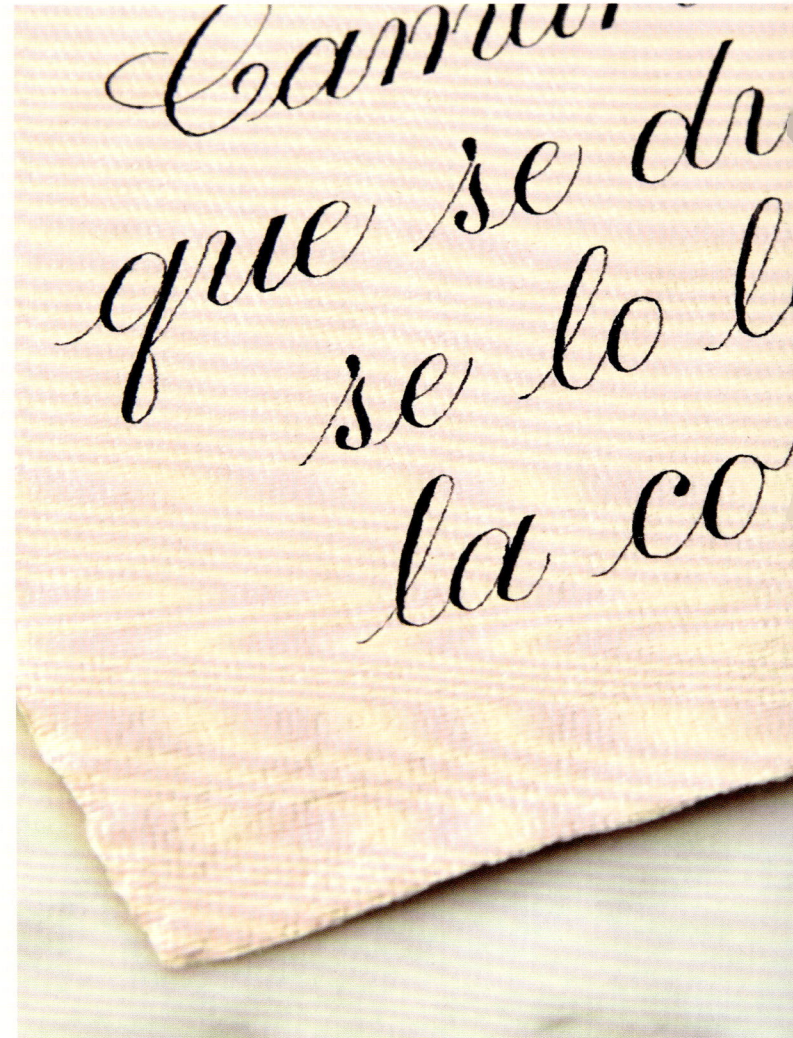

Cotton paper tends to pair best with inks that have a thin viscosity, such as iron gall (shown here). Its crevices can prove more difficult for thicker inks.

surfaces and exceptional ability to handle ink. They provide a luxurious feel and often feature a beautiful deckled, ragged edge. Look for cotton papers with a high rag content (100 percent cotton or close to it) for the best performance. Pointed pen nibs that have a fairly blunt tip, like the Brause EF66 or the Brause Rose, and watery inks, like iron gall and walnut, work well with cotton paper.

Watercolor paper

Hot-pressed watercolor paper has a smooth surface that works well with pointed pen nibs. It allows for precise strokes and helps facilitate fine details in calligraphy work. It's a great paper to experiment with. Cold-pressed paper is favored by many calligraphers (myself included) for its unique texture. However, the same texture and small indentations can pose difficulties for those new to calligraphy.

Cotton

Watercolor

Building your kit

You don't need expensive tools to begin your pointed pen calligraphy journey. There are just a handful of items you need to get started, and you can add to your collection as you gain more experience.

A good nib to begin with is the Nikko G, which is widely available. It's a good idea to buy two so you have a backup. Laserjet paper, such as HP Premium 80lb (120gsm), is the most reliable practice paper, and you can use your home printer to print practice lines on it. Sumi ink is a fantastic ink to start with because it has a nice flow and dries to a dreamy matte sheen. For the nonfibrous cloth, choose something that's tightly woven, like a cloth dinner napkin, so that the fibers don't affect your work.

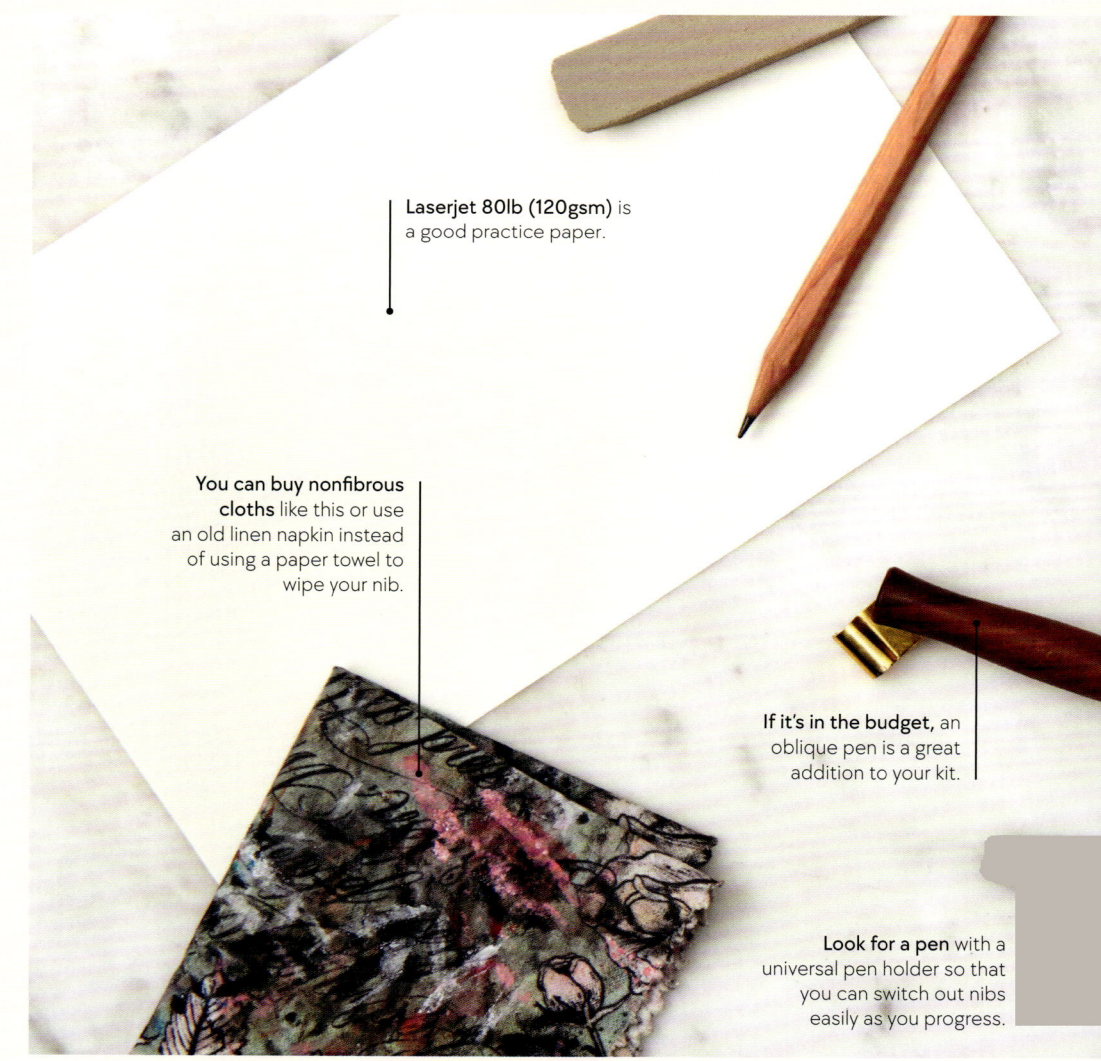

Laserjet 80lb (120gsm) is a good practice paper.

You can buy nonfibrous cloths like this or use an old linen napkin instead of using a paper towel to wipe your nib.

If it's in the budget, an oblique pen is a great addition to your kit.

Look for a pen with a universal pen holder so that you can switch out nibs easily as you progress.

"Sumi ink is a fantastic ink to start with because it has a nice flow and dries to a dreamy matte sheen."

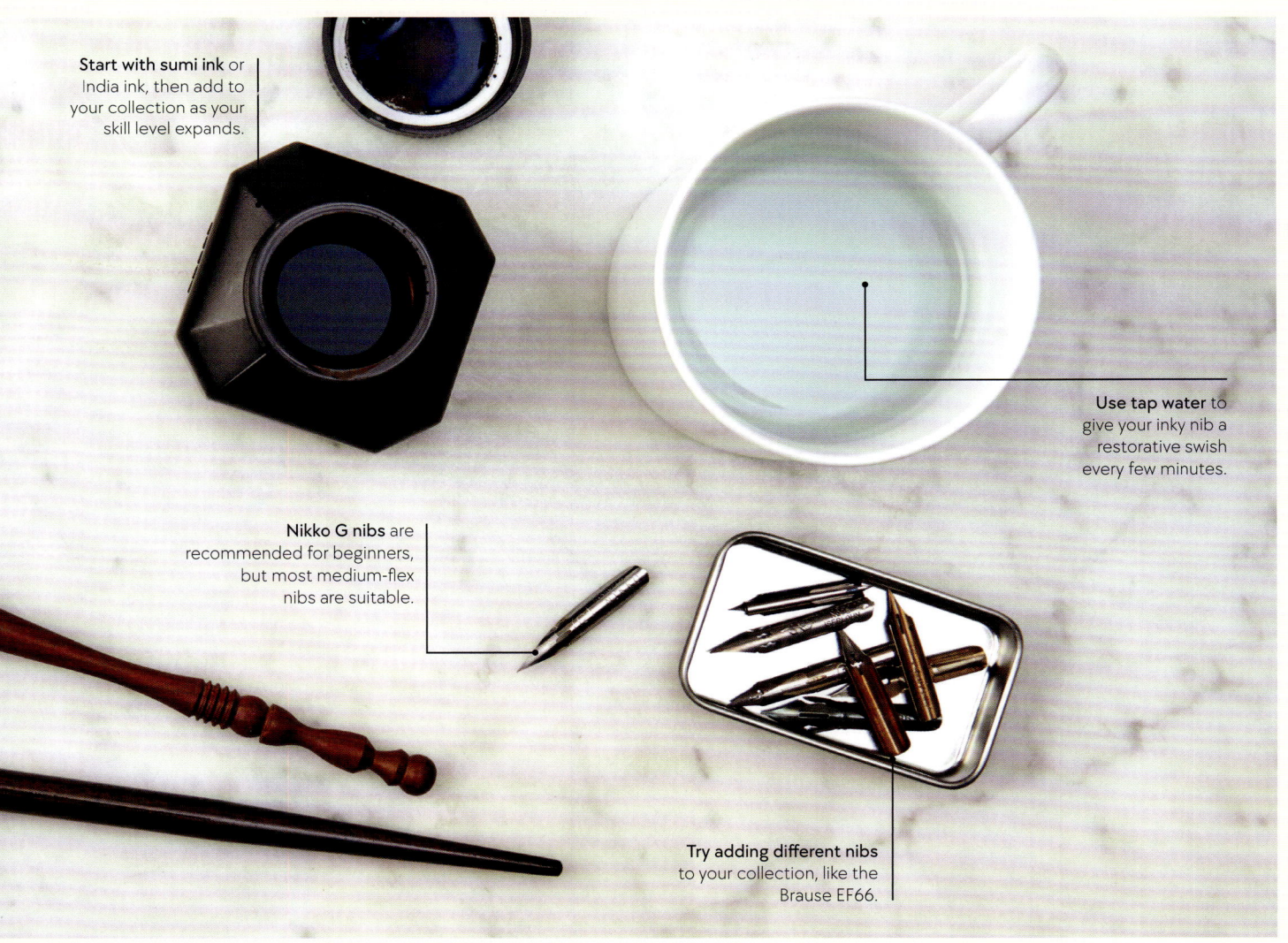

Start with sumi ink or India ink, then add to your collection as your skill level expands.

Use tap water to give your inky nib a restorative swish every few minutes.

Nikko G nibs are recommended for beginners, but most medium-flex nibs are suitable.

Try adding different nibs to your collection, like the Brause EF66.

Building your kit

Other tools

After you master calligraphy using the basic kit, you might want to raise the level of your creations with some extra supplies. Here are some suggestions for tools that you may find useful. You don't need to buy everything all at once and you may already have some of them in your toolbox.

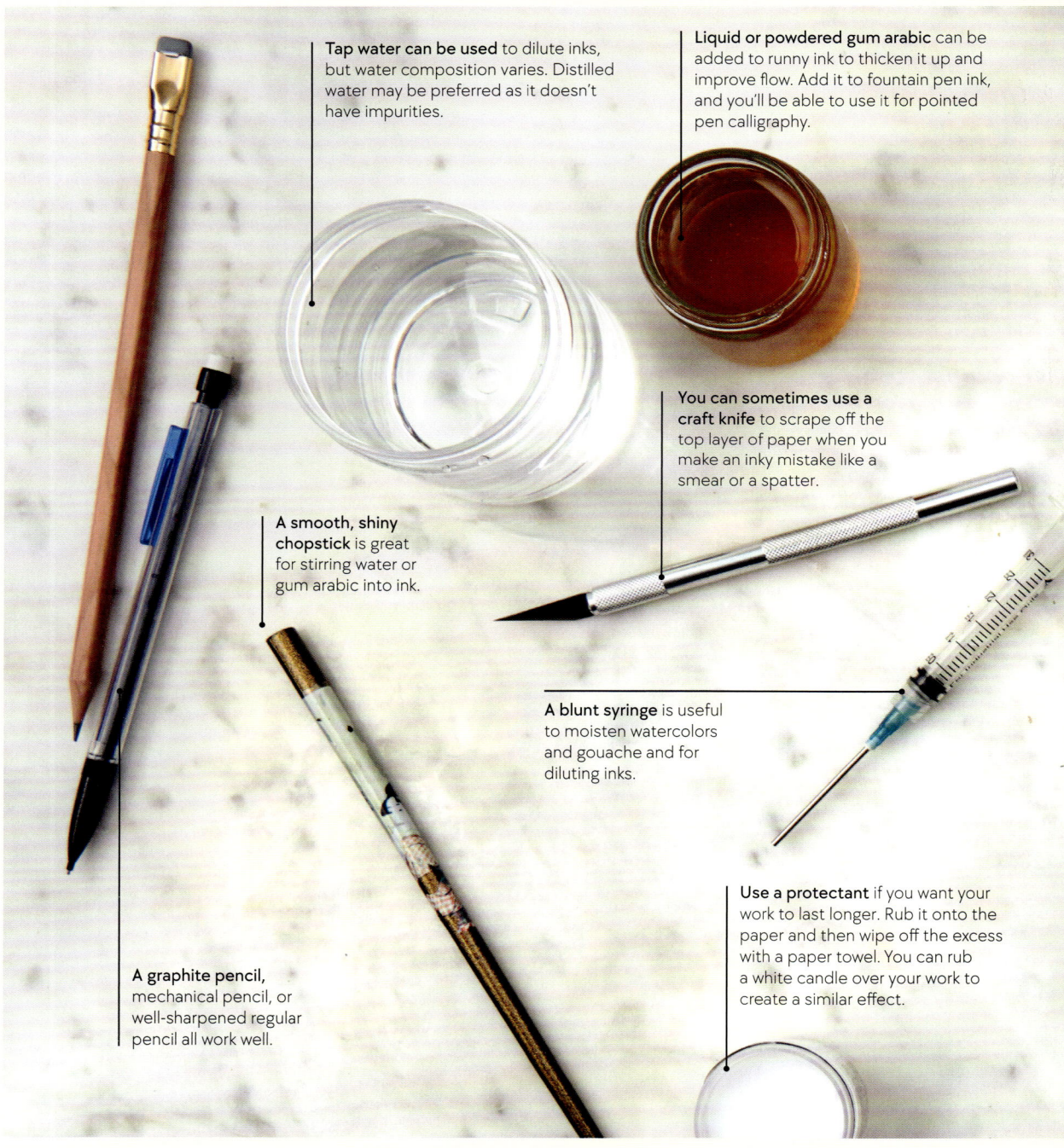

Tap water can be used to dilute inks, but water composition varies. Distilled water may be preferred as it doesn't have impurities.

Liquid or powdered gum arabic can be added to runny ink to thicken it up and improve flow. Add it to fountain pen ink, and you'll be able to use it for pointed pen calligraphy.

You can sometimes use a craft knife to scrape off the top layer of paper when you make an inky mistake like a smear or a spatter.

A smooth, shiny chopstick is great for stirring water or gum arabic into ink.

A blunt syringe is useful to moisten watercolors and gouache and for diluting inks.

Use a protectant if you want your work to last longer. Rub it onto the paper and then wipe off the excess with a paper towel. You can rub a white candle over your work to create a similar effect.

A graphite pencil, mechanical pencil, or well-sharpened regular pencil all work well.

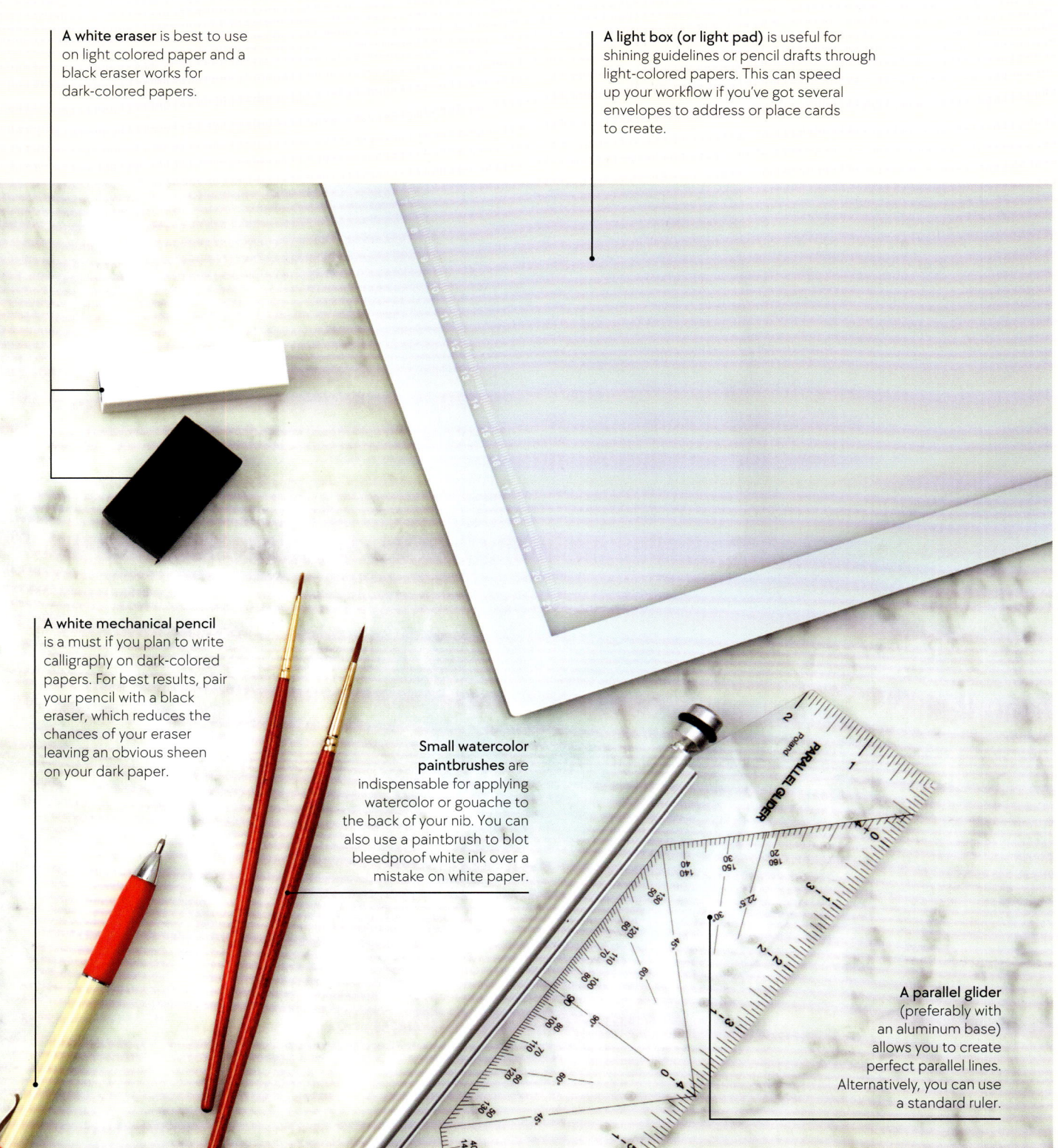

A white eraser is best to use on light colored paper and a black eraser works for dark-colored papers.

A light box (or light pad) is useful for shining guidelines or pencil drafts through light-colored papers. This can speed up your workflow if you've got several envelopes to address or place cards to create.

A white mechanical pencil is a must if you plan to write calligraphy on dark-colored papers. For best results, pair your pencil with a black eraser, which reduces the chances of your eraser leaving an obvious sheen on your dark paper.

Small watercolor paintbrushes are indispensable for applying watercolor or gouache to the back of your nib. You can also use a paintbrush to blot bleedproof white ink over a mistake on white paper.

A parallel glider (preferably with an aluminum base) allows you to create perfect parallel lines. Alternatively, you can use a standard ruler.

Supply storage

We all have different living situations and tendencies when it comes to keeping things organized, so there will be variations from artist to artist as far as how you store your calligraphy tools and equipment.

Pen holders can simply be stored in a mug, nibs inserted and ready to go. If you choose to store your pens in an enclosed container, make sure your nibs aren't in danger of sustaining an impact. If they are, remove the nibs and store them separately.

Nibs can be stored in any container as long as it keeps them dry and safe. You also need to make sure they're protected from any knocks that could splay their tines.

Inks often come in containers into which you can dip your pen. However, if you need to transfer your ink to a different container, look for containers with screw-top lids. You can either buy new jars or upcycle containers (like jelly jars) for this purpose.

Water for cleaning nibs and brushes can be kept in any vessel that you find practical and easy to use. For example, you could keep your water in a favorite old mug that is sturdy enough not to tip over easily.

Paper is best stored flat in a drawer or on a shelf. If space is limited, upright storage is possible, but make sure the paper is tightly packed to avoid curling.

Old calligraphy practice pages and/or filled-out worksheets can be stored in a binder. It's always a good idea to keep examples of your calligraphy around as you are learning and creating. You can look back at your progress when you flip back through those pages.

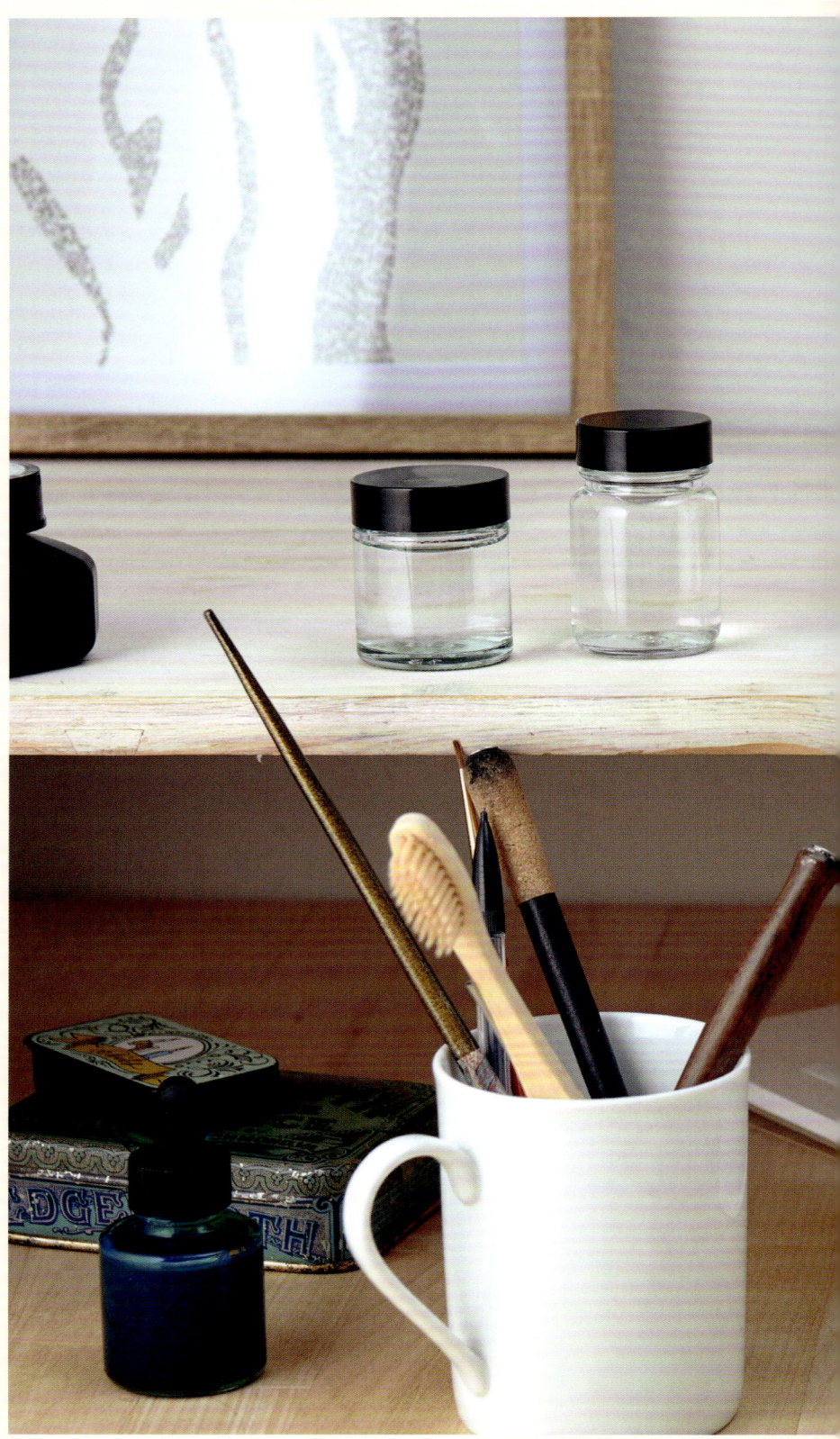

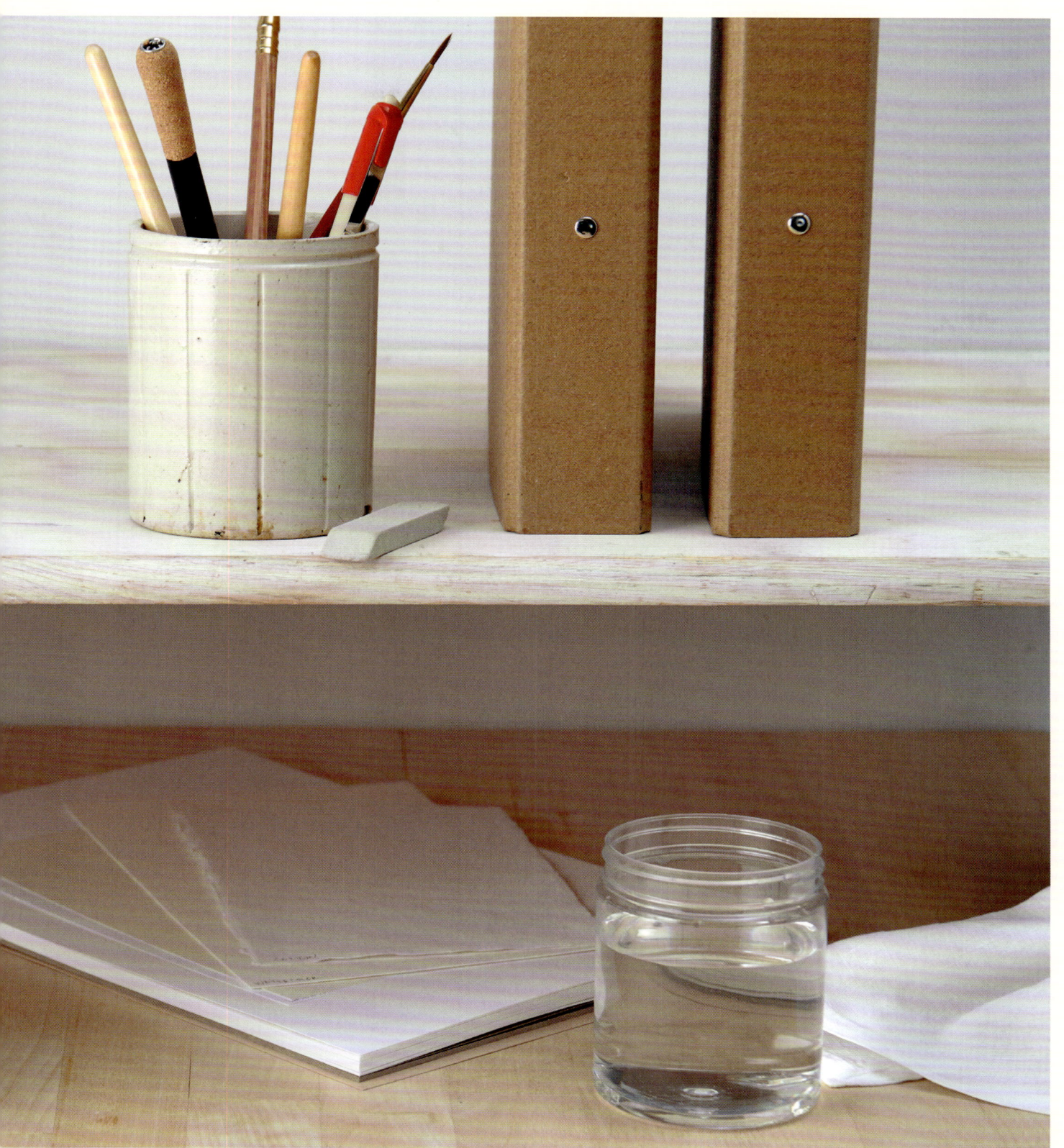

Building your kit

The preparation

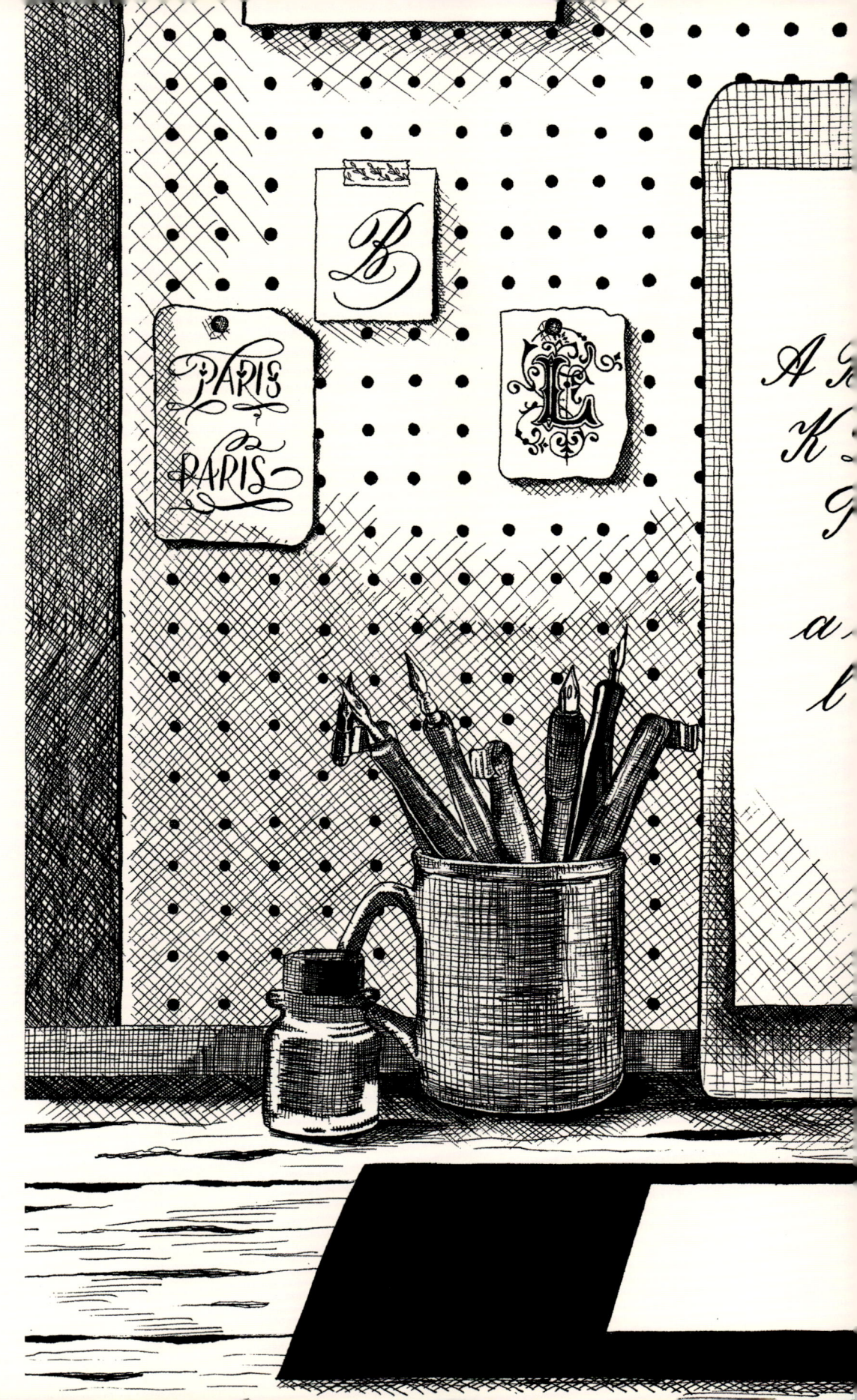

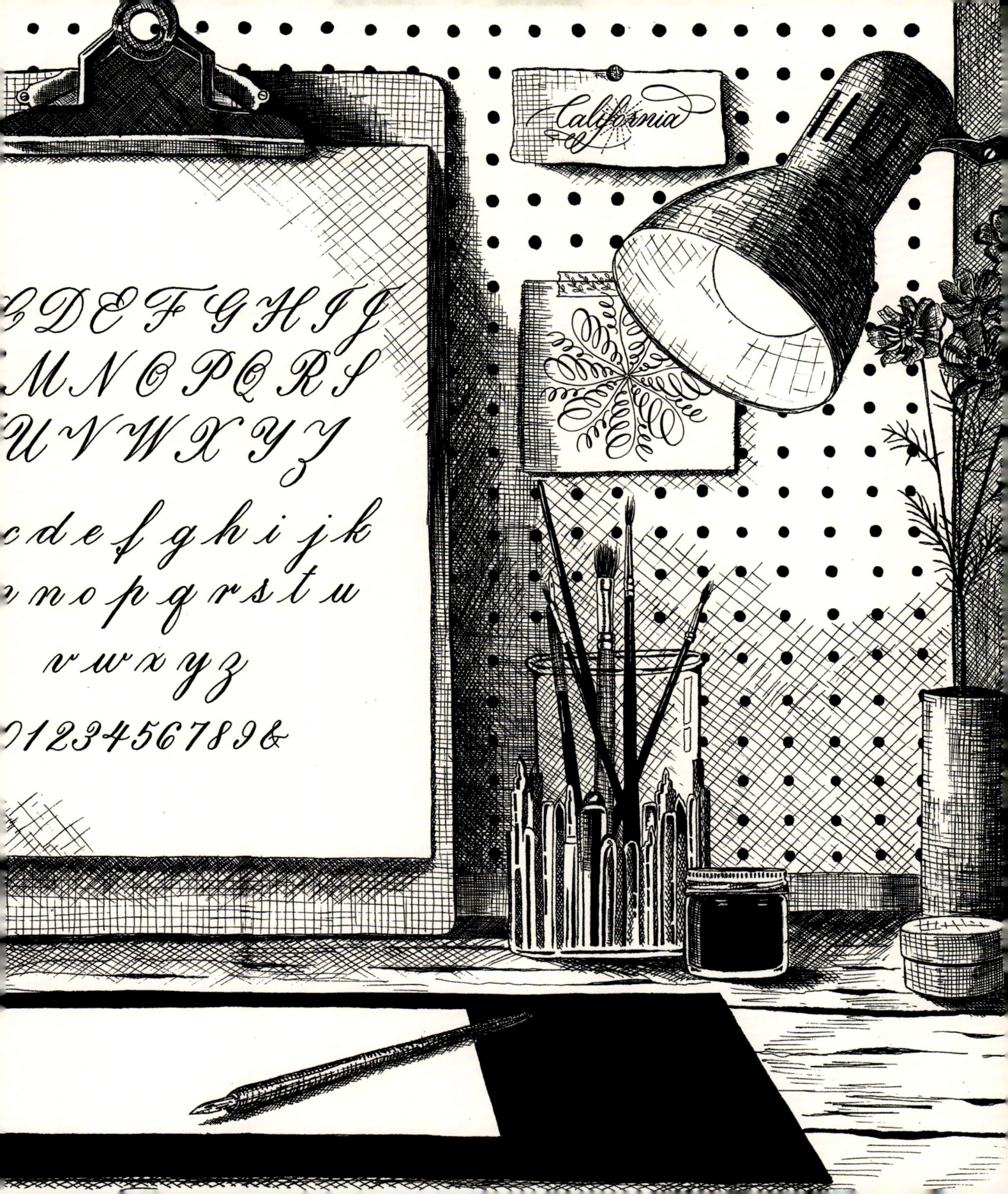

Preparing for success

While the right supplies and good techniques make a world of difference, your workspace is another important factor to consider. Set yourself up at a table with plenty of elbow room and a comfortable chair that's conducive to good posture.

Your workspace

Ensure that you have a flat, smooth writing surface, and a chair that supports good posture and allows you to write comfortably for extended periods. Set up your workspace so that your ink and water are nearby, but not so close that you'll accidentally knock them over while writing. Remember, too, that you need to keep a smooth scrap piece of paper—"padding paper"—under the paper you're writing on. The padding paper should be equal in size or larger than your project page. This subtle cushioning allows you to achieve the desired pressure for your strokes and ensures a pleasant, smooth writing experience. (Padding paper isn't vital to successful envelope calligraphy because envelopes have a built-in double layer of paper.)

Dress code

It's also important to dress comfortably. If possible, wear loose clothing that allows you to breathe freely, and, if temperature allows, wear a long-sleeved shirt. That way, your forearm can glide across the table instead of sticking to its surface, which leads to impeded stroke fluidity. If you can't wear a long-sleeved shirt, try keeping a scrap piece of fabric under your arm to encourage that forearm glide. If you have long hair, it's a good idea to keep it tied back while working so that it doesn't get in the way.

Good lighting

Natural light is ideal, but if that's not possible, opt for a bright and adjustable lamp that you can position to illuminate your work area effectively. The better you can see your work, the better that work will be!

A joyful experience

It is also important to make each calligraphy creation session a pleasurable experience that you anticipate with joy. That could mean brewing up a cup of your favorite tea and grabbing a couple of pieces of chocolate. You might turn on a good audiobook, a podcast, or some relaxing music. In addition to these ambient joys, it's a good idea to personalize your workspace with elements that inspire and motivate you, if possible. Decorate the walls with artwork, calligraphy quotes, or anything that resonates with your creative spirit. A space that sparks joy and enthusiasm will make your calligraphy sessions all the more uplifting, enjoyable, and rewarding.

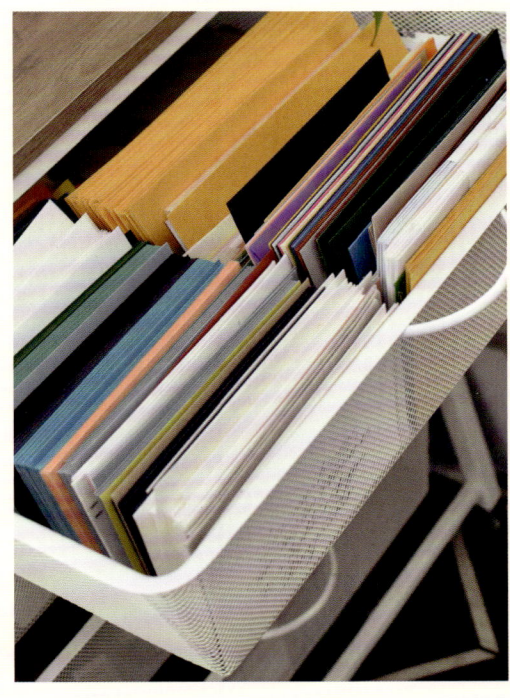

Having all your materials organized helps create a calm working environment.

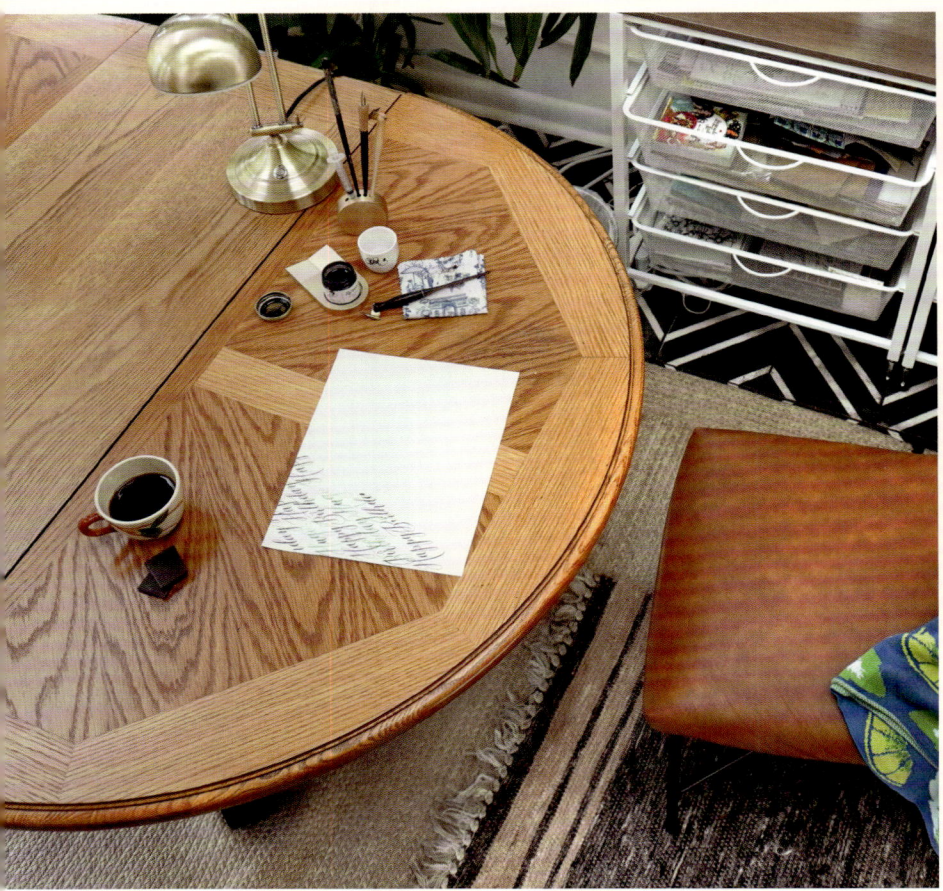

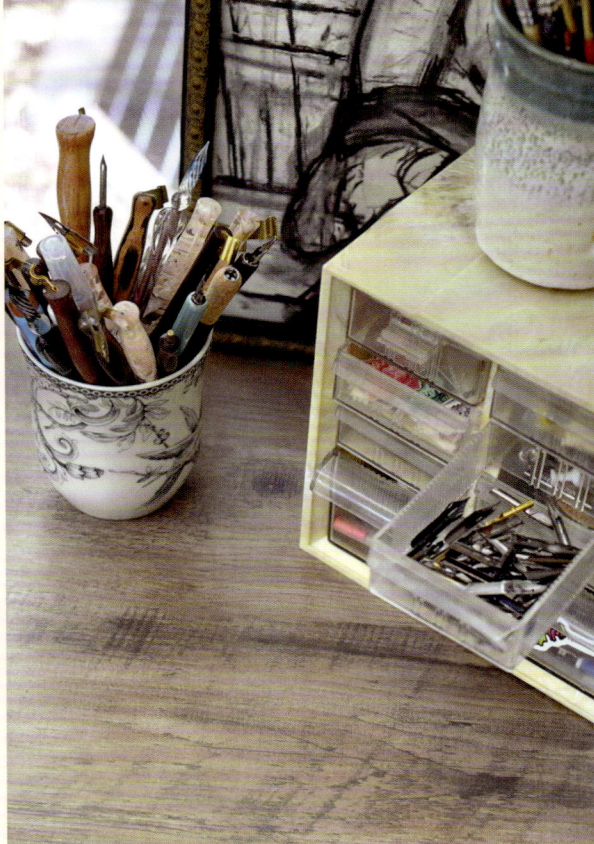

The right supplies

Before you start working, there are several factors to consider to help you gather together the best supplies for your project. These include the colors you're going to use, the paper, and the type of nib and holder.

For your first projects, it's a good idea to keep things simple and use black ink on white paper while you get used to creating calligraphy strokes and lettering. However, if you're preparing something special, like a birthday card or an invitation, you'll want to think more carefully about the materials you're using. Everyone has their own preferences, and the choices available are limitless. Here are a few ideas to get your inspiration flowing.

Elegant color combinations
Dark paper tones and metallic ink or watercolor paint. This classic combination exudes sophistication and luxury, perfect for formal invitations or menus.
Dark paper tones and white ink. White ink on dark paper creates a stunning contrast, adding an air of elegance and drama to your calligraphy projects. To add a luxurious boost, incorporate some gold as well.

Cream or white paper and iron gall ink. Iron gall ink on cream or white paper evokes a timeless and vintage feel, making it an excellent choice for traditional or historical-themed projects.

Playful color combinations
Pink paper and white ink. This vibrant combination adds a burst of energy and fun to your calligraphy projects. It's ideal for cheerful greeting cards and invitations.
White paper and rainbow watercolor paints (used as ink). Alternate the watercolors that you load onto your nib to achieve a rainbow effect. This is a lovely combination for birthday party paper goods like place cards or food labels.
Purple paper and pink gouache. This lively and vibrant combination brings a playful feel to your calligraphy projects. It's great for adding a touch of whimsy and charm to love letters and cute greeting cards.

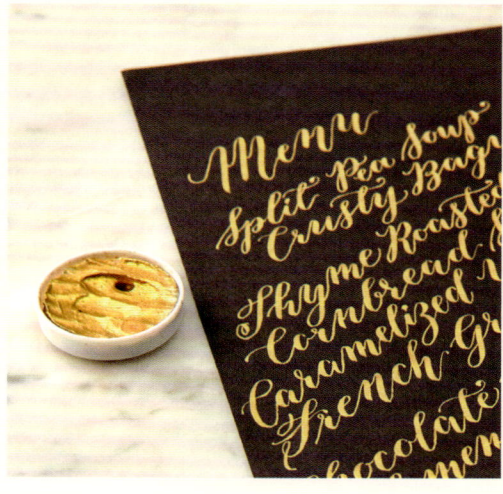

Dark paper and gold watercolor has been used here to create a menu that looks rich and luxurious.

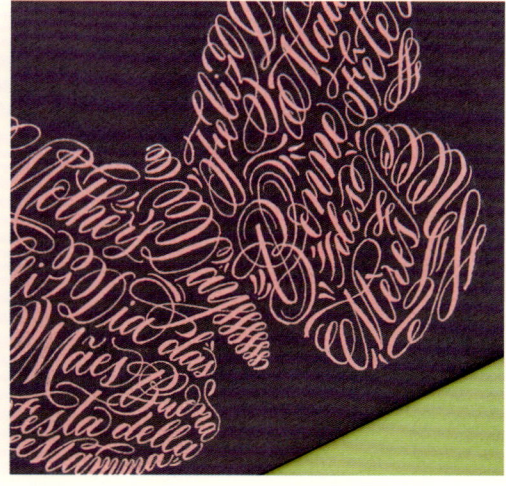

Purple cardstock and pink is a beautiful combination for this Mother's Day card (see pp.158–161).

Turquoise paper with gold ink or watercolor paint. This is a stunning combination that is perfect for adding a luxurious and eye-catching element to your projects such as greeting cards or gift tags.

Paper texture

Smooth paper works well for beginners or those looking for a crisp and clean finish to their lettering. It allows the nib to glide smoothly, resulting in precise and defined strokes. On the other hand, textured paper adds character and uniqueness to your calligraphy. The tactile surface of handmade cotton paper, for example, leads to a look that's simultaneously rustic and elegant. Experiment with different paper textures to find the one that complements your calligraphy style and enhances the visual appeal of your project.

Draft materials

An effective pencil draft makes all the difference for most calligraphy projects, so it's important to find the right supplies that set you up for success. For light-colored papers, use a graphite pencil and a white eraser. When you're working with dark-colored papers, it makes sense to use a white pencil and a black eraser to prepare your drafts.

Pen holders and nibs

In general, it's good to choose low-flex nibs when you're pressed for space or want the ability to create smaller letters. High-flex nibs are better for larger lettering and filling up a generous writing area. To choose your pen holder, consider the calligraphy style you are going to use. If you want to create lettering with a right-leaning slant and you're right-handed, try a right oblique pen. If the lettering doesn't have much of a slant or if you're left-handed, a straight pen is often the best choice.

Finishing agents

If you're creating a project that won't be exposed to moisture or curious fingers, then there's no need to add a finish. If, however, you've created something that will be handled, like an envelope, it's a good idea to put a finish over your calligraphy. A waxy protectant is useful for this, while a waterproof spray finish works for large batches of envelopes or invitations.

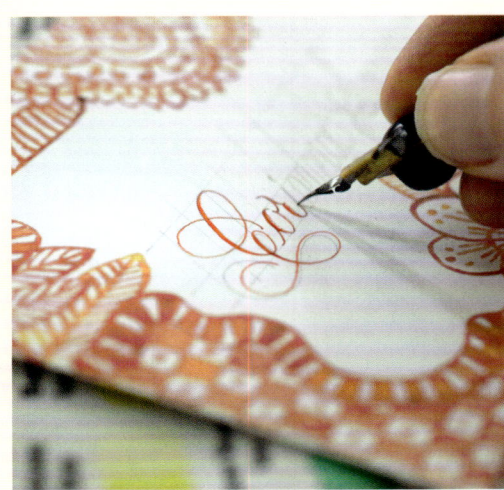

Calligraphy with a rainbow effect can be achieved by alternating different watercolors as you write.

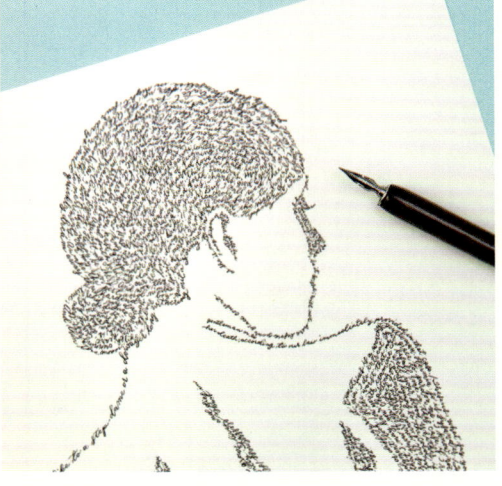

The simple combination of black ink on white paper is sometimes the best choice for a dramatic piece.

The right supplies

Preparing new nibs

Calligraphy nibs are treated with an oil or wax coating to ensure they stay in good condition until use. It's important to remove this coating because it will cause the ink to bead up on the nib and stop it from reaching the paper.

Removing your nib's oily coating and then waiting a few weeks or months to use it won't cause the nib any harm (provided you protect the nib from excessive moisture). The nib will just look a bit duller than brand-new nibs. There are several different ways to clean new calligraphy nibs.

Potato

Take a raw, white- or yellow-fleshed potato. Gently press your nib into the potato and leave for 15 minutes (make sure not to leave for any longer than this or your nib may rust).

The natural acidity of the potato and its slightly abrasive texture helps remove oils and residues from the nib. After the allotted time, rinse your nib with water and pat it dry with a cloth.

Cleaning liquid

Moisten a soft-bristled toothbrush with water, apply some cleaning liquid, and scrub the nib for about 30 seconds. Then, drop the nib in a cup of water and let it sit for a few seconds to get the soap off. Finally, dry the nib with a cloth.

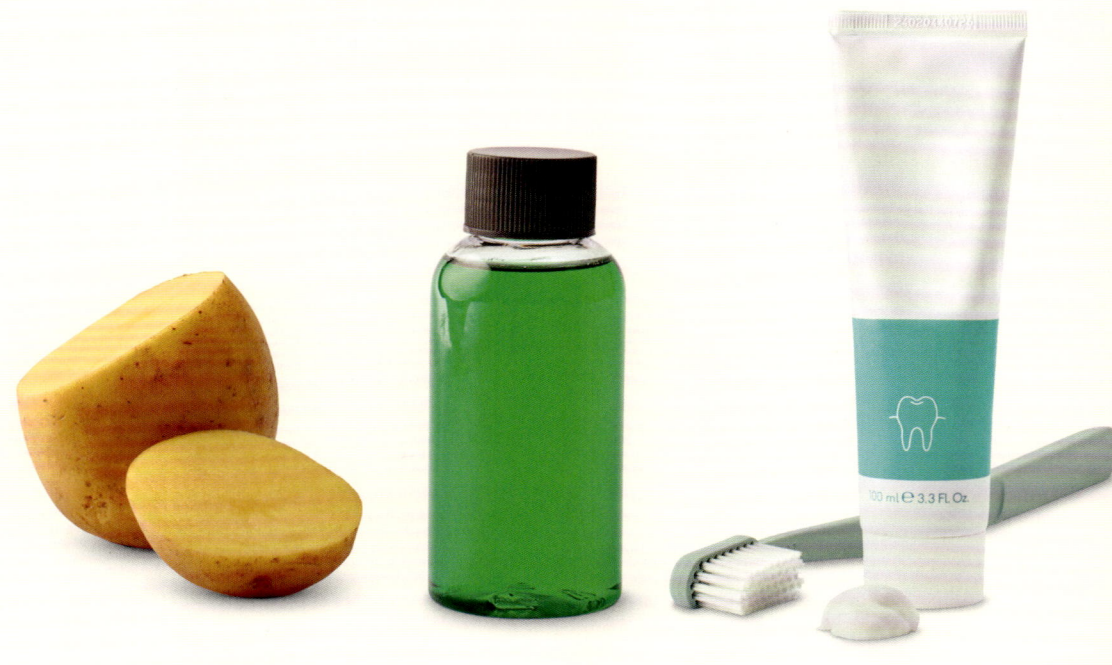

Potato   Cleaning liquid   Toothpaste and a toothbrush

Toothpaste and a toothbrush

Apply toothpaste to a toothbrush, then scrub the nib for 30 seconds. Once you finish scrubbing, drop the nib in water and let it sit for a couple of seconds. Finish by drying the nib with a cloth.

Rubbing alcohol

Pour a small amount of rubbing alcohol into a cup or container, then dip the nib into the alcohol for a few seconds. This helps dissolve any oil or grease on the nib's surface. Afterward, remove the nib and let it air-dry or pat it dry with a cloth.

Acetone

This strong solvent can be used to clean stubborn residue or ink stains from calligraphy nibs. However, it is essential to use acetone with caution as it can be harsh on certain nib coatings. If using acetone, dip the nib briefly, then rinse it with water immediately and dry it thoroughly.

Nontoxic pen cleaner

You can buy specialized nontoxic pen cleaners that are designed to remove ink, oils, and residue from nibs without damaging them. Follow the package instructions.

> **"Removing your nib's oily coating and then waiting to use it won't cause it any harm."**

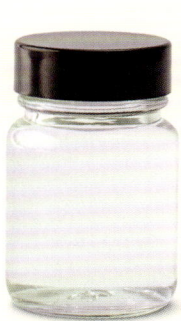

Rubbing alcohol

Acetone

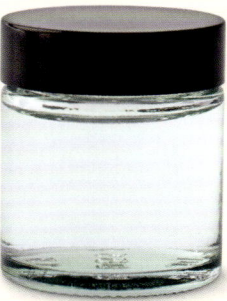

Nontoxic pen cleaner

Preparing new nibs

Adjusting your pen

Many first-time calligraphers purchase a plastic-flanged oblique holder, as these tend to be cheaper. However, it is worth investing in a brass-flanged oblique pen holder instead, as this gives you the opportunity to adjust the angle and nib position to suit your comfort and writing style.

Pen angle

A common problem that beginner calligraphers experience is the nib catching on the paper. This is often caused by the pen angle. If you're holding the pen too upright, then the nib comes at the paper from an aggressively vertical angle and digs into the paper fibers. Oblique pens work to correct that vertical angle. While the pen is straight, the flange tilts the nib up, helping you come at the paper with a gentler angle. You can adjust the flange to increase that angle, if need be. In contrast, plastic-flanged oblique calligraphy pens have a flange that stays in line with the pen. That really doesn't help as far as softening your angle goes. In fact, if you have trouble with nibs catching on the paper when you're using regular straight calligraphy pens, you'll probably experience the same issue with a plastic-flanged oblique.

Nib position

When you insert a nib into an oblique calligraphy pen, the tip of the nib should touch an imaginary line running through the middle of the pen. This ensures that the pen holder and the nib are in alignment. Improper alignment can make it challenging to maintain control over your pen strokes, especially when trying to achieve smooth, flowing lines. With a brass-flanged oblique pen, it's easy to achieve the proper alignment. Unless your nib is very short, plastic-flanged oblique pens cannot fulfill this requirement. Most of the time, the nib extends well past the center line of the pen, which makes it more difficult to perfect your calligraphy skills and get a smooth line.

Adjustment potential

The biggest advantage of brass-flanged oblique pens is that they can easily be adjusted. If you find, for example, that the pen holds your nib at too severe an angle, then you can grip the brass flange firmly with your left thumb and index finger as you slightly rotate the pen holder counterclockwise with your right hand. Doing this will adjust the position of your flange so that the nib meets the page at a less severe angle. If you want to adjust the nib to meet the page at a more upright angle, rotate the pen in a clockwise direction instead.

A brass flange also gives you the opportunity to tighten or loosen its grip on a nib. If your nib won't quite slide into the slit in the flange, try gripping the flange with your left thumb and index finger as you gently rotate the pen counterclockwise, then clockwise. Repeat the process a couple of times, and you'll find that the slit has widened slightly. To get the flange to narrow, try using cylindrical jewelry pliers (or needle-nose pliers) to pinch the flange's opening slightly to the required size.

Pen is straight

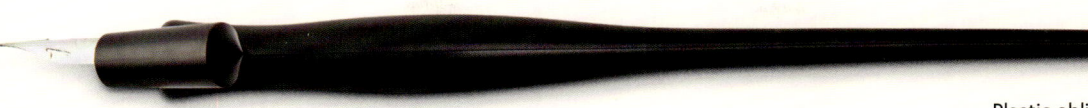

Flange is straight

Plastic oblique calligraphy pen This pen offers some of the advantages of an oblique calligraphy pen at a low price point.

Pen is straight

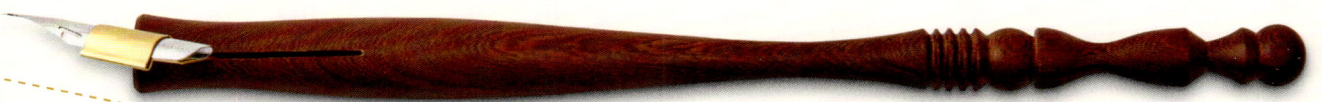

Flange is slanted

Brass-flanged pen holder With the nib tilted upward, the nib meets the paper at a gentler angle.

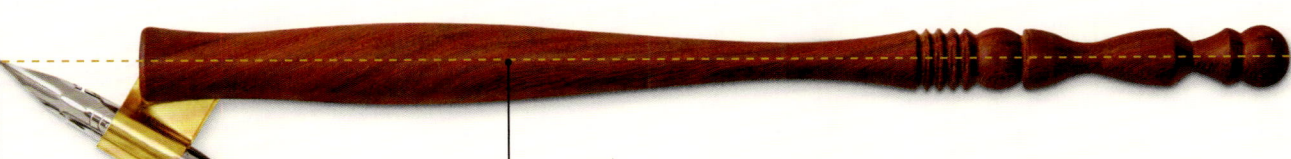

The tip of the pen With a brass flange, the nib can be aligned with the center of the pen.

Center line of the pen Pen holder and nib should be in—or nearly in—alignment.

Brass-flanged oblique pen holder With this pen holder, you can make adjustments to the angle of the nib to suit your style.

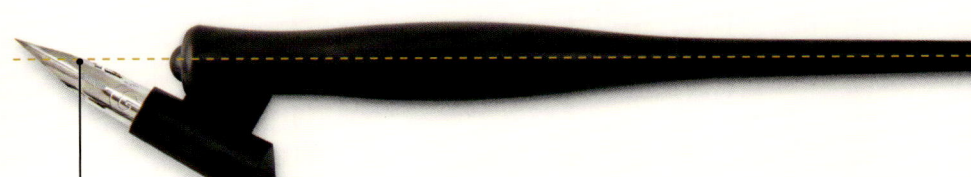

The nib position With a plastic flange, your nib often won't be in line with the center of the pen.

Plastic-flanged oblique calligraphy pen There is no possibility of adjusting the angle of the nib when using a plastic pen holder like this one.

Adjusting your pen

Finding your grip

While there are recommendations on how to grip your pen, these are just starting points. Ultimately, the best grip for you will depend on your personal preferences, hand size, and the specific calligraphy style you are practicing.

It's essential to experiment with different grips and observe how they impact your writing. Don't be afraid to try unconventional approaches and adapt your grip as needed to achieve the results that you're looking for.

Straight pen grip

Think about how you write with an everyday pen. You probably maintain a curled grip around the barrel, letting your fingers control the pen's movements. Pointed pen calligraphy is tricky at the beginning because the pen is so similar to the pens you're used to writing with every day, but the grip should be different. Try to keep your grip relatively relaxed and hold the pen at a 45-degree angle to the paper. The grip is the same whether you're right- or left-handed.

If you are finding that your grip just doesn't feel right, check for these common issues.

What to avoid

Holding the pen vertically increases the probability of your nib digging in to the paper, impeding your movement. A vertical position also generally results in ink flow issues. Instead of gliding smoothly onto the paper, the ink may come out in a blob.

Holding the pen too far up on the barrel can lead to a lack of control over the pressure applied to the nib. To achieve better control, try holding the pen about ½in (1.25cm) from its end. This grip allows for more precise pressure control and better guidance of the nib's direction.

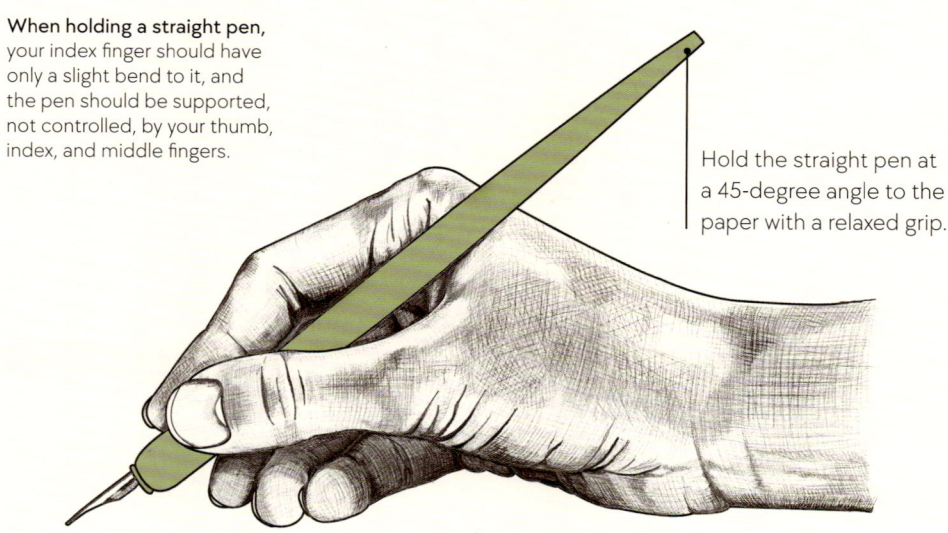

When holding a straight pen, your index finger should have only a slight bend to it, and the pen should be supported, not controlled, by your thumb, index, and middle fingers.

Hold the straight pen at a 45-degree angle to the paper with a relaxed grip.

Oblique pen grip

Pointed pen calligraphy purists tend to think that there's only one grip to use with the oblique pen. This grip involves putting your index finger on the top of the pen and letting the tip of your thumb rest just above the flange. Your thumb and index finger will be on the top of the pen while your middle finger rests under the pen. This grip is similar to how you hold a straight pen, but the difference is the middle of the thumbnail making contact with the flange.

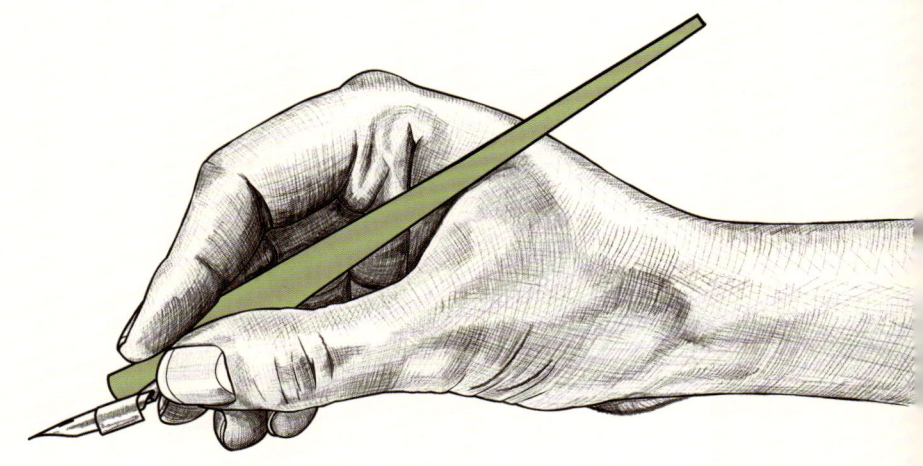

To hold an oblique pen, put your index finger on top of the pen and your thumb just above the flange.

Alternative grips

You may find that the traditional oblique pen grip, shown above, works for you. If not, there are ways to break these rules. See if one of these variations works better for you.

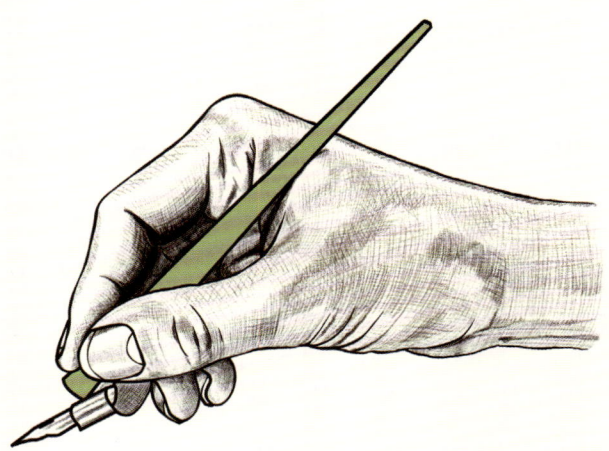

Rest the left side of your thumb on the flange if you have long thumbnails or the traditional grip doesn't feel right for you. Then use your index finger and thumb to pinch the barrel of the pen in a three-point grip, while your three other fingers stay under the pen.

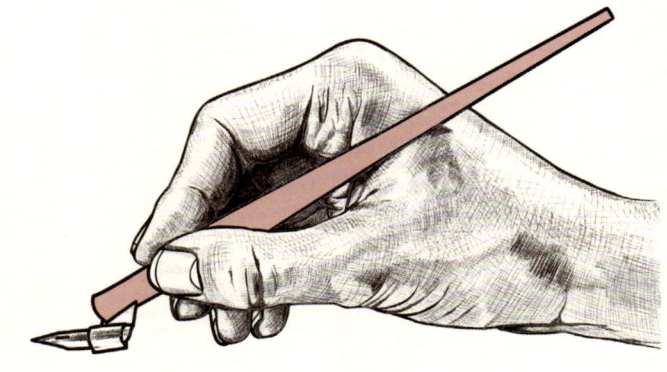

Holding the pen slightly farther up the barrel is another effective oblique pen grip. Instead of positioning your fingers so that your thumb touches the flange, move your grip up slightly. This grip allows for a looser, more relaxed hold, which can be beneficial for some writers.

Finding your grip

Dipping and refiling

When you first start practicing calligraphy, you may automatically dunk your pen in water as you would with a paintbrush. It is important to avoid doing this with dip pens for several reasons.

When you're working on a calligraphy project, you'll need to dip your nib into the ink frequently to keep an even flow. You'll know it's time to redip your nib when your nib starts "railroading" (p.57) or stops writing. You'll also need to use water to clean your nib regularly. Just fill up a cup with tap water and keep that cup beside you. When the ink starts to thicken or accumulate on the nib, wash the ink off in the water, quickly pat the nib dry with a cloth, and start writing again.

Smart dipping

It's important to dip the nib in ink or water only as far as the reservoir or just slightly higher. Try not to push the pen and nib

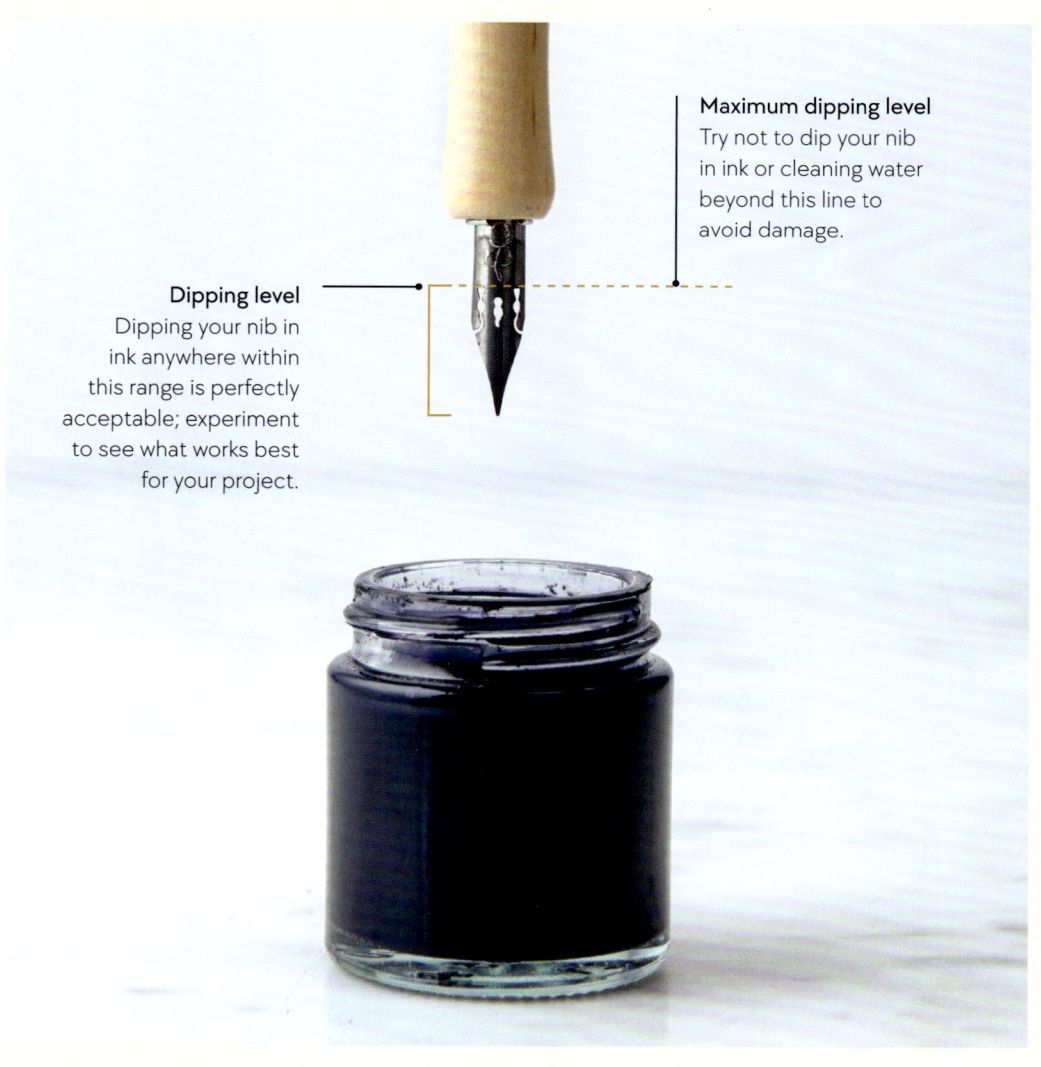

Maximum dipping level
Try not to dip your nib in ink or cleaning water beyond this line to avoid damage.

Dipping level
Dipping your nib in ink anywhere within this range is perfectly acceptable; experiment to see what works best for your project.

further into the ink or water because the nib and/or the pen's universal insert will rust. If a nib develops rust inside your pen, you'll have a lot of trouble getting it out. If ink gets inside the pen, it eventually solidifies like glue, and it is almost impossible to pull the nib out.

If you do dip your pen too far into ink or water, immediately remove the nib and try to get the moisture out of the pen. When working with a straight pen, you might be able to do this with a cotton swab. If you are using an oblique pen, remove the nib and let it dry.

If surface rust does develop, it doesn't necessarily mean that you can't use the nib again. Some inks are more forgiving with rusty nibs, while others might clog.

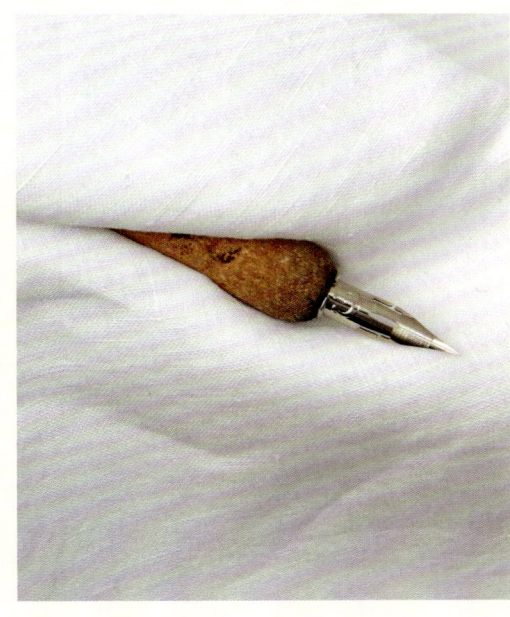

Drying the nib using a cloth made of cotton or linen is ideal. When you're finished, give your nib a final swish in the water, then dry with a nonfibrous cloth.

Cleaning the nib

To clean your nib after a writing session, simply dip it into some water and dry it with a cleaning cloth. Ink stains on the nib don't affect ink flow, but if you want to keep your calligraphy supplies looking extra clean, you can use a toothbrush to try and scrub the ink off between calligraphy sessions. To be even more thorough, you can use some baking soda, too. The baking soda particles might encourage ink to lift out of the little grooves in the nib.

New nib

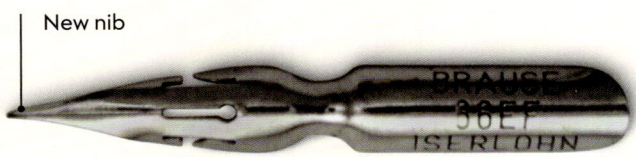

Used nib

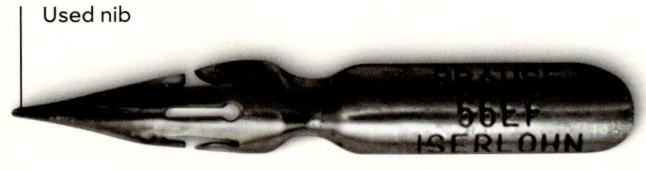

Avoiding paper towels

While you can use paper towels to dry nibs, stray paper towel fibers tend to get caught on the shoulders or the tip of the nib. You often won't see those fibers until you begin to write and it makes a mess of your work, as the fibers drag ink across the page. It is safer to use a nonfibrous, tightly woven cloth, such as a cotton dinner napkin.

While it's important to clean your nibs, it is impossible to keep them looking like new. A slightly dull nib shows that you've been practicing your calligraphy.

Tip
When to replace your nib

If your nib's tines have split, your nib feels uncomfortable and scratchy, or your upstrokes are too wide, it's time to replace your nib.

Try not to dip your nib into water or ink beyond the lines shown here to avoid your nib becoming rusty.

Dipping and refilling

The practice

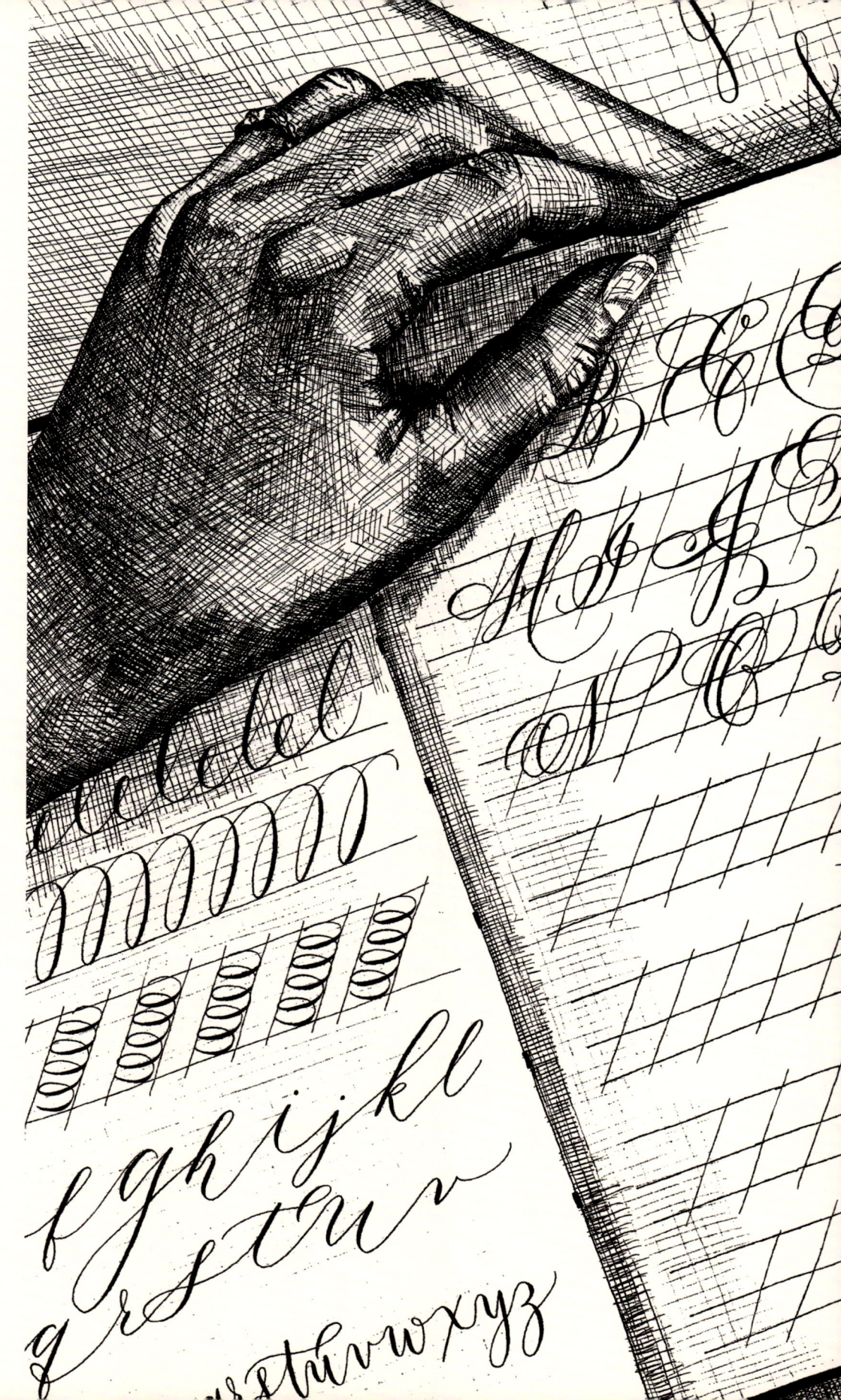

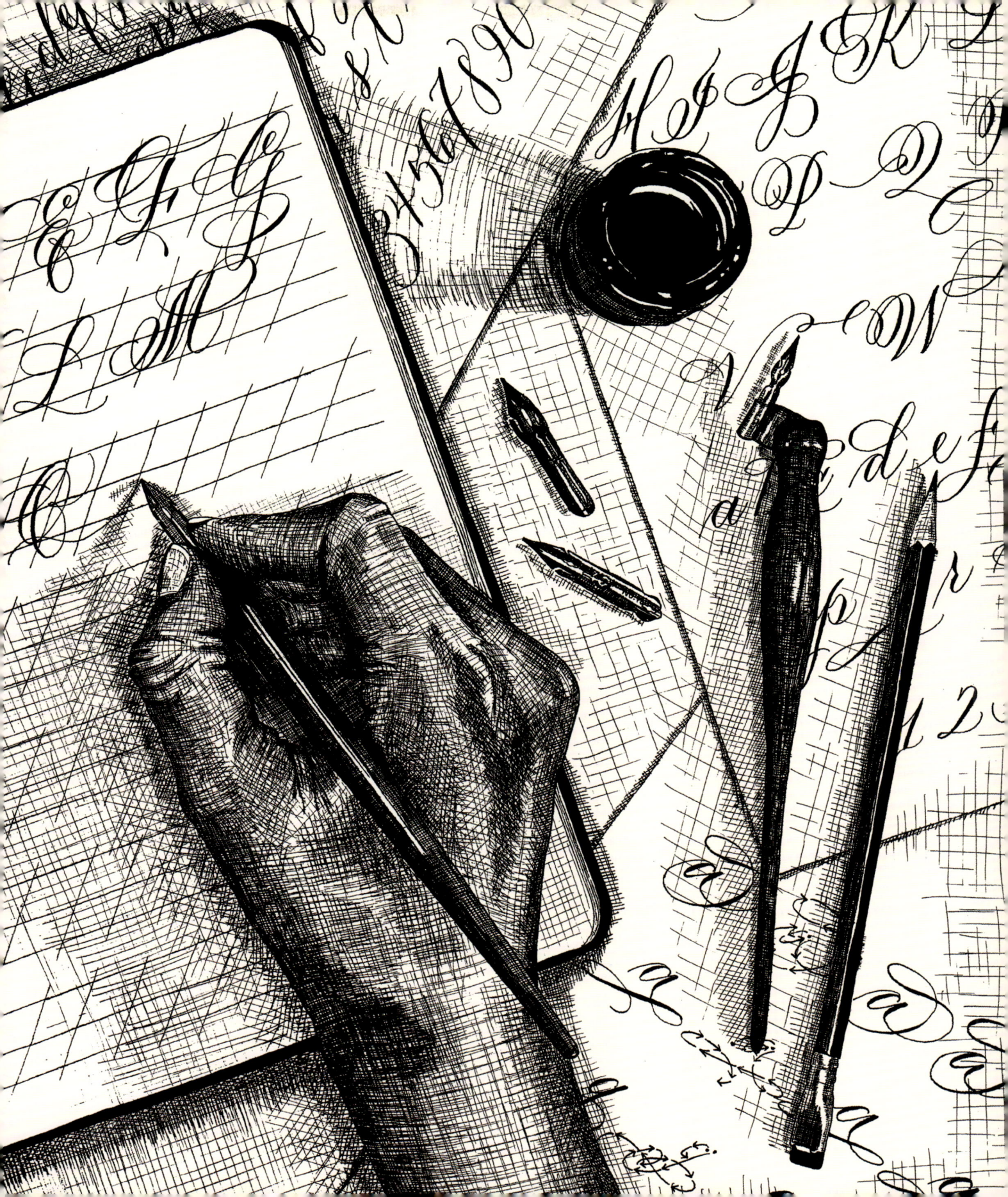

The basic strokes

Pointed pen calligraphy can be divided into three simple strokes: upstrokes, horizontal strokes, and downstrokes. Practicing these strokes is the foundation of all calligraphy, so it's important to master them and give them the practice time they deserve.

The best way to practice is to use drill sheets (see pp.62–63), or you can repeat strokes on a scrap piece of paper until the interaction between nib and ink feels intuitive. When you're ready to begin writing, dip the pen into the ink. The quantity of ink on the nib is a personal preference; just make sure it doesn't go too far above the nib's reservoir (see pp.46–47). If you suspect there may be too much ink on the nib, give your pen a firm shake over the open ink jar or your cleaning water to remove the excess.

Downstrokes
Try not to write too fast, which results in sloppy, uneven strokes. Take a deep breath, relax, and pull your pen down in a slow, consistent movement. Let's say you're making a downstroke that's 1in (2.5cm) long: try to make that downstroke in no less than two seconds. Your pen holder should not lever up as you write a downstroke. Maintain a 45-degree angle of pen to paper and be mindful of exerting balanced pressure to both tines of your nib.

Upstrokes
Unlike downstrokes, where you apply pressure to the nib to achieve a thick line, upstrokes require a gentle glide of the pen. Barely touch your inky nib to the surface of your paper and smoothly push it up. Try to aim for a featherlight touch to create thin, elegant lines that contrast beautifully with the bold downstrokes. The trick is to maintain a steady rhythm and consistent pressure, avoiding any sudden stops or jerky movements. Practice the motion slowly and deliberately.

Horizontal strokes
Horizontal strokes occur when you move your pen right or left to create a horizontal (or mostly horizontal) line. Horizontal strokes require the same delicate pressure that upstrokes do. Apply too much pressure to the nib, and one of your tines will snag on paper fibers.

Equal pressure
If you apply more pressure to one tine of the nib than the other, your ink flow will be uneven, resulting in thicker or thinner strokes in your calligraphy. This inconsistency can make your writing look unbalanced and less visually appealing. By exerting equal pressure to both tines, you will ensure that the ink flow remains consistent, leading to smooth and uniform calligraphy strokes. Balanced pressure also helps prevent issues like scratching the paper or snagging the nib, which often occurs if one tine is under more pressure than the other.

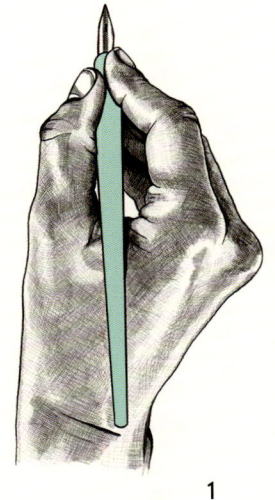

1

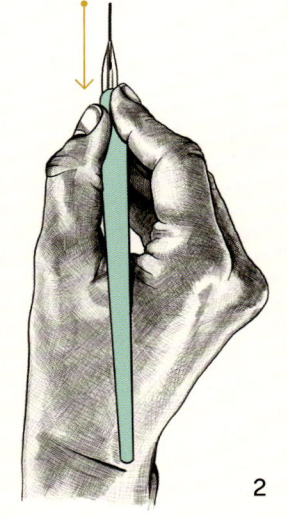

2

Downstroke

For downstrokes, press gently but firmly on your pen so that the tines of your nib split apart (**1**). Then, pull the pen down, keeping it at a 45-degree angle to your writing surface. As you pull down (**2**), the width of your stroke should match the width of your nib's split tines, creating a thick stroke.

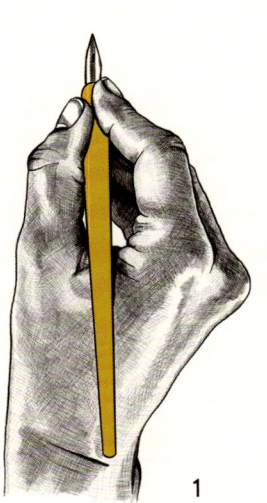

1

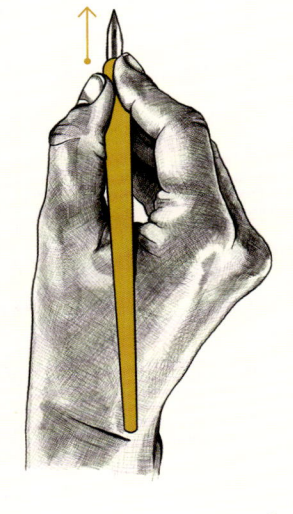

2

Upstroke

To make an upstroke, push your pen up (**1**), exerting as little pressure as possible on the nib. The tines of the nib will stay together as you write, resulting in a thin stroke (**2**).

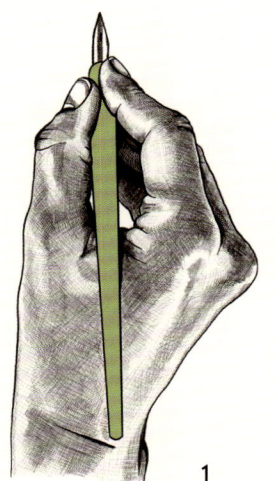

1

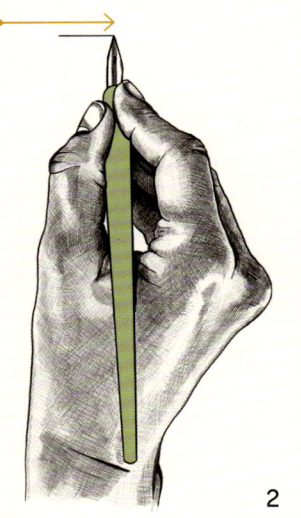

2

Horizontal stroke

To create a horizontal stroke, move your pen over in a horizontal movement (**1**). Apply very little pressure on the nib to ensure that the tines stay together to make a thin stroke (**2**).

The basic strokes

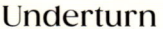

Tip

Hold the pen straight

It's common for beginners to hold the pen sideways while practicing upstrokes, relying on only one of the nib's tines for fineness. However, this technique doesn't translate well to actual writing. For cohesive letters and words, keep your pen grip consistent to write all types of strokes.

Letter slant

As you write, the shank of your nib should be parallel to the letter slant that you're trying to achieve. This goes for whether you're using a straight pen or an oblique pen. If your calligraphy style has a 55-degree slant, the position of your nib should reflect that. You may need to rotate the paper to make this work. If the upstrokes and horizontal strokes in your calligraphy are vertical (90 degrees), the positioning of your nib should reflect that. For right-handed people, it can be difficult to exert balanced pressure on both tines of a nib when you're writing in a slanted style with a straight pen. Using an oblique pen, the flange does the nib angle work for you. (You will probably still need to slightly rotate your paper to write comfortably.)

Curves

Drawing curves requires a quick yet gradual transition of pressure to make downstrokes and letting up on pressure to make upstrokes (or vice versa). Practicing this transition will pay off because every alphabet character requires a curve of some kind.

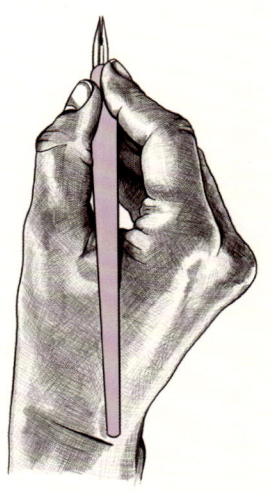

1

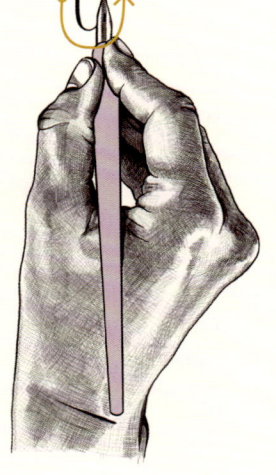

2

Underturn

To make an underturn (a "u"-shaped curve), begin by exerting pressure to your nib to split the tines apart to make a downstroke (**1**). As you reach the bottom of the curve, gently let up on your pressure exertion to allow the tines to spring back together. Then finish the "u" shape with a delicate upstroke (**2**).

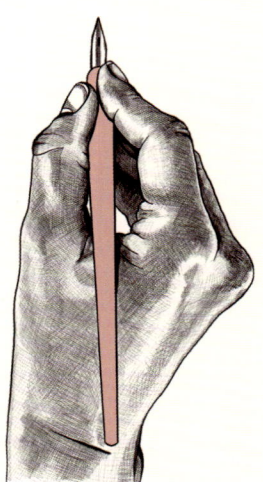

1

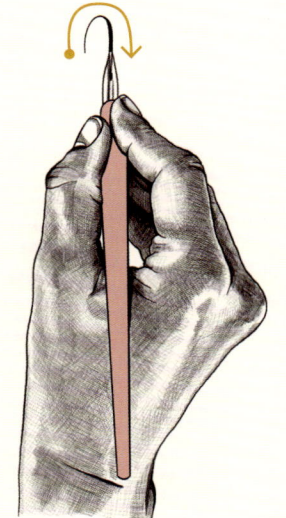

2

Overturn

To make an overturn (a hill-shaped curve), begin by exerting minimal pressure to your nib to make an upstroke that curves to the right at the top (**1**). As the curve turns down, ease into applying more pressure to the nib to encourage the tines to spring apart, resulting in a thick downstroke (**2**).

Other strokes

Calligraphy involves moving your pen upward, downward, or across to create the three types of foundational strokes. However, it is useful to be aware of other terms that are used to describe a wider range of shapes or strokes.

1 Entrance stroke The first stroke used to start a letter or word, setting the foundation for the following strokes.

2 Flourish An embellishment or decorative extension added to letterforms or words, enhancing their visual appeal.

3 Loop A circular or elliptical shape created by the movement of the pen, often found in flourishing and decorative elements.

4 Compound stroke A smooth, continuous stroke that combines both downstrokes and upstrokes. It's used to enable the smooth connection between thick and thin strokes.

5 Oval A curved stroke resembling an oval shape, commonly used in the construction of certain letters.

6 Swell A gradual thickening of the stroke, often seen in flourishing or decorative elements.

7 Hairline An extremely thin and delicate stroke, typically an upstroke or a horizontal stroke.

8 Exit stroke The final stroke used to finish a letter or word, leading smoothly into the next element.

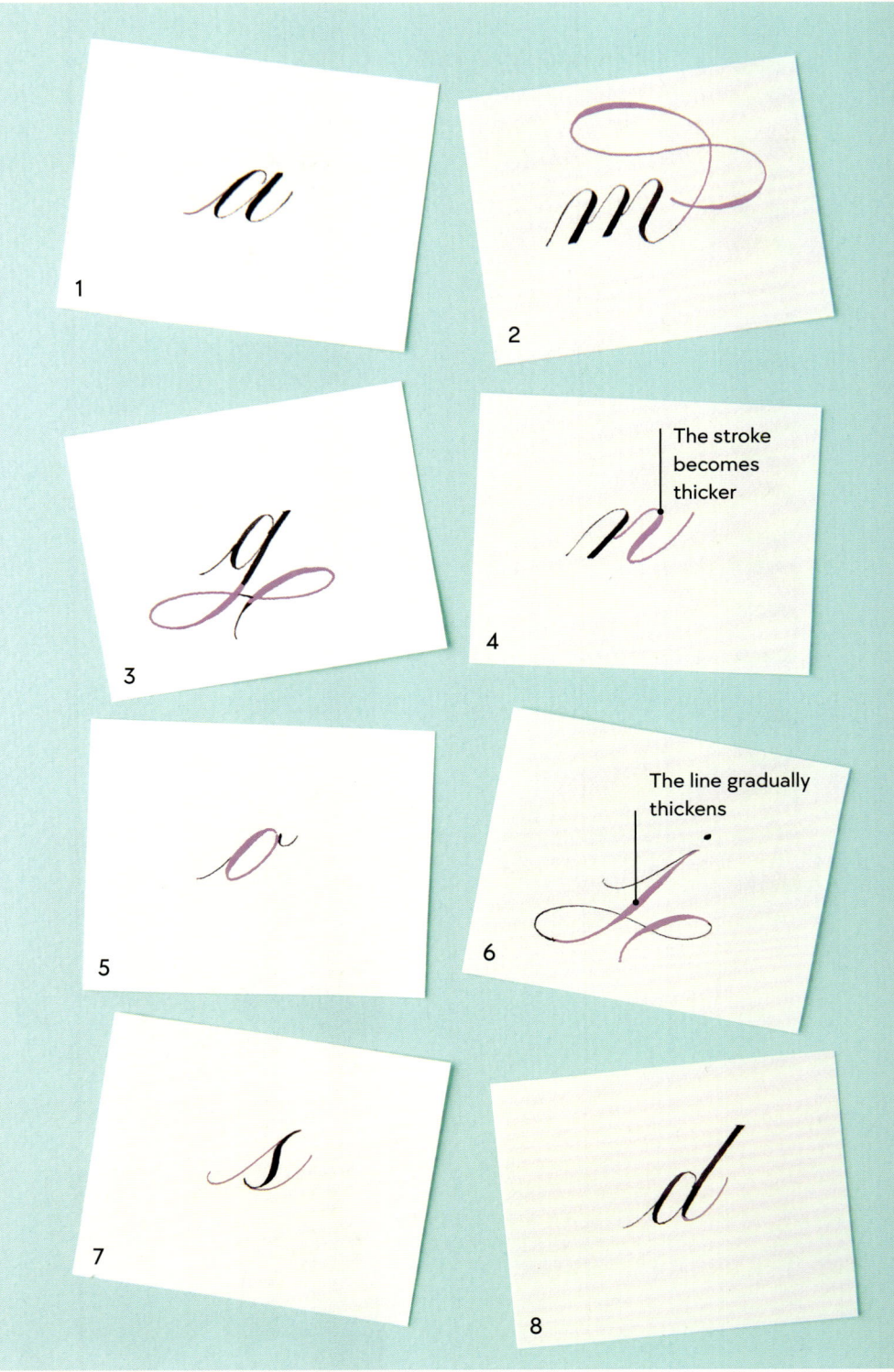

The basic strokes

The movement

In pointed pen calligraphy, your movement is key. Fully understanding how to move your pen is a huge milestone, and one that takes quite a bit of trial and error to reach. Here are the three key aspects to keep in mind as you write.

Angle of pen holder to paper

As you're writing, your pen holder itself should only barely change position. Your job is to glide the pen across the page without letting it dramatically lever up or down. Beginners often want to lever the pen from a 45-degree position to a 90-degree position as they draw a stroke from top to bottom, but it's critical to avoid that. The pen should not wiggle in reaction to overly active fingers as you write. Instead, you should aim to keep the pen mostly static as it travels across the page, only slightly moving in reaction to the pressure that you exert when you create downstrokes. This may feel unnatural at first, but it will become easier with practice.

Use your entire arm to write

As you're writing, your finger movement should be about 25 percent of that used when you write with an everyday pen. To ensure smooth strokes, most of your movement will come from the elbow, forearm, and wrist, with your fingers mainly acting to exert pressure on the nib. Imagine your elbow as a pivot, providing sweeping motions, and your fingers as gentle adjusters that ensure stroke contrast. Many beginners hear "use your arm to write," and think they need to hold their forearm and elbow uncomfortably aloft. There is no need for this. Your forearm should rest on your writing surface, where it can comfortably

When you write with a regular pen or pencil, your fingers do most of the work, causing the pen to shift positions and move in various directions.

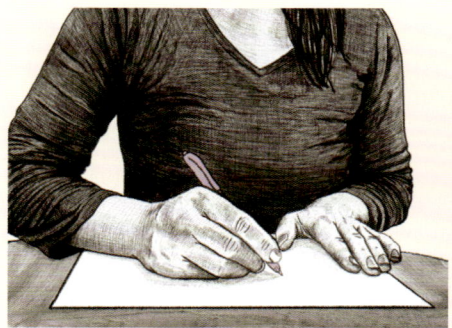
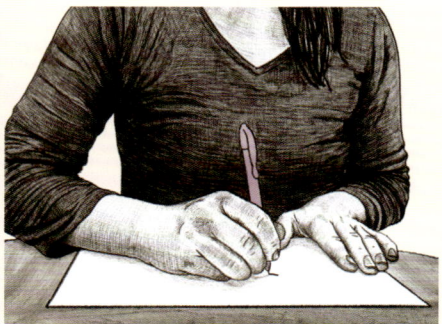

With a pointed pen, keep the holder steady and glide it smoothly, allowing only slight pressure-induced movements.

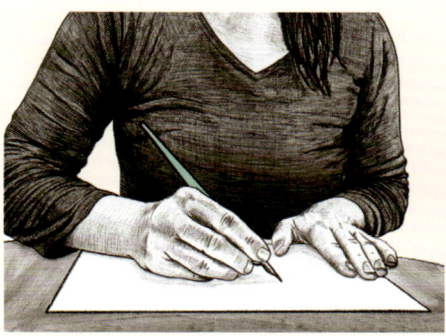
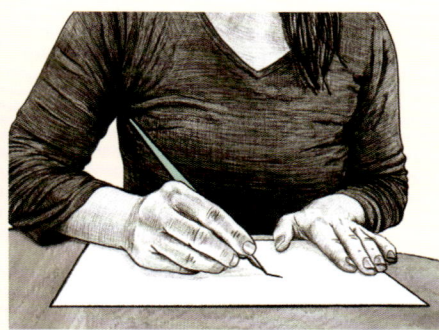

glide back and forth as you write your strokes. To keep your arm from sticking to the table as you work, try wearing a long-sleeved shirt or placing some fabric under your arm.

Maintain good posture

As you write, continually assess your body position and breathing patterns. So many of us have a tendency to curl up, limit our breathing, and become tense while we concentrate on our calligraphy creation. The more relaxed your body is, the easier it will be to make professional-looking, beautiful calligraphy. So if you notice that you're starting to hunch, do the following:

straighten your back, roll your shoulders a few times, and take a deep breath. Start writing again in that upright position. When you maintain good posture, you'll be able to write for longer and you won't suffer the unpleasant consequences of staying in a hunched position for a long time.

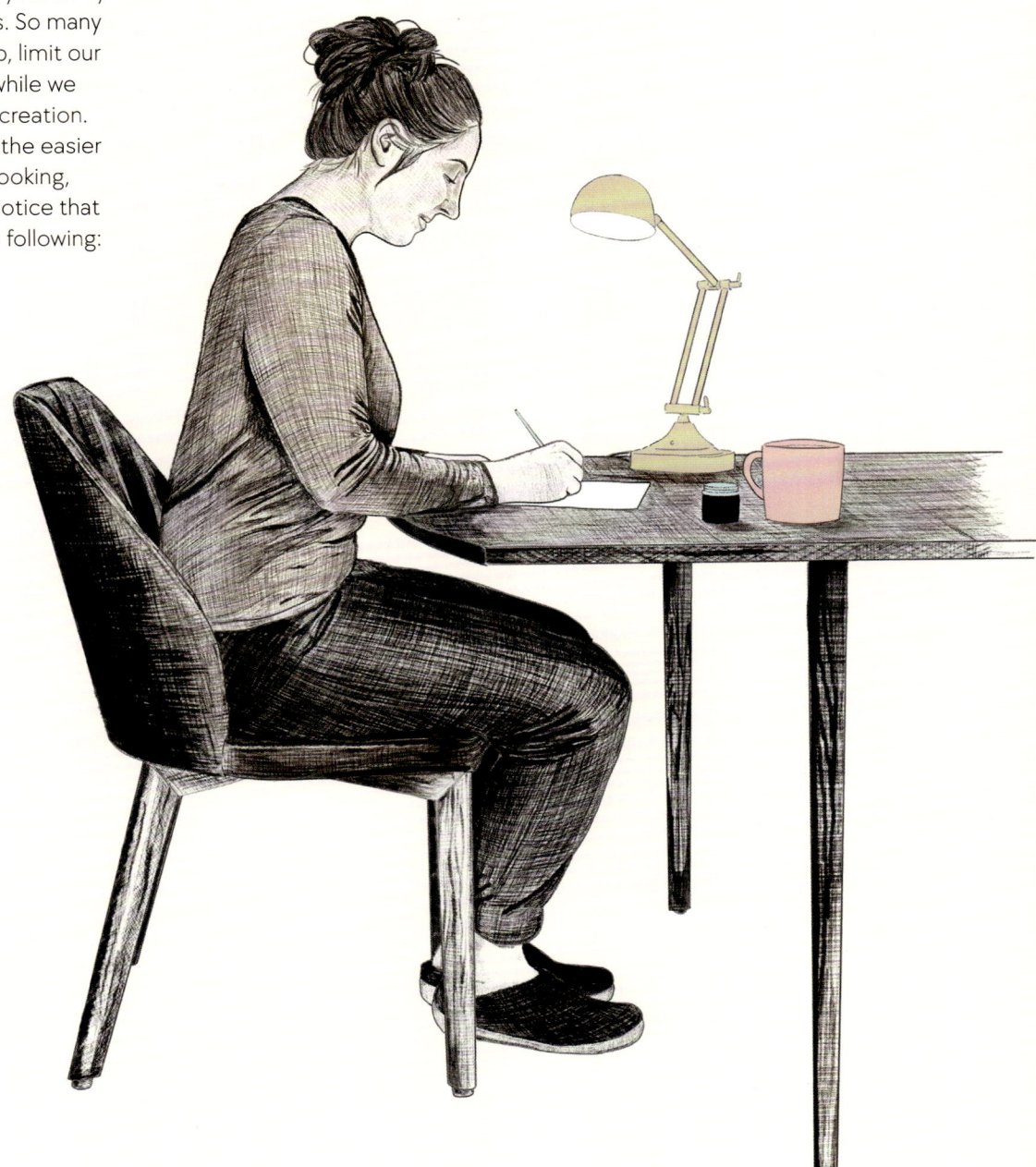

It's important to maintain good posture while writing. If you catch yourself hunching, gently correct your position.

The movement

Effective practice

Once you can write the basic strokes, it's time to begin practicing them. The more you do this, the more confident you'll become and the easier it will be to make consistent strokes when you set out to work on a project. Get your workspace set up and settle down for your first calligraphy session.

Begin by setting up your workspace with cleaning water, padding paper (this can be spare paper), and a cleaning cloth. Choose the pen holder, nib, paper, and ink combination that you wish to use. If you're a beginner, try using a straight pen, a Nikko G nib, sumi or India ink, and laserjet paper or a calligraphy practice pad. Then, place your paper on top of the padding paper (if you're working on a single piece of paper).

1 Grip the pen (see pp.44–45). Then, pull the pen holder down to make a downstroke. Exert even, balanced pressure on both tines of your nib to ensure a clean stroke. Make several more downstrokes until you like how they look (and how you feel making them).

2 Now, try an upstroke. Remember to apply very little pressure to the pen as you push up, and try to keep your pen in the same position it was in as you created downstrokes. Make several more upstrokes, then create a few horizontal strokes.

3 Once you've written those three basic strokes, try more complicated strokes like loops, flourishes, and ovals (see p.53). These types of strokes show up often in letterforms and are so important both for practicing and for warming up before creating a project.

4 Depending on your skill level, you can keep practicing strokes and making drills, or you can move on and start working on a project. Although it's tempting, never skip a warm-up; otherwise, you're likely to experience shaky, uneven strokes.

5 When you're finished writing for the day, swish your nib off in cleaning water and dry it with a nonfibrous cloth.

6 Store your pen holder and nib according to your preference (see pp.32–33).

Railroading

As you create downstrokes, you might notice that the ink eventually splits off into two thin lines instead of making one thick line. That's called "railroading," and it happens when you don't have enough ink on your nib. To address that issue, redip your pen in the ink, then position it where the railroading began to occur. Apply pressure to the nib to split the tines into a downstroke position, then continue making your downstroke.

Keeping the flow

Every couple of minutes, when your ink flow starts to get impeded by water evaporating from the ink on the nib, swish the ink off in your cleaning water for a second or two. Make sure that water interacts only with the part of the nib that has ink on it. Remember: no moisture should ever enter your pen holder. Once you've swished the nib off, quickly pat it dry—or almost dry—with your cleaning cloth and start writing again.

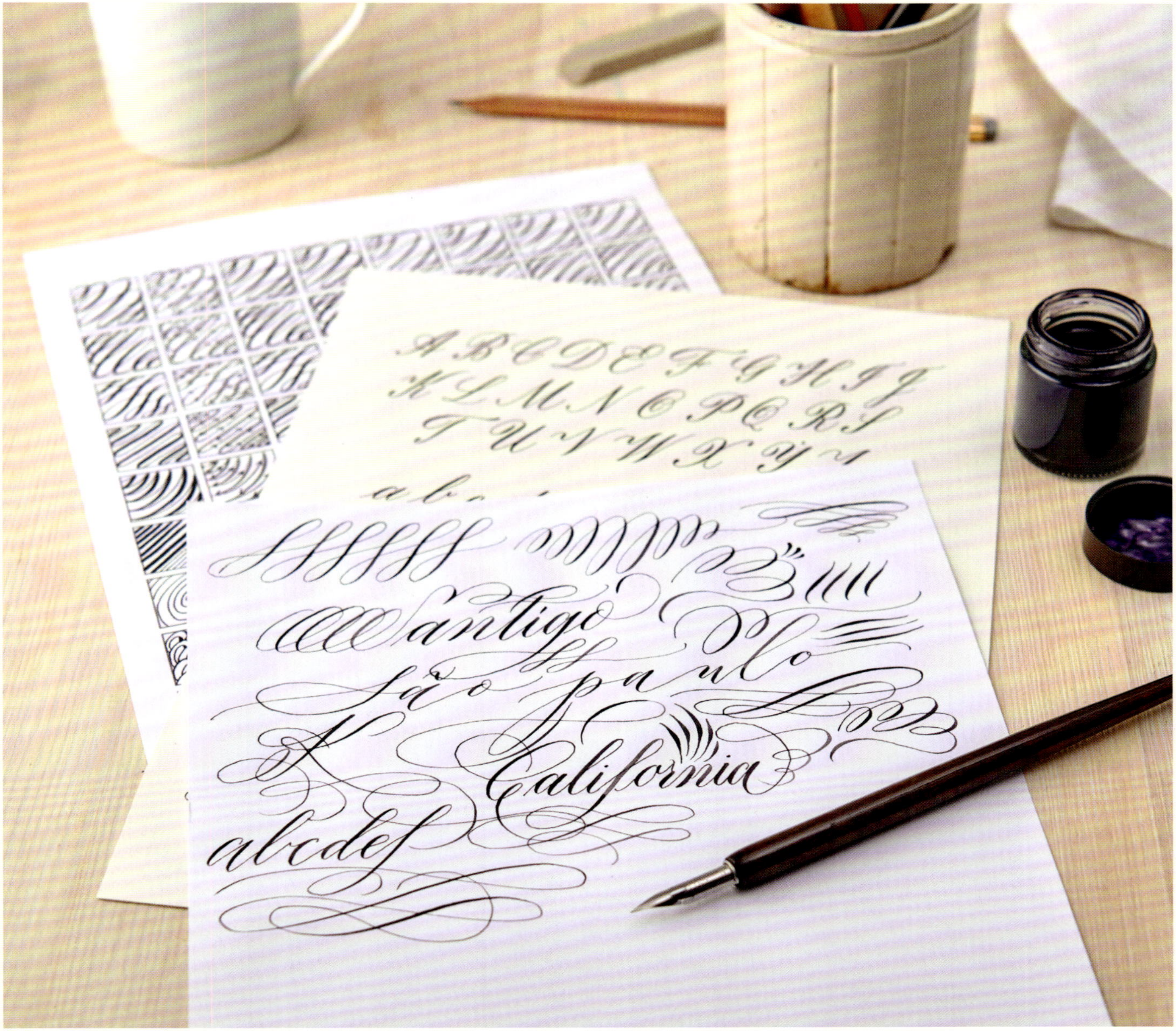

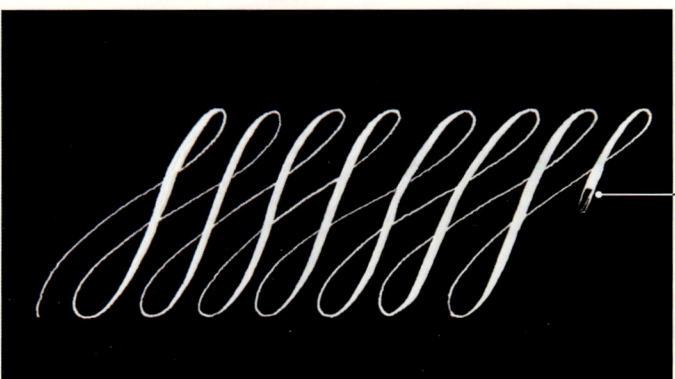

Above: It's a good idea to practice calligraphy on a piece of paper or a drill sheet before getting started on a project.

Railroading

Left: You need to dip your pen in the ink regularly to avoid "railroading," as shown at the end of this flourish.

Tip

Ink flow

Note that good ink flow is especially important for delicate upstrokes. If you find that your nib is "skipping" on upstrokes, it could be because the ink is too thick. Try diluting it with some water to see if that solves the problem.

Effective practice

Guidelines and planning

Guidelines serve as essential tools for ensuring uniformity and precision as you write. They provide a framework for your letters, helping you maintain consistency. They're usually drawn with a graphite pencil (on light-colored papers) or a white chalk pencil (on dark-colored papers).

Guideline ratios and placements depend on your project requirements, like the space you have available and the look you want to achieve. For densely packed compositions, you'll need guidelines that are closer together. Larger papers (and fewer words) allow for larger guideline ratios.

Key steps to creating guidelines

1 Draw evenly spaced guidelines: Use a ruler and your pencil to draw multiple sets of guidelines, maintaining consistent spacing between each set. Parallel gliders can help you draw straight and evenly spaced guidelines. You can also use a computer program like Photoshop to create and duplicate evenly spaced guideline sets to make a template. There are also calligraphy guideline generators available online that can help you create custom guidelines quickly and easily.

2 Determine the lowercase to uppercase height ratio: Depending on the calligraphy style you plan to use and your personal preference, begin by establishing the ratio between lowercase and uppercase letter heights. While traditional calligraphy styles typically have a set ratio of ascender height to x-height (ascenders are often twice as tall or 1.5 times as tall as the x-height), you can do whatever you want with guideline ratios in modern pointed pen calligraphy. It just depends on what looks right for you and the effect that you're going for.

3 Assess spacing requirements: Evaluate the size of your paper and adjust the spacing between your guidelines accordingly. It's a good idea to make a draft version of the longest line of your calligraphy, then design the guidelines to work with that.

4 Figure out line spacing: Experiment with different line spacings to find the right balance for your specific project. Write a few test lines and adjust the spacing until you achieve the desired visual effect.

5 Letter slants: Depending on the calligraphy style you're using, add the appropriate slant lines using a parallel glider. This alignment will ensure that your letters maintain a consistent angle.

6 Write and erase: Once your calligraphy is complete, allow the ink to dry thoroughly before erasing the guidelines.

Slanted guidelines

Slanted guidelines are good for creating consistent right-leaning (slanted) calligraphy styles.

The slant angle is typically around 55 degrees.

The middle line indicates the height of the lowercase letters (the "x"-height).

Draw a baseline and top line based on the size of the letters you'll be using.

½in (14mm)

⅓in (8mm)

Line spacing depends on the calligraphy style, the length of ascenders and descenders, and letter size.

The baseline shows where each letter should sit.

Straight guidelines

For upright modern calligraphy styles, you'll need guidelines with a 90-degree angle.

Vertical strokes like upstrokes and downstrokes are parallel to the upright slant lines.

The center line shows where the top of the lowercase letters reach.

Spacing your lines evenly helps achieve uniformity in your work.

Center line placement depends on your preference.

Guidelines and planning

Centering

For calligraphy that makes an impression, it's a good idea to center your words. If you skip this step, you may find that your calligraphy doesn't fit correctly within the space you have or it looks unbalanced. The only foolproof way to center your calligraphy is to make a full pencil draft of your work. There are, however, a couple of shortcut techniques. Although less precise, these shortcuts can help when time is limited.

Partial computer centering

Draw your guidelines and a center line through the page. Then, make a pencil draft of the longest line of calligraphy. If you don't get that first line centered, measure it, erase it, then write it again using the measurements. Next, type your text into a word processor with a script-style font and center them. From there, you can see the spatial relationship between calligraphy lines to ensure that each line is roughly centered compared to the longest line.

Full computer centering

If you're using a bouncy calligraphy like Kaitlin Style (see pp.74–81), you can use a word processing program to type whatever you plan to write. Select a script-style bouncy font to type the words, then center the script on the computer, and adjust the spacing between letters and the leading if necessary. Once you're happy with the layout, print out the computer-generated script. Put the paper you plan to write on over the printout, then place both papers on a light box. Use what you see through the page as a rough guide to help you center your own calligraphy.

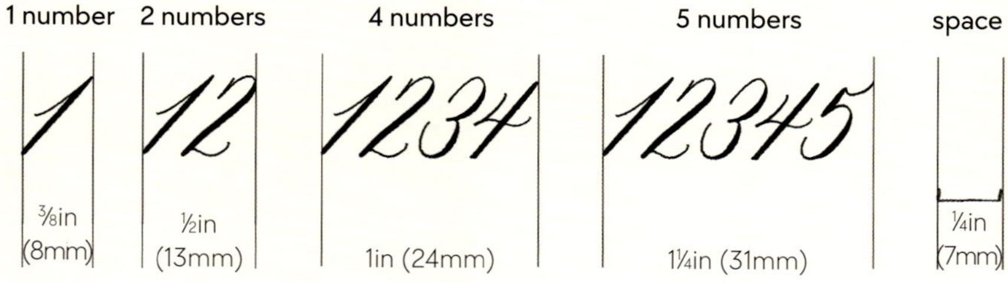

Some examples of letters you might add to a cheat sheet are shown here. You will need to include all the different word lengths you'll be using.

Spacing "cheat sheet"

If there is a calligraphy style you use often, it's worth creating a "cheat sheet" so that you don't need to make a pencil draft every time. Write examples of small and large 1-letter words, 2-letter words, and so on. Measure each word and the length of a typical space between any two words or characters. Some words contain large letters that take up more space (such as the letter "M"), while others will have more narrow letters (such as "i") that need less space. Decide whether the word you're writing contains mostly small or large letters, then you can use your cheat sheet to guess how much space is needed.

Tip

Decorative elements

If you're working on a fairly casual project and you have a word or a line that isn't centered, you can always add a decorative element at the beginning or the end to help make the line look centered.

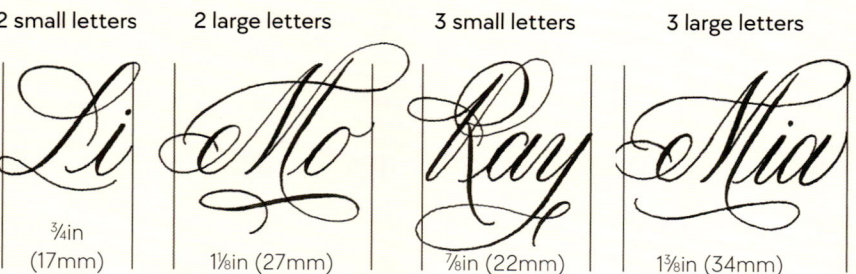

2 small letters	2 large letters	3 small letters	3 large letters
¾in (17mm)	1⅛in (27mm)	⅞in (22mm)	1⅜in (34mm)

6 small letters	6 large letters
1⅜in (34mm)	2in (50mm)

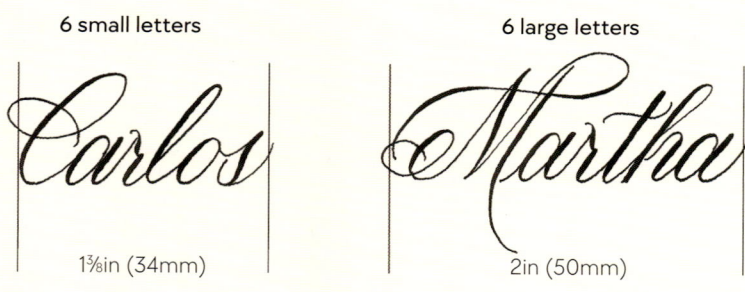

1 number	2 numbers	4 numbers	5 numbers	space
⅜in (8mm)	½in (13mm)	1in (24mm)	1¼in (31mm)	¼in (7mm)

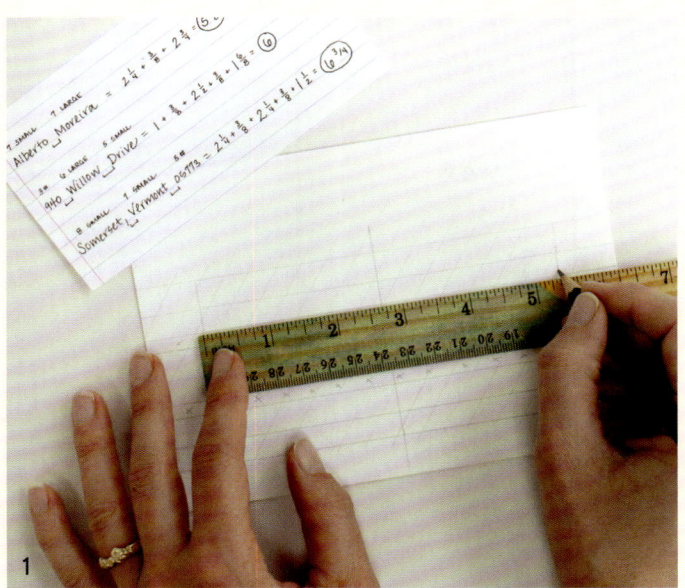

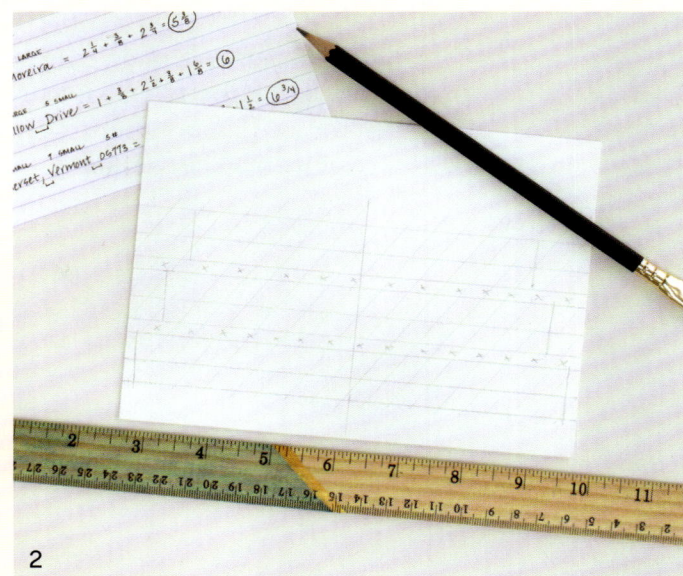

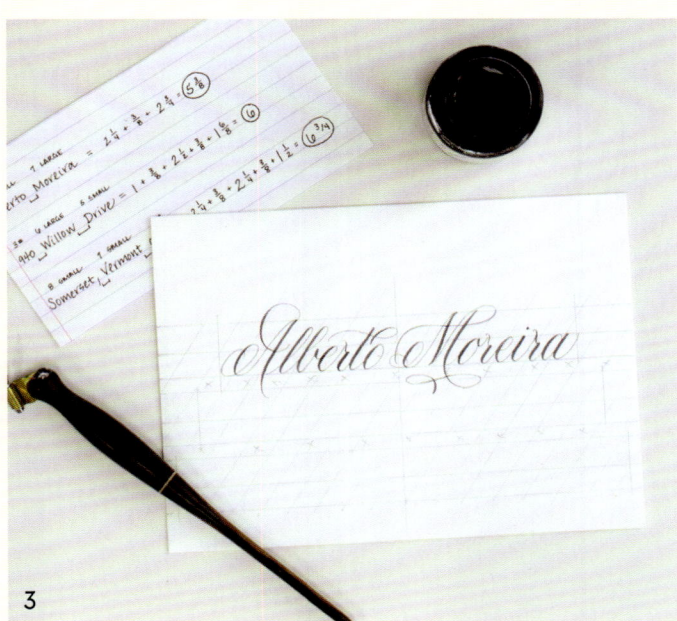

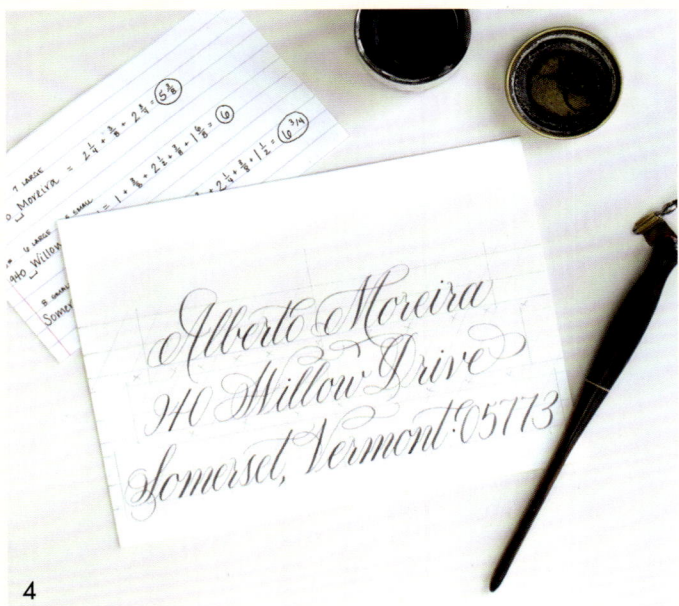

Centering envelopes

Being able to create perfectly centered, cleanly calligraphed envelopes is a core skill. Follow these steps to get this right:

1 Using your cheat sheet, figure out how long each address line should be by adding up the length of each word and space needed. Draw horizontal guidelines on your envelope and a vertical central guideline.

2 Use your measurements to mark where each line will start and finish. Little crosses can help you see where the letters fit into the guidelines and where the baseline is.

3 Write the first line of the address. Make sure that your first letter touches the left vertical guideline and the last letter reaches the right vertical guideline (some of the flourishes may go just outside of the guidelines).

4 Add the rest of the address between the vertical guidelines. Wait for the ink to dry, then carefully erase any pencil guidelines. Voilà! Your envelope is ready.

Guidelines and planning

Practice drills

Calligraphy drills are practice exercises designed to help improve and refine the basic skills required for calligraphy. These drills focus on fundamental elements such as letterforms, strokes, spacing, and consistency.

Calligraphy drills are a great way to cultivate your skills. Regular practice will develop your pen control and hone your hand-eye coordination. Some drill suggestions are shown below, but practicing any type of stroke configuration that's seen in calligraphy is a good idea. For example, you could try repeatedly writing any of the "Other Strokes" on page 53. Despite being called "drills," which might call to mind a dull task, your drills don't have to be boring. As long as you're practicing different loops and strokes, you can write whatever you want. Try calligraphing your own name several times with added flourishes, or draw a storm of tornadoes across your

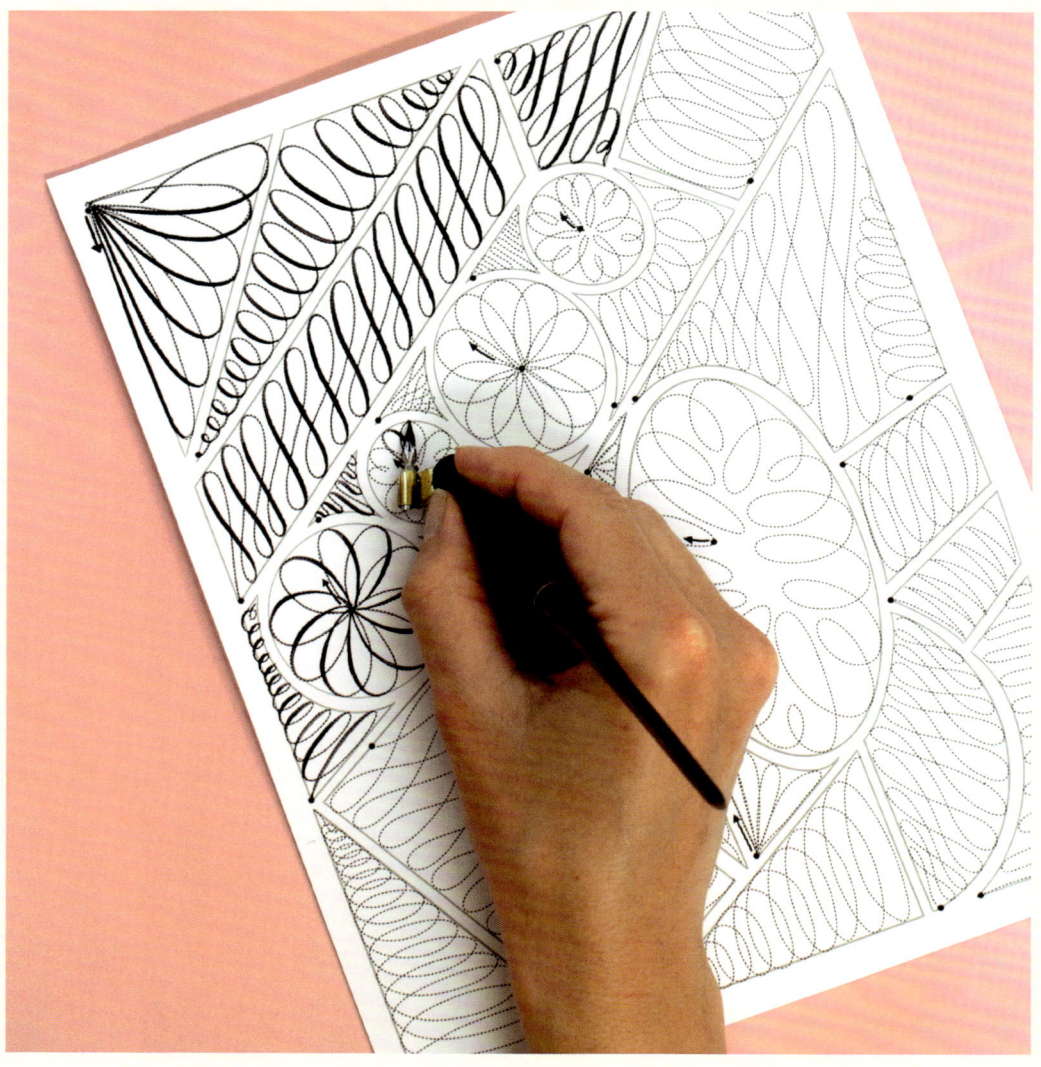

In addition to drawing simple strokes, you can practice more complex drills. Any sequence of loops, curves, and ovals are excellent practice.

page. As you write, focus on applying balanced pressure to both tines of your nib, maintain a relaxed grip on your pen holder (see pp.44–45), and glide your forearm across the table.

The idea is to work on your pen control and your stroke contrast. Using practice drills can help you adapt to a new nib and ink combination, especially if you're preparing for an important project.

Regular practice
Drills aren't just for beginners. Even experienced calligraphers do a couple of minutes of drills to warm up before starting a project. Many people also find them a relaxing way to spend a few minutes. Drills will always be part of your calligraphy routine, first in a big way and then in a smaller way.

Choose your drill
Try some of the examples shown below and then seek out the many free downloadable calligraphy drills available online. You can also buy practice books containing drills, which can be useful if you want to take them on your travels. Alternatively, you can do your own drills on a blank sheet of paper.

Drill suggestions
You can find printable drills like these online, or improvise and draw skill level-boosting swirls and loops on your paper.

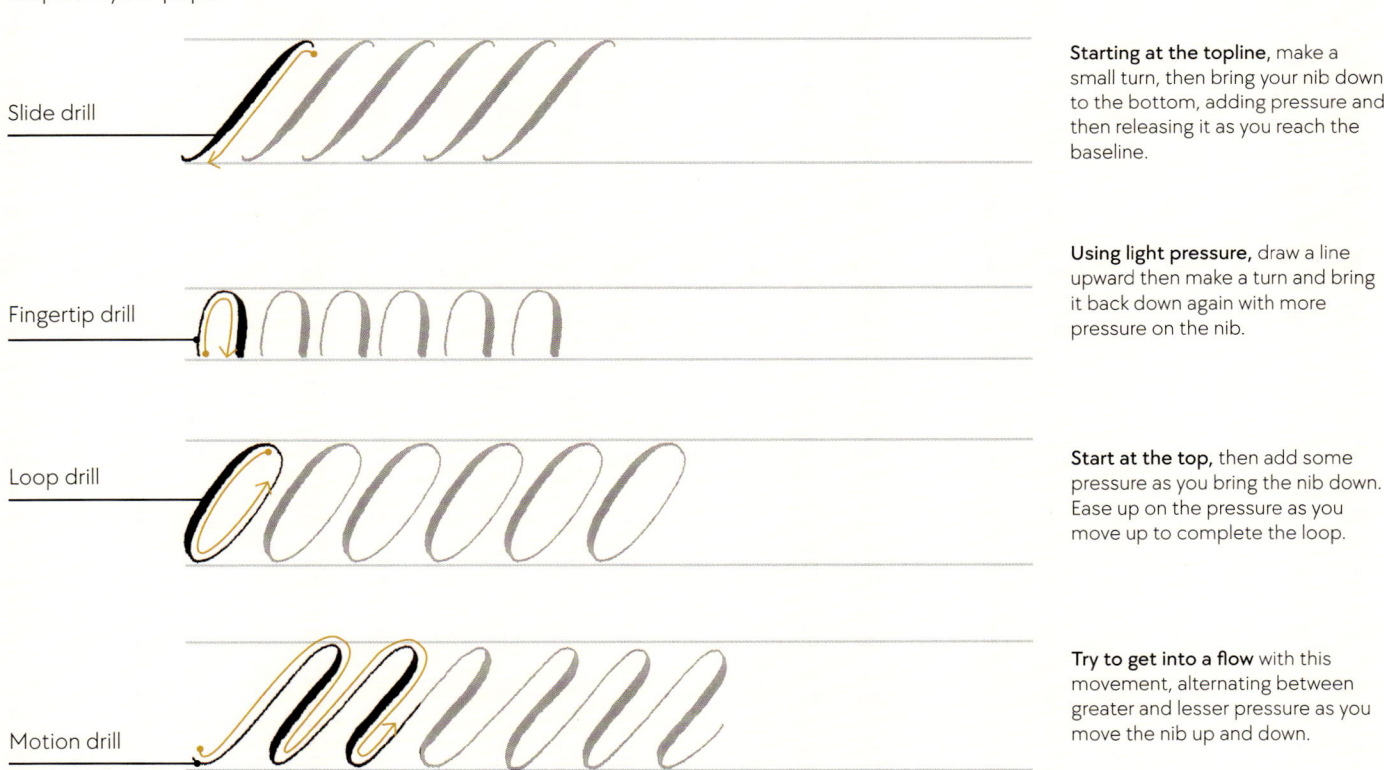

Slide drill

Starting at the topline, make a small turn, then bring your nib down to the bottom, adding pressure and then releasing it as you reach the baseline.

Fingertip drill

Using light pressure, draw a line upward then make a turn and bring it back down again with more pressure on the nib.

Loop drill

Start at the top, then add some pressure as you bring the nib down. Ease up on the pressure as you move up to complete the loop.

Motion drill

Try to get into a flow with this movement, alternating between greater and lesser pressure as you move the nib up and down.

Practice drills

Calligraphy exemplars

An exemplar serves as a reference guide for mastering different calligraphy styles. It provides helpful examples of letterforms, spacing, and—in some cases—connections between letters.

In addition to the alphabet, exemplars can also include flourishes, decorative elements, and variations on basic letterforms. It is worth keeping an exemplar close on hand as you write, regardless of your skill level. Even if you don't need the exemplar for most of the letter formations, it's a useful reference to ensure consistency.

It's crucial to have a reference exemplar if you're working on formal projects (such as wedding stationery) that require a uniform and professional look. To make that reference, copy out an exemplar in the style you plan to use and add elements that are relevant to your project.

On the following pages, you'll find five different exemplars. Four of these are my own modern calligraphy creations, while Copperplate is a traditional style. Each exemplar includes letters, numbers, and a smattering of special characters.

Make sure to look at the sample words that have been written in the lettering style after each exemplar so you can see how the letters come together to form words. If you like one of the exemplars, try copying its letterforms to make your own exemplar, and feel free to modify the styling as desired or create your own from scratch (see pp.110–113).

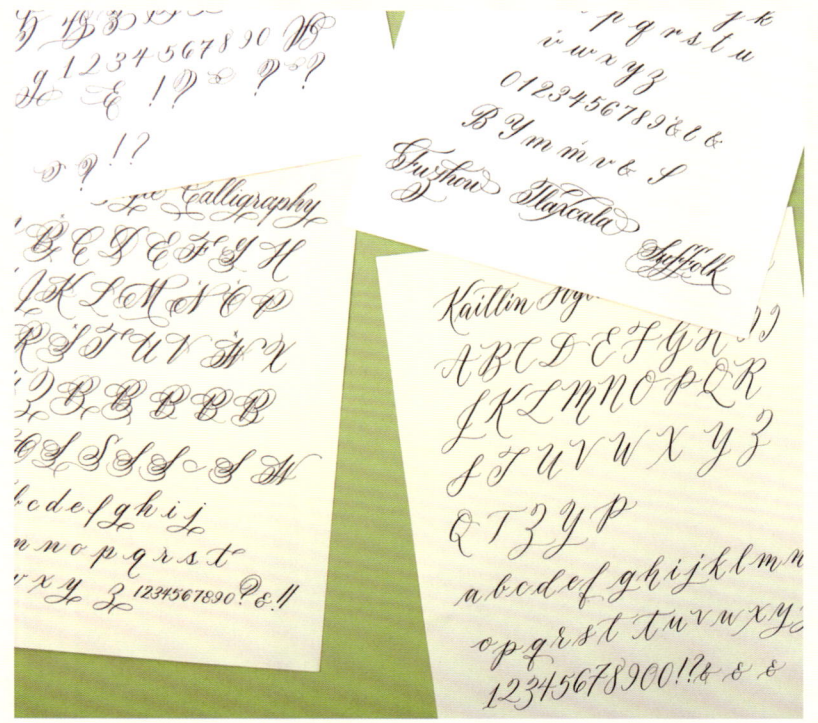

A few calligraphy exemplars in different styles, showing the alphabet, numbers, and characters.

Tip

Doodles

If you're creating your own style, start with doodles. Try experimenting to see what letterforms you like best. You can clean up these forms and ensure a uniform slant when you write the letterforms in the exemplar.

Using the exemplars in this book

When you're working on a project or want to practice drills, pick a style you want to try, then copy the guidelines and follow the stroke lines to recreate each letter, number, and character in that style.

KEY
- stroke 1
- stroke 2
- stroke 3
- stroke 4
- stroke 5

Start with the green stroke then follow the other colors in this order.

VARIATIONS

Exemplars are a great starting point, but once you feel confident, you can experiment with letter variations. For example, try extending the tails of letters like "y" and "g" for a more dramatic flair, or add serifs to uppercase letters for a classical appearance.

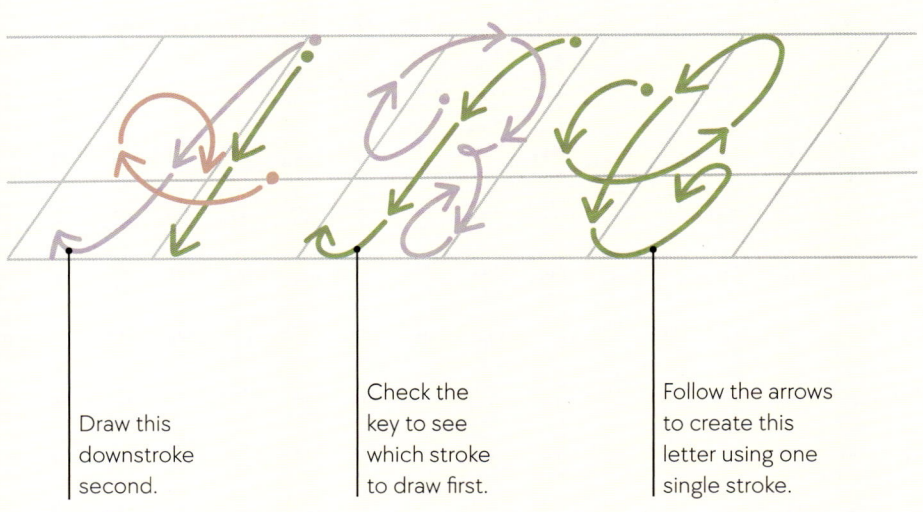

Copy the upper and lower guidelines and the slant lines to get the letters right.

Draw this downstroke second.

Check the key to see which stroke to draw first.

Follow the arrows to create this letter using one single stroke.

Tip

Following stroke guides

Stroke color changes and their starting dots denote places where you should briefly pick up your pen. At that point, you can refill your nib with ink and/or take a quick breather. Dot your "i"s and cross letters like "t" and "x" after writing the entire word.

Calligraphy exemplars

Amy style

This calligraphy style appeals to artists for a variety of reasons. Some love it for its legibility, others appreciate the flourish, and some are just relieved that they don't have to deal with a right-leaning letter slant.

This modern calligraphy style came about in 2013, when I created an early version of "Amy style" calligraphy for Philadelphia bride Amy's wedding envelope and escort card calligraphy. Amy wanted calligraphy that was elegant but not too stuffy. She sent me a few photos of different styles that she liked, and I used her preferences and examples to formulate an upright calligraphy style with unique details. "S" and "s," for example, are inspired by print lettering styles, and crosses on letters like "A" and "t" are wavy. An Amy-style descender doesn't connect to the letter beside it. Because this calligraphy style has no slant, I recommend creating it with a straight pen holder.

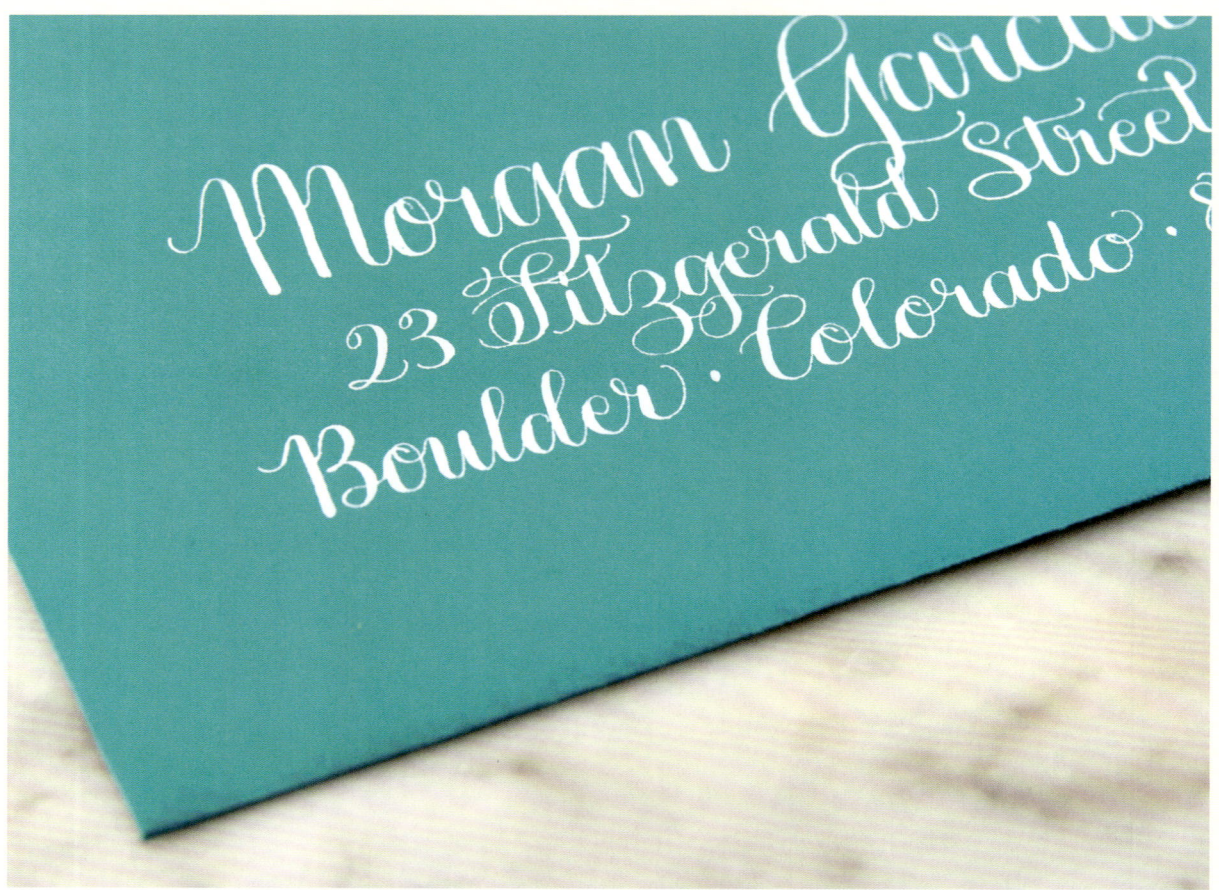

The circular loops and upright style of Amy calligraphy are evident in this name and address.

Amy-style exemplar at a glance

This calligraphy style is approachable both for the reader and the writer. Its loops look more like circles than traditional ovals, and its flourishes are short and playful.

ABCDEFGHIJK
LMNOPQRSTUV
WXYZ

abcdefghijklmno
pqrstuvwxyz
1234567890!?&

Uppercase

Follow the order of strokes shown in the key
(see right) to form each letter shown here.

KEY
- stroke 1
- stroke 2
- stroke 3
- stroke 4

⅜in (10mm)

⅓in (8.5mm)

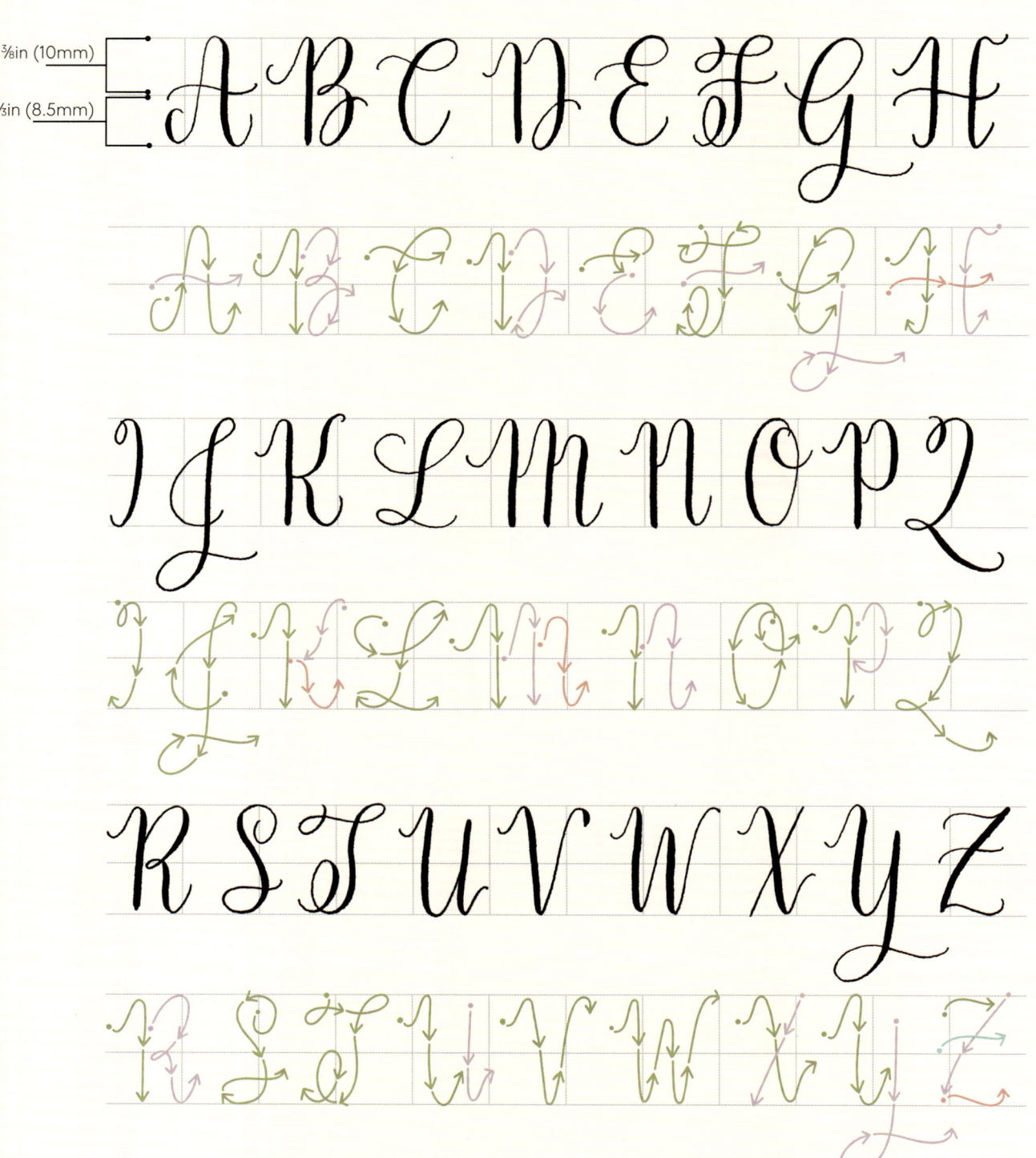

Lowercase

Use the key for the correct order of strokes
to form the lowercase letters shown here.

Tip

Trial and error

The letter "s" in this style
resembles the one you find
in block lettering. It can be
difficult to get right with a
pointed pen. If you wish,
you can replace it with a
traditional (triangle-
shaped) cursive letter "s."

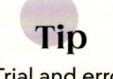

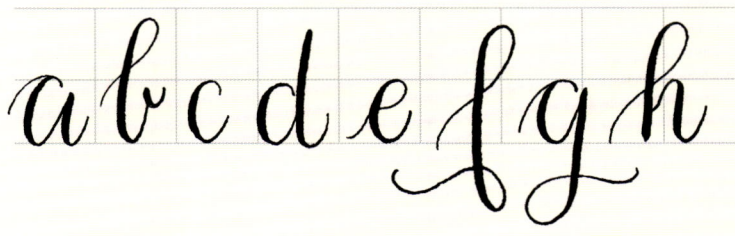

Ascenders on
lowercase letters
should end just below
the top guideline.

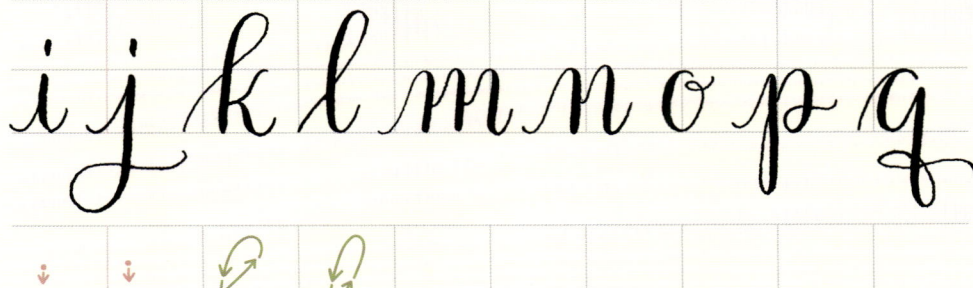

The cross on "x"
might be a
downstroke, but
be sure to give it
the thin width of
an upstroke.

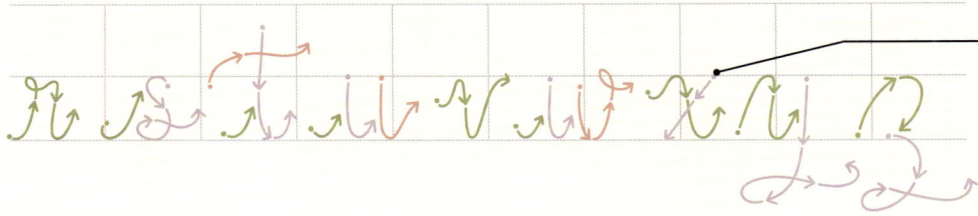

Amy style

Numbers, accents, and punctuation

Once you've mastered the alphabet, it's useful
to know how to draw these extra digits and letters.

Numbers
shouldn't
touch the
top guideline.

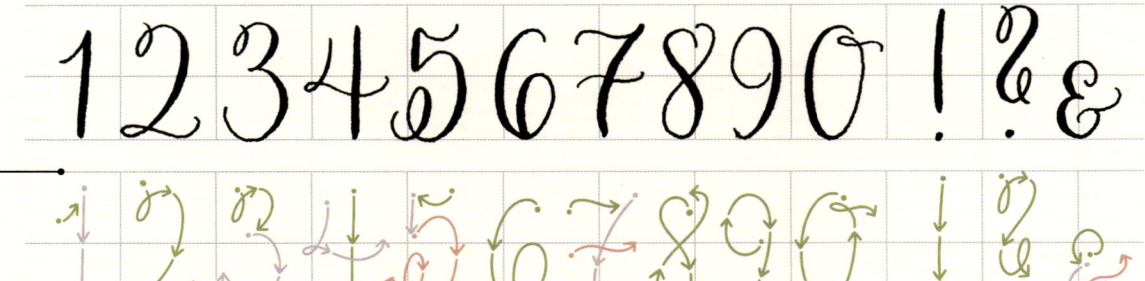

Take your time

Don't rush through
writing these characters;
intentional movements will
result in the best outcome
for your project.

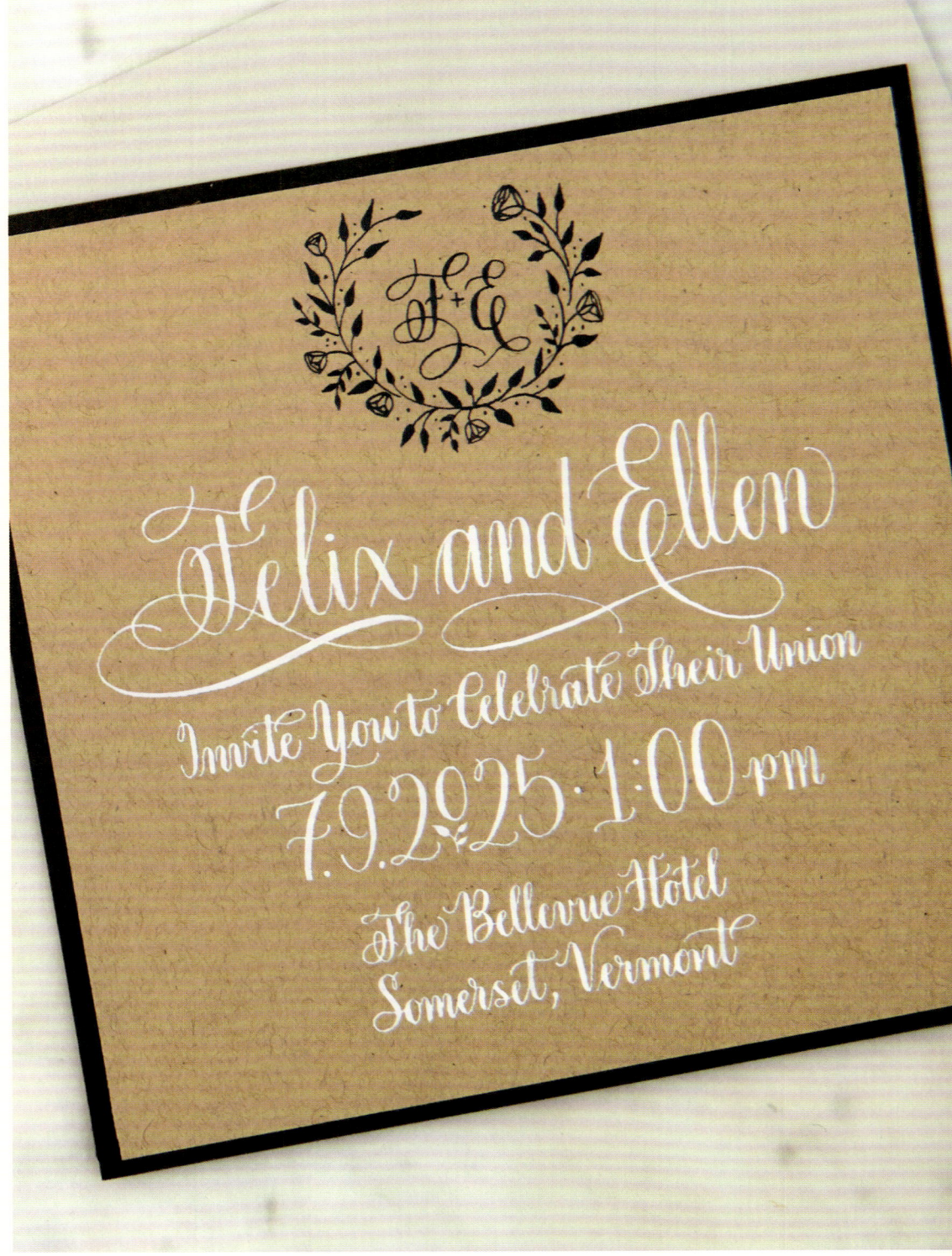

This Amy-style calligraphy wedding
invitation features gray gouache
and white ink (see p.173).

Joining letters

These Amy-style words include challenging letter combinations to help you figure out how to connect letters in your own projects. For quality practice, try writing these words on your own.

Follow this key for the stroke order. Once the word reaches stroke number 5, the stroke colors reset.

KEY
- stroke 1
- stroke 2
- stroke 3
- stroke 4
- stroke 5

Leave a gap equivalent to the width of one lowercase letter.

New York

Tlaxcala

Spacing is important in words with loopy letters like this. It might take a couple of tries to get it right.

Fuzhou

Suffolk

Amy-style descenders don't connect to the letter that follows.

In words with double "f's," consider the positioning of their descender loops.

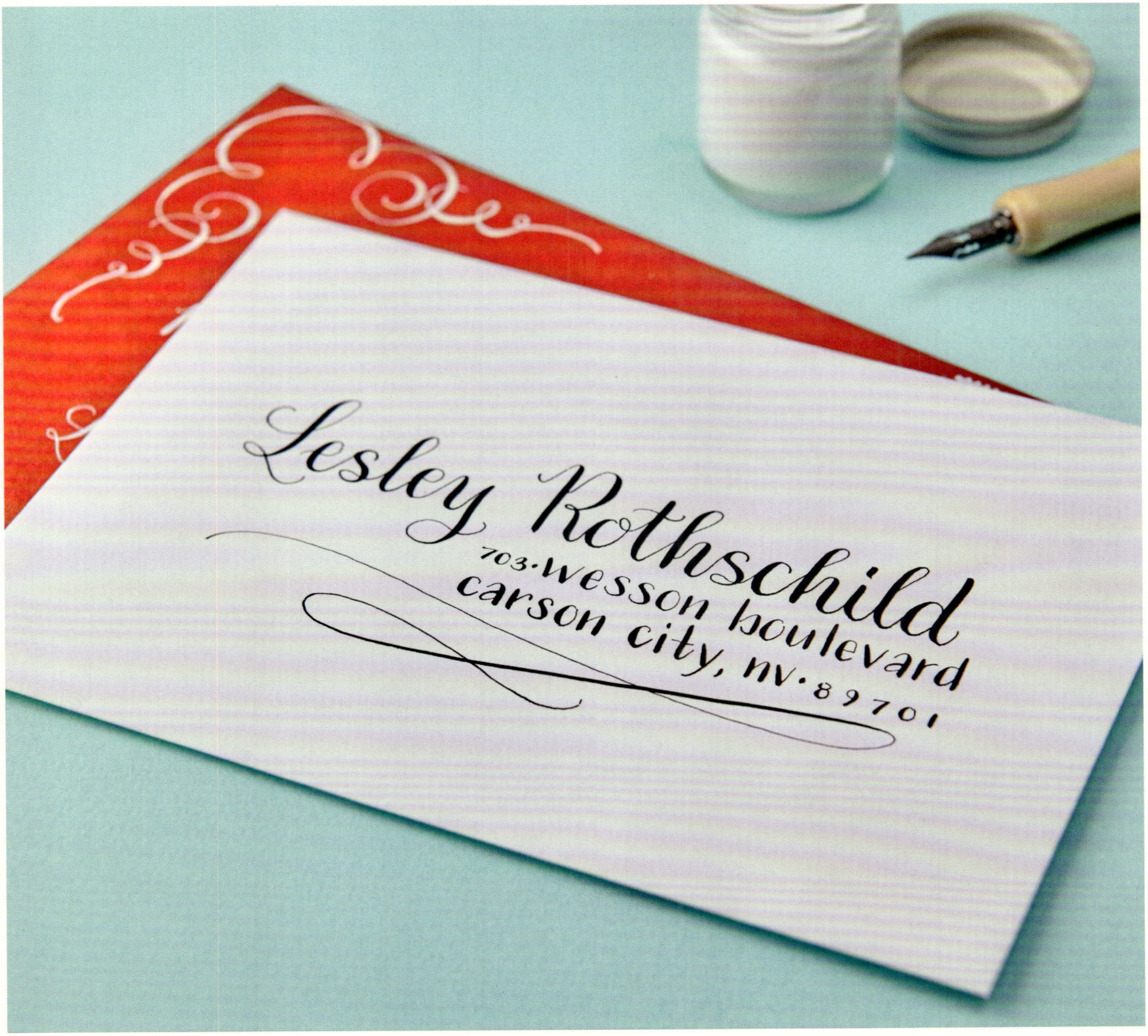

Tip

Joining letters

In Amy style, some letters don't join together. For example, any letter that has a descender (with the exception of "p") doesn't connect with the letter that follows.

Like all modern calligraphy styles, Amy style pairs well with sans serif hand lettering (see p.109).

Amy style

Kaitlin style

This is a versatile calligraphy style that can be dressed up or down. It can be written in freehand for more informal projects, or you can make it more consistent and clean for elegant paper goods.

The beauty of Kaitlin style is that it can be written freestyle, meaning that you don't have to start by drawing guidelines. That said, using guidelines will result in neater, more consistent letterforms. You can add a guideline group that includes a baseline, a top line, and slant lines if you are looking for a more formal look. For example, simple guidelines might be used for a wedding invitation suite to ensure that the calligraphy looks neat and consistent. In contrast, an informal project like the calligraphy ampersand (see pp.188–189) or the wrapping paper in Kaitlin style (see pp.162–165) doesn't need guidelines because the intended effect is more casual.

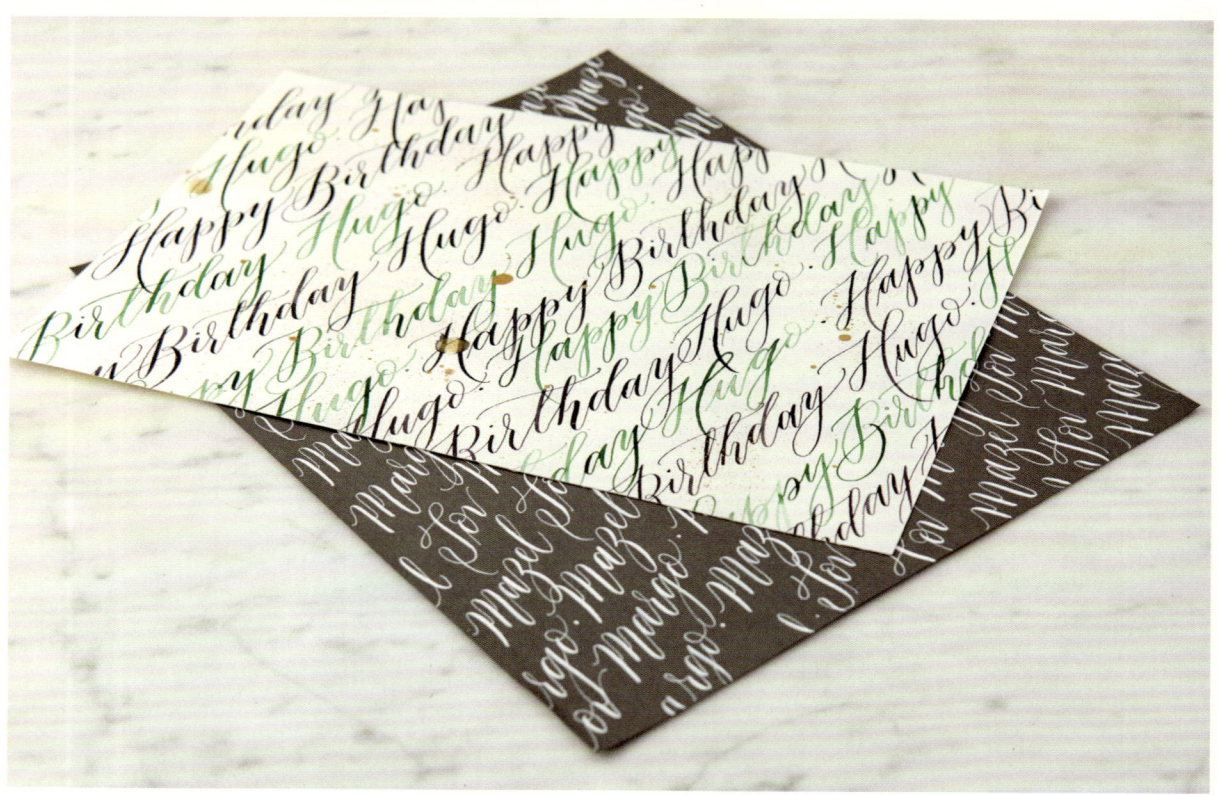

This is a good style to use for an informal personalized wrapping paper design.

Kaitlin-style exemplar at a glance

This page shows the free and flexible nature of Kaitlin style.
These letters are somewhat restrained compared to how
you might use them in real life. Feel free to elongate
strokes and play with letter formations.

A B C D E F G H I
J K L M N O P Q R
S T U V W X Y Z

a b c d e f g h i j k l m n
o p q r s t u v w x y z
1 2 3 4 5 6 7 8 9 0 ! ? &

Uppercase

Follow the order of strokes shown in the key to form each letter shown here. Note that the guidelines help with the letter slants and general positioning. A Kaitlin style letter's relationship to the top and bottom guideline should be different every time you write that letter.

KEY

● stroke 1
● stroke 2
● stroke 3
● stroke 4

⅜in (10mm)

⅓in (8.5mm)

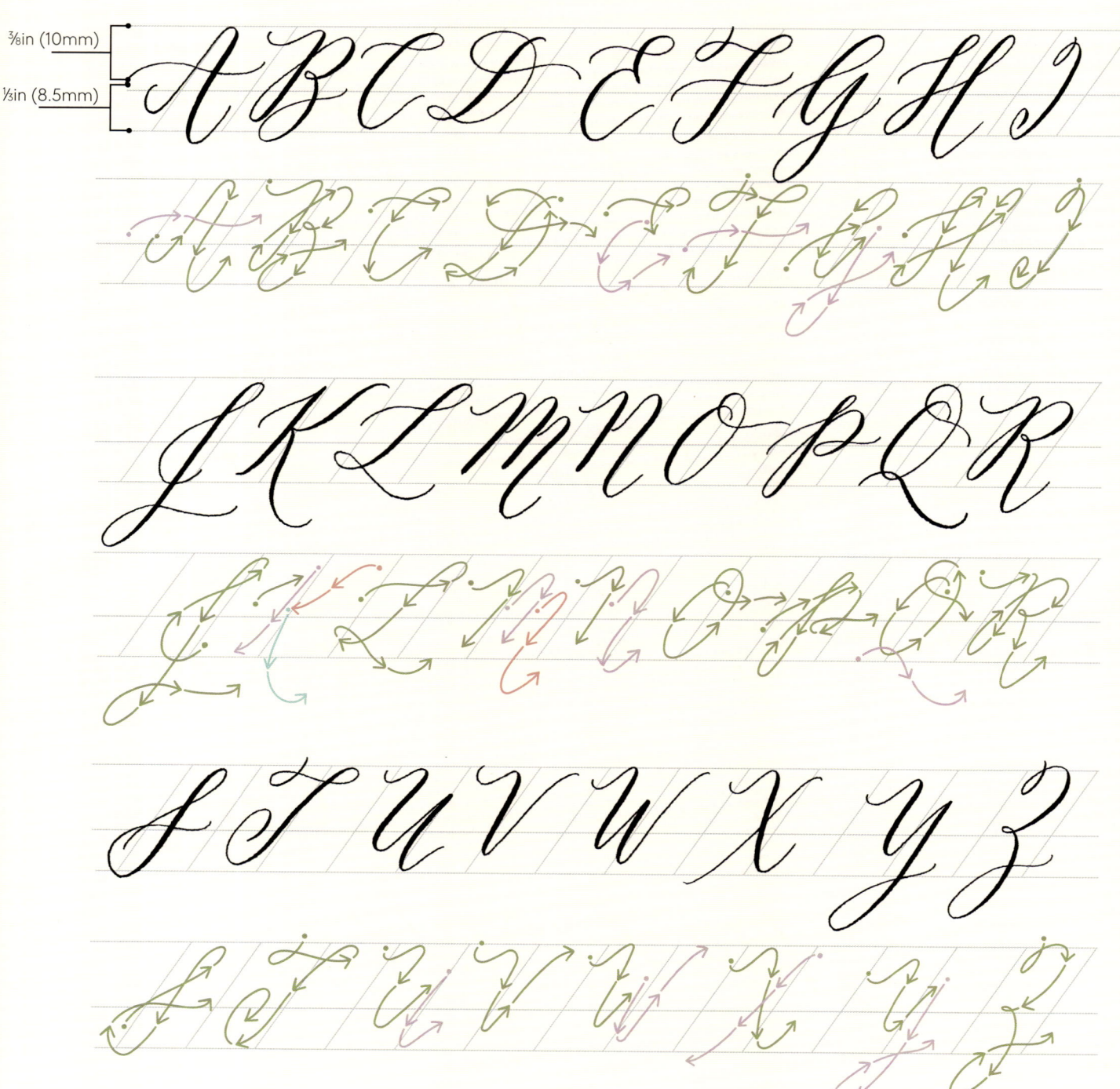

Lowercase

Practice these letters with and without guidelines to achieve the playful, free look of Kaitlin style.

Tip

Dropping the guidelines

While these letters are shown with guidelines, they are optional. Guidelines do lead to neater, more consistent letters, but sometimes, it's good to let go of perfection.

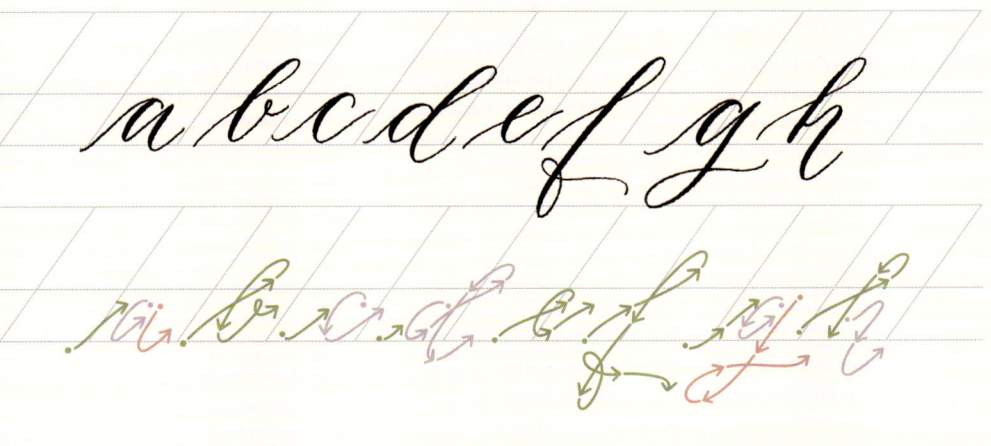

Extend strokes like these as far as you want to. Long, sweeping strokes are part of the style.

If you're using guidelines, don't forget to "bounce" the letters so they don't all rest on the baseline.

Kaitlin style

Numbers, accents, and punctuation

Once you've mastered the regular alphabet, take a look at some of the other characters you may need to draw.

1234567890!!?&

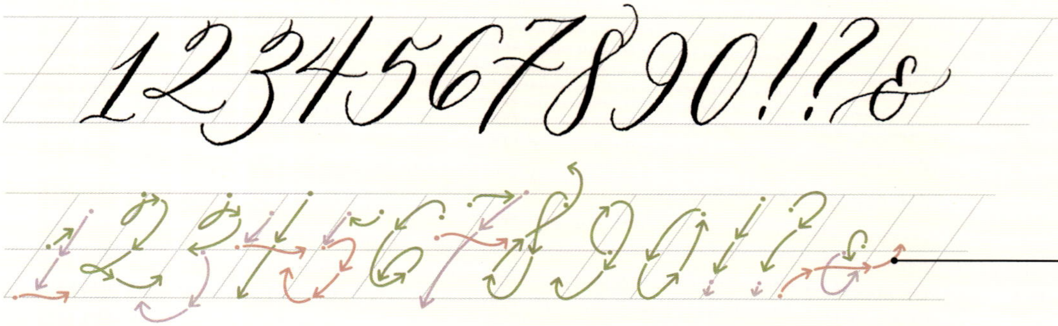

Try different ampersand formations (or simply a "+") to make this calligraphy style your own.

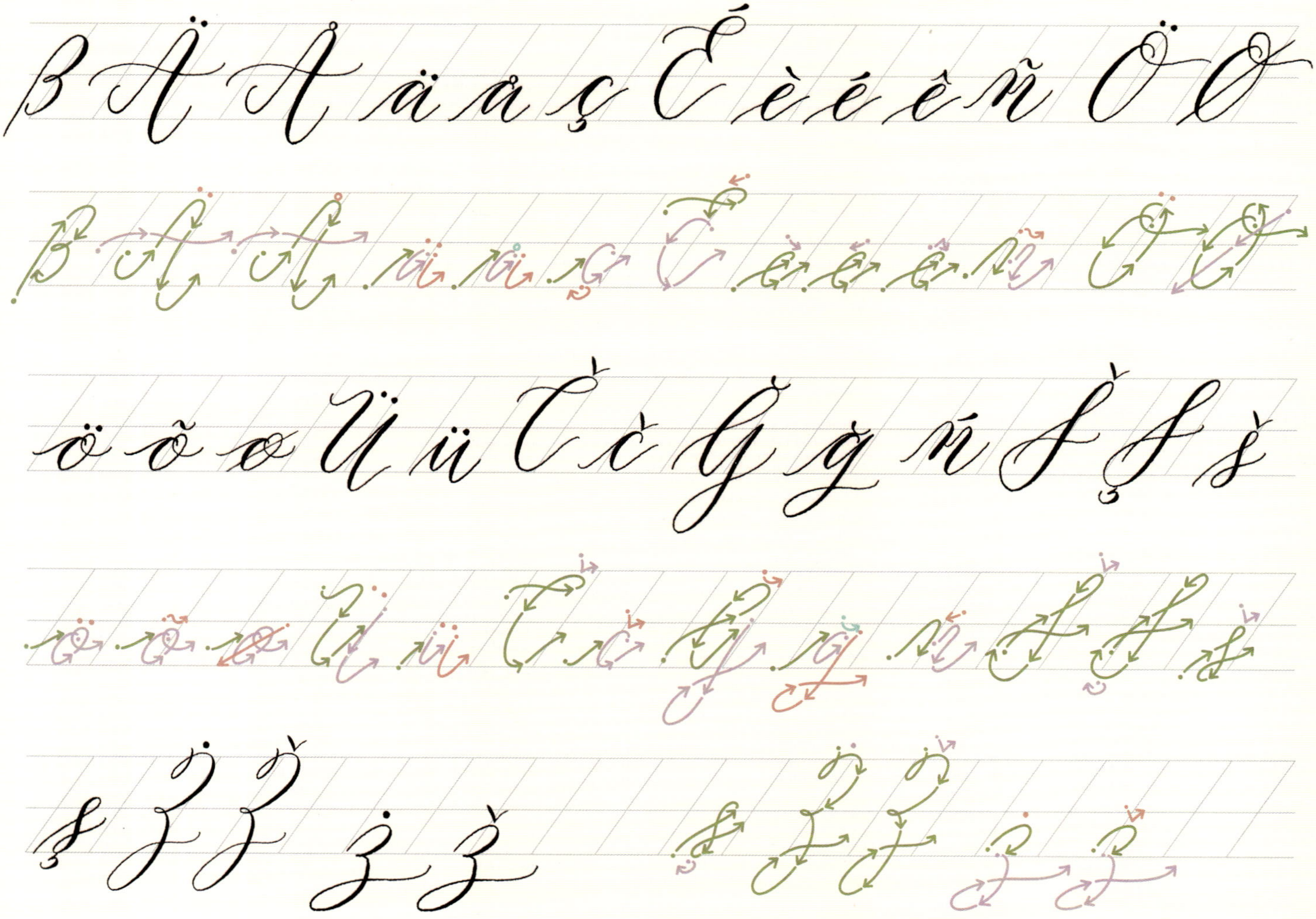

ẞ Ă Ă Ä ä å ç Ĉ è é ê ñ Ö Ö

ö õ ø Ü ü Ĉ Ĝ ğ ń Ş Ş š

ş ẑ ž ż ž

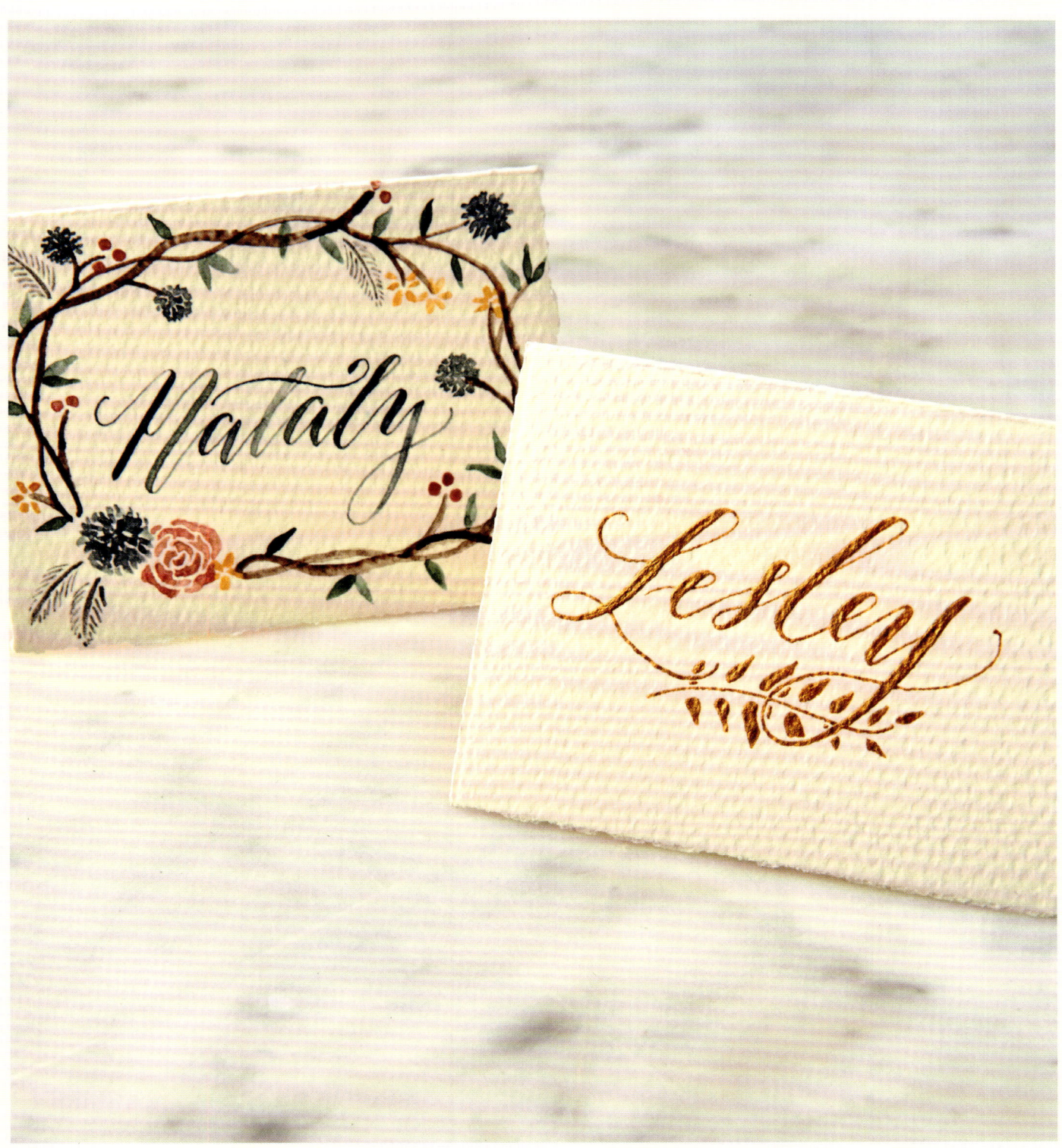

These Kaitlin-style calligraphy place cards strike an elegantly casual tone, especially with added illustrative touches.

79

Joining letters

There are many ways to make Kaitlin-style calligraphy your own, and no two words will ever look exactly the same. Play with elongating strokes, adding more bounce, or increasing the space between letters. For quality practice, try calligraphing these words as shown, then again twice more with your own changes.

You can allow entry strokes or descenders to enter the space of the word before.

New York

Fuzhou

Try elongating descender strokes so they "hug" the rest of the letters in your word.

Keep the entry stroke of the "D" shorter so it doesn't cross the "l," making it look like a "t."

For a fun variation, try writing the second "f" of this word with a long exit stroke that extends all the way to "k", similar to the "z" in "Fuzhou".

Delhi

Suffolk

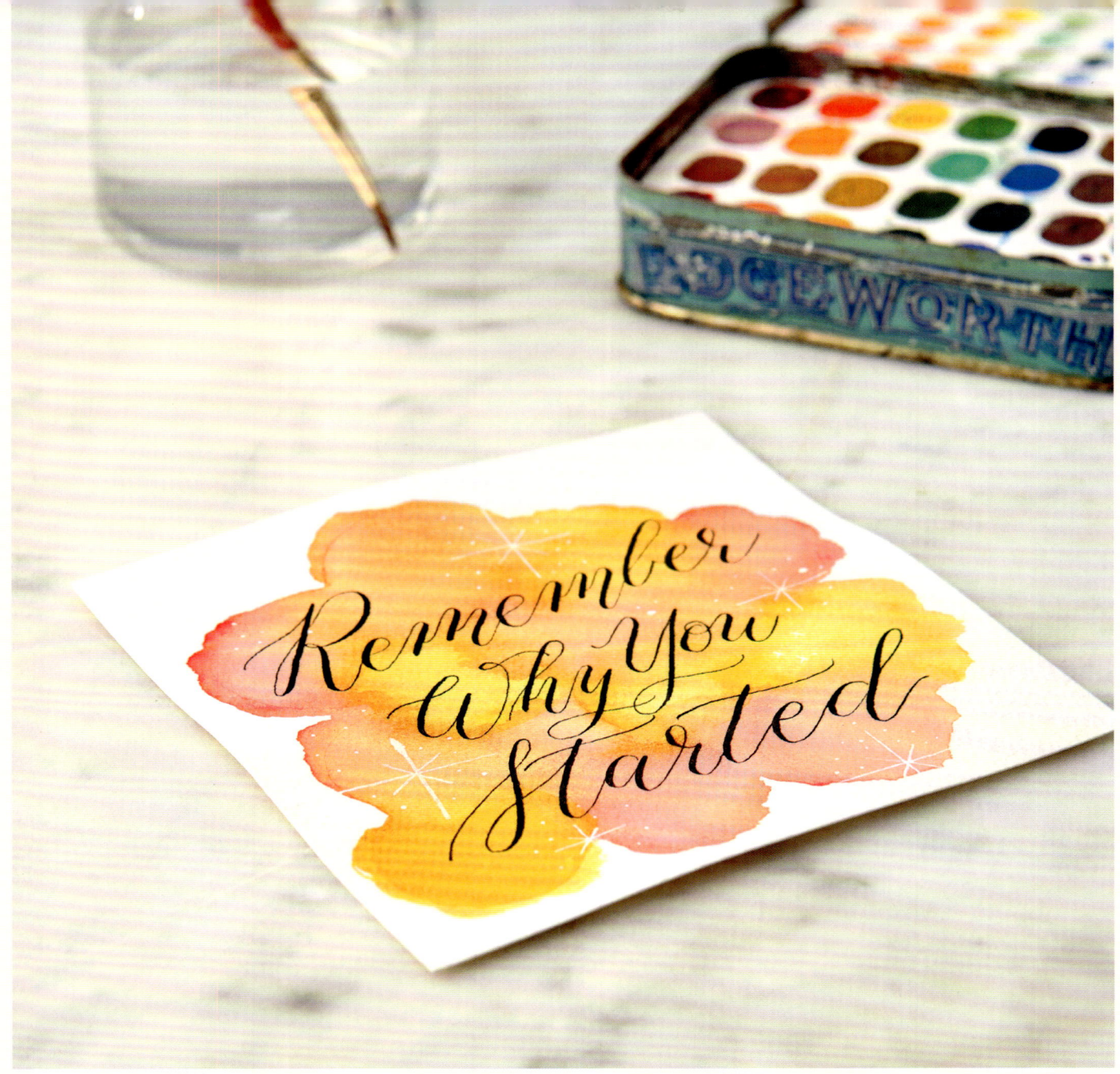

This colorful piece combines waterproof ink and abstract watercolor touches, resulting in an eye-catching design with just a few words of calligraphy.

Don't fret about creating this style perfectly. It's very forgiving and you can add your own new letterforms. I love to make a block letter-style "S" every once in a while or draw letters like "G" in a more ornate cursive style.

Kaitlin style

Copperplate style

If modern calligraphy isn't for you or you're just looking for a change of pace, try Copperplate. This is a traditional style of pointed pen calligraphy that originated in England during the 17th and 18th centuries.

Copperplate calligraphy is known for its elegant and flowing letterforms, which are clean and somewhat restrained. The name "copperplate" comes from the use of copper plates that were engraved with the letterforms for printing. While my passion is contemporary calligraphy styles, I like to create Copperplate letters every once in a while. They're precise and traditional, perfect for when I feel like taking on a challenge. Try them out when you find yourself at a solid intermediate level.

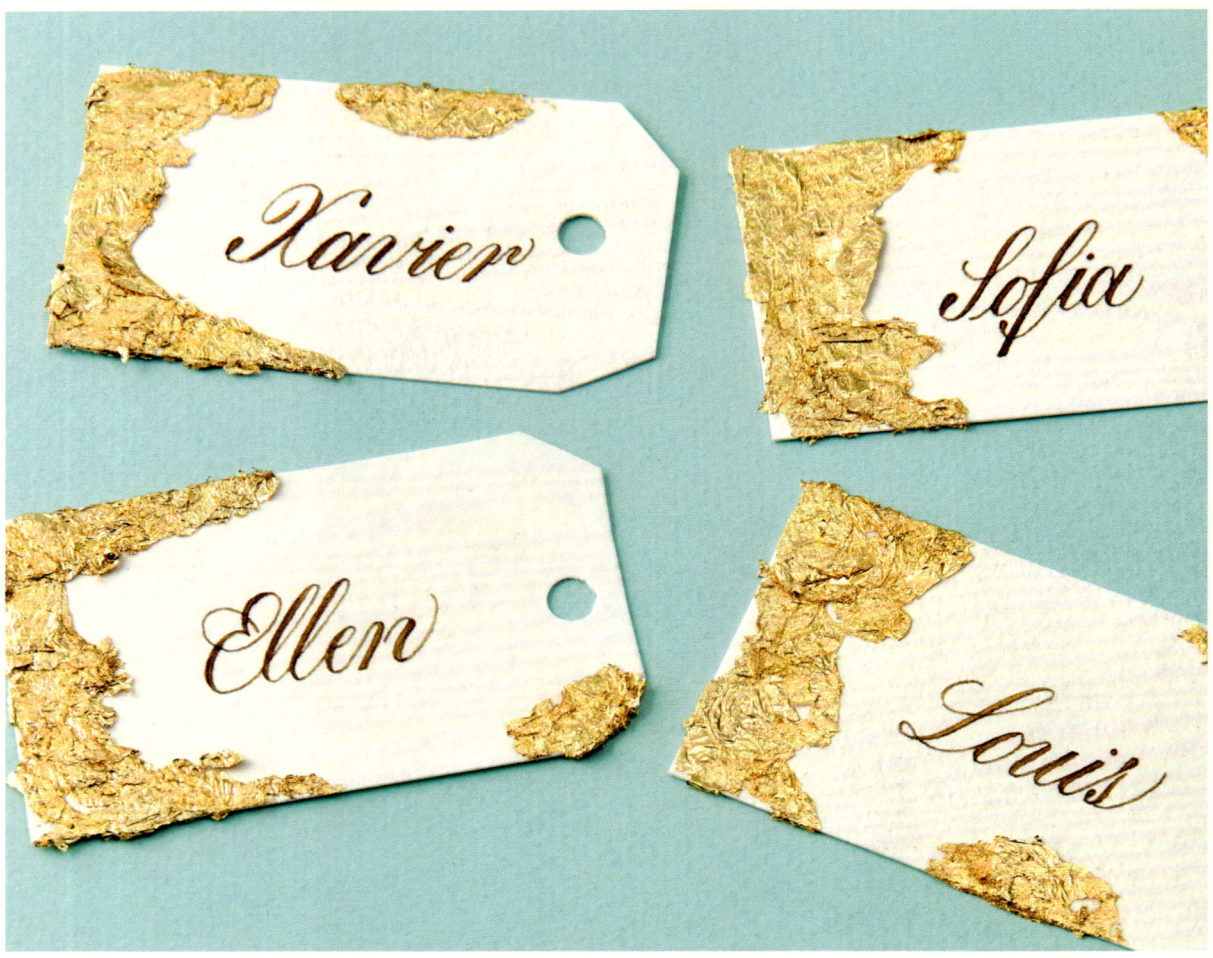

Copperplate-style calligraphy has been used on these gift tags adorned with gold-leaf decoration.

Copperplate-style exemplar at a glance

The alphabet in uppercase and lowercase Copperplate calligraphy is shown here. You can see the clear, regular, rounded shape of the letters; use this to refer back to once you've practiced the style on the following pages.

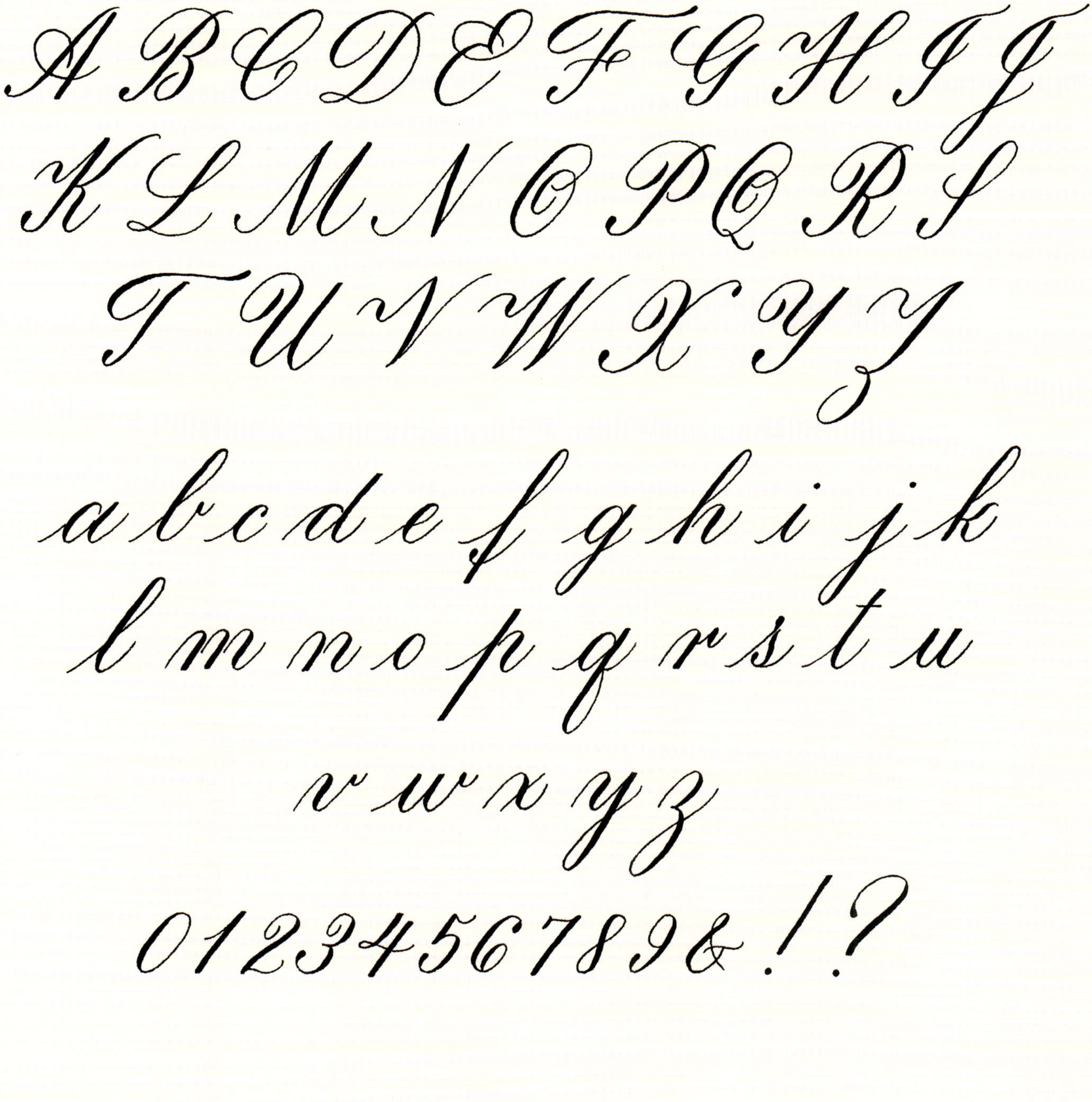

$$A\ B\ C\ D\ E\ F\ G\ H\ I\ J$$

$$K\ L\ M\ N\ O\ P\ Q\ R\ S$$

$$T\ U\ V\ W\ X\ Y\ Z$$

$$a\ b\ c\ d\ e\ f\ g\ h\ i\ j\ k$$

$$l\ m\ n\ o\ p\ q\ r\ s\ t\ u$$

$$v\ w\ x\ y\ z$$

$$0\ 1\ 2\ 3\ 4\ 5\ 6\ 7\ 8\ 9\ \&\ !\ ?$$

Copperplate style

Uppercase

You can follow the measurements shown here or scale them up or down depending on the space you're working with.

KEY
- stroke 1
- stroke 2
- stroke 3
- stroke 4
- stroke 5

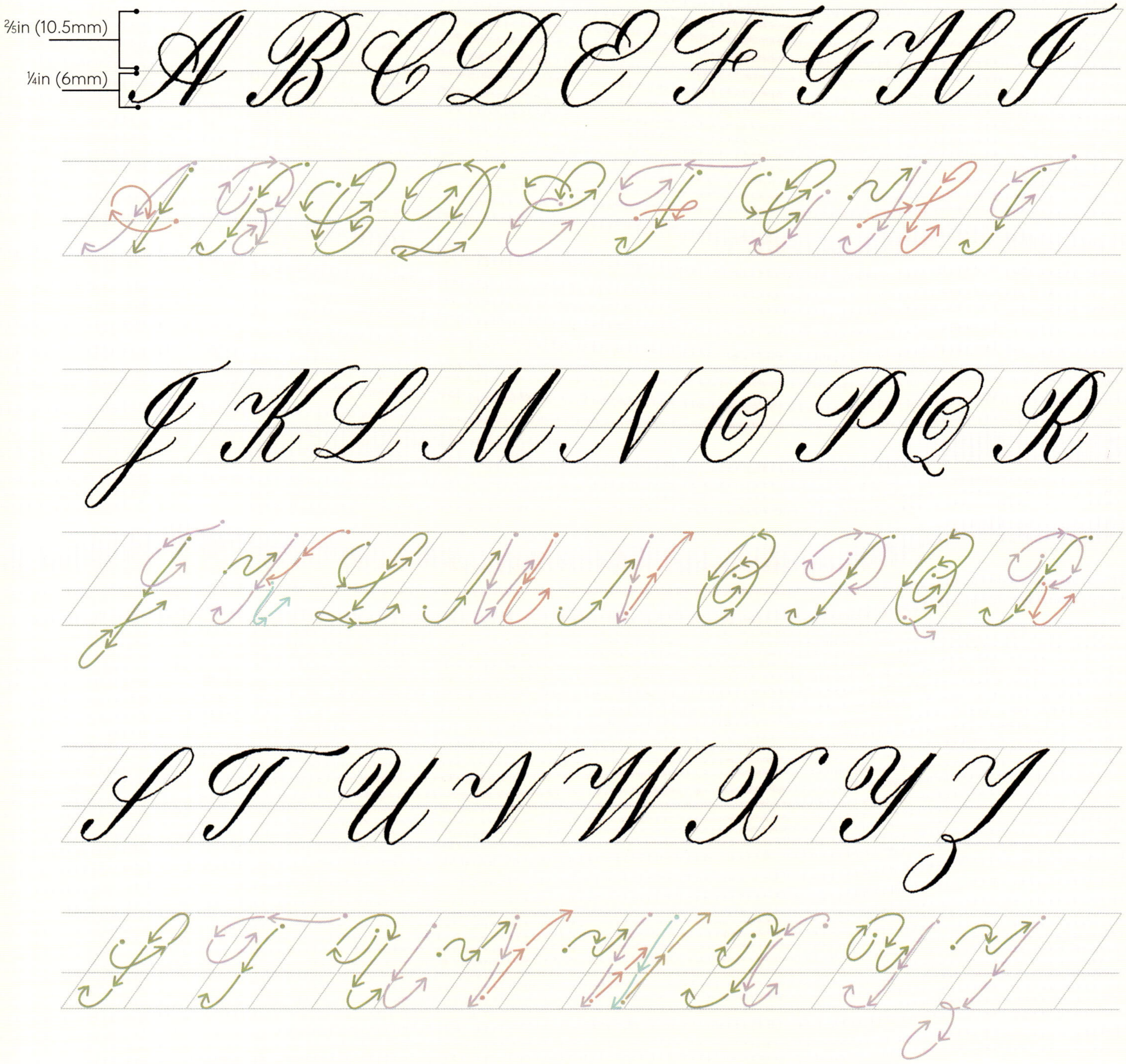

⅖in (10.5mm)

¼in (6mm)

A B C D E F G H I

J K L M N O P Q R

S T U V W X Y Z

Lowercase

The precise, clean lines of this style are evident in every letter.

Tip

Squared off

In Copperplate, it's a good idea to manually draw squared-off edges on stroke endings to make them look neater.

a b c d e f g h i

j k l m n o p q

"p's" are open and end in a compound stroke.

All lowercase letters connect to each other in a word.

You can either extend the ascenders of lowercase letters all the way to the top guideline or just below it.

r s t u v w x y z

Copperplate style

Numbers, accents, and punctuation

You'll need to write the numbers often if you're working on addresses, so it's worth practicing these alongside the regular letters.

0 1 2 3 4 5 6 7 8 9 & ! ?

Numbers follow the same slant as letters.

ß Ä Å ä å ç Ć è é ê ñ Ö Ø

ö õ ø Ü ü Ć ć Ğ ğ ń Ś Ş ś ş

ý ÿ ž ż ž

This little "v" stroke combines a short downstroke with a delicate upstroke.

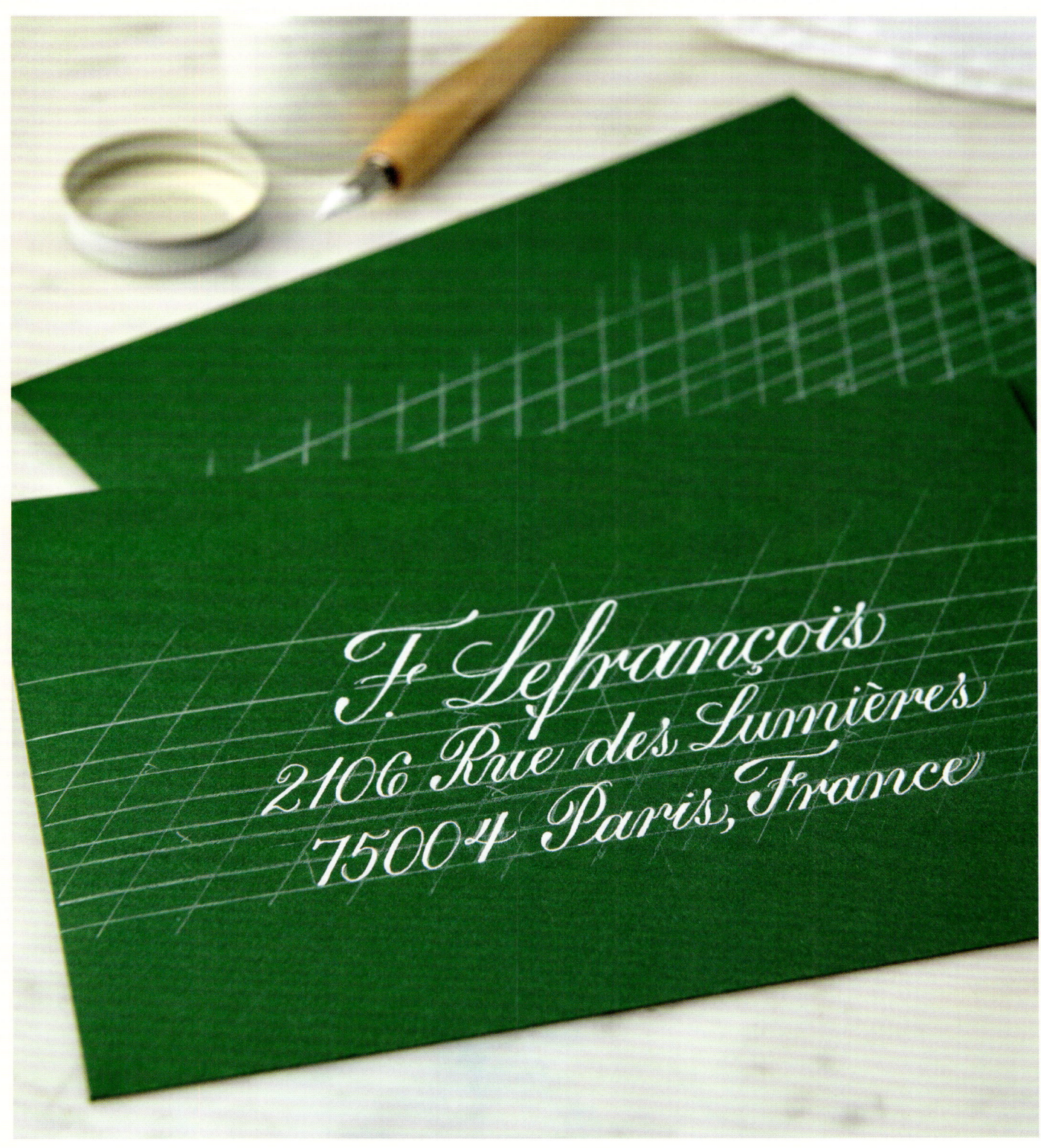

F. Lefrançois
2106 Rue des Lumières
75004 Paris, France

For tips on centering the calligraphy
on your envelope, see pp.60–61.

Copperplate style

Joining letters

Once you've practiced writing individual letters, you'll need to think about joining them together to write words. Sometimes, knowing how to join the letters is not clear. Here are a few examples to show you how this style works.

New York

Fuzhou

Add the line across this "F" before writing the rest of the word to ensure it doesn't intersect with the neighbouring letter.

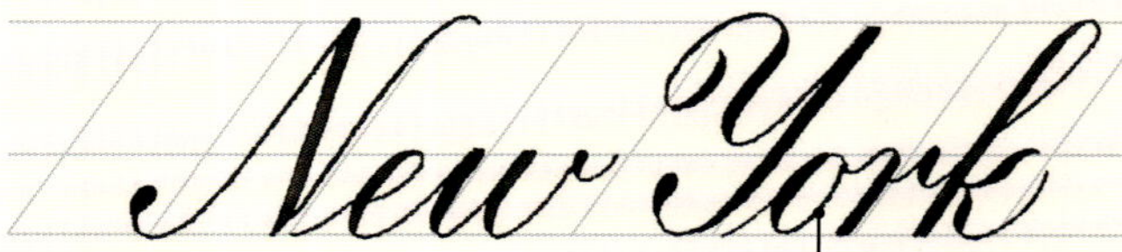

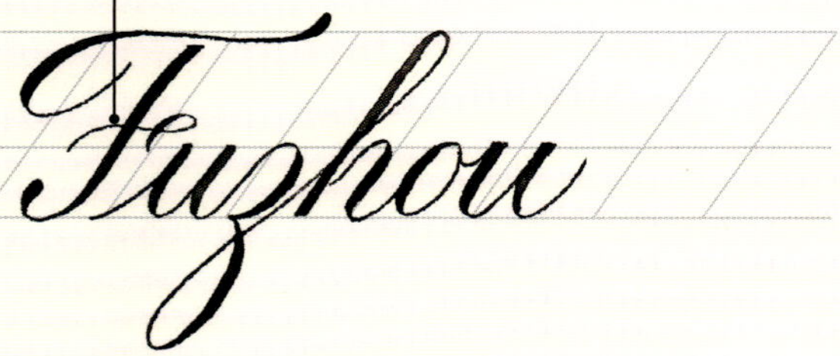

In traditional Copperplate calligraphy, all lowercase letters connect to one another.

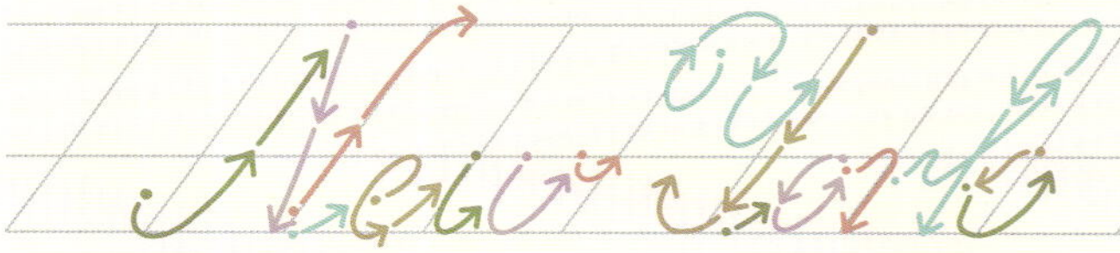

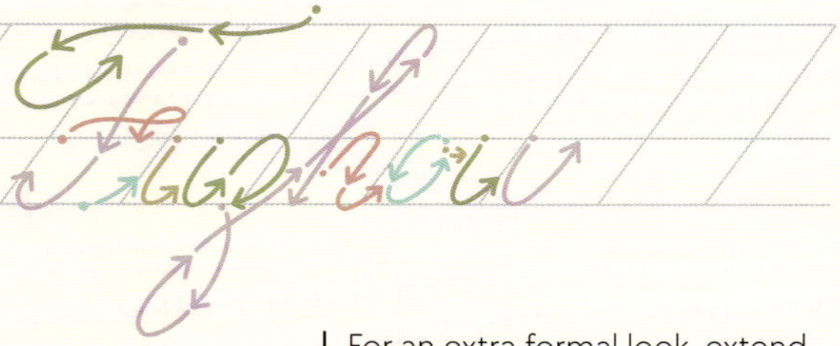

Delhi

Suffolk

For an extra formal look, extend your lowercase ascenders to the top guideline.

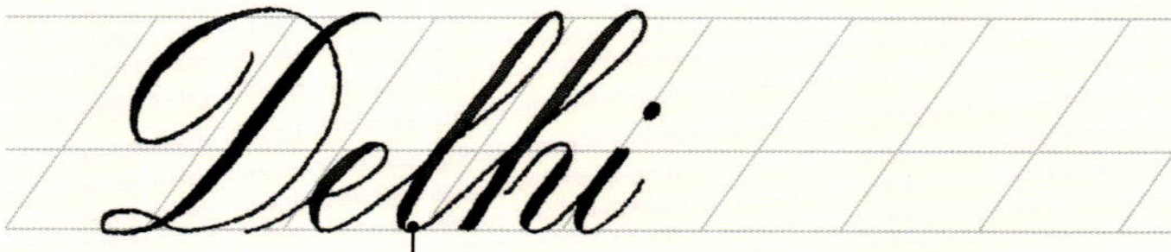

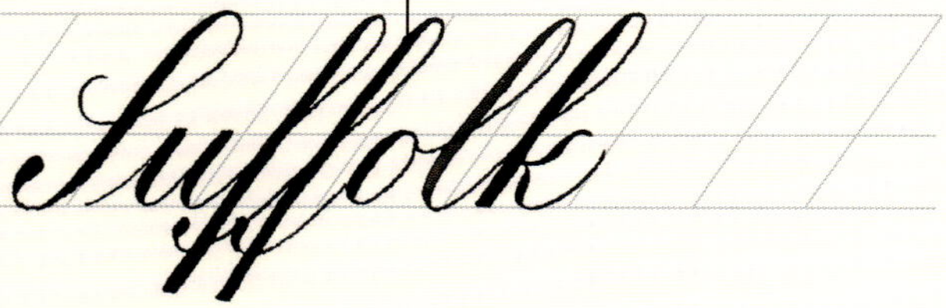

Copperplate relies heavily on consistency. Make sure all of your vertical strokes stay true to your slant lines.

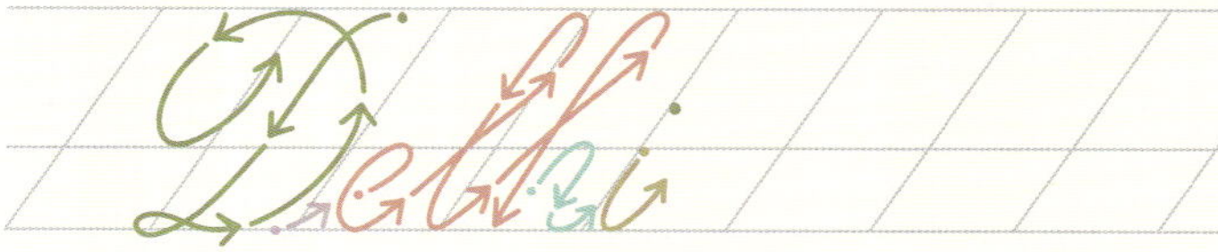

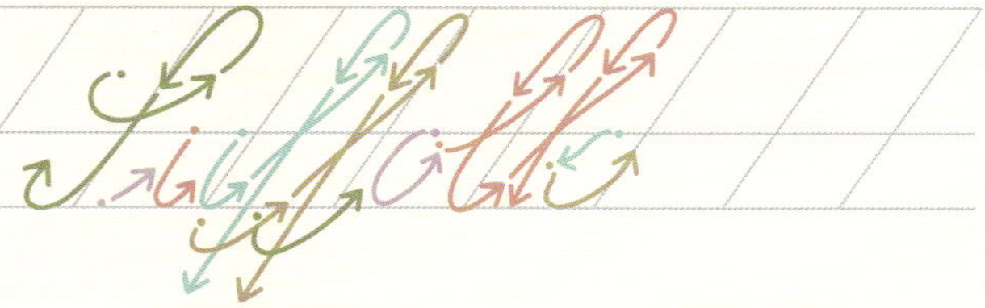

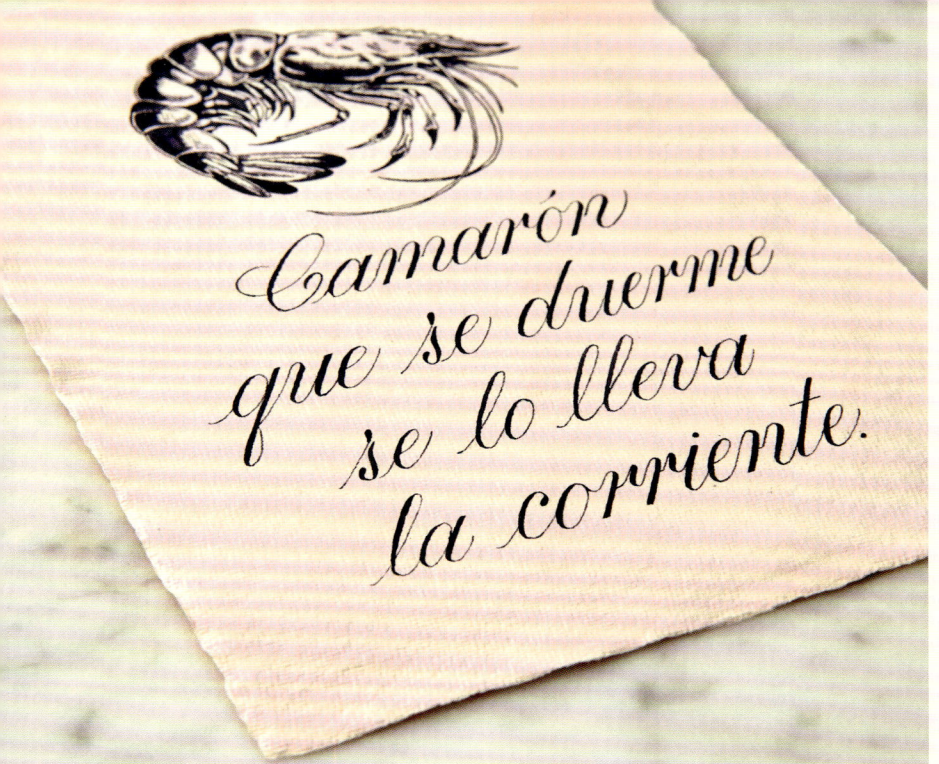

Camarón
que se duerme
se lo lleva
la corriente.

Above: This piece shows that all lowercase letters join together in copperplate.

Right: A slightly embellished Copperplate style has been used to add a classic look to this bookmark (see pp.192–195).

STYLE

Copperplate calligraphy takes a lot of practice, so don't worry if it doesn't look perfect the first few times that you try to create it. Every time you pick up your pen, you're improving.

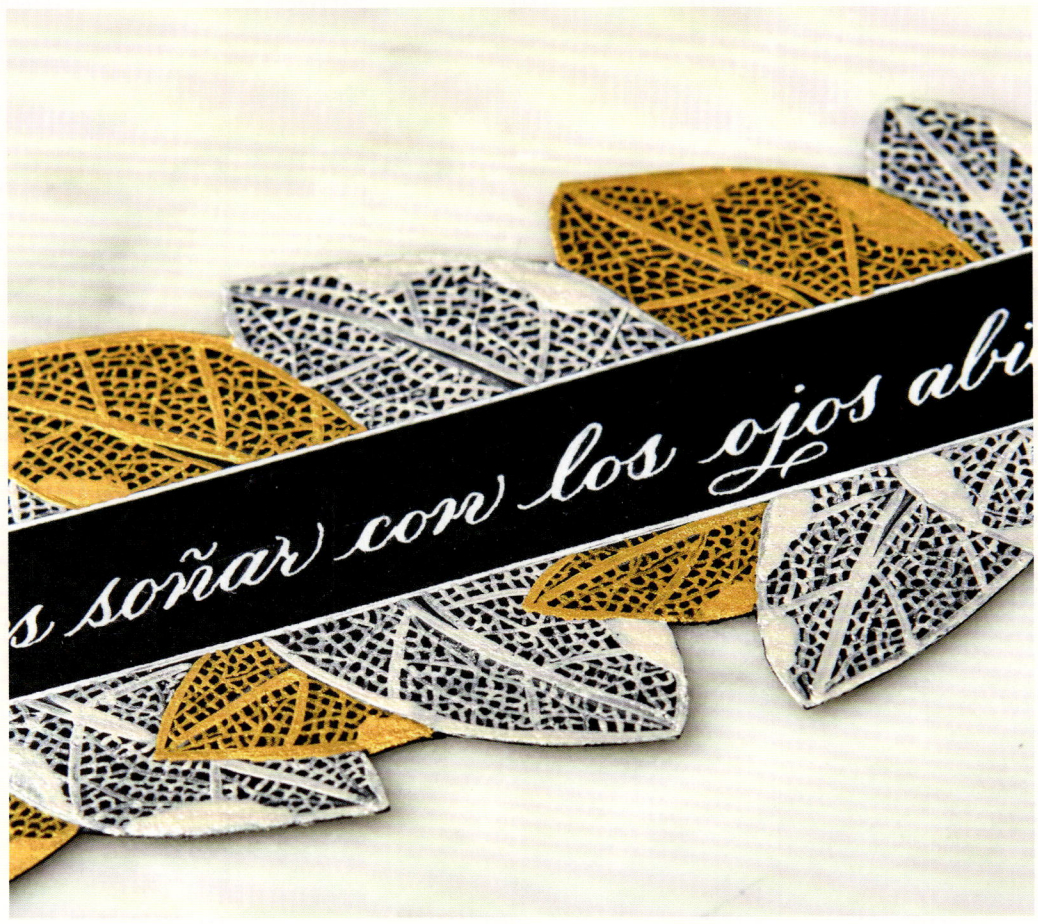

s soñar con los ojos abi

Janet style

When you want to create legible calligraphy that marries traditional elegance with modern embellished flair, opt for Janet style. This style impresses without going over the top.

In 2015, a Boston bride named Janet asked me to create a traditional-looking calligraphy style for her wedding invitation envelopes. After some research and tweaking, I came up with "Janet style" calligraphy, named after that bride. It is inspired by Copperplate (see pp.82–89), borrowing several elements like the 55-degree slant and certain lowercase letter formations. The similarities end there, though—Janet-style calligraphy boasts fun flourishes and flexible letter formations. It's the perfect style to use when you're looking to make classy, traditional calligraphy with a modern twist.

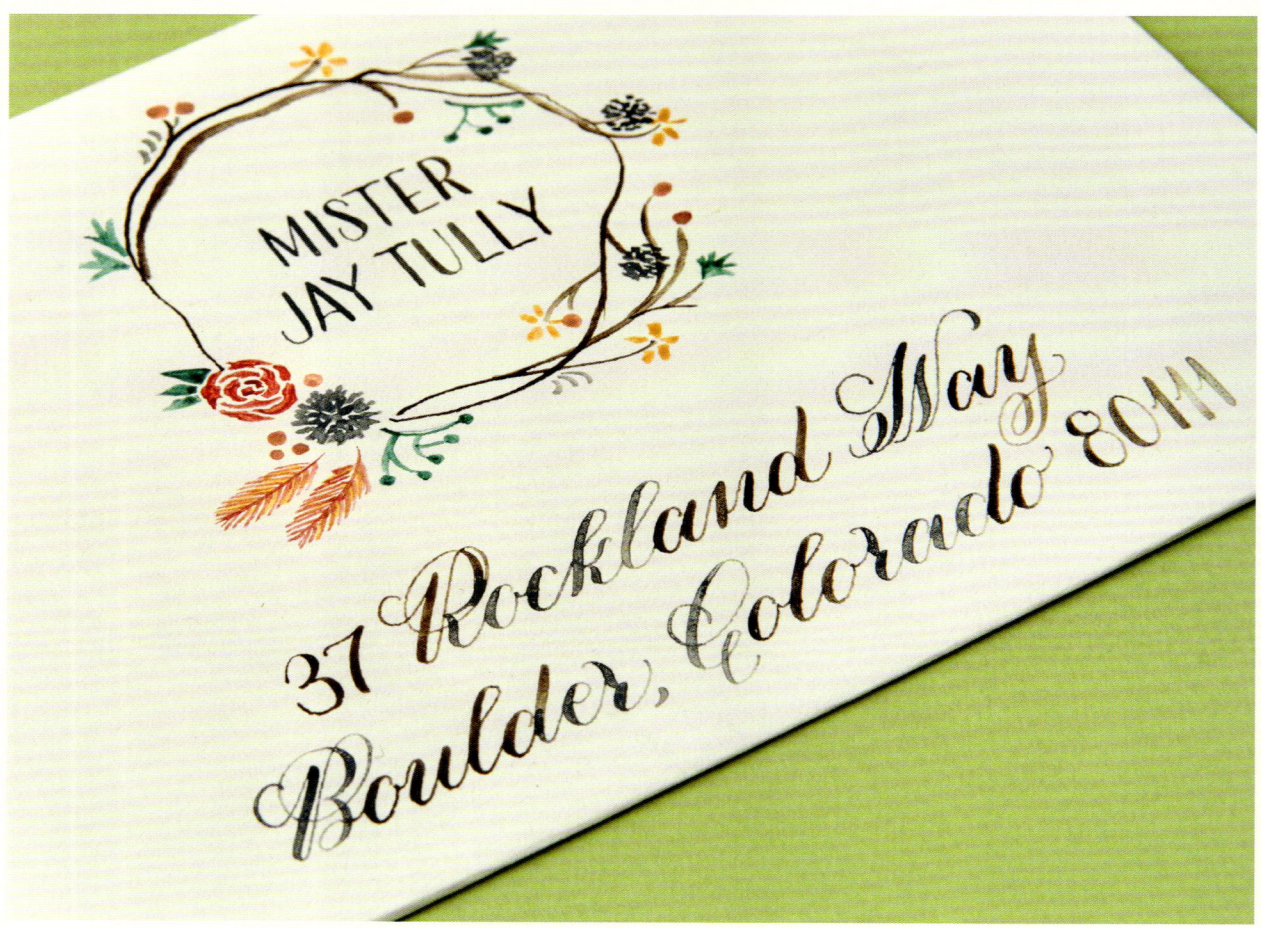

In this example of Janet style, some of the letters have been simplified and the name of the recipient is in block letters to help legibility.

Janet-style exemplar at a glance

This calligraphy style relies on a delicate balance of legibility and embellishments. It has elegant flourishes with just a little bit of restraint. For a more showy style, see Flourish style (pp.98–105).

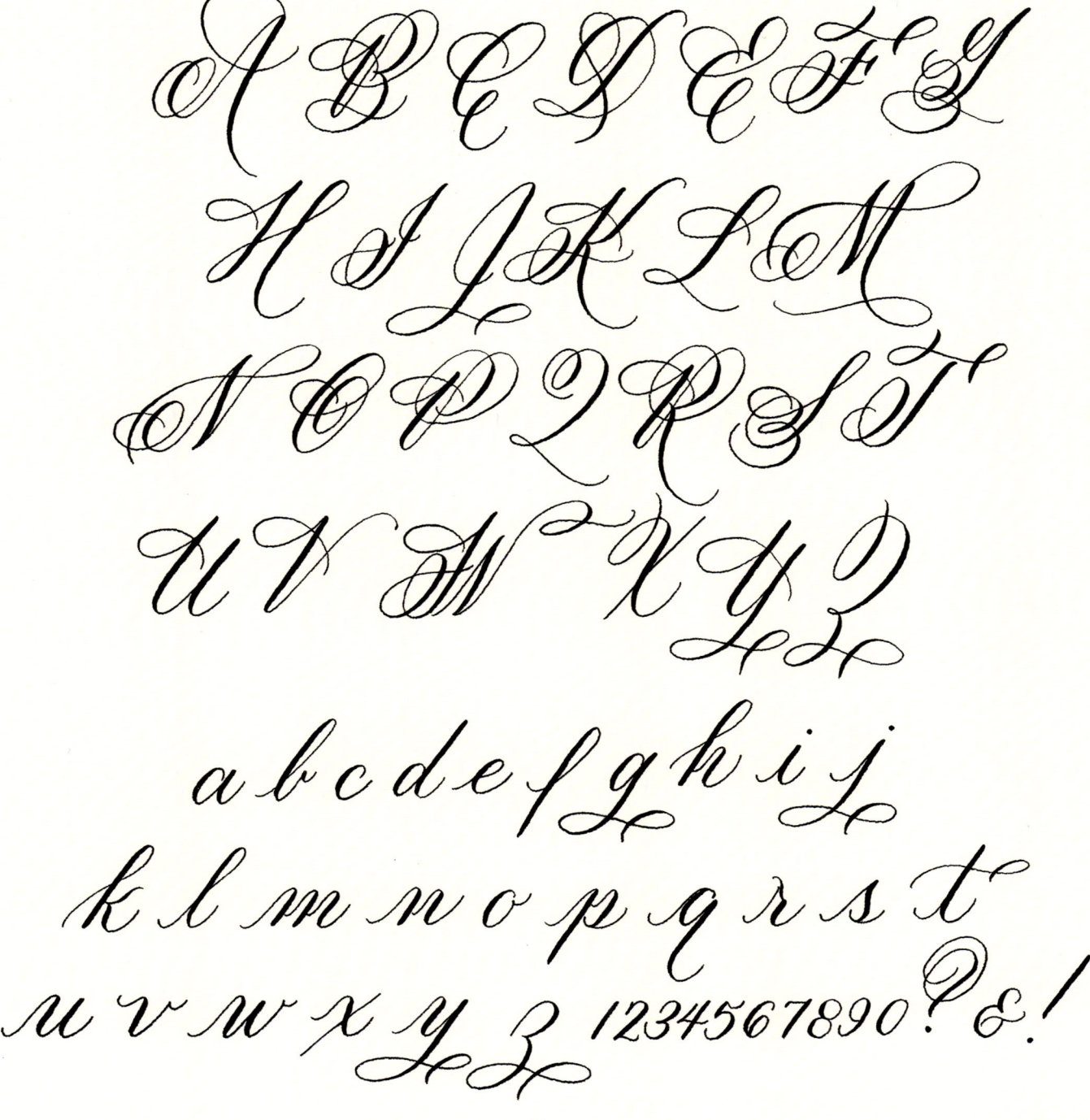

Janet style

Uppercase

Use the key to form each letter correctly,
starting with stroke 1 and then stroke 2,
and so on.

⅖in (10.5 mm)

¼in (6 mm)

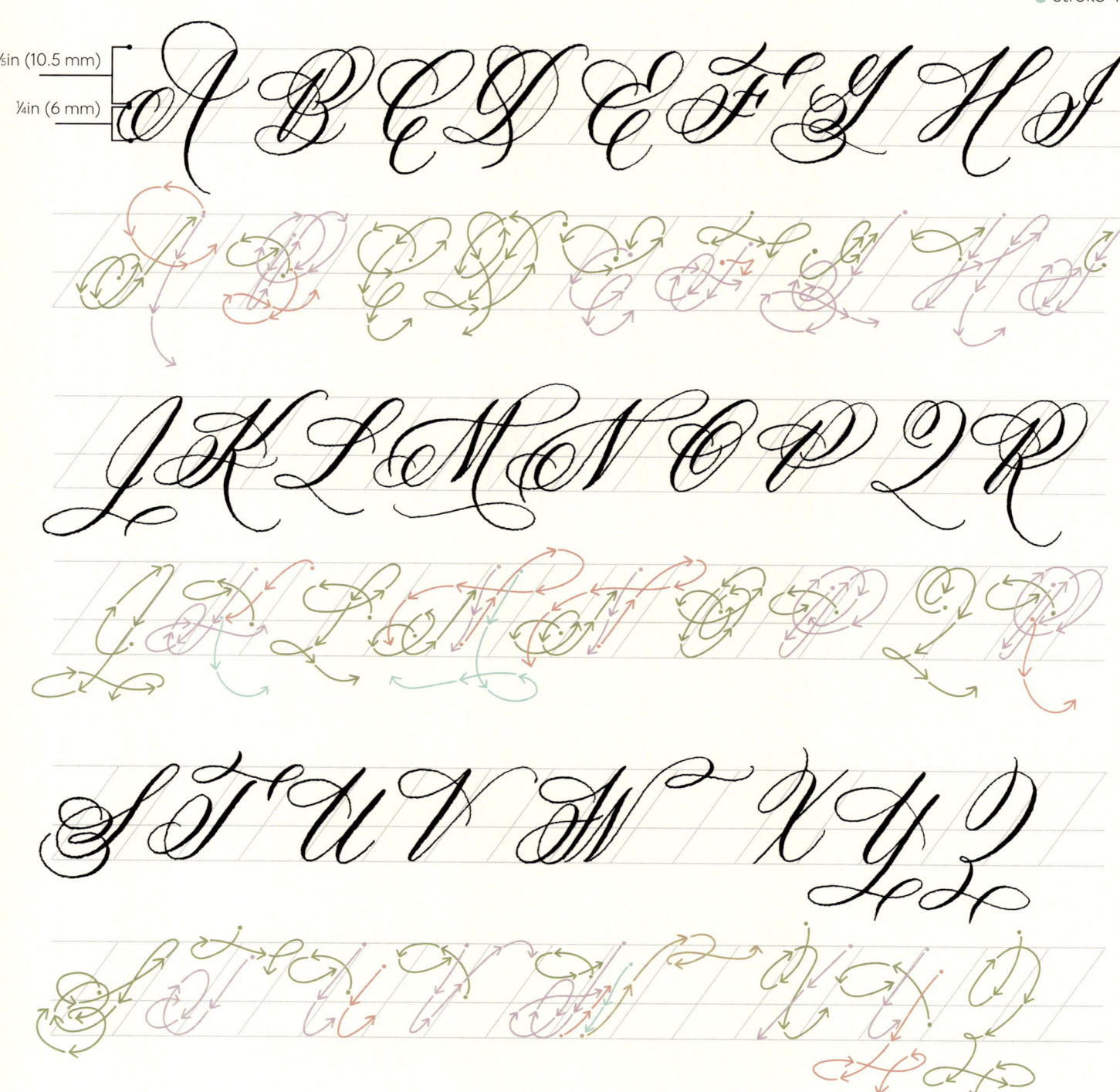

Lowercase

Some of the lowercase letters have flourishes, which you can play with to make them your own style.

Tip

Slant lines

Pencil guidelines are imperative to writing in this style. Don't skip the slant lines!

a b c d e f g h i

You can connect a descender to the next letter or end it in a flourish.

j k l m n o p q r

s t u v w x y z

The cross on the "x" doesn't need to be parallel to the slant lines.

Janet style

Numbers, accents, and punctuation

Once you've mastered the regular alphabet, it's useful to know how to draw these extra digits and letters.

1234567890 ? & !

Janet-style numbers are a little taller than the x-height so the letters remain the focal point.

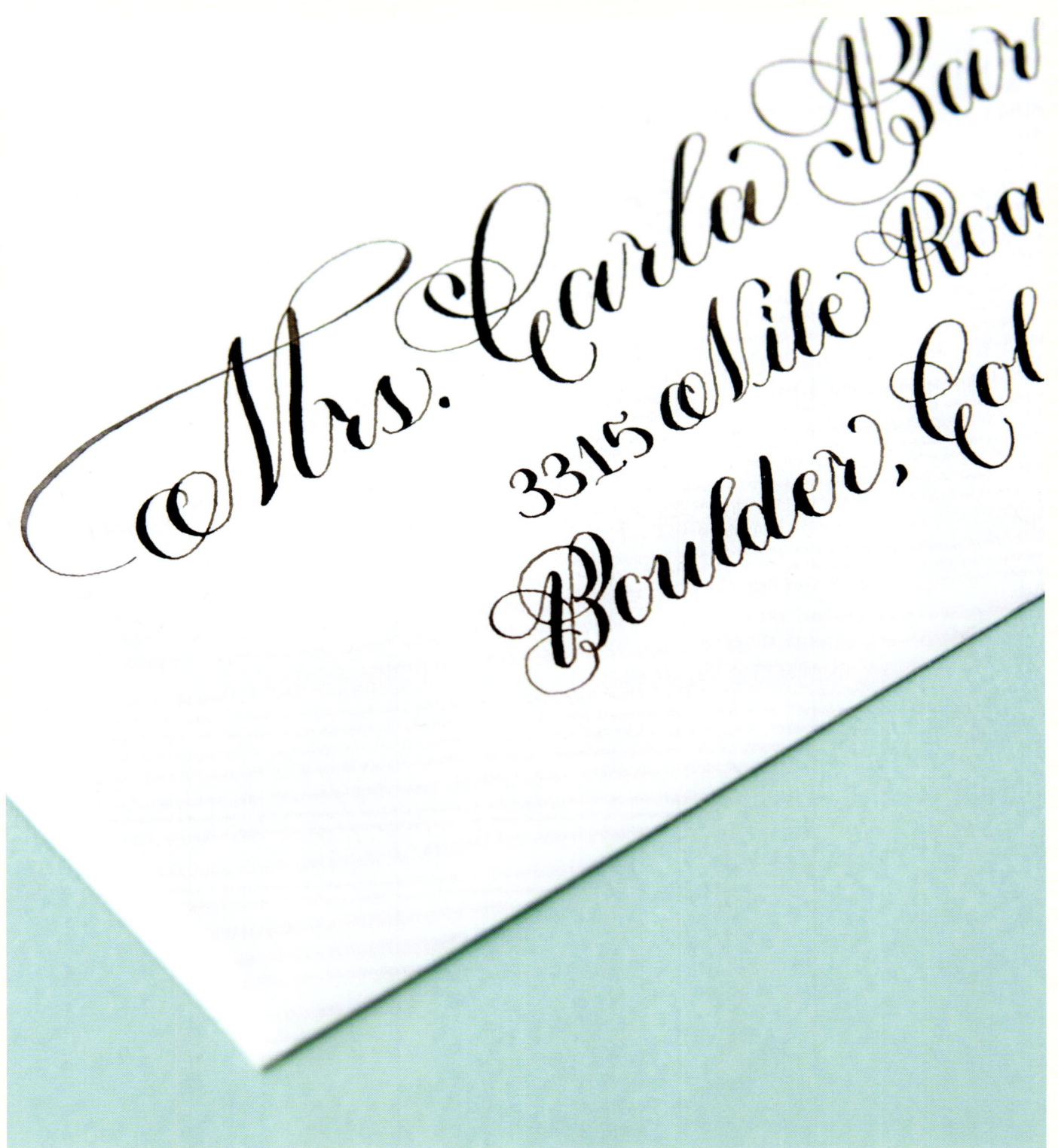

The embellishments of this style are evident in this example of a name and address on an envelope.

Janet style

Joining letters

Making individual letters is only half of the battle, but having the confidence to write any word that might come up in real life can be more difficult. Here are some sample words with tricky letter combinations that may be useful.

If you've got a word with double "t's," you can cross both with one stroke.

Gyumri

Ottawa

Descenders can connect to the letter beside them or end in a flourish.

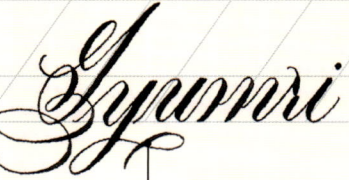

Some letters are slightly smaller than the guidelines, but this won't be noticeable once the lines are removed.

New York

Fuzhou

Flourishes may sometimes intersect other letters.

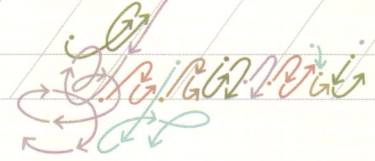

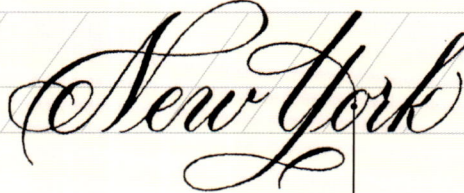

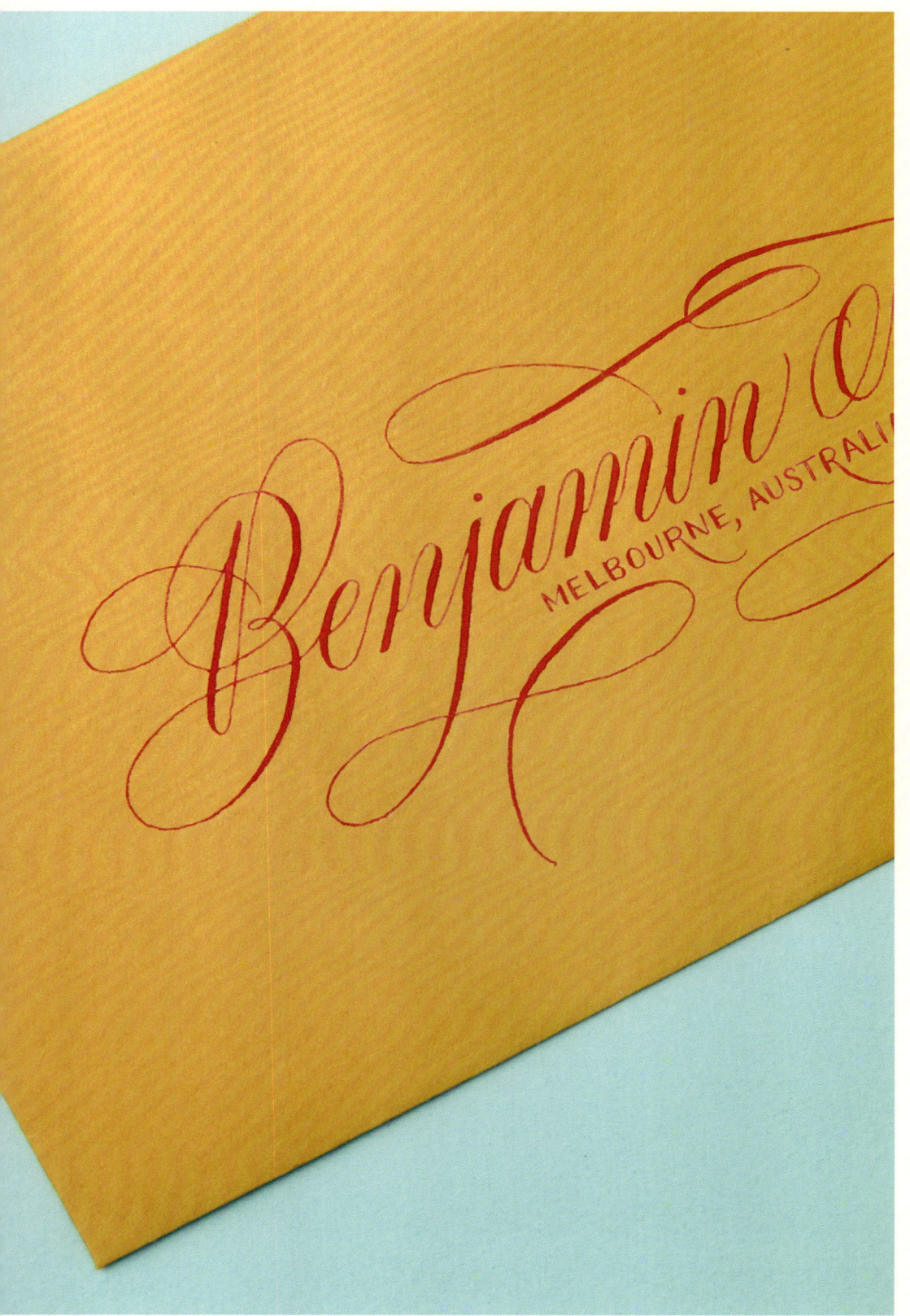

To make this calligraphy style your own, connect descenders in words to the letter that follows, or break up the word with a flourish. The level of embellishment is up to you: Janet style looks good dressed up with copious loops and swirls, but it can be refreshing and classy to keep things simple.

With Janet style, you can manually square-off the edges of stroke endings (as in Copperplate) to add extra elegance.

Flourished style

You can embrace the opportunity to dazzle and shine with this calligraphy style. It's all about opulence and flamboyance, enriched by lavish swirls and twirls.

Sometimes it's refreshing to create calligraphy that is unashamedly over the top. It's not minimalistic and doesn't hold anything back. While the other calligraphy styles in this book can be taken quite literally (letters can be formed and joined together exactly as demonstrated), this style requires discretion and modifications. You can't flourish every single letter or else your calligraphy won't be legible.

Note: I created the Flourished style for my intermediate students. If you find it intimidating, you can come back to it when you've built up your skills to a higher level.

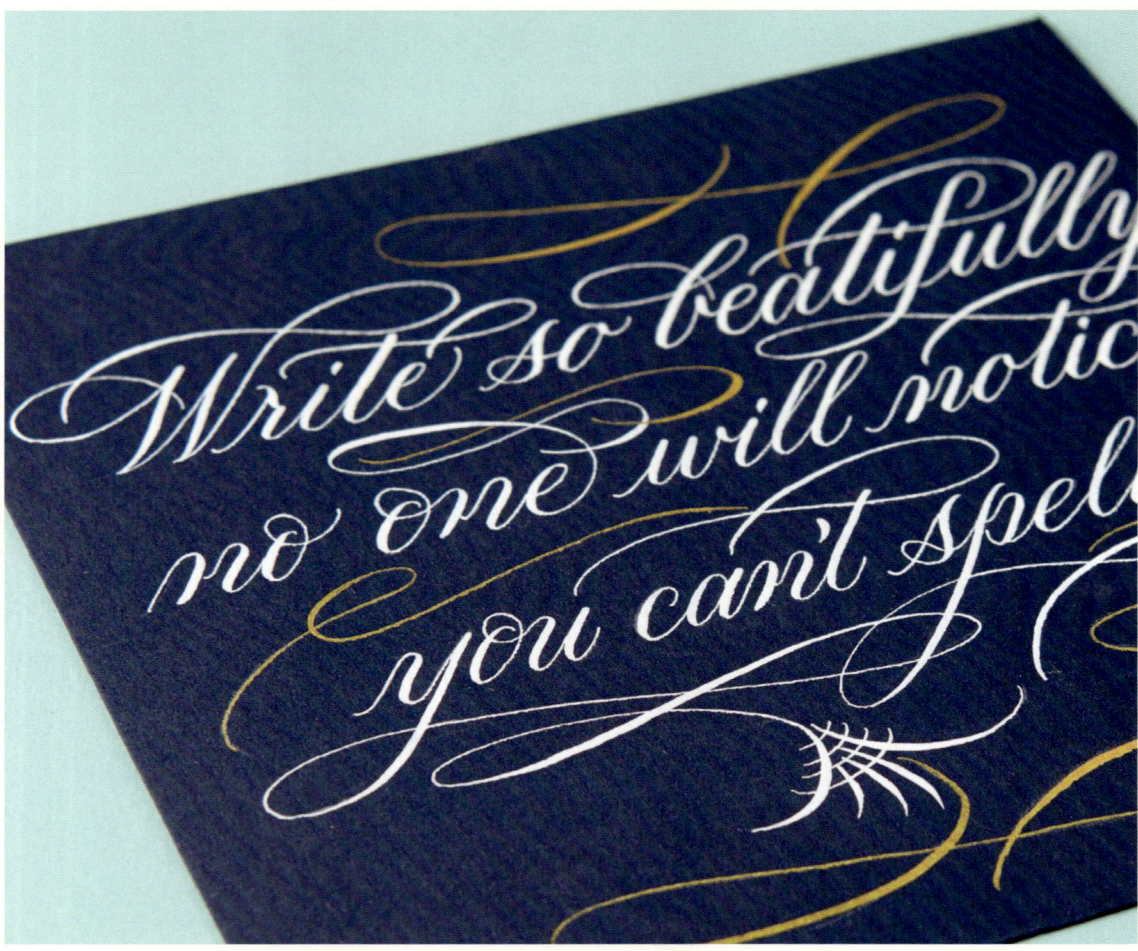

This piece is so heavily flourished, it takes time to notice that there is a spelling mistake in the text!

Flourished-style exemplar at a glance

Notice the extra swirls and flourishes in this style. This alphabet is a starting point for you to create your own flourished calligraphy style.

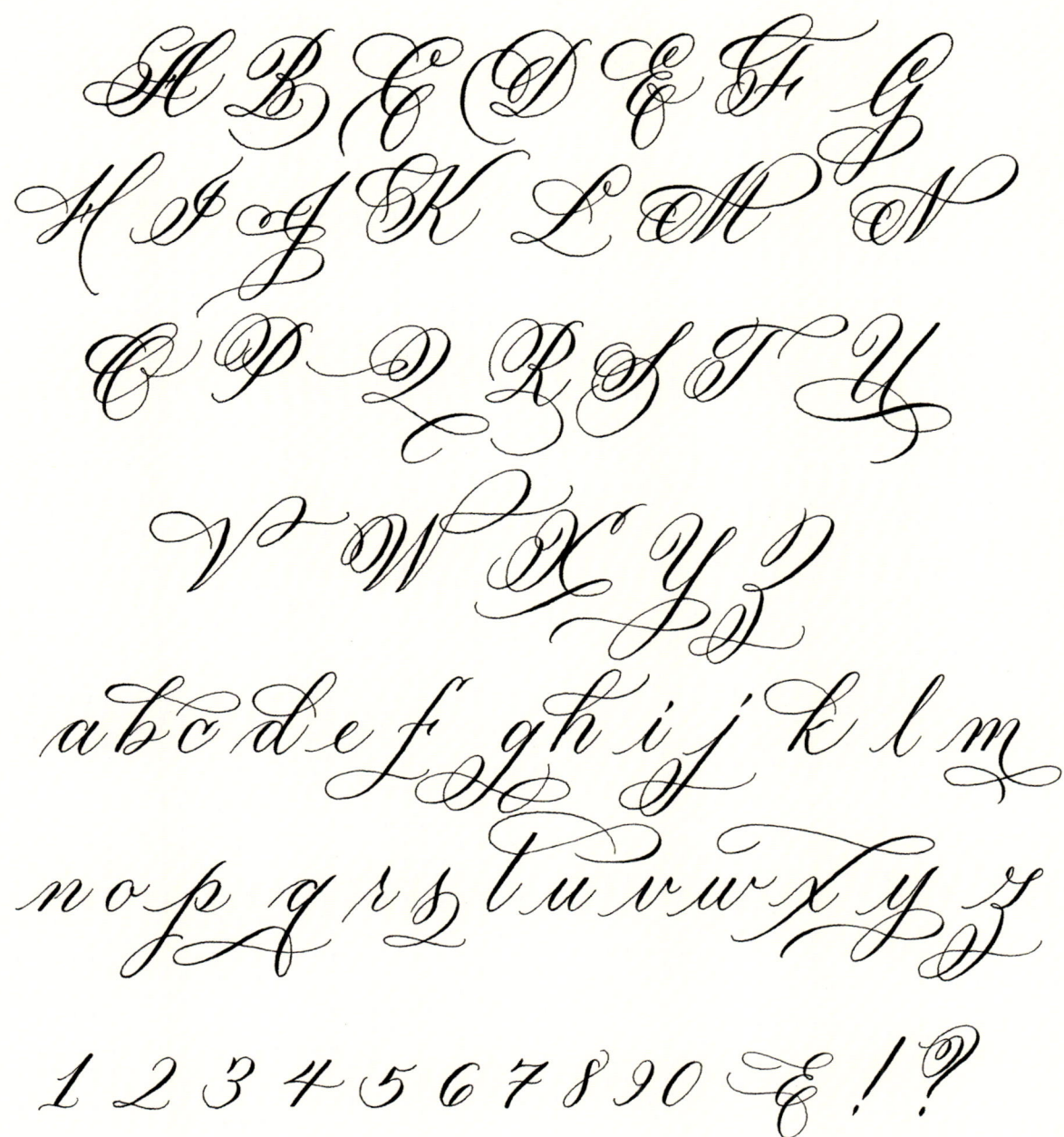

Flourished style

Uppercase

Follow the order of strokes shown in the key to form each letter shown here. Note that these letters have been reduced in size and can be recreated at a size that suits your project.

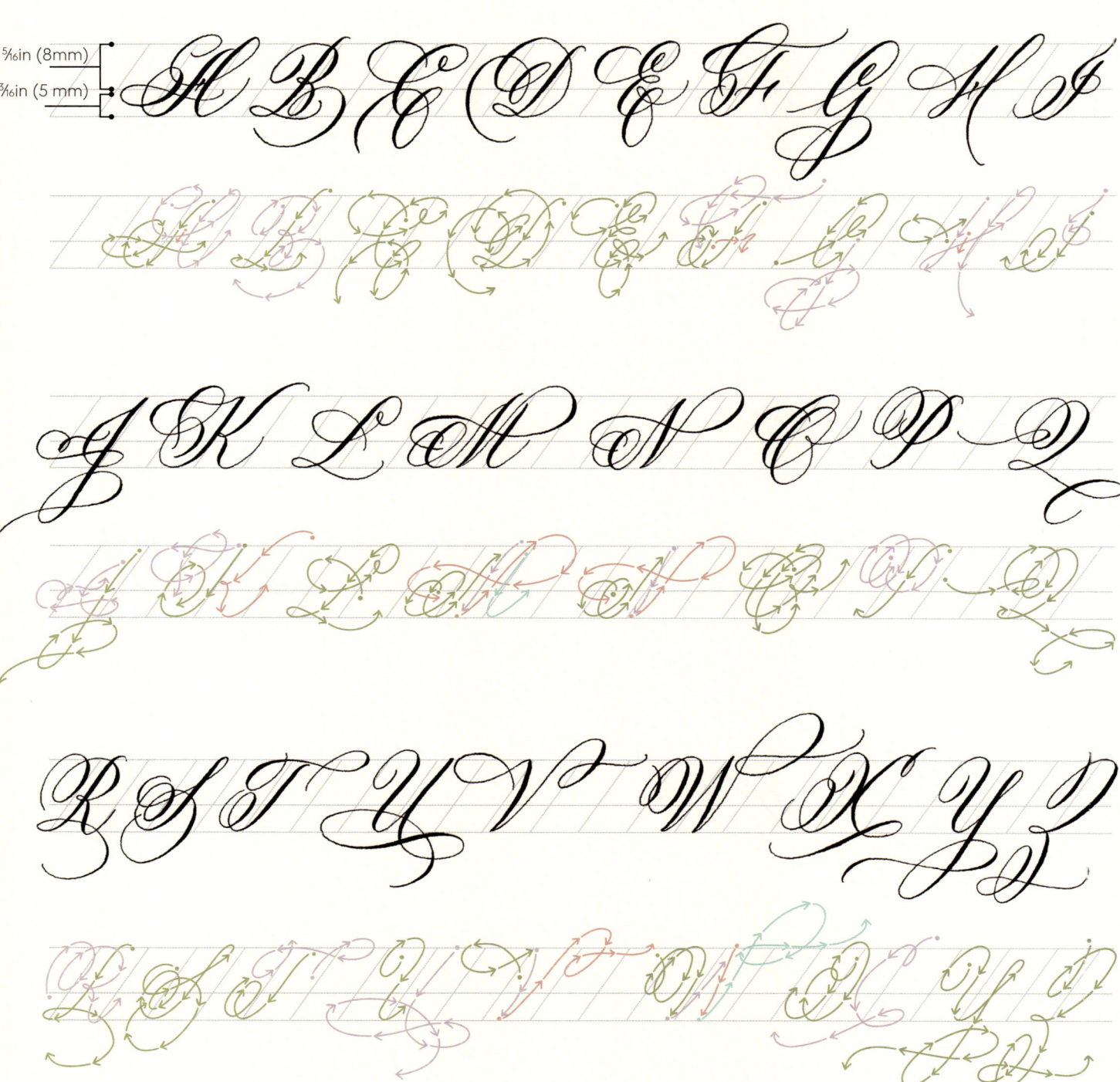

⁵⁄₁₆in (8mm)
³⁄₁₆in (5 mm)

Lowercase

Some ideas for flourishes are shown here.
Practice these then you can add your own
ideas for flourishes.

Tip

Adding flourishes

Smart flourishing is all about
balance. Try taking one word
and experimenting with
different ways to flourish it.
Once you've made a word that
marries legibility with fabulous
embellishments (and you're
happy with how it looks),
you've got a winner.

If you want to vary your
flourishes, you could
end the "j" like the "g."

You can use a
Copperplate-style "s"
instead of this highly
embellished version.

All of the flourishes
shown are customizable.
You can play with your
own versions.

101

Flourished style

Numbers, accents, and punctuation

The numbers remain relatively unflourished to help with legibility, but some other more unusual characters are more swirly.

1 2 3 4 5 6 7 8 9 0 & ! ?

ß H̎ H à â ç É è é ê ñ Č C

ö õ ø Ü ü Ć č G ğ ń Ś Ś

ś ş Ź Ž Ž

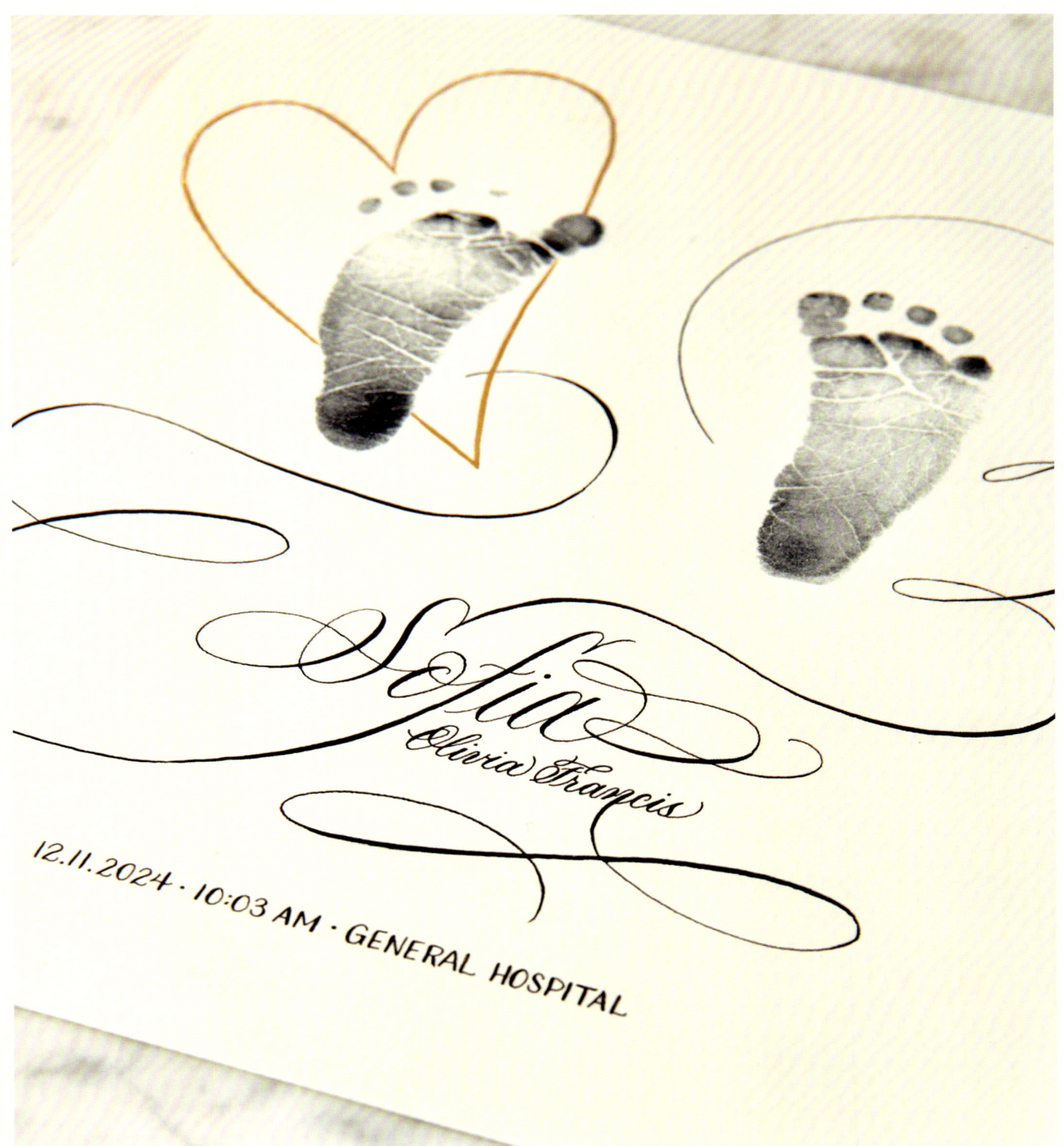

Sofia

Olivia Francis

12.11.2024 · 10:03 AM · GENERAL HOSPITAL

Here, a beautifully swirly "S"
has been done with Flourished
calligraphy (see pp.182–185).

Flourished style

Joining letters

As with Kaitlin-style calligraphy, no two Flourished calligraphy words will be the same. That's because there are so many different routes that you can go with your embellishments. Try writing these words as shown, then rewrite them, adding your own flourishes.

Try playful flourishes on the last letter of a word.

New York

This style allows you to extend your flourishes

Fuzhou

Crosses on "x's" give you a bonus flourishing opportunity

Tlaxcala

Suffolk

It's fine for your strokes to intersect as long as your words remain legible and visually pleasing

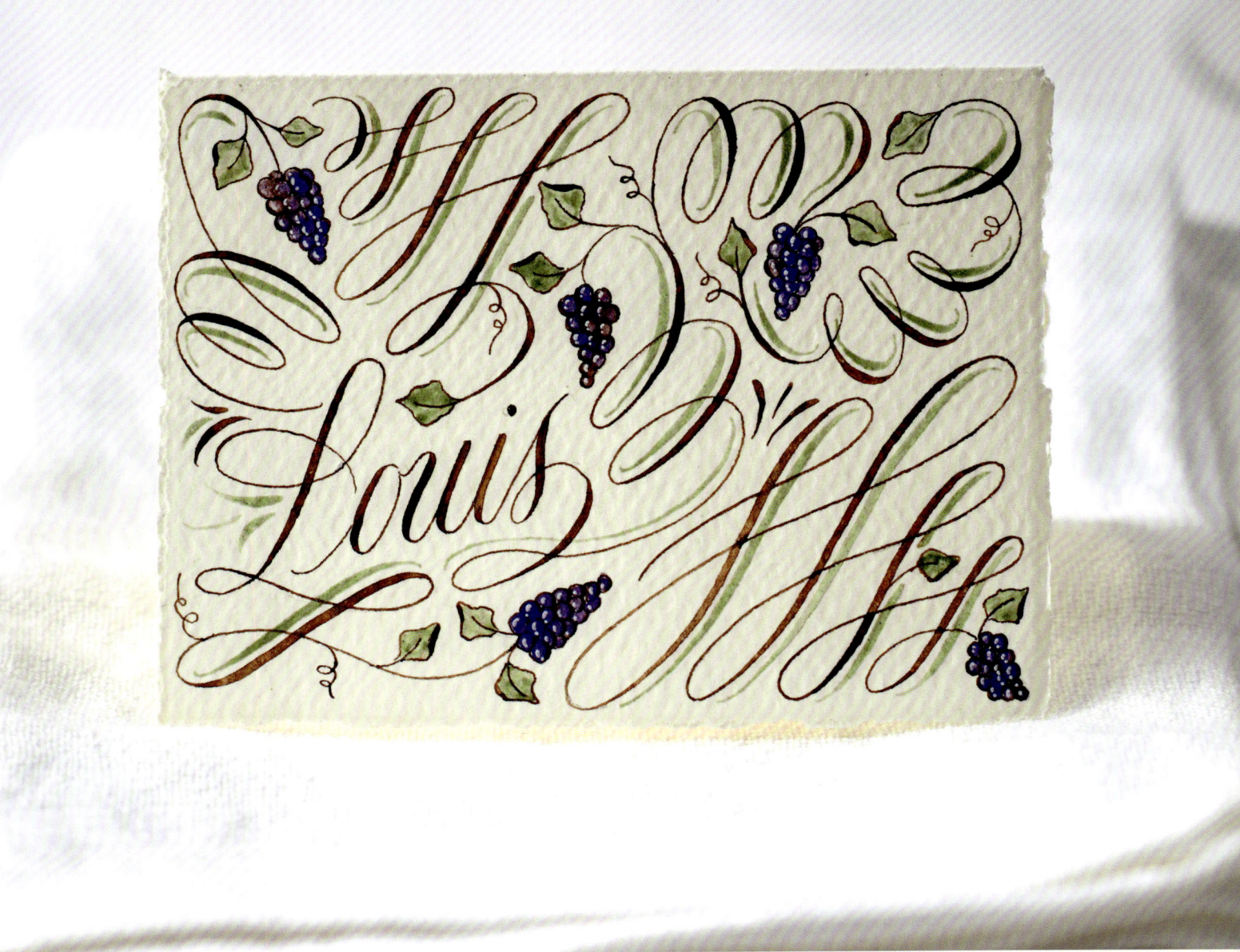

STYLE

Flourished calligraphy is all about balance. It takes practice to write legible calligraphy that has a lot of loops and swirls. The first few times you write this style, try not to overdo the embellishments. As you practice more, you can level up with your flourishes.

The flourishes on this place card help fill the space in a decorative way (see pp.174–177).

Flourished style

Hand lettering

You don't need specialized tools or expertise for hand lettering; any writing instrument, from a ballpoint pen to a pencil, will do. Hand lettering pairs beautifully with calligraphy, so it is worth taking the time to practice it.

Hand lettering is a term used for letters that are drawn as unique, separate pieces. Where calligraphy focuses on the art of beautiful writing with an emphasis on fluidity and stroke contrast, hand lettering allows for more personalized expressions of each letter, often incorporating a variety of styles, embellishments, and layouts to convey a specific mood or message. Calligraphy and hand lettering can be combined to stunning effect. They make for a powerful duo, one that you'll often see used on paper goods like wedding invitations and beautiful hand-decorated envelopes.

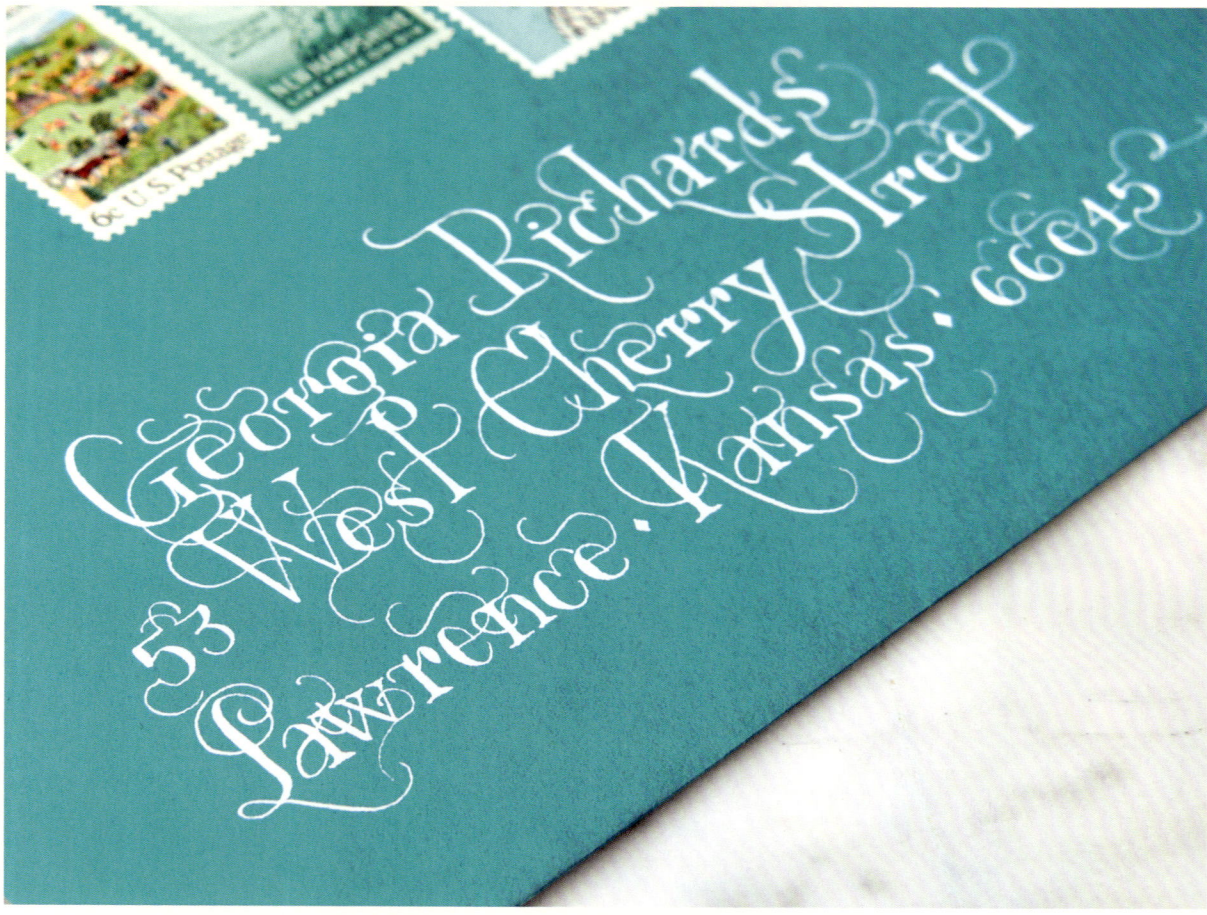

Lasso lettering takes time; this envelope took over 45 minutes to create, from drawing guidelines to completing the letterforms.

Lasso-style lettering

In this style, the flourishes are delicate enough not to affect the legibility of words, but they add a considerable amount of artistic personality. When you look at a Lasso lettering word, your brain immediately registers what the word is. It is usually a split second later that you see (and begin to appreciate) the flourishes.

Lasso lettering is a good choice for projects that require dense coverage, like the Flourished Map (pp.190–91). You can extend the flourishes to reach any guideline boundary without affecting legibility.

ABCDEFGHIJK
LMNOPQRSTU
VWXYZabcdefg
hijklmnopqrstu
vwxyz1234567890&

Block lettering

Block lettering is a type of hand lettering where letters are individual and distinct, without any connecting strokes between them. Calligraphy often benefits enormously from being paired with block lettering, and many block lettering styles look incredible when written with a pointed pen. So while the examples in this section aren't technically considered to be calligraphy, they will help you create stunning calligraphed creations.

George-style lettering

George-style lettering has straight, clean lines with a hint of quirk and artistry. It's an excellent go-to for cards, envelope art, place cards, and any other project that seeks to make a bold statement with clear readability. Because it is clean and hyper-legible, it's a good lettering style for pairing with flourished calligraphy. Try creating an envelope address where the recipient's name is written in George-style lettering and the address is written in flowy calligraphy. The resulting stylistic contrast can be very visually appealing.

This style is customizable. Notice that a few letters have variations.

These letters are shown with parallel diagonal lines inside, but you can use a different pattern or a color instead.

George-style numbers are the same height as uppercase letters.

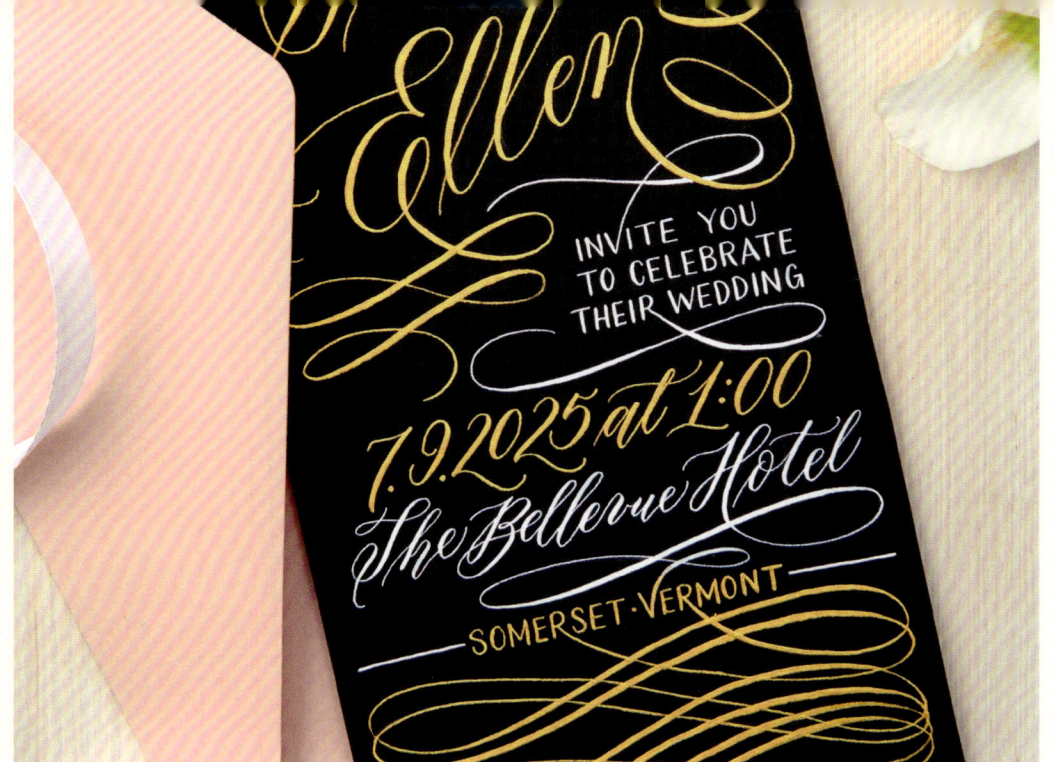

Legible block lettering always pairs well with flowy script.

Sans serif lettering

Sans serif lettering is a basic style of lettering that every calligrapher needs in their back pocket. Sans serif lettering is a favorite for two reasons: first, its legibility virtually guarantees the quick delivery of any hand-calligraphed envelope.

You can write your recipient's name with glorious, sweeping flourishes, then write a no-nonsense address using sans serif lettering. The second reason calligraphers love to use sans serif lettering is it makes projects quicker to do. After all, it takes much less time to write no-frills lettering than it does impressive calligraphy. Consider interweaving this lettering style into your projects when you need stylistic contrast, legibility, and/or efficiency.

Sans serif lettering is best written with a medium-flex nib in a straight pen for a clean, legible effect

ABCDEFGHIJ
KLMNOPQRS
TUVWXYZabcd
efghijklmnopqrs
tuvwxyz
1234567890

Hand lettering

Creating your own style

Once you've mastered the basics of pointed pen calligraphy and learned how to write a couple of styles, you might want to come up with your own styles. There are a few ways that you can help the process when it comes to designing your own calligraphy letters and characters.

Set rules

If you're struggling to get started, try thinking about the following points to get your thoughts in order:

Slant: Does your calligraphy style lean to the left or to the right or have no slant?

Connections: Are all, none, or some letters connected in a word?

Adjectives: Once you've developed this style, how do you want to be able to describe it? It could be neat and elegant or cute and messy, for example.

Embellishments: Do you want your style to include additional flourishes every time a particular letter is used?

Use: How do you see this style being used? This will affect how elaborate or simple it needs to be.

Experiment

Once you've considered the parameters given here, try writing five (or more) versions of a sentence using your aesthetic wish list. Try a sentence that uses all the letters of the alphabet, like "The five boxing wizards jump quickly," or copy out a section of lorem ipsum nonsense text (see right), which can be generated easily online. After you've written out the test sentence several times, identify the different elements that you like. Perhaps in one version, you wrote a

particularly inspired "q." Maybe a different version of the sentence boasts flourishes that look unique and confident. Take note of what you like and what you don't like. Keep that in mind as you write a final version of the test sentence, one that incorporates all of your self-feedback.

Make an exemplar

The next step is to make an exemplar that includes the full alphabet in upper and lower-case, numbers, and any other characters that will be useful to you, similar to the examples on pp.64–105.

Test and adjust

Referring to your new exemplar, write out a few longer passages of text. Step back and see whether the style meets all your rules and whether any clusters of words look awkward or difficult to read. Make any adjustments you need, then jot down notes or make modifications to your exemplar.

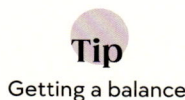

Tip
Getting a balance

Not all of the letters in your exemplar need to be aesthetic heavy hitters. Eye-pleasing calligraphy is all about balance; some letters will be plainer than others.

Points to consider

Here are five examples of calligraphy styles with their rules to
show you how you might get started.

Quo zephyr flavit ex viridi monte.

Slant: Upright **Connections:** Don't connect uppercase letters or descenders **Adjectives:** Modern, legible, cheerful
Embellishment: Lots of flourishes but nothing too excessive **Use:** Casual events and personal projects

Quo zephyr flavit ex viridi monte.

Slant: 55 degrees **Connections:** Almost all letters connect **Adjectives:** Elegant, traditional, restrained
Embellishment: Minimal **Use:** Formal events

Quo zephyr flavit ex viridi monte.

Slant: Unspecified, right-leaning **Connections:** Uppercase letters don't connect to following letters, lowercase letters all connect
Adjectives: Free-spirited, bohemian, modern elegance **Embellishment:** Minimal with the exception of long, wavy strokes used to cross
letters like "t" **Use:** Weddings/events with bohemian flair, quick and casual calligraphy

Quo zephyr flavit ex viridi monte.

Slant: Upright **Connections:** Don't connect uppercase letters or tails **Adjectives:** 1930s, dainty, rounded
Embellishment: Minimal **Use:** Nostalgic event stationery

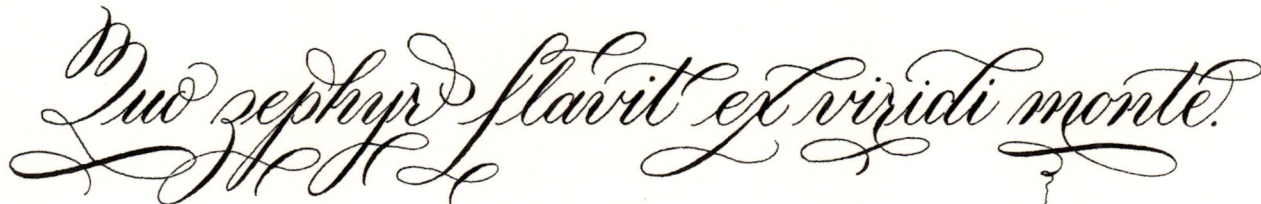

Slant: 55 degrees **Connections:** Minimal; disconnect letters when the opportunity to flourish arises
Adjectives: Striking, over-the-top **Embellishment:** Excessive **Use:** Extravagant events

Creating your own style

Finding the right mood

Another approach to creating your own calligraphy style is to write out the same word or sentence over and over, each time keeping in mind a different adjective. Here are a few ideas to get you started, and some examples of how they can translate into calligraphy forms.

1 Bohemian Spacing your letters farther apart than usual can channel an elegantly whimsical aesthetic. A bit of flourish adds the perfect touch.

2 Spooky The stiff and abrupt nature of these strokes gives the impression of being written by Frankenstein's creation.

3 Clean Consistent loops and squared-off tips contribute to a look that's legible and squeaky clean.

4 Festive There's nothing more festive than a confetti cannon. That's why this word includes plenty of flourishes and appears to shoot confetti at the end.

5 Sloppy With its uncertain baseline and carefree variation in letter sizes, this word is delightfully messy.

6 Cutesy Copious circular strokes and an upright slant make the letters in this word cute as a button.

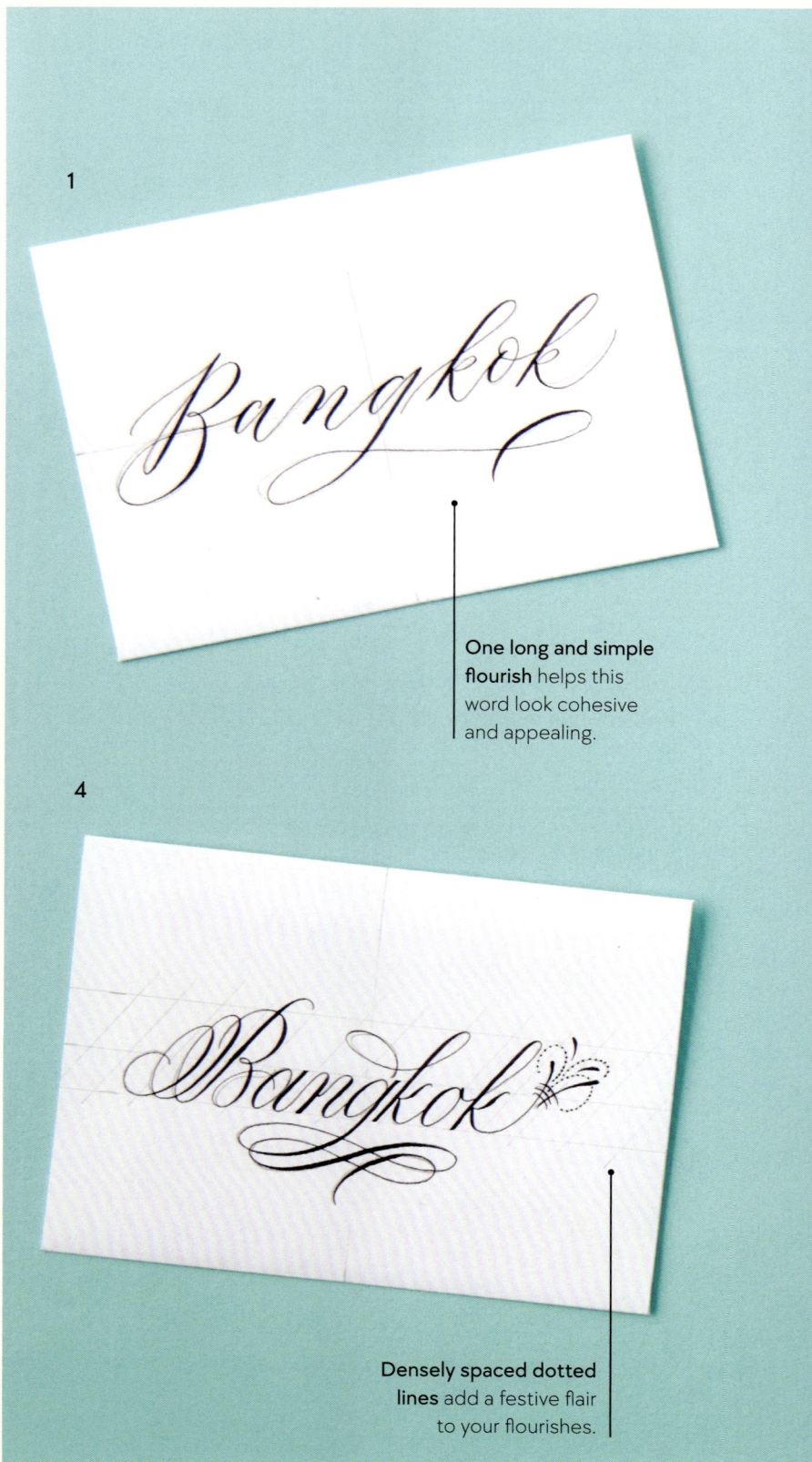

1

One long and simple **flourish** helps this word look cohesive and appealing.

4

Densely spaced dotted **lines** add a festive flair to your flourishes.

2

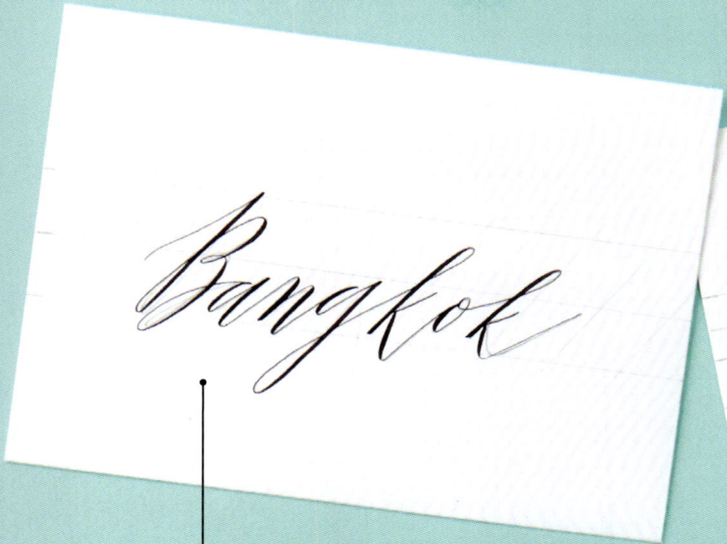

Bangkok

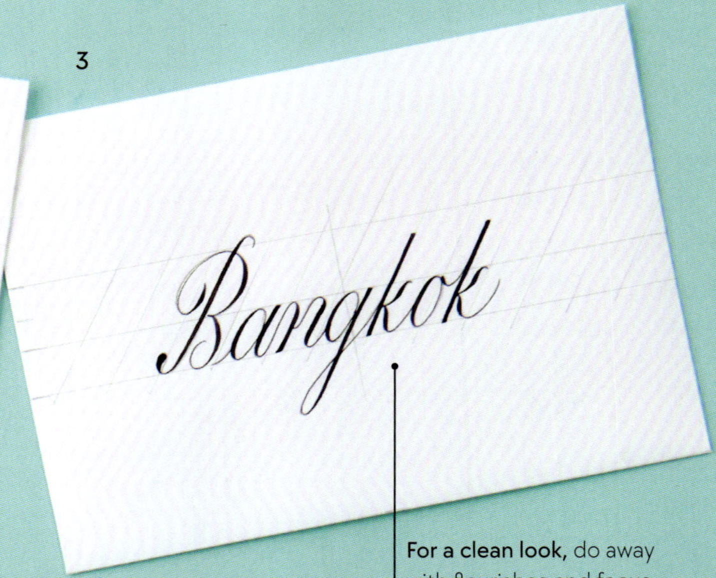

Letters that look like they were written under strain tend to channel Halloween vibes.

3

Bangkok

For a clean look, do away with flourishes and focus on squared-off strokes.

5

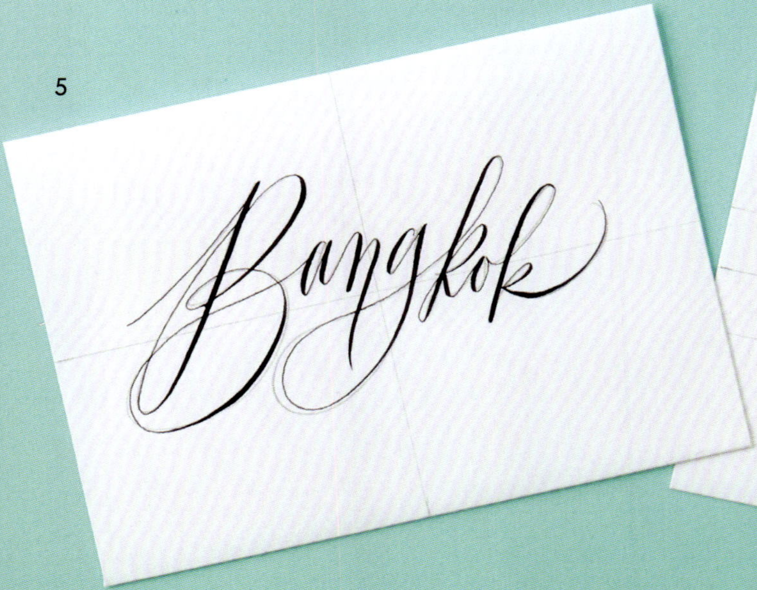

Bangkok

6

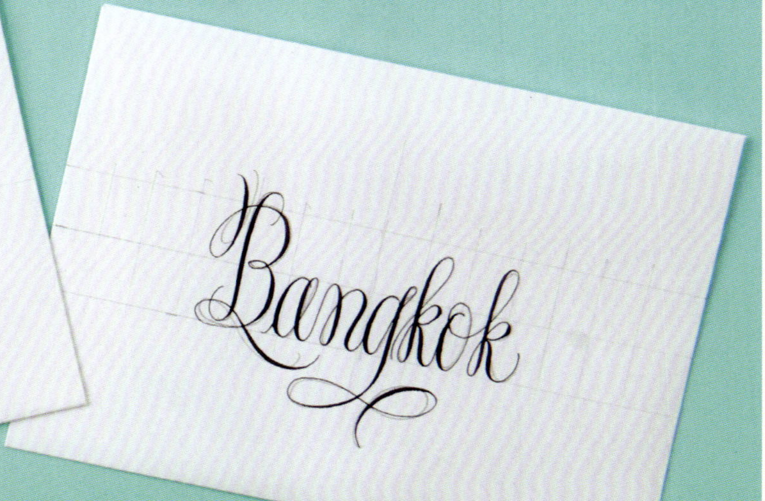

Bangkok

Mastering the technique

When you embark on your calligraphy journey, it can be hard to resist the urge to jump straight into creating projects. However, it is important to embrace the value of regular practice—not only to improve your skills but to enjoy the process, too.

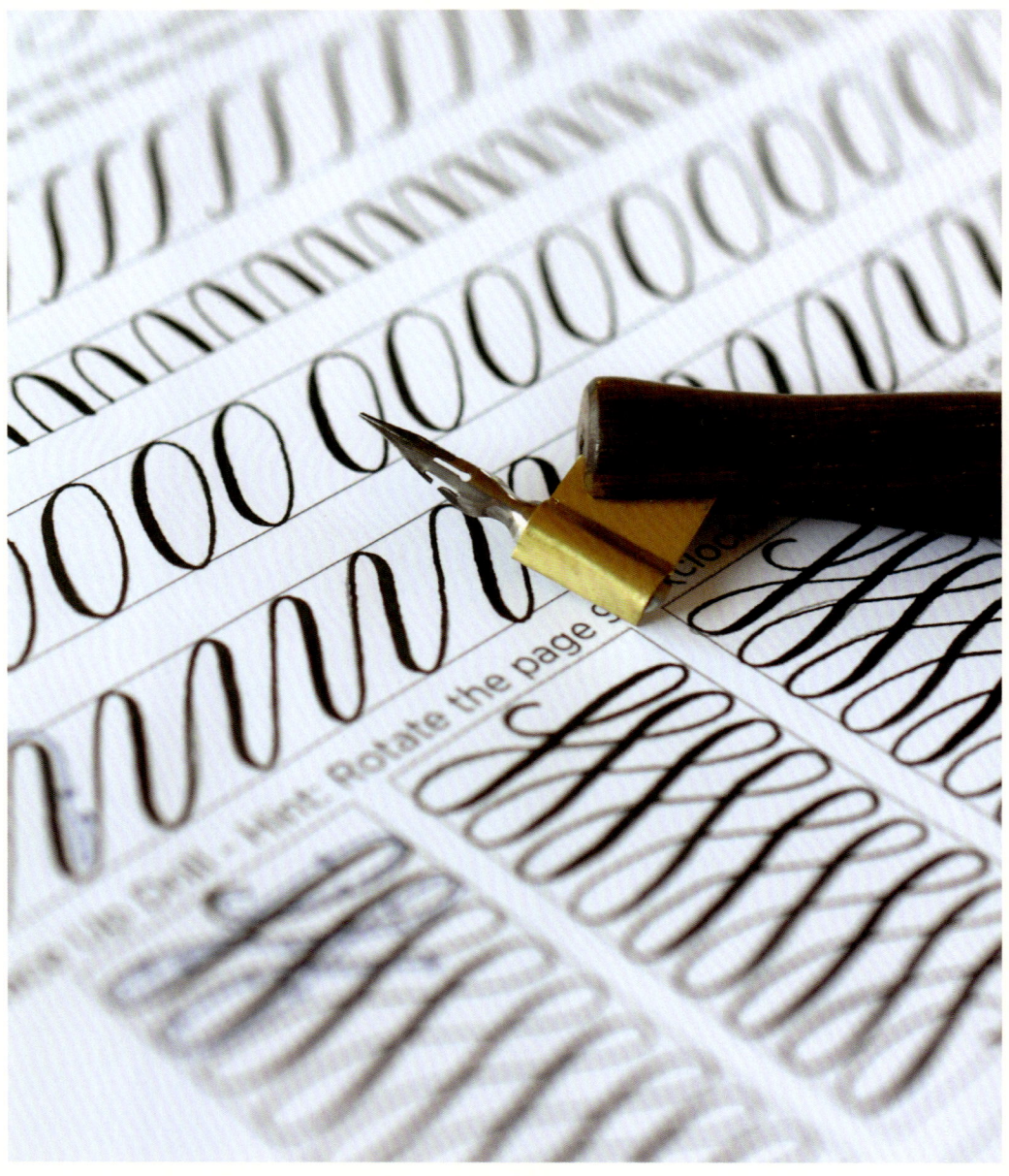

Kick off your calligraphy practice with the basics (see pp.50–53). Work to create the three main types of pointed pen calligraphy strokes and do plenty of drills until you feel comfortable handling your pointed pen.

As with anything you have decided to learn, you've got to make practice enjoyable. You will master the calligraphy basics quickly if you like what you're doing. Part of this will come down to ensuring you have a comfortable setup (see pp.36–37), but you also need to set the right mood. You might like to work in silence, or perhaps heavy metal music helps you focus best. Maybe you'll sip tea between strokes or enjoy a square of chocolate every time you complete a drill.

Repetition and variation

There's no getting away from the fact that practicing drills can be repetitive, and that can get boring over time. Once you begin to feel confident with your letterforms, begin to introduce projects (see pp.138–195) into your routine. I recommend a 1:2 ratio of structured practice to joyful projects. In other words, for every 20 minutes you spend doing calligraphy drills, try to give yourself 40 minutes of making something enjoyable.

Another way to keep things interesting is to introduce different inks into your practice: instead of using sumi ink, try gouache, or play with metallic watercolors to make glittery, golden letters (see pp.130–131). It helps to get a feel for new materials and mediums with practice drills before you commit to a project using them.

Get into the habit of warming up with some calligraphy drills at the beginning of each session.

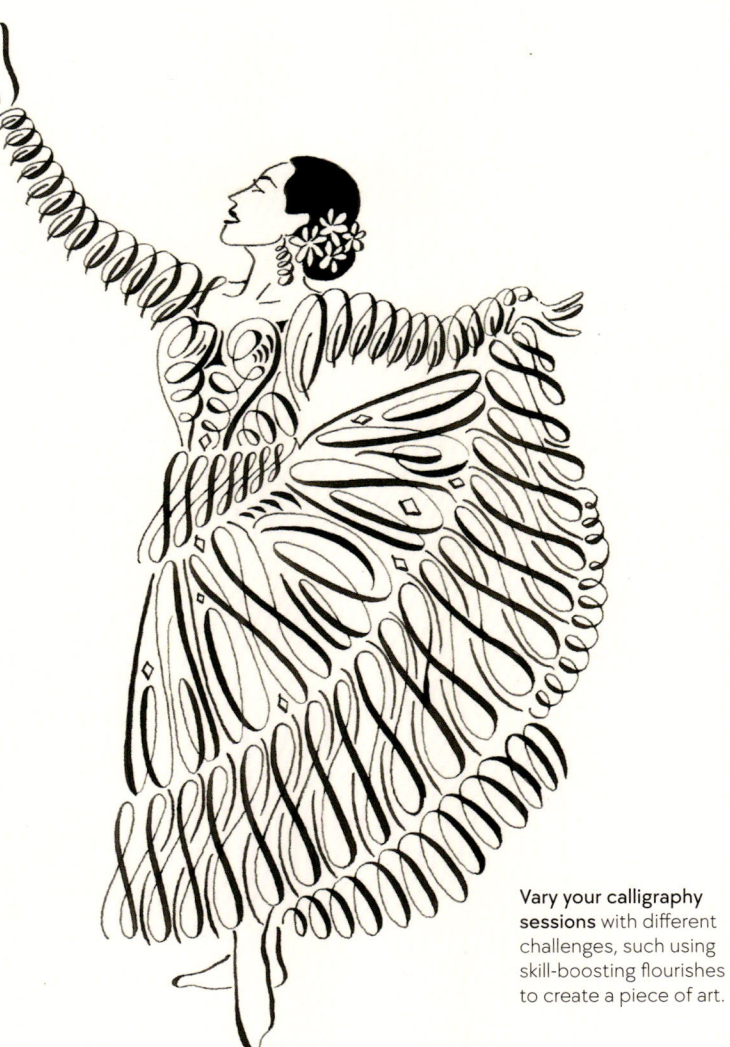

Vary your calligraphy sessions with different challenges, such using skill-boosting flourishes to create a piece of art.

Eventually, you might feel that that drill sessions no longer seem necessary. However, it still helps to keep up a routine of completing drills and practicing letterforms from time to time, to keep your skills sharp.

Appreciate the journey

As you practice calligraphy, try to always keep in mind that nothing will ever be perfect. Even the most experienced calligrapher makes mistakes and continues to learn. You will always see flaws in what you make. The trick is to realize that those flaws are exactly what makes the work special.

Tip

Take your time

If you begin with quality instruction and understand the hurdles you may face, you're less likely to abandon your calligraphy efforts when you run into problems.

Mastering the technique

Tracking your progress

Your calligraphy will evolve over time. Embrace the small triumphs along the way—the moment you nail a tricky letter, the smoothness of your transitions, or the consistent spacing between words.

Keep a record

It can be easy to feel frustrated and feel that you're not progressing as quickly as you'd like to. Very often, though, you just don't realize how far you've come from when you first put nib to paper. It is very likely that you have learned more than you know. A great way to check your progress is to keep a photographic record of your work, even if only occasionally. Then you can look back to track your improvement over time, particularly if you attempt the same letter style or project a few times.

How you keep records of your calligraphy skills is up to you. You might put select practice pieces in a binder in chronological order. Alternatively, you can take photos of your work and keep them in a special folder on your computer or your phone.

You don't need to keep every piece of practice paper or take a photo of every project you do. Instead, try to keep a record of anything that seems significant. Whenever you make something you like—especially if it's something that won't stick around, like a pretty envelope—take a photo

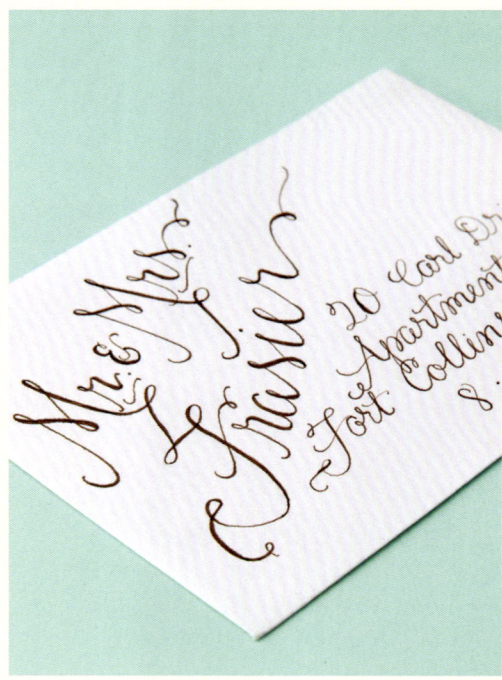

I created this envelope in 2013, before I'd discovered the magic of slant lines and flexible nibs.

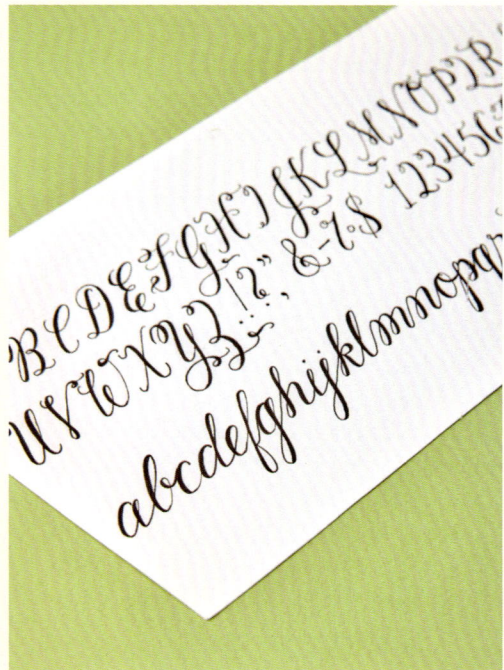

This alphabet was painstakingly written using faux calligraphy (see p.10) back in 2012.

of it. Perhaps you could keep one practice piece or take one photo every month, and after a year, you'll be astonished at how your skills have grown.

Repeat your projects

If in doubt, try remaking a project from your early calligraphy days. Choose something you did as a beginner—like an envelope or a quote—and remake that project at your current skill level. The differences will be astonishing and encouraging.

In short, remember to cherish your journey and celebrate every step of progress. When discouragement creeps in, look at your early work to remind yourself how far you've come. Growth in calligraphy takes time, practice, and—most of all—motivation.

"A great way to check your progress is to keep a photographic record of your work."

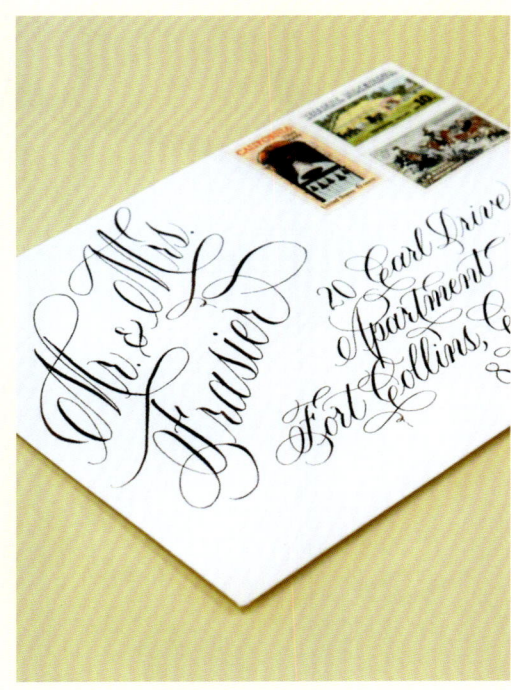

My 2024 envelope redo is more fluid and relaxed, with consistent slants and contrasting stroke widths.

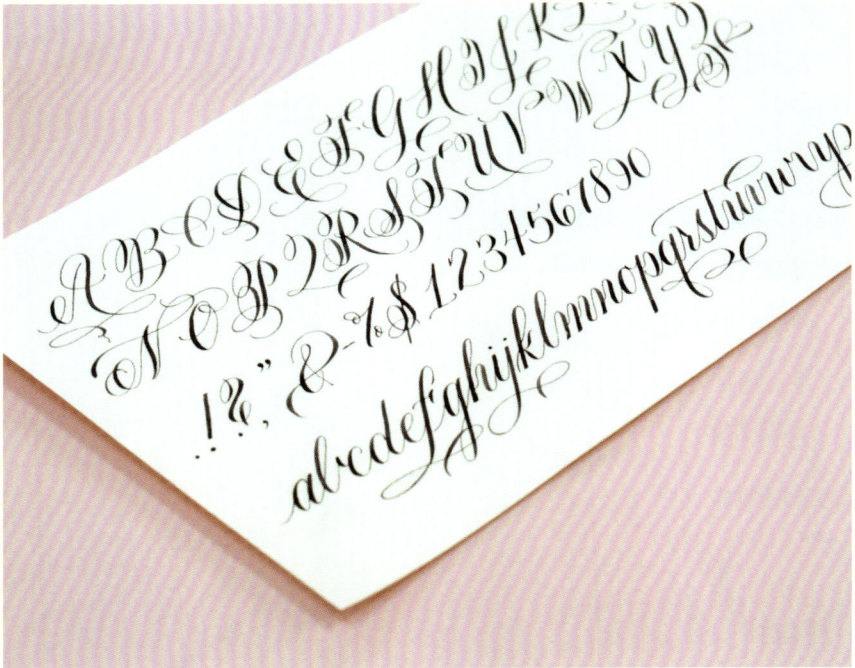

This recent alphabet features letters that look more playful and confident than my 2012 attempt.

Tracking your progress

Challenges and opportunities

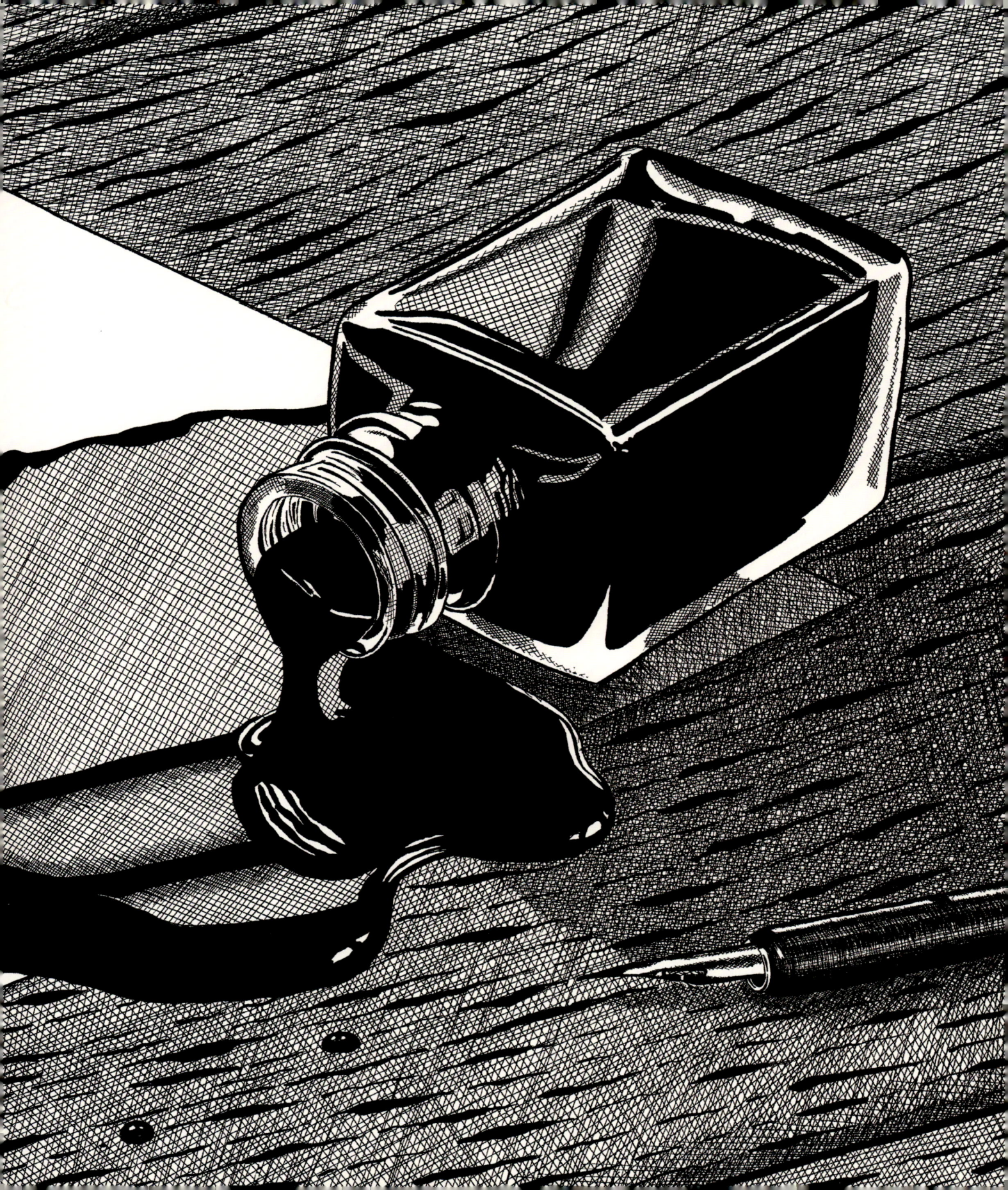

Nib challenges

Even if you've followed the advice given on pp.36–47 of this book, it's common to encounter nib issues like ink not flowing or uneven strokes. Many of these problems can be fixed with simple solutions, though sometimes replacing the nib is the most effective remedy.

Here are some of the most common nib problems you might encounter and how to fix them.

The nib refuses to write

After dipping your nib, you may find that the ink does not flow onto the page. There are a few potential solutions for this:

- **Remove the wax.** Make sure you've removed the wax from the nib (see pp.40–41). Oils and wax on the nib can make the ink bead up, preventing it from flowing down the nib.
- **Dilute the ink.** If the ink is too thick, it will stay on the nib. Try diluting it with some water to see if that fixes the problem.
- **Clean the nib.** Use some water and a nonfibrous cloth. As you write, the moisture in the ink evaporates from the nib, leading to residue that disrupts the ink flow. Make it a habit to regularly clean your nib as you write.
- **Adjust your writing angle.** Our instinct is to write holding our pens vertically. While this writing angle feels natural, it will cause the nib to dig in to your paper, pick up paper fibers, and hamper ink flow. For the best results, try levering the pen down to achieve a softer angle to the page.

Replace the nib

If you have tried these fixes and the ink still isn't flowing correctly, the upstrokes are less delicate, or the nib feels scratchy and unpleasant to use, it may be time to replace it. It's very difficult to predict how long pointed pen nibs will last. Their lifespan depends on factors, including the type of ink you use (and its acidity), how often you use the nib, how much pressure you apply to the nib, and the kind of nib you're using.

A nib's tines are delicate and can be damaged quite easily. If you press too hard or unevenly, so that one tine is getting more pressure than the other one, nibs can split permanently. This can also happen if your pen rolls off the table or sustains an impact. If a nib's tines are scissored or split, it's time to replace the nib.

The nib is stuck in the pen

If you can't get the nib out of your pen, it may be rusted or dried up ink inside may be acting as a glue. Neither water nor ink should ever enter your pen (see pp.46–47). The only part of the pen that should interact with any type of moisture is the nib itself. If this does happen, however, you can try pulling out the nib with pliers.

Strokes are uneven or skipping

If you're experiencing uneven or skipping strokes, take a look at how you're holding the pen. Are you exerting balanced, even pressure on both tines of the nib? If not, adjust your technique. Make sure, too, that the shank of the nib is parallel to the letter slant that you want to write (see pp.54–55). If you're having trouble with that, rotate your page. Another culprit could be the ink's viscosity—you may need to add a little water to improve the flow.

A new nib has a
pointed tip.

Remember to
remove the
manufacturer's
wax before use.

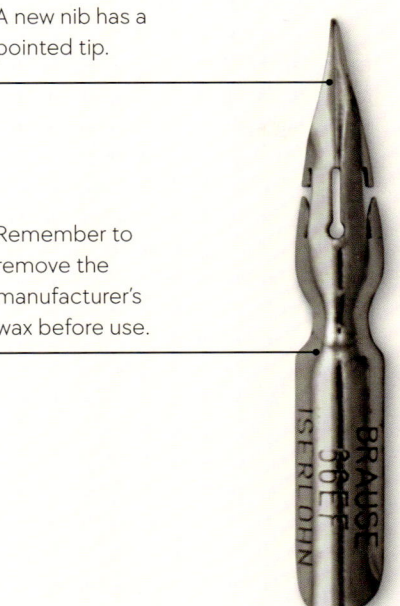

A new nib has a shiny,
clean appearance.

Ink stains don't affect
the utility of your nib.

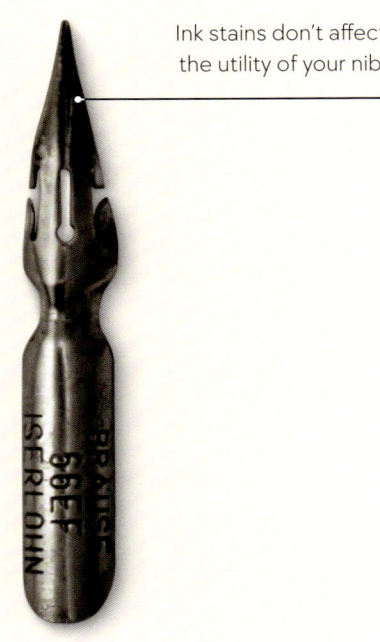

As long as your nib is
enjoyable to use, it doesn't
matter how grimy it looks.

A blunt tip is a
sign of a worn-
out nib.

This well-used nib
no longer writes
smoothly.

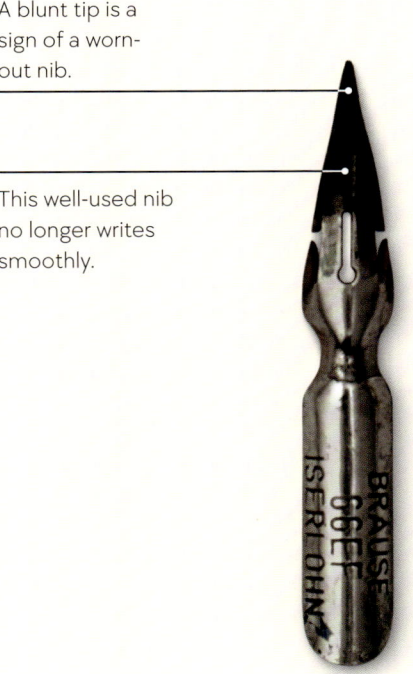

Replace a worn nib that
doesn't create clean stroke
contrast or smooth strokes.

Damage to the
tip of the nib.

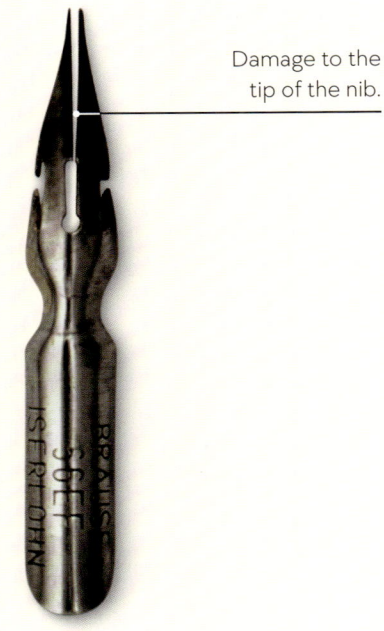

Damaged nibs have
scissored tines. You'll need
to replace a nib like this.

Nib challenges

Ink issues

If your nib is working fine but something else isn't right, you might need to check that your ink isn't causing the problem. Some common ink problems involve its viscosity and compatibility with your paper.

If you're struggling to make your ink work effectively, try some of these suggestions:

Ink is feathering/bleeding
This common issue usually happens for two main reasons:
- **Ink/paper incompatibility.** If the ink is too thin and/or the paper is fibrous, the ink will bleed. If that's the case, either try writing on a different paper (watercolor paper rarely allows feathering or bleeding) or mix some gum arabic—liquid or powder—into your ink a little bit at a time. Keep mixing and testing until the ink no longer bleeds.
- **Uneven nib pressure.** If you're exerting uneven pressure on the tines of your nib, it will cut into the page slightly, disturbing your paper fibers. These fibers may then soak up and spread the ink, resulting in a fuzzy stroke. To fix this, exert balanced, even pressure on both tines of the nib as you write.

The ink has dried up in its bottle
Many inks can be revived by adding water, waiting overnight, and stirring to incorporate the water into the ink. If possible, use distilled water to dilute your ink. Depending on the quality of the water where you live, adding tap water can encourage mold to form, so using distilled water is the safest option. If you try this, the ink might not be quite as good as new—but you'll be able to write with it again.

The ink is blobbing
If your ink is coming out in blobs, it can descend to the page in a series of beads and dots. Try adding half a teaspoon of water, then repeat until it flows smoothly.

You can also try shaking your nib over the ink bottle or water cup after loading it with ink. This will encourage the excess ink to come off the nib before it hits the page. Finally, try holding your pen at a closer angle to the paper. If the nib has too much of an upright angle, the abrupt parting of the tines when you exert downstroke pressure can result in the ink being dumped onto your paper.

The ink isn't sticking
If you find that the ink is not adhering to your writing surface, it may be because the paper is too smooth or has a coating that repels the ink. The best thing to do at that point is to use a different paper. If this is not possible, try other inks to see whether any of those work. If all else fails, you can try using the faux calligraphy technique (see p.10) with a permanent marker.

The ink smears
If your ink smears while you are erasing your guidelines, it is not yet fully dry. You may be able to remove the ink smear (see pp.136–137), but if not, just be extra careful next time. If possible, wait overnight before using an eraser on your calligraphy.

Tip

Color consistency

Some inks like iron gall and walnut naturally have a bit of gradation to them. However, if you're sure a color is supposed to be consistent and it's not, give it a vigorous stir to evenly distribute the pigment.

Right: Here, iron gall ink creates both darker and lighter gray areas.

Below left: The upper example was created by applying balanced pressure to both nib tines, while the lower example was created with more pressure on the right tine.

Below right: Thin ink combined with budget inkjet paper results in heavy feathering in this calligraphy.

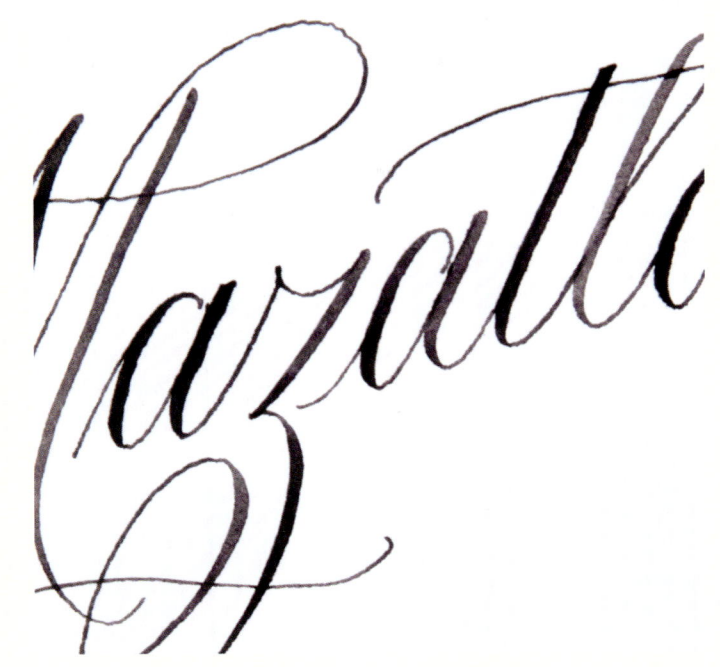

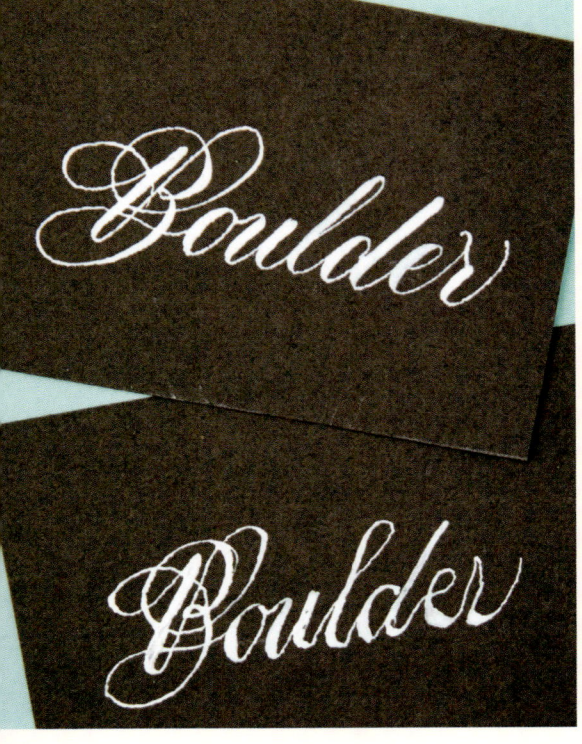

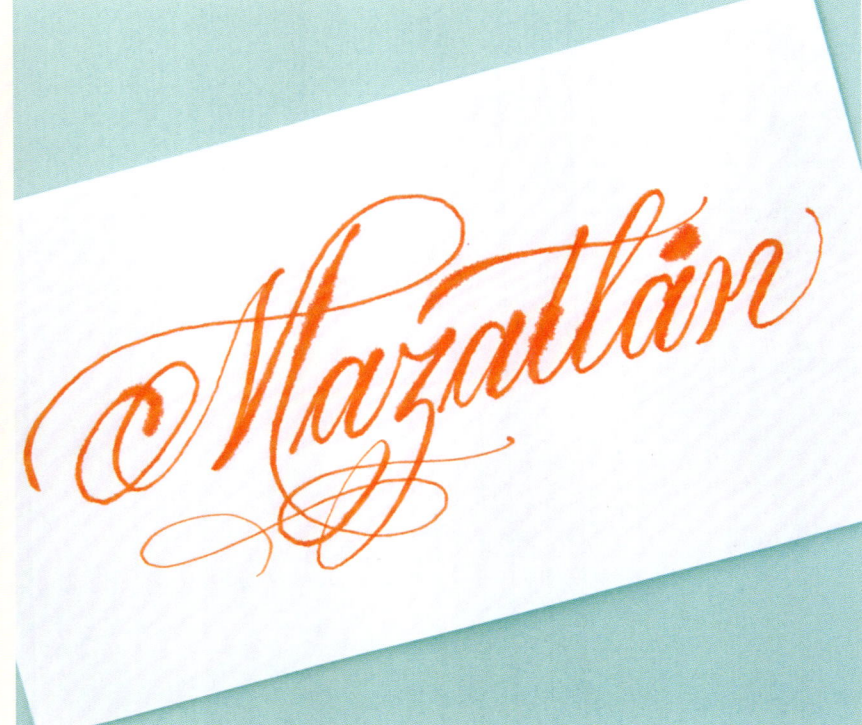

Ink issues

Paper challenges

Certain papers perform better for pointed pen calligraphy projects than others. Choosing the right paper can significantly impact the appearance and quality of your finished work.

These are some of the most common problems that calligraphers have with paper and solutions to help resolve them.

The texture is too rough

As your calligraphy skill level increases, you'll be able to write on toothy (rough) paper surfaces. That said, there are some papers that are too fibrous even for the most skilled of calligraphers. Is it upcycled paper that you made at home or artisan paper that has a lot of visible fibers? In that case, it's probably best to skip using a pointed pen on that paper. If you're sure that it's possible to

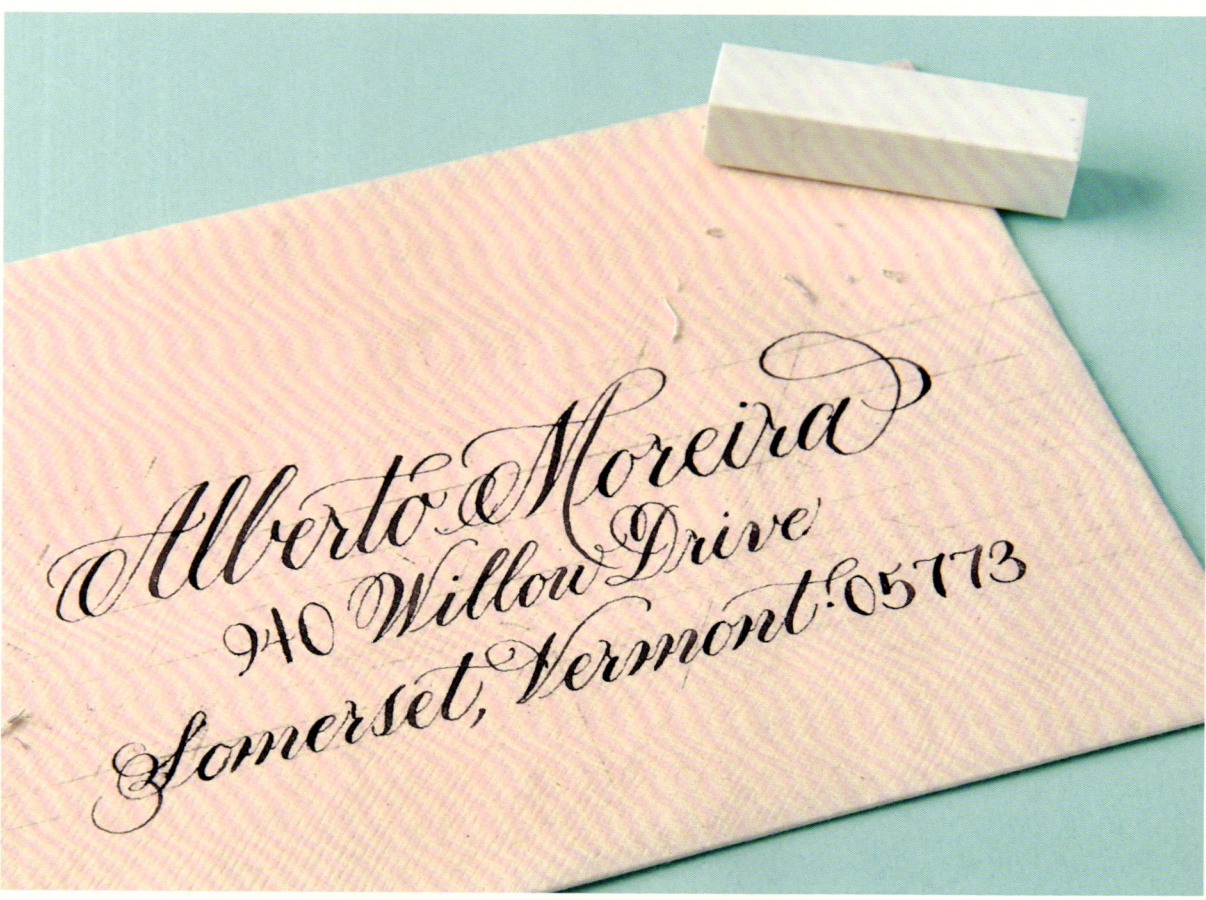

Heavily textured, luxe papers tend to hold on to pencil lines. For that reason, it is important to use a light touch when drawing guidelines.

Tip

Beware of the fibers

In general, any paper that has visible fibers is a no-go. Similarly, papers with unique, highly grooved texture, such as those that are designed to simulate wood, won't work with your pointed pen.

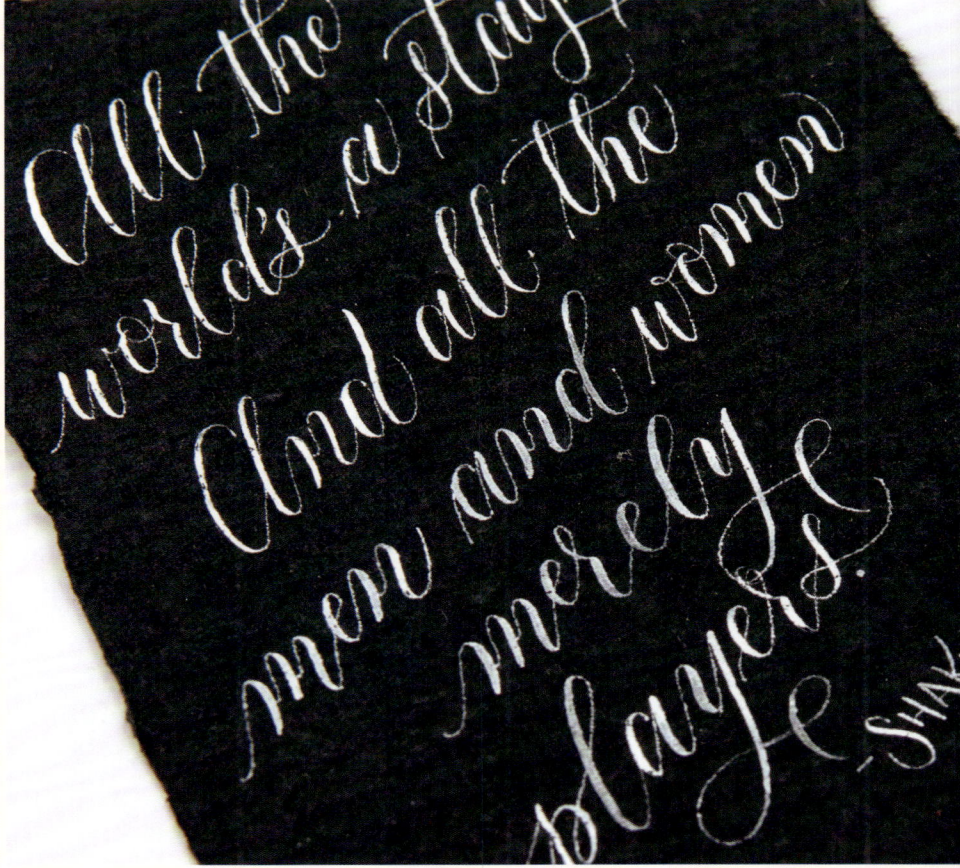

Writing on soft, cottony paper causes inconsistent upstrokes. You'll notice that your nib catches on rogue fibers regularly, resulting in an unpleasant halting motion.

create calligraphy on the paper, try using a fairly blunt, flexible nib such as the Brause Rose. Poky, sharp nibs like the Nikko G will often get stuck on dips and divots in the paper. Try experimenting with different inks too. It could be that a more paintlike ink or a thin, watery ink will work best on papers with a rougher texture.

The texture is too smooth

Counterintuitively, a paper that is too smooth can also cause problems, whether that is less-than-ideal stroke contrast between thin or thick strokes or ink that beads up on the paper's surface. For this reason, it is best to avoid writing on coated papers.

The paper is warping

Warped paper is a problem that will happen sometimes when you paint over your calligraphy with watercolors. You can fix the warping, to an extent, by placing the (dried) piece of paper under a heavy stack of books. If you use paper designed for watercolors, you'll avoid this problem altogether.

Pencil guidelines won't erase

If your paper is fairly soft or dense, you'll sometimes find that the impression from pencil guidelines remains after you've run an eraser over them. To prevent from this happening again, use a soft pencil (such as a 2B) and exert less pressure on your pencil when you're drawing guidelines.

The eraser leaves a residue

This issue doesn't happen often on white paper, but it is a concern for colored papers, especially if the paper is a dark color. Try using a black eraser instead of a white eraser. Black erasers are formulated differently than white erasers and may be gentler on the paper surface and less likely to alter its sheen or texture.

Paper challenges

Pushing the boundaries

The ideas shown on these pages are designed to inspire your calligraphic journey and push the boundaries of what you can achieve as a modern calligrapher. These are just a few suggestions that may lead to further experimentation and your own unique designs and projects.

You don't have to limit your calligraphy creation to straightforward, highly legible lines. Instead, consider the art that you can make using calligraphy. The exciting thing about calligraphy is that you can make a statement with both your written message and the way that you write it. Calligraphy also has a knack for drawing the viewer in. They want to get closer to see all of those tiny details that aren't visible from afar.

Remember to keep an open mind when it comes to calligraphy, and never hesitate to experiment. Your offbeat idea might just turn into the best thing you've ever created.

Unusual surfaces

As long as a surface is smooth with just a bit of tooth or texture, you can write on it. Surfaces like agate, marble, and ceramic tiles make for surprisingly effective canvases. I've

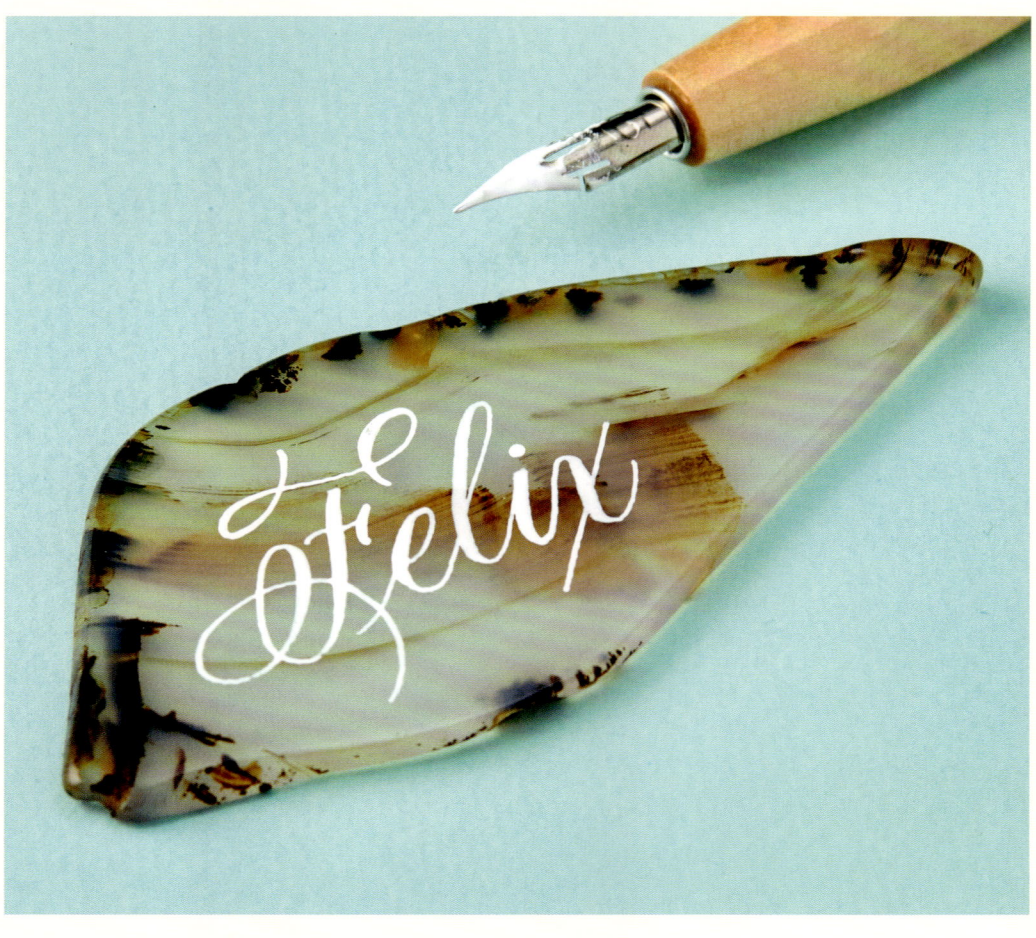

Experiment with writing on different surfaces like agate.

also successfully written on avocados, mangoes, waxy leaves, and smooth leather. When in doubt, try it out.

Breaking free

You've learned about how to make guidelines and slant lines (pp.58–61) and what a difference that can make in helping your calligraphy to look neat and consistent. Sometimes, though, ignoring the need to make guidelines can feel freeing and lead to spontaneous and breathtaking projects. Experiment with stream of consciousness calligraphy and see where it takes you. Try writing words with some letters that balloon out, while others remain small. Ignore convention and write vertical calligraphy or calligraphy that intertwines with block lettering. You could also think about embellishing your calligraphy with colors, ink spatters, or little doodles. Remember, the most important thing is to have fun and embrace calligraphy as a mood-boosting creative activity.

Calligraphy as art

You can arrange your calligraphy to be an important stand-alone artistic element, or intentionally use your strokes to make projects like calligraphy medallions or calligraphic drawings. Consider how you might use your art to enhance your surroundings or an experience. Can you write out an embellished quote to enhance

your workspace, or perhaps draw a calligraphy silhouette to display in your home? What sorts of projects can you make for your loved ones? Remember that opportunities to create are everywhere.

Try unconventional layouts

Try writing within the confines of a shape to convey a message in a visually compelling way. Draw the outline of your shape in pencil. This could be as straightforward as a heart or a star, or it could be as abstract as the outline of a bird (see pp.128–129). Just make sure the shape is immediately recognizable from a distance. Then fill it with calligraphy shapes and letters.

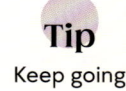

Tip

Keep going

Don't become discouraged if a project idea turns out to be a dud. Sometimes, the coolest project concepts are born out of techniques that didn't quite work or mistakes that require a creative fix.

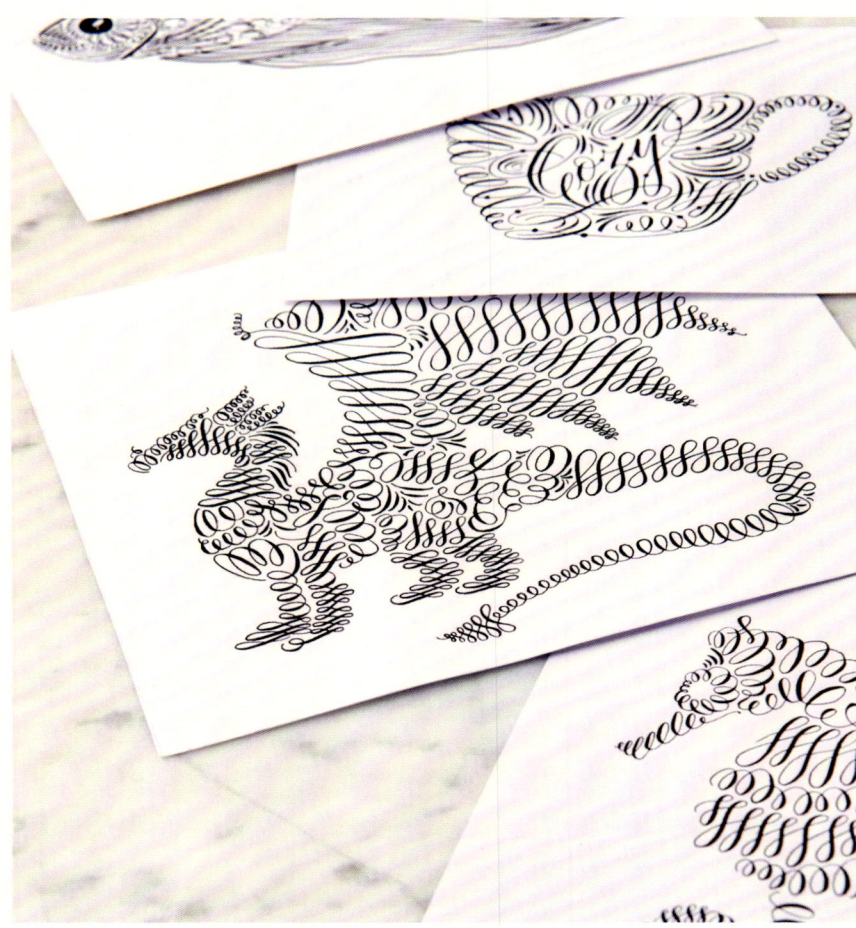

You can use a silhouette of any shape as the starting point for flourished art.

Pushing the boundaries

Flourished pictures

You can use a series of flourished strokes and dots to create a variety of flourished subjects, like the owl on the right. Start with a pencil outline of your chosen subject. Make sure that it is recognizable as a silhouette, then make a pencil draft of various flourishes and strokes that complement the different components of a piece. Be sure to include any features that are visually important and will help the observer to recognize what they're looking at. In the case of an owl, a solid diamond-shaped beak, stylized eyes, and the dramatic ruffs (the eyebrowlike feathers) are all important, as are the feet and the division between the owl's wings and the rest of its body. Once you've drawn the pencil guideline, fill it in with various strokes until the intended subject is obvious and the artwork looks intricate and abundant. You can change the stroke types to signify various body parts or to show the difference between a bird's wing and breast, for example. Warm up with a drill (see pp.62–63) before going to work on your main image to ensure your flourishes flow smoothly.

KEY
- stroke 1
- stroke 2
- stroke 3
- stroke 4
- stroke 5

The process

These three steps will walk you through the techniques needed to create a flourished image like this owl. You can apply them to any picture you like.

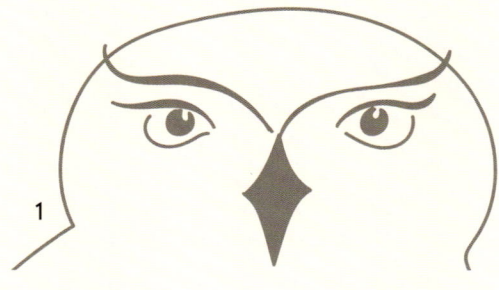

1 Draw the outline and add specific features.

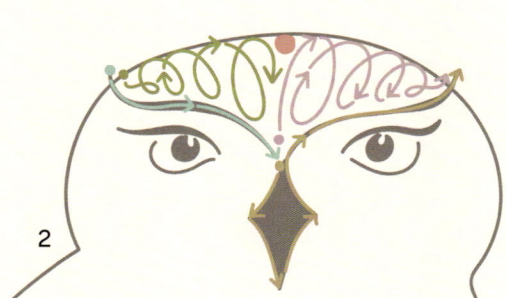

2 Identify an area within the design where you want to begin. A self-contained section is a good starting point. Begin adding swirls or flourishes. If you are creating a symmetrical shape, you may want to lift the pen midway through the shape and begin a new line.

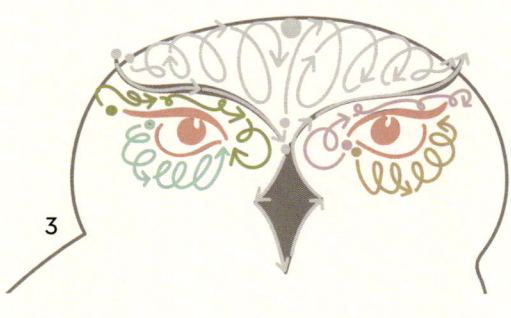

3 Larger open spaces can be broken down into smaller flourished areas to give definition and add focus, such as around the eyes here.

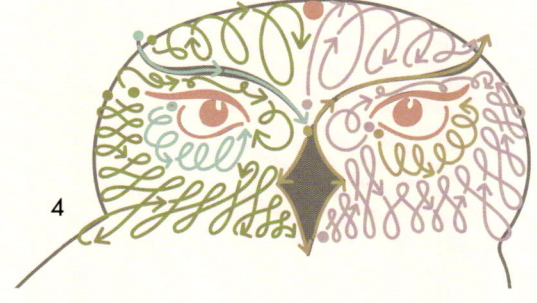

4 Alternate between flourishes and swirls as you continue to fill in the design, varying the size of each depending on the available space. If you have time, create a pencil draft first to experiment with different strokes and densities in order to achieve a balance that works.

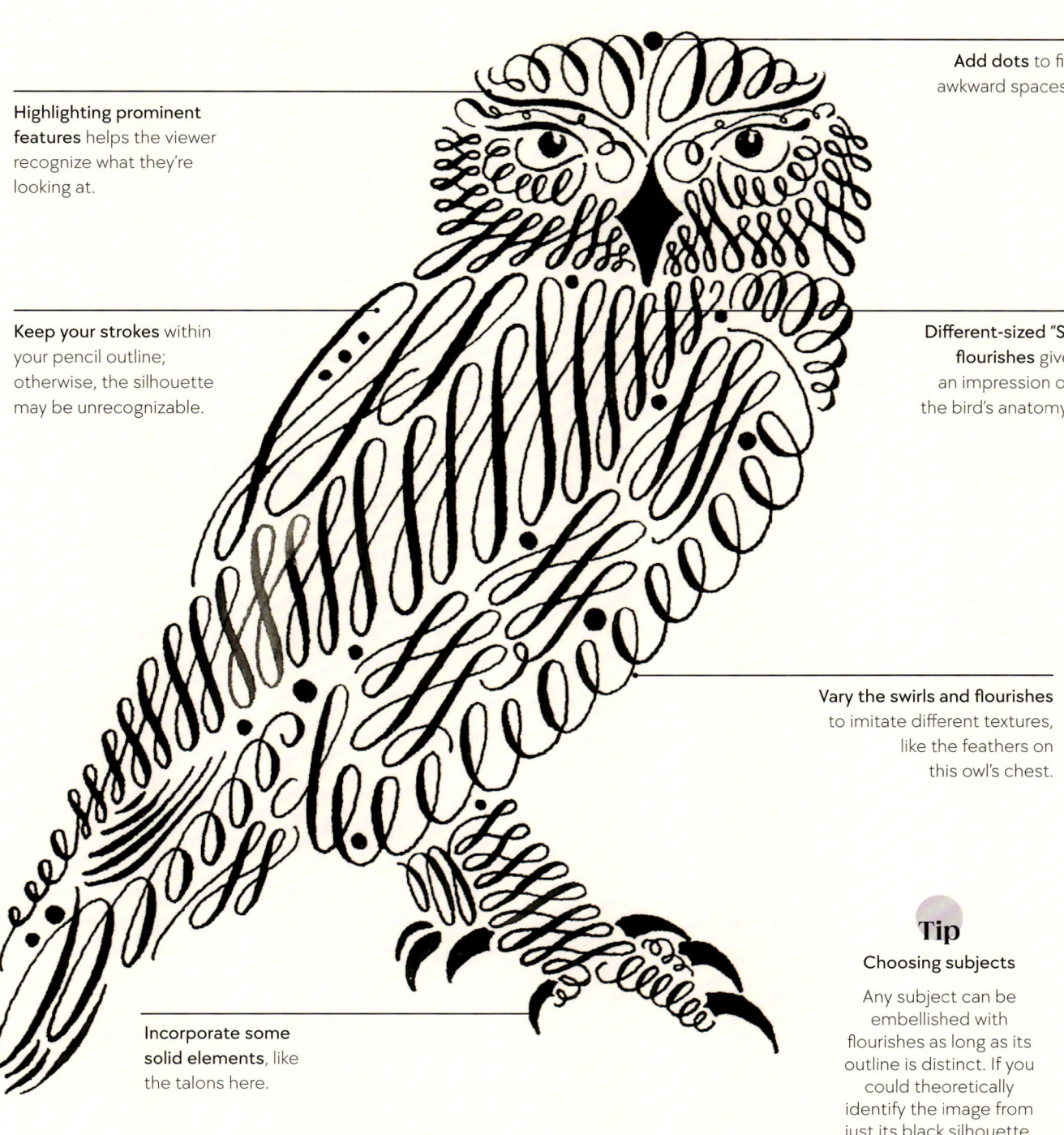

Highlighting prominent features helps the viewer recognize what they're looking at.

Keep your strokes within your pencil outline; otherwise, the silhouette may be unrecognizable.

Incorporate some **solid elements,** like the talons here.

Add dots to fill awkward spaces.

Different-sized "S" flourishes give an impression of the bird's anatomy.

Vary the swirls and flourishes to imitate different textures, like the feathers on this owl's chest.

Tip

Choosing subjects

Any subject can be embellished with flourishes as long as its outline is distinct. If you could theoretically identify the image from just its black silhouette, it's suitable for this method.

Pushing the boundaries

Alternative inks

Once you've tried standard inks such as sumi and India ink, you may want to try some alternatives. There are many different options that you can use for calligraphy, and you'll find your favorites as you experiment and work on new projects. You can find specific recommendations on page 197.

Watercolor paint

A watercolor palette can be used as an instant, portable, and varied ink collection. It is easier to transport than ink so can be taken on your travels. To use it as an ink, moisten the paint with a small amount of water (around half a teaspoon). Then, wait a minute or two for the water to soak in. Moisten a small paintbrush with water, and mix it with the paint until it resembles the viscosity of cream. Use your paintbrush to brush the watercolor on the underside of your calligraphy nib and give the nib a firm shake over your cleaning water to remove excess watercolor. Then, put your nib to paper and write. An ombré effect can be achieved by adding different colors and shades of watercolor to your nib.

Metallic paint and ink

If you are looking for a metallic finish (for example, gold or silver), metallic inks and watercolors are available. For smaller amounts, metallic watercolors may be preferable as the pigments of metallic inks tend to coagulate at the bottom of the bottle.

White ink

White calligraphy ink is opaque and highly pigmented, allowing calligraphy to stand out against a dark background. It is essential to use a high-quality white ink that flows smoothly to achieve crisp lines. The consistency of the ink is also important.

Some white "ink" products, such as Dr. Ph. Martin's Bleedproof White, are watercolor-based products, not traditional inks. These products are often referred to as "ink" because they are commonly used for calligraphy and lettering purposes. While they behave like ink, they require a little more attention. You will need to dilute your white ink with water before every writing session, and stir it to a creamy consistency.

Gouache

Gouache is an opaque paint that contains pigment, a binding agent, and water. To use gouache, squeeze some onto a plate or palette. Then add a little water and mix to a creamy ink consistency. Brush the gouache onto the back of your nib and use it to write. You can adjust the "ink" with more water (if too thick) or add more gouache (if too thin). If you need to use a lot of gouache, you can transform it into a dippable ink by mixing gouache and water in an airtight jar.

Not all gouache is suitable for calligraphy use. Look for options with very finely ground pigment particles that flow off your pen.

Waterproof ink

It is useful to have a waterproof ink on hand, especially if you plan to combine your pointed pen work with watercolor. Look for an ink that is totally smudge-proof, waterproof, and can be diluted with water when needed to improve ink flow.

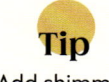

Tip

Add shimmer

To create ink that sparkles, stir in a small amount of mica powder (such as PearlEx powdered pigment). This will create an ink that has just a bit of shimmer to it.

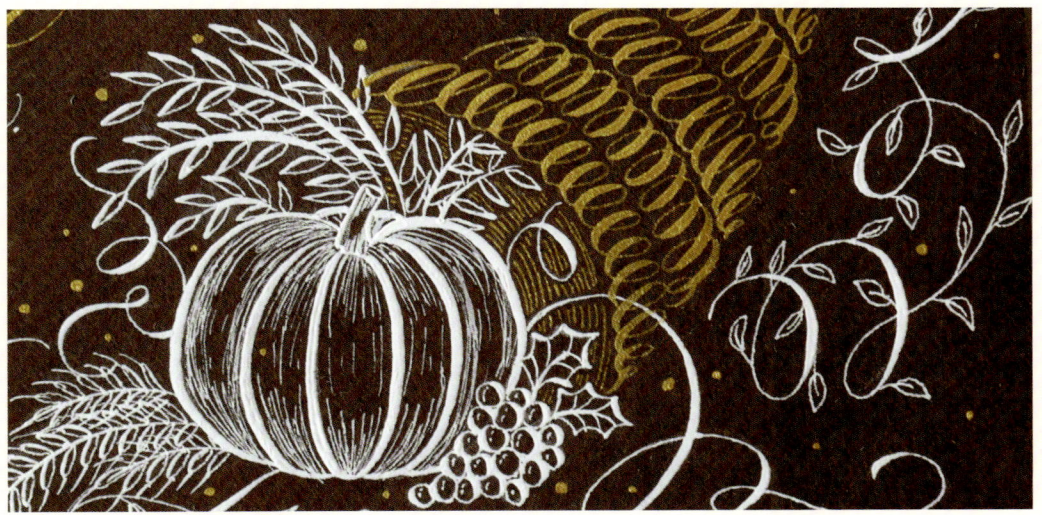

Left: **Gold watercolor paint used as ink** shimmers and catches the light, in contrast with the white flourishes and artwork.

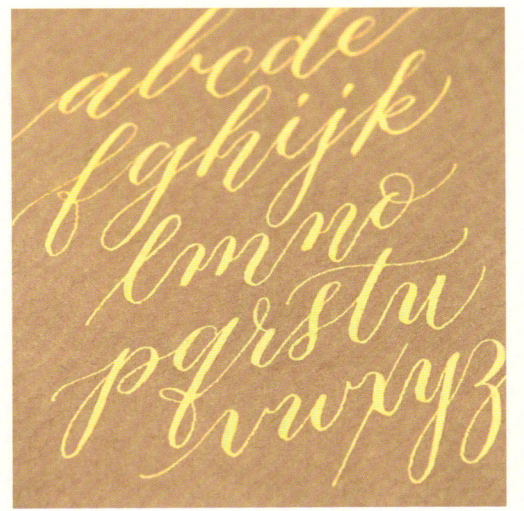

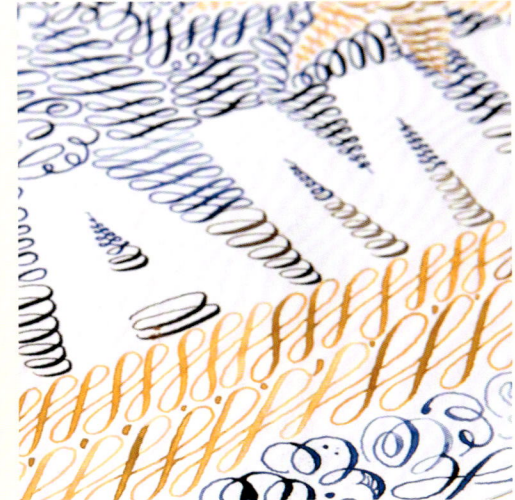

Far left: **Gouache** gives you the ability to write opaque, slightly chalky calligraphy.

Left: **Writing and adding flourishes with watercolors** often results in a gradated, ombré effect.

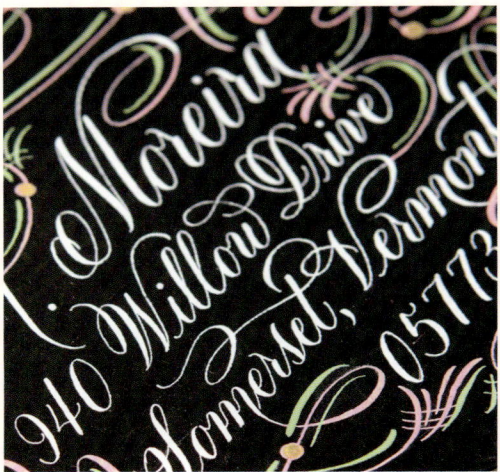

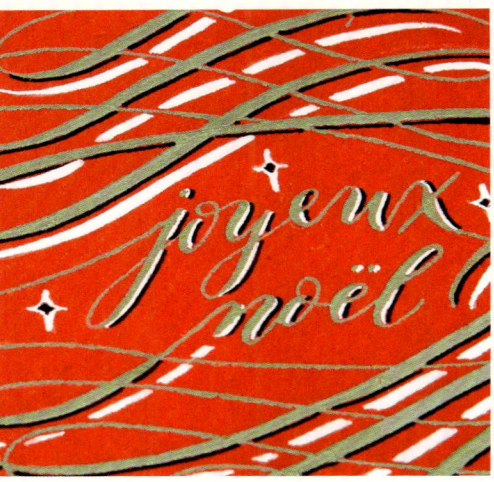

Far left: **White ink** may be a little fussy to write with, but the stunning opaque results are worth it.

Left: **Metallic watercolors** come in many shades including gold.

Alternative inks

This calligraphy was created with masking fluid. Notice that the negative spaces are well preserved, giving a striking contrast.

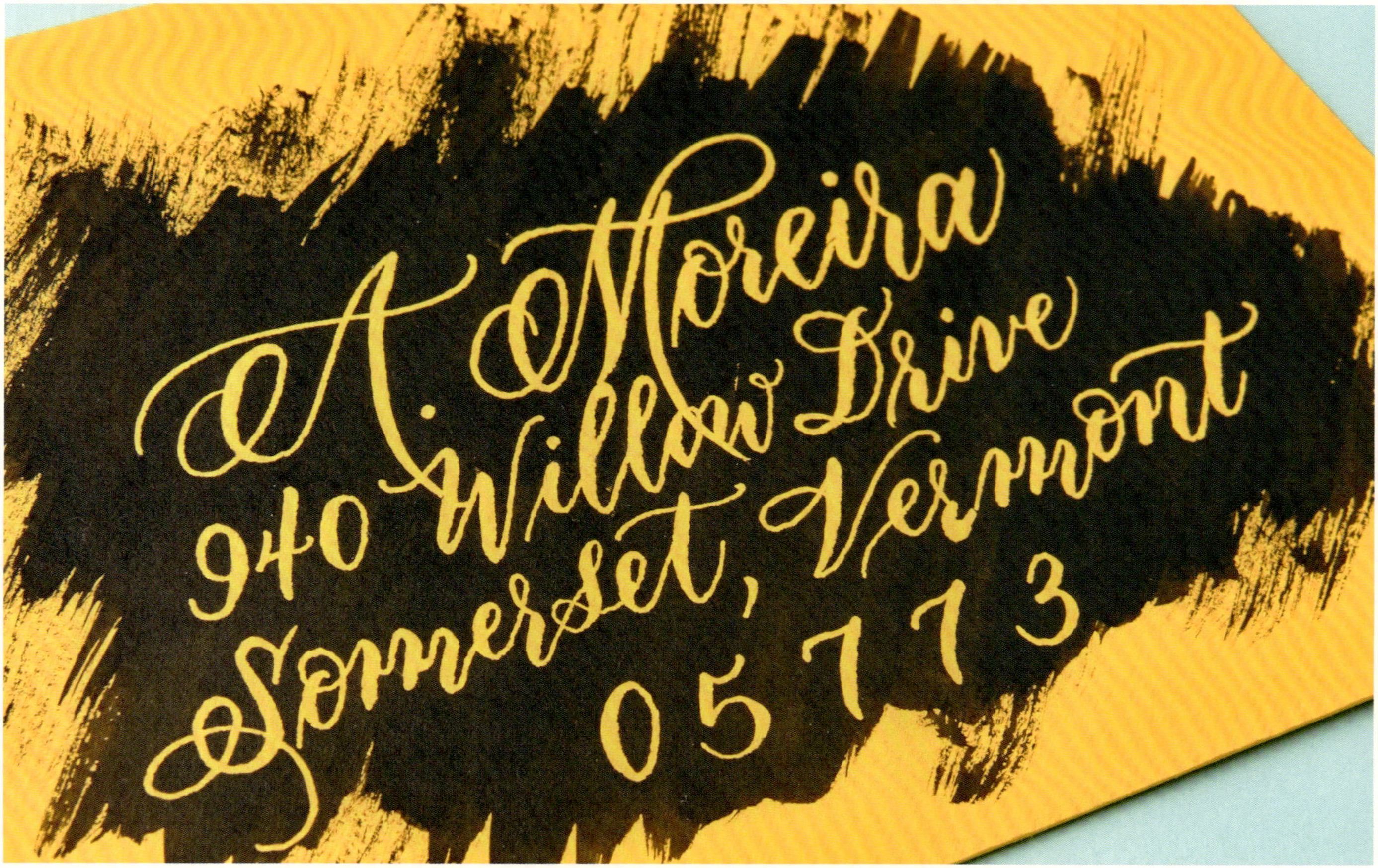

Using masking fluid as ink

Make a pencil draft of your calligraphy first (optional), then dip your pointed pen into the masking fluid and write. Once the fluid has dried, use a wide paintbrush to slather a contrasting color of watercolor paint or ink over your calligraphy. Wait for all the moisture to evaporate out of the paint, then peel off the masking fluid, leaving only your calligraphy visible on the page.

Naturally derived inks

You can use any natural material that stains to make a unique calligraphy ink. In addition to the options given below, you can try: red wine, soy sauce, turmeric powder (mixed with water), or blueberry or pomegranate juice.

- **Tea:** Boil some water, pour it onto plenty of tea bags or tea leaves and brew for about 15 minutes. If using loose tea, strain the liquid into a bowl using some coffee filters or a mesh strainer. Once the brew is dark and strong, try writing with it.
- **Coffee:** Make strong coffee using a 1:1 ratio of instant coffee and water to prepare your "ink." Coffee is not as lightfast or hardy as traditional inks, so it's best suited for practice pieces or projects that you won't keep long-term.
- **Beet juice:** Take a beet and cut it into thin (about ¼in [5mm]) slices. Simmer it in 8oz (250ml) of water until the slices are tender. Allow everything to cool, then strain the liquid and discard the solids. Add a tablespoon of vinegar to improve the longevity and vibrancy of your new ink.

Note that natural inks are not suitable for long-term storage. For best results, make your ink, pour it into a jar, then use it within a couple of weeks. You'll know the ink is no longer good because it will smell rancid or start to develop mold.

Making it resilient

Remember that natural inks are far from waterproof. If you're using them to write something that could potentially be exposed to moisture, like an envelope, be sure to apply a fixative. Otherwise, one raindrop can render your words illegible.

Coffee used as ink gives a sepia-toned effect, creating a vintage and warm aesthetic.

"You can use any natural material that stains to make your own ink."

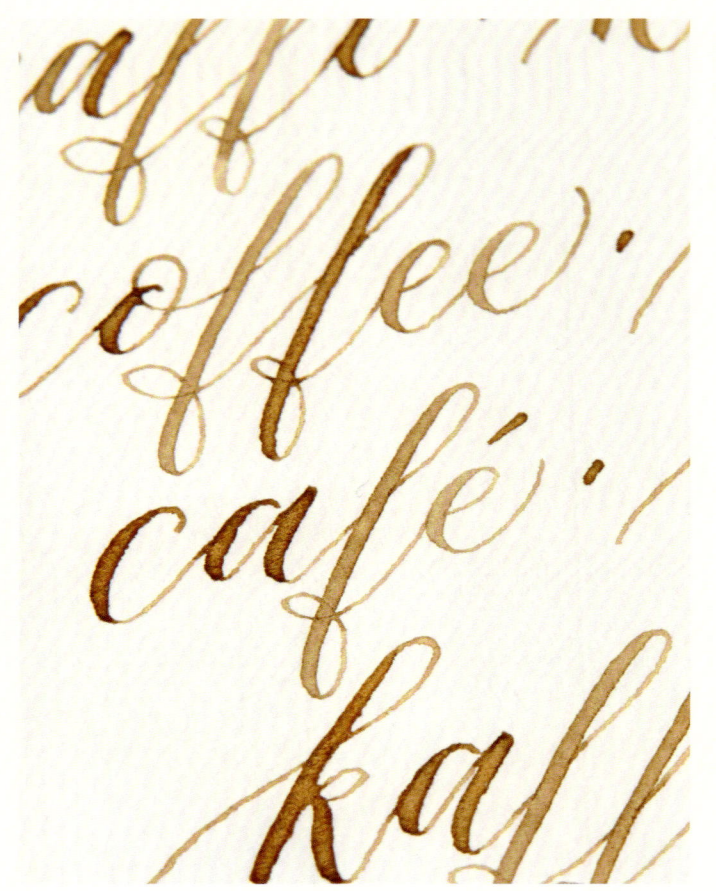

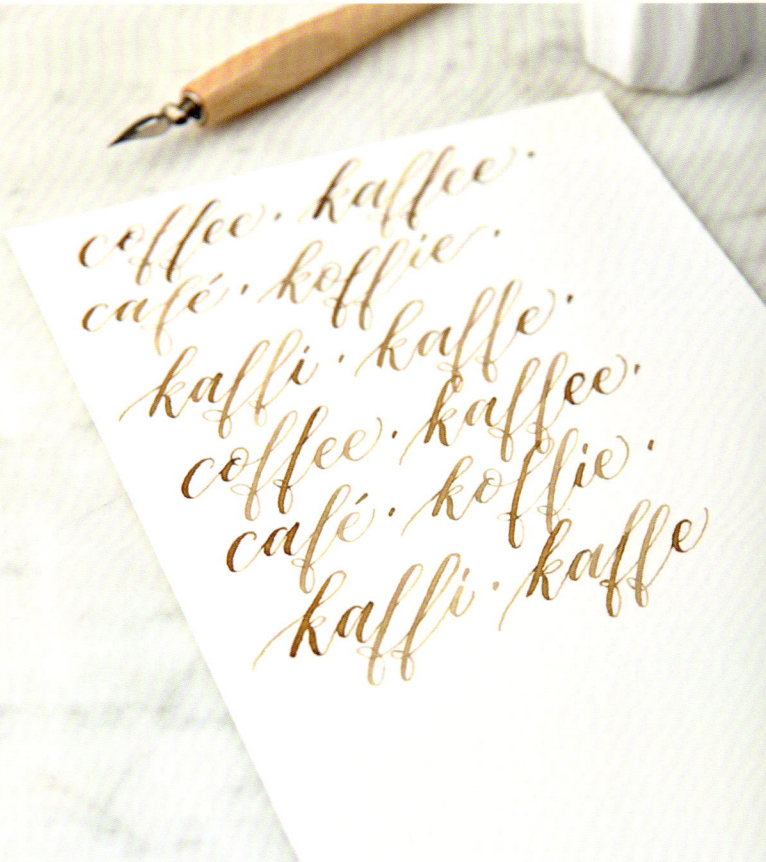

Alternative inks

Ink spatters

Ink spatters can be used to emphasize that your calligraphy was created by hand and is a one-of-a-kind piece. They're best suited to casual projects with a slightly bohemian feel because they offer a quick, easy, and artistic way to fill up negative space.

It is vital to test out your ink spatters on a scrap piece of paper before you add them to your project to make sure that you've got the consistency of the ink or paint right. If it's too watery, your paint or ink will run down the page, ruining your calligraphy. Conversely, if it's too thick, you won't be able to produce fluid, casual-looking spatters. Once you've got the consistency of the ink and your method right you can get started. Try to embrace the randomness of this method; the point is that you can't quite predict how

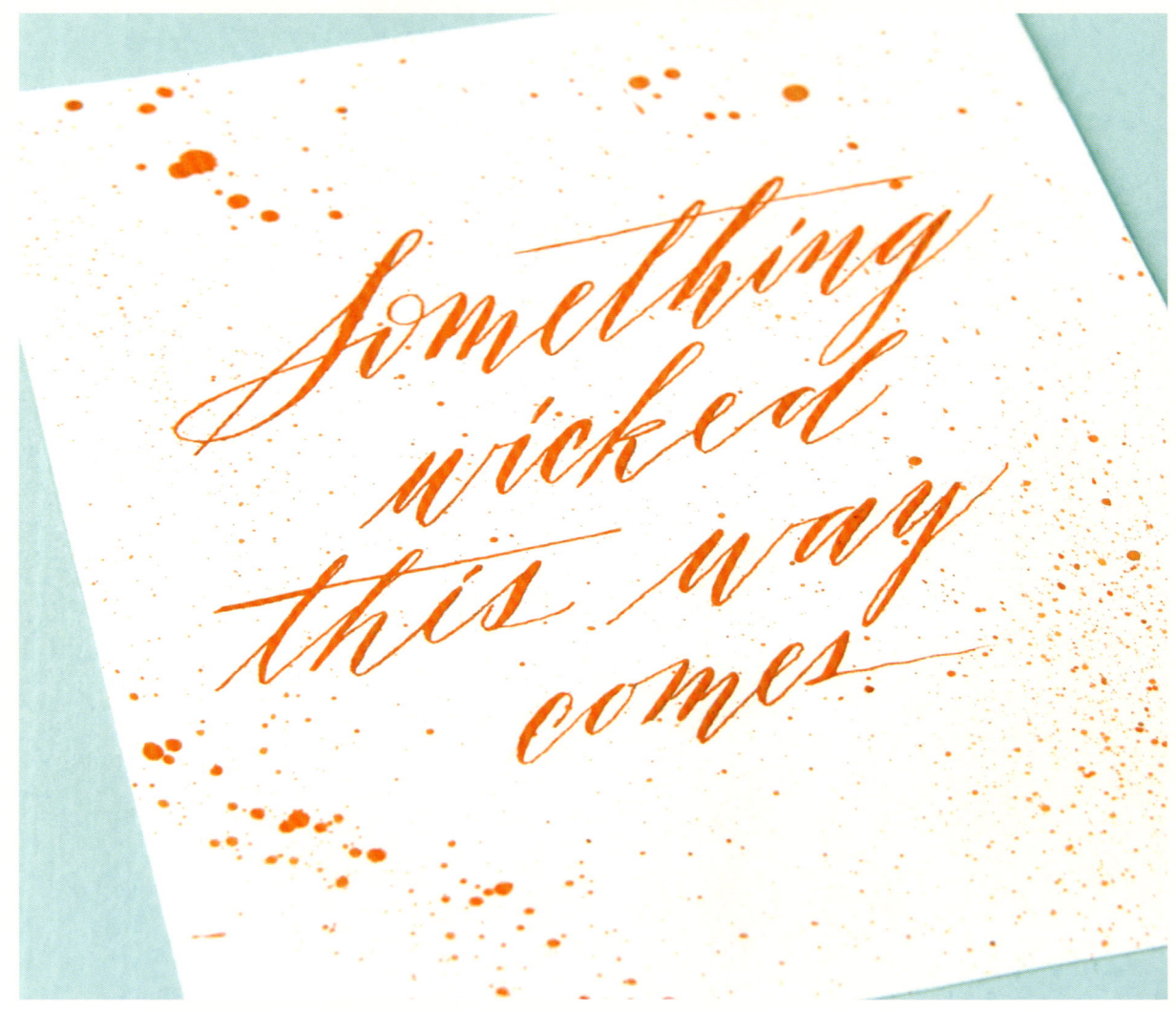

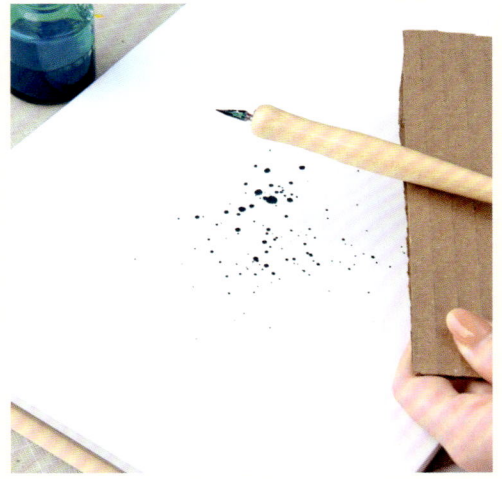
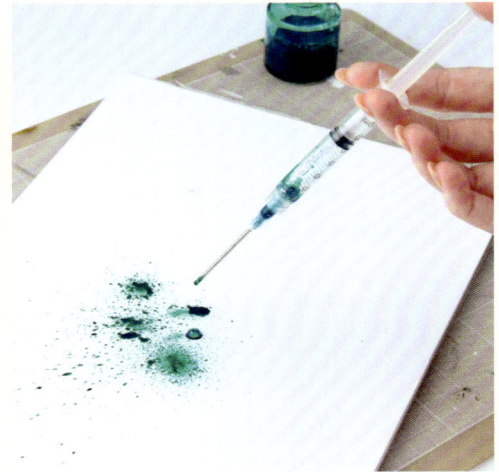

the ink is going to fall on the page. You can either make spatters with the same ink that you used to write your calligraphy, or you can use a different ink for contrast and visual interest. There are three main methods for creating ink spatters:

Nib flicking

To make ink spatters using this method, fit a straight pen with an old, damaged nib. Load the nib with ink, then flick it against the edge of thick cardstock or an old credit card. The result will be a delicate, targeted spray of ink.

Syringe droplets

If you want larger, dramatic splotches of ink, a blunt syringe is the most effective method. Begin by sucking up a bit of ink into the syringe, then empty the syringe back into the ink. Then, position the syringe over your

paper and forcefully push the plunger down to spray out the remainder of the ink.

Toothbrush flicking

Using a toothbrush results in a bit more spray than nib flicking because a toothbrush can hold more ink. Begin by dipping the tips of your bristles into ink, then use a quick, sharp movement of your thumb against the bristles. This action will force the ink out of the toothbrush in small, fairly controlled droplets.

Above left: Use an old nib and some cardstock to create a spatter effect.

Above middle: A blunt syringe filled with ink can give some interesting results on the page.

Above right: Spattering ink with a toothbrush may give you a controlled result.

Ink spatters are especially effective on spooky or Halloween-themed pieces, evoking a sense of messiness and chaos that is perfect for the occasion.

Ink spatters

Fixing mistakes

All calligraphers know the sinking feeling that occurs when you realize you've made a mistake in a project. Maybe a small paint speck has gone in the wrong place, or perhaps you've made a typo in your calligraphy. Don't despair!

Before you discard your work and start again, here are some tried-and-true methods that you can try to get your project back on track. If these don't work, keep your mistake pieces; you might be able to reuse them.

Scrape off unwanted marks

Craft knives are good for correcting small mistakes. The goal is to remove the top layer of paper, which is the layer that contains the mistake. Before you do anything, wait for the ink to dry. Then, use the tip of your craft knife to carefully scrape back and forth over the unwanted stroke or splatter. Unfortunately, the paper texture will be a bit "off" from all the scraping, so the fix might be noticeable. You can minimize that by rubbing a smooth stone over the scrape.

Rub off mistakes with an eraser

Some manufacturers make erasers out of a mixture of rubber and a fine sandlike material. The eraser is abrasive and intended to gently scrape off the top layer of paper. Wait until your ink is totally dry before using the eraser; otherwise, you'll just spread the wet ink around more. Sand erasers are best for mistakes that have a larger surface area, like unintentional ink spatters or fingerprints.

Paint over the mistake

If these methods don't work, consider covering the mistake with an ink or paint that matches the color of your paper. Note, however, that this technique will lead to a noticeable difference in texture and sheen. Use this method on especially "busy" pieces, where it's hard to see discrepancies.

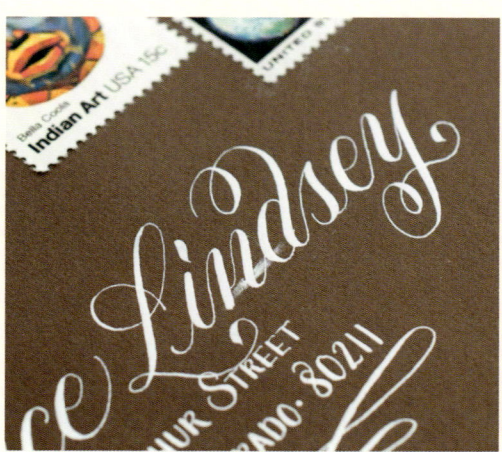

Some of the white ink has smudged here.

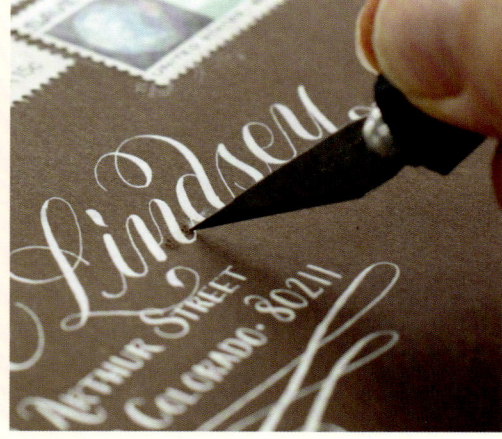

Use a craft knife to try to carefully scrape away a mistaken ink mark or smudge.

Just go with it

In certain cases, embracing your mistake might not be an option. However, some projects have room for experimentation. If you accidentally make a spatter, consider adding several intentional spatters to make a piece look artistic and deliberate.

If saving your piece is futile, consider ways that you can remake the piece relatively quickly. For example, if the original piece was created on light-colored paper, you can use a light box to trace over the original. For some projects, a complete redo is necessary. Take comfort in the fact that you learn something from every mistake.

Avoiding mistakes

There are some things that you can do to avoid making a mistake in the first place. Some of them may mean that your project takes a little more time, but there's a better chance of desirable results.

- **Set up your workspace** in a way that minimizes the potential for spills and mishaps. Make sure your cleaning water and inks are positioned so you won't accidentally bump into them, and find a good spot to place your brushes and pens when you're not using them so they won't roll off the table or onto what you're working on. If you're snacking while creating, make sure your fingers remain clean and won't stain the page.
- **Warm up with a drill** before you start. If you go into a project "cold," you're much more likely to create shaky, awkward strokes. It's important to start any creation session by writing several strokes and loops on a scrap piece of paper to warm up your hand and get into the writing groove.
- **Start with a pencil draft.** Pencil drafts require extra time, but they will help you avoid spelling and spacing mistakes.
- **Be extra vigilant with words or names** that can be spelled in multiple ways (like Catherine, Katherine, Cathryn). It's easy to default to the spelling you're most familiar with, so double-check to avoid mistakes.

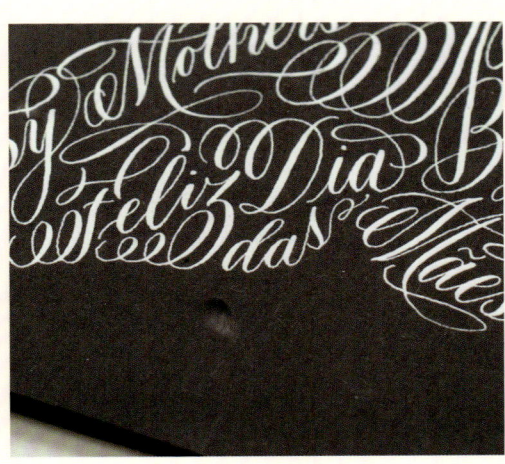

The paper has become damaged after the calligraphy is complete.

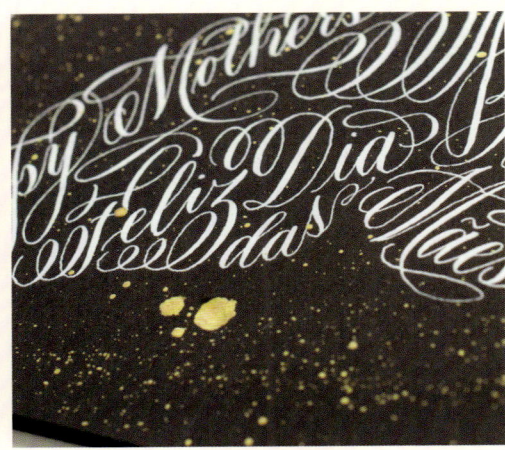

Work with your mistake by adding more splatters or marks and incorporating them into your work.

Fixing mistakes

The projects

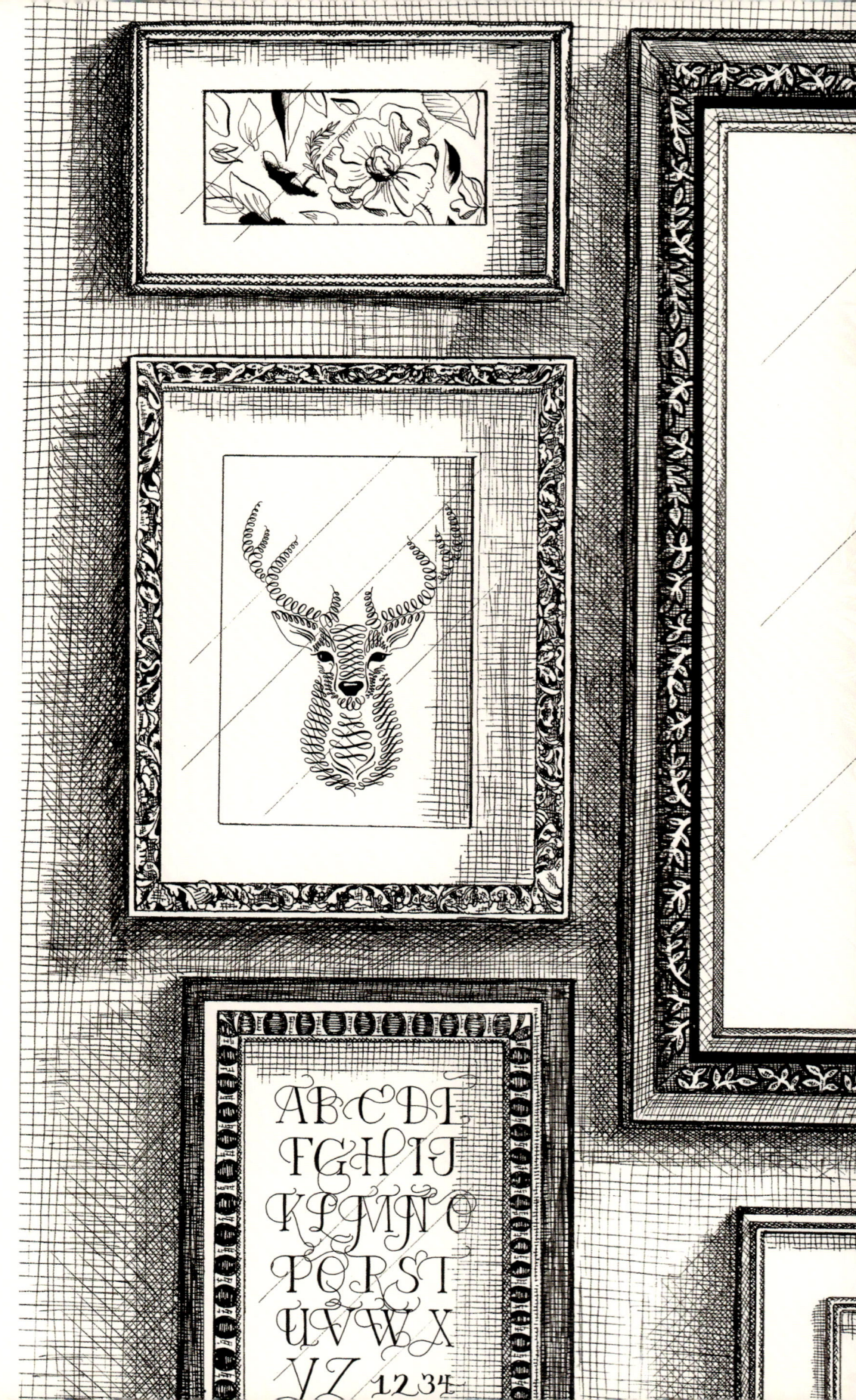

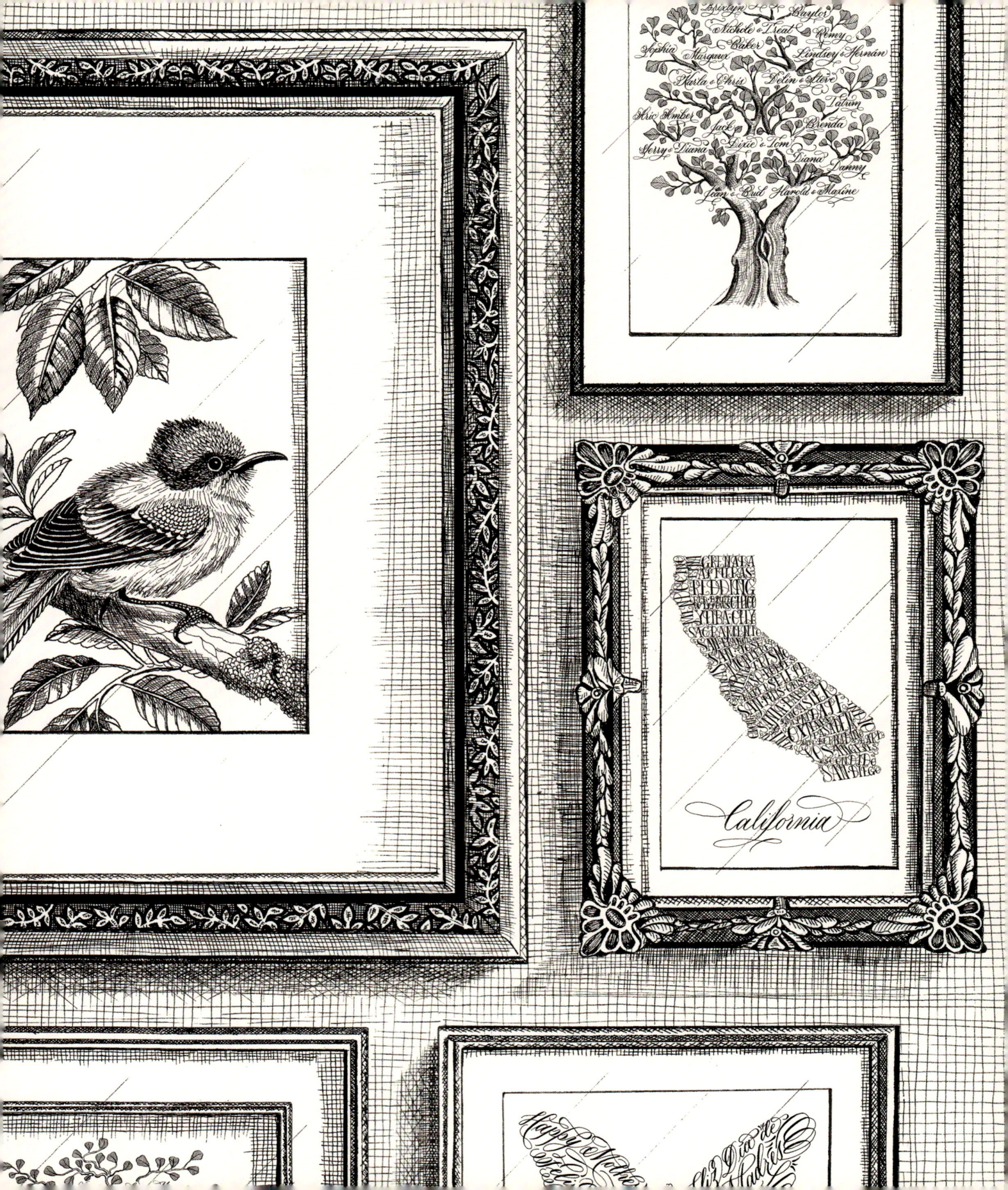

Elaborate mail art

Envelope art is a great starting place for those who are new to calligraphy. In a world that's dominated by electronic communication, many of us still enjoy the tactile experience of receiving and opening an envelope.

● **DIFFICULTY**
beginner to advanced

Who wouldn't be intrigued and delighted by seeing their name and address written with care and artistry? The envelope art itself is only one part of the experience. It piques the recipient's interest, making them eager to open the envelope and see what's inside. Every blank envelope in your collection is an opportunity to unleash creativity through embellished lettering, original illustrations, and carefully selected and positioned postage stamps.

One way to approach envelope art is to start with a theme. If you know the recipient well enough, you can often tailor the theme to something that reminds you of them. For example, you could draw an intricate teacup on an envelope for someone who loves their tea. Or you might be interested in a specific topic, like the natural world, and this may become the theme of your project.

This mail art concept is perfect to send to anyone who lives in the mountains (or who wishes they did). It uses playful hand lettering, flourishes, and a vibrant mountain motif to make an eye-catching treat. When it comes to adding a postage stamp, see if you can find one that complements the colors in the mountains mail art.

SUPPLIES

Kraft A7 envelope

Graphite pencil

Ruler

Compass (optional)

Eraser

Iron gall ink

Watercolor paints

Tiny paintbrush

A flexible nib (such as the Brause EF66) in the holder of your choice

STYLE

The lettering style used here is a thick serif that connects to loops and twirls. The calligraphy is Janet style with a little more flourish than usual.

You can illustrate envelopes with any theme you like, leaving space for the address to be seen clearly.

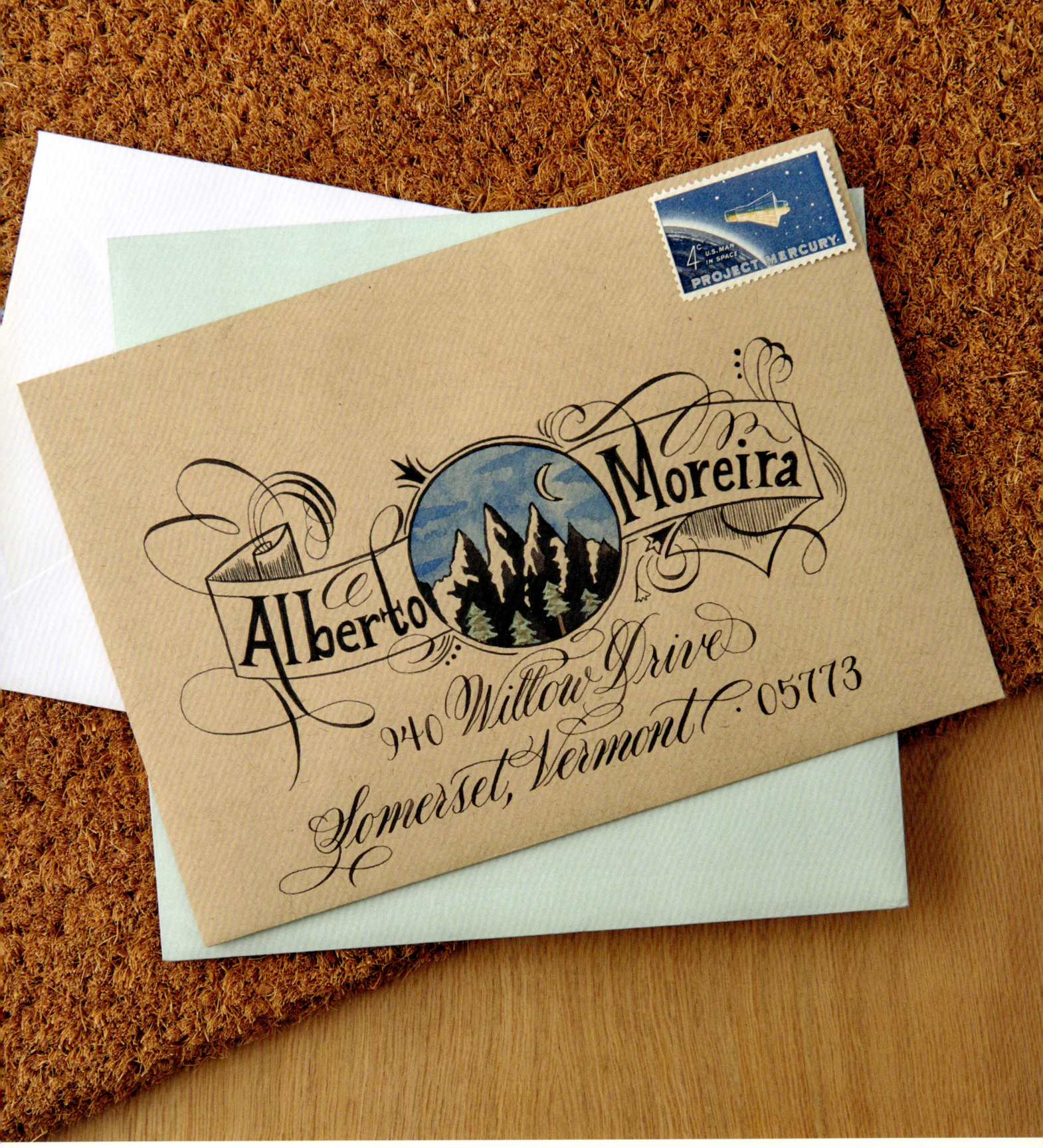

Alberto Moreira

940 Willow Drive

Somerset, Vermont 05773

Elaborate mail art

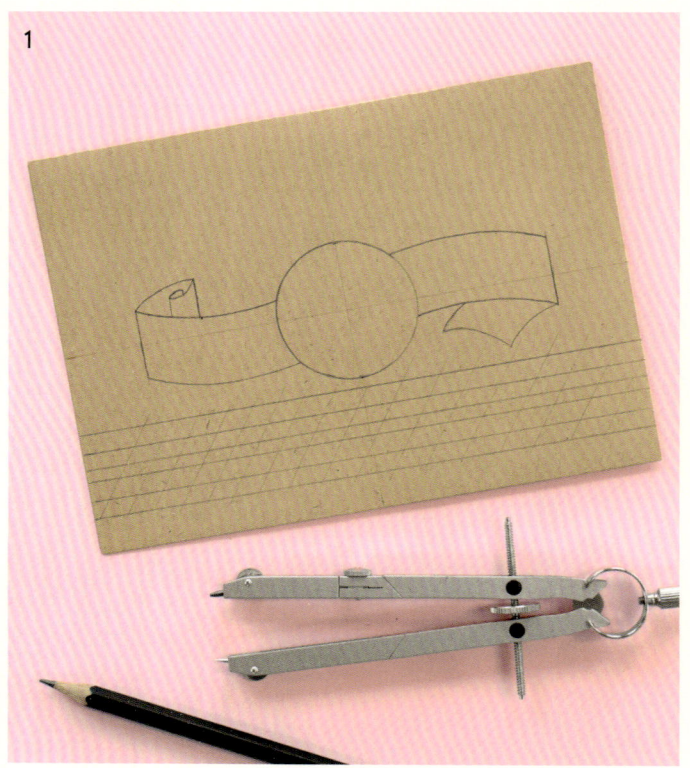

1

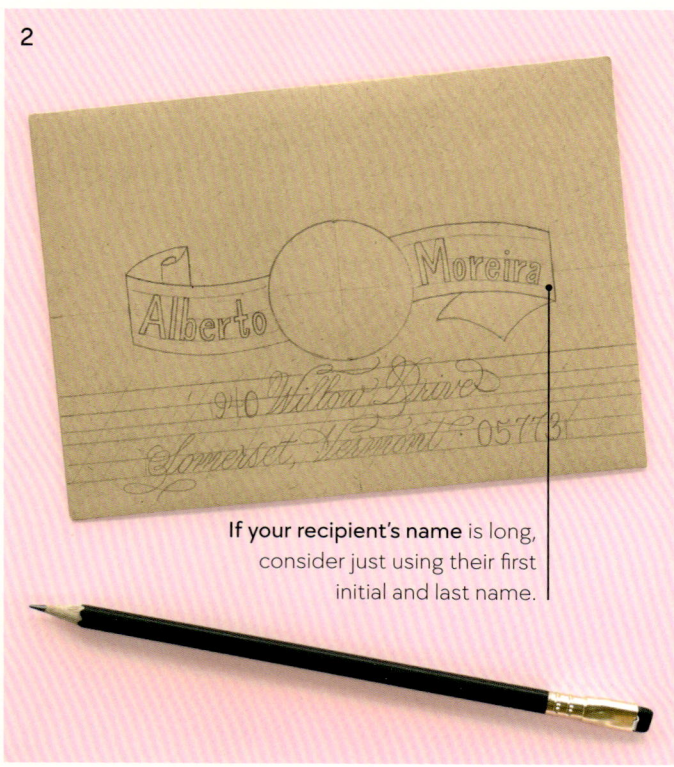

2

If your recipient's name is long, consider just using their first initial and last name.

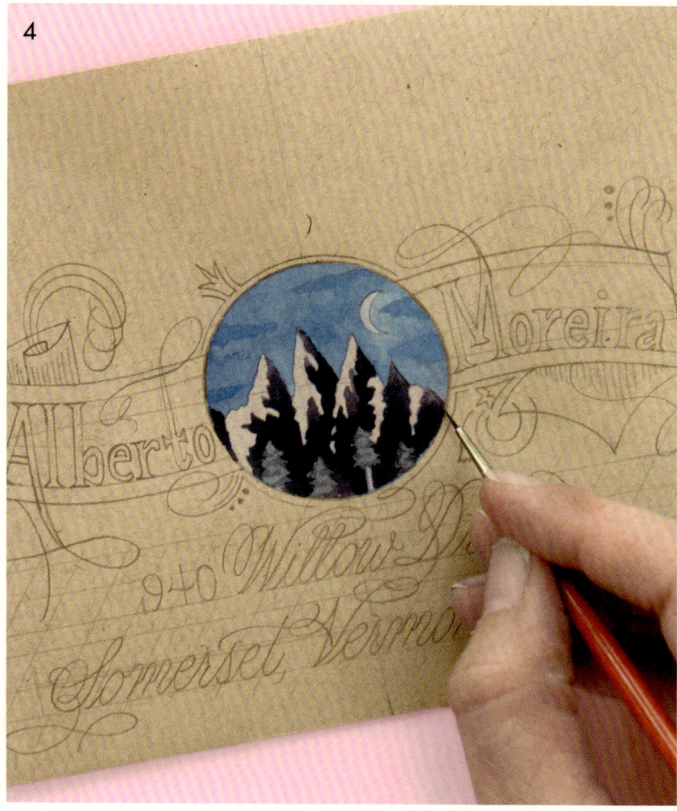

4

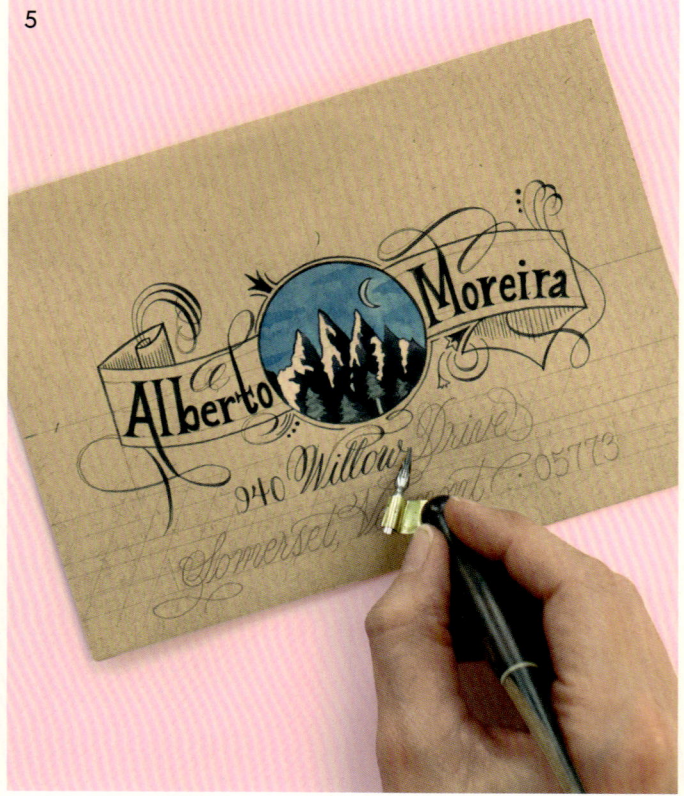

5

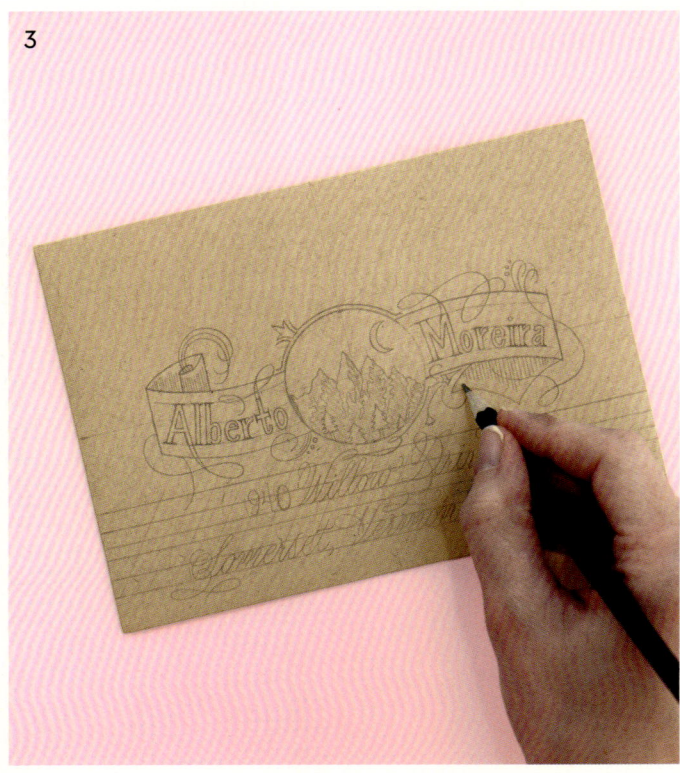

3

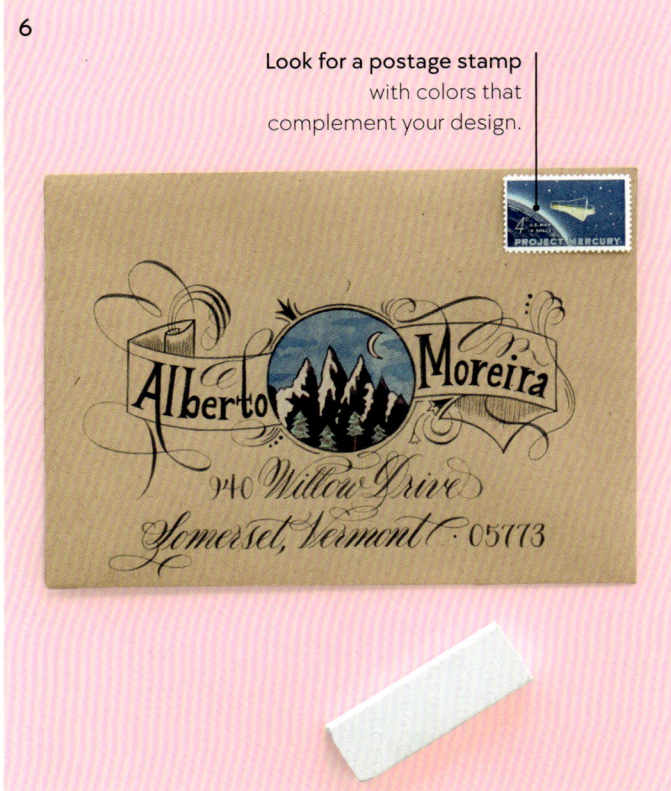

6

Look for a postage stamp with colors that complement your design.

1 Use a pencil and ruler to divide the envelope into four quarters. Then, either use a compass or draw around a circular object to draw a circle measuring about 1¾in (4.5cm) in the center of your envelope. Next, draw a banner extending from either side of the circle. Finish by drawing two sets of guidelines below the banner measuring about ½in (1.5cm) from the baseline to the top line, with a ⅜in (1cm) x-height and ⅛in (5mm) between the address lines.

2 Use a pencil to draft playful block lettering in the banner on either side of the circle. Your recipient's first name will go on the left side of the banner, and their last name on the right. Then, sketch out the calligraphy for the address below. It works well to pair an elegant script style with the casual block lettering.

3 Use your pencil to draft the mountains, flourishes, and embellishments. This will fill in the space and add interest to the banner, the lettering, and the calligraphy.

4 Use a fairly dark blue watercolor paint to fill in the sky behind the mountains. When that is dry, layer on more paint to imply the presence of clouds. Then, fill in the trees with a medium green tone. Once dry, layer on a little more

green paint in select areas to add depth to the trees. If there are any tree trunks, fill those in with brown. Then, add contrast to the mountains with iron gall ink (the ink is best applied with a paintbrush for this step).

5 Using a flexible nib and iron gall ink, trace over your lettering, calligraphy, and embellishments. Trace around the mountains, the moon, and the circle.

6 When the ink is dry, use your eraser to remove any pencil guidelines. At this point, you may spot areas that could use further decoration. Use your pointed pen to fill in these gaps, then your mail art is complete and ready to send to the lucky recipient.

Tip

Sketch out ideas

It is a good idea to develop any envelope art concepts with a pencil draft first. Draw the illustrations and write the address on a separate piece of paper, then adapt as needed to ensure that all the elements complement each other.

Elaborate mail art

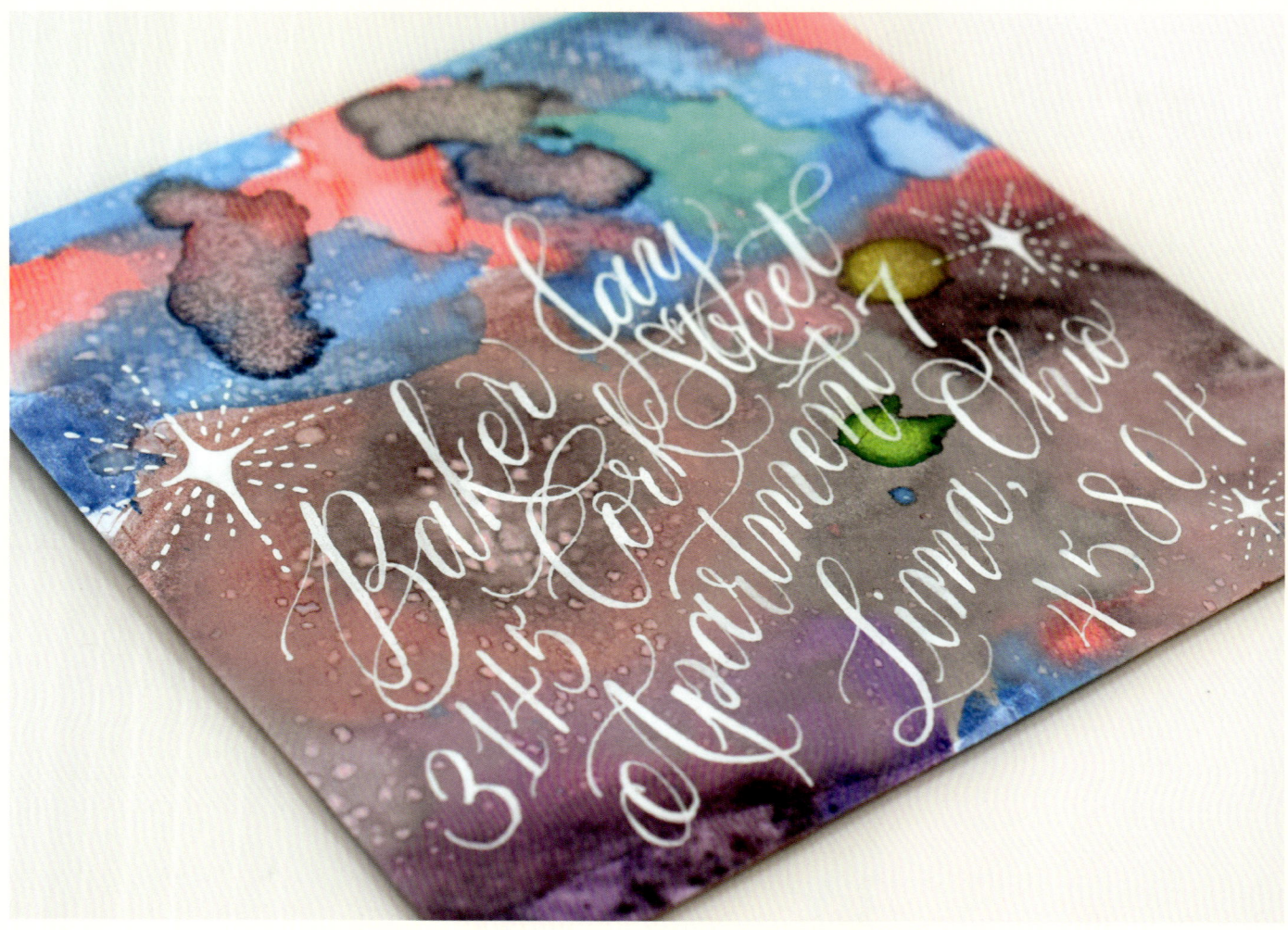

A blend of different colors creates an interesting backdrop for the white ink used on this envelope.

Mail art tips

The right envelope

Look for high-quality, calligraphy-friendly envelopes. You don't have to be picky, though; you can always take it as a challenge to work with a stock of standard envelopes that you may have sitting around.

Make your own envelope

To make your project even more special, try making your own handmade envelope. Find an envelope with a shape and size that you like. Then, carefully disassemble it. Trace around the unfolded envelope on an interesting piece of paper, then cut it out. Fold in and glue all the flaps to complete your envelope.

Legibility

It's important to make sure that your recipient's address is legible; otherwise, it may never arrive. Make sure the postcode is clear enough for a machine to read it. For the rest of the address, it's generally alright if your lettering is intricate as long as it's legible.

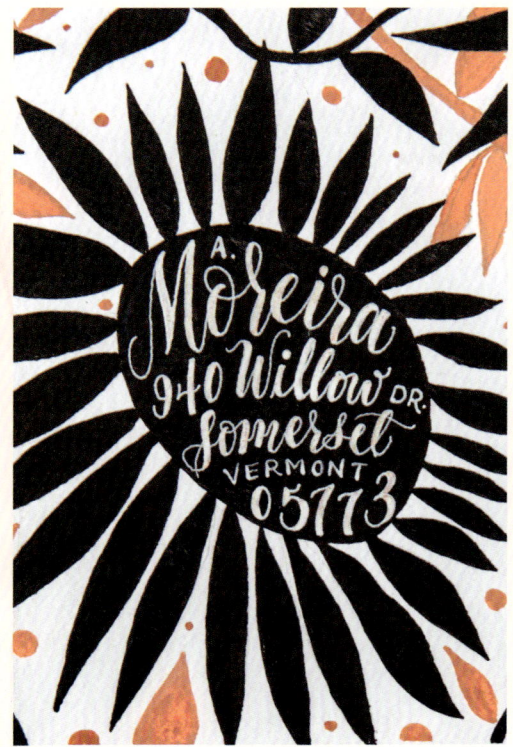

Use the graphics below as inspiration for your next piece of creative mail art.

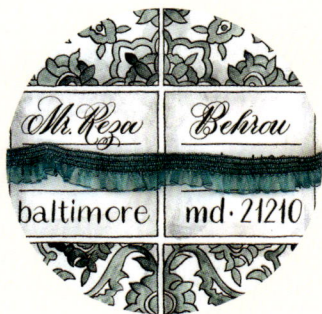

A combination of calligraphy styles on an elaborate background is easy on the eye.

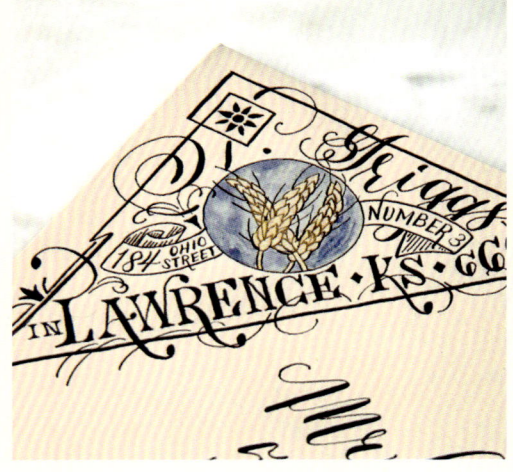

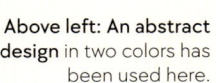

Above left: An abstract design in two colors has been used here.

Above right: Consider decorating the back of the envelope to match the front.

Right: Adding a return address in one corner gives you the chance to add more decoration.

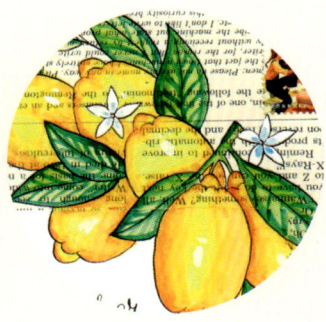

Fresh colors for zesty lemons could be used to decorate your envelope.

Notes for posting

Most envelopes are sorted through a machine, which will tear off any loose découpaged elements. So if your envelope design includes découpage, make sure you get everything glued down well. If in doubt, you can always send your envelope in a plastic sleeve.

Stamps vary by country. Do some research to find out if you can use vintage and/or foreign stamps (and, if so, where you can buy them). If you live in a country where you don't have much of a selection, take that as a challenge to make an amazing envelope design anyway.

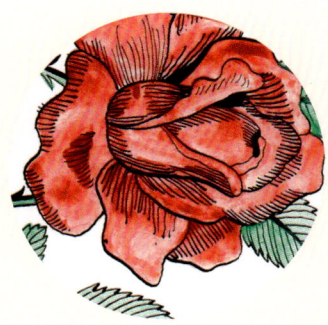

Draw flowers with waterproof ink, then use watercolor to bring them to life.

Gallery

Mail art is one of my very favorite ways to use my calligraphy skills. Envelopes offer a relatively small canvas to work on, and embellishing them is a bite-size project that makes a big difference. You will be surprised at how much your recipients appreciate you going the extra mile to make a beautiful surprise for their mailbox.

1

Although this envelope is heavily flourished, the white address stands out clearly. Notice that the color scheme was inspired by the postage stamp: pink, green, white, and gold.

2

This chic floral envelope design uses black sumi ink, gold watercolor, and a few thin white ink smudges. The address here is a great example of how pointed pen calligraphy and sans serif lettering can complement each other.

3

Stamps can offer great mail art inspiration. This envelope's flourishes emanate from the postage stamp, and the goldenrod watercolor circles echo the coin in the stamp.

4

In this mail art, calligraphy plays second fiddle—and that's okay! The koi and their pond—drawn with a Nikko G nib, waterproof ink, and watercolor—steal the show in the best of ways.

5

The design for this envelope was inspired by simple floral art from the 1950s. A blank border helps frame the design, making it more compelling.

6

I'm a big fan of vintage bird illustrations, so I indulged myself with this envelope design. If you can think of a subject you'd enjoy exploring through illustration, consider incorporating it into your mail art.

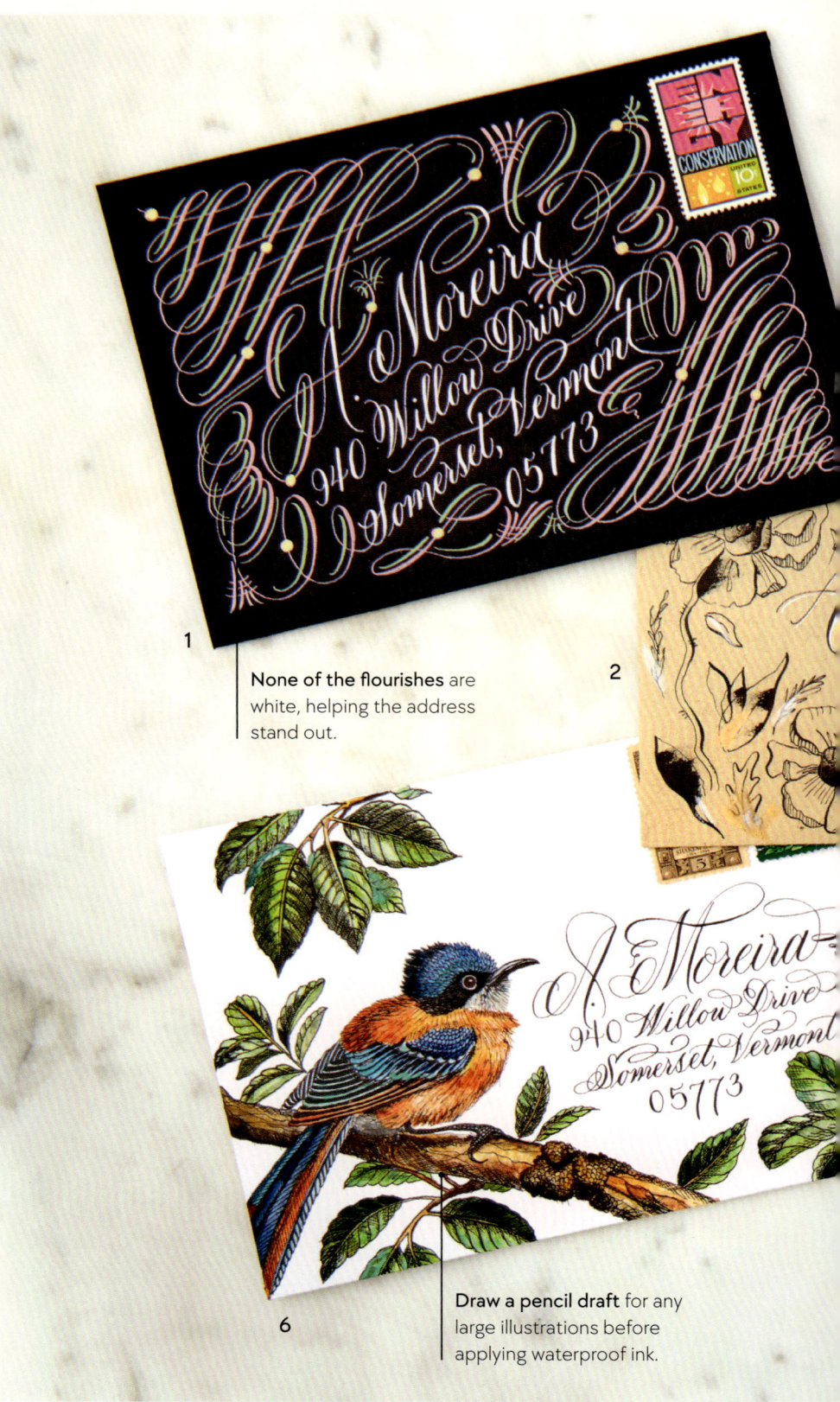

1

None of the flourishes are white, helping the address stand out.

2

6

Draw a pencil draft for any large illustrations before applying waterproof ink.

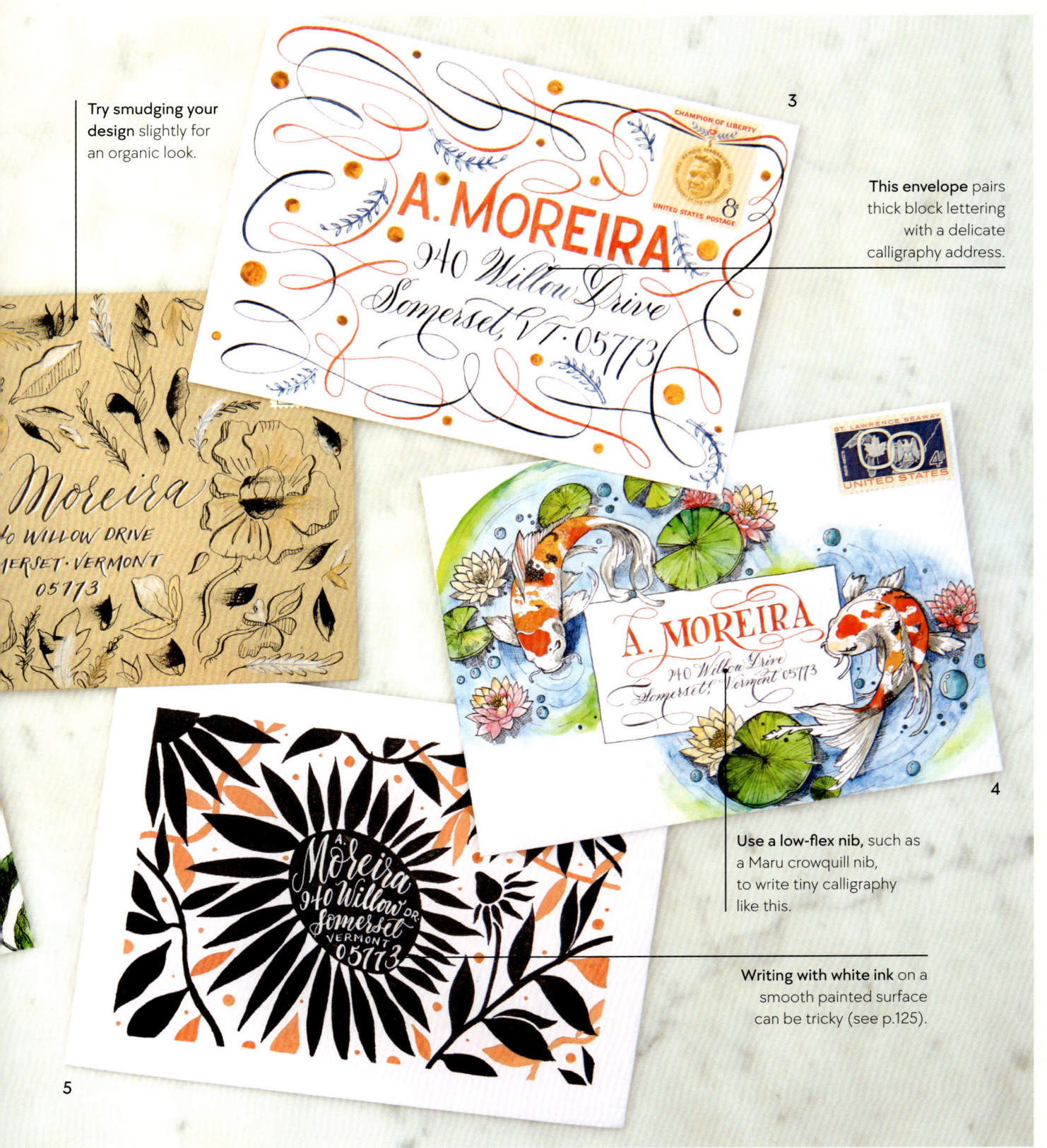

Try smudging your **design** slightly for an organic look.

3

This envelope pairs thick block lettering with a delicate calligraphy address.

Use a low-flex nib, such as a Maru crowquill nib, to write tiny calligraphy like this.

4

Writing with white ink on a smooth painted surface can be tricky (see p.125).

5

Elaborate mail art

Twist-out tree holiday card

Even without a traditional greeting, this card exudes holiday cheer. It's got twinkling stars, a tree outline that twists for contrast, and just the right amount of drama.

● **DIFFICULTY**
intermediate

Make a few of these gorgeous cards whenever the mood strikes and stockpile them for the holiday season. You won't regret having a couple of extras to send to your friends and family members. With its luscious and repetitive flourishes, this project serves as one big calligraphy drill, meaning it's great practice. Create this card, and you'll be putting together something stunning and improving your pointed pen calligraphy skills at the same time.

Try using an oblique pen to draw the flourishes on the tree. The oblique holder will help keep your hand out of the way as you write, resulting in smudge-free strokes. Then, to reduce the risk of the stars smudging as you're drawing them, mentally divide the tree into four quarters. If you're right-handed, begin by drawing stars in the upper left quarter, then the upper right. Then, move on to the lower left quarter, and finish in the lower right quarter. Left-handed calligraphers will probably have the most success working from the top right to left and then down.

If you're sending this card to someone flat in an envelope, add a written message on the inside of the card encouraging the recipient to retwist the tree for display.

SUPPLIES

White mechanical pencil

Black cardstock folded in half to make a card measuring around 5x7in (13x18cm)

Ruler

Pen holder and nibs of your choice (such as a Brause EF66 nib for the flourishes and a Nikko G nib for the gold stars)

White ink

Gold watercolor paint

Paintbrush

Craft knife

Cutting mat (optional)

Black eraser

This card with a twist is sure to dazzle anyone lucky enough to receive it.

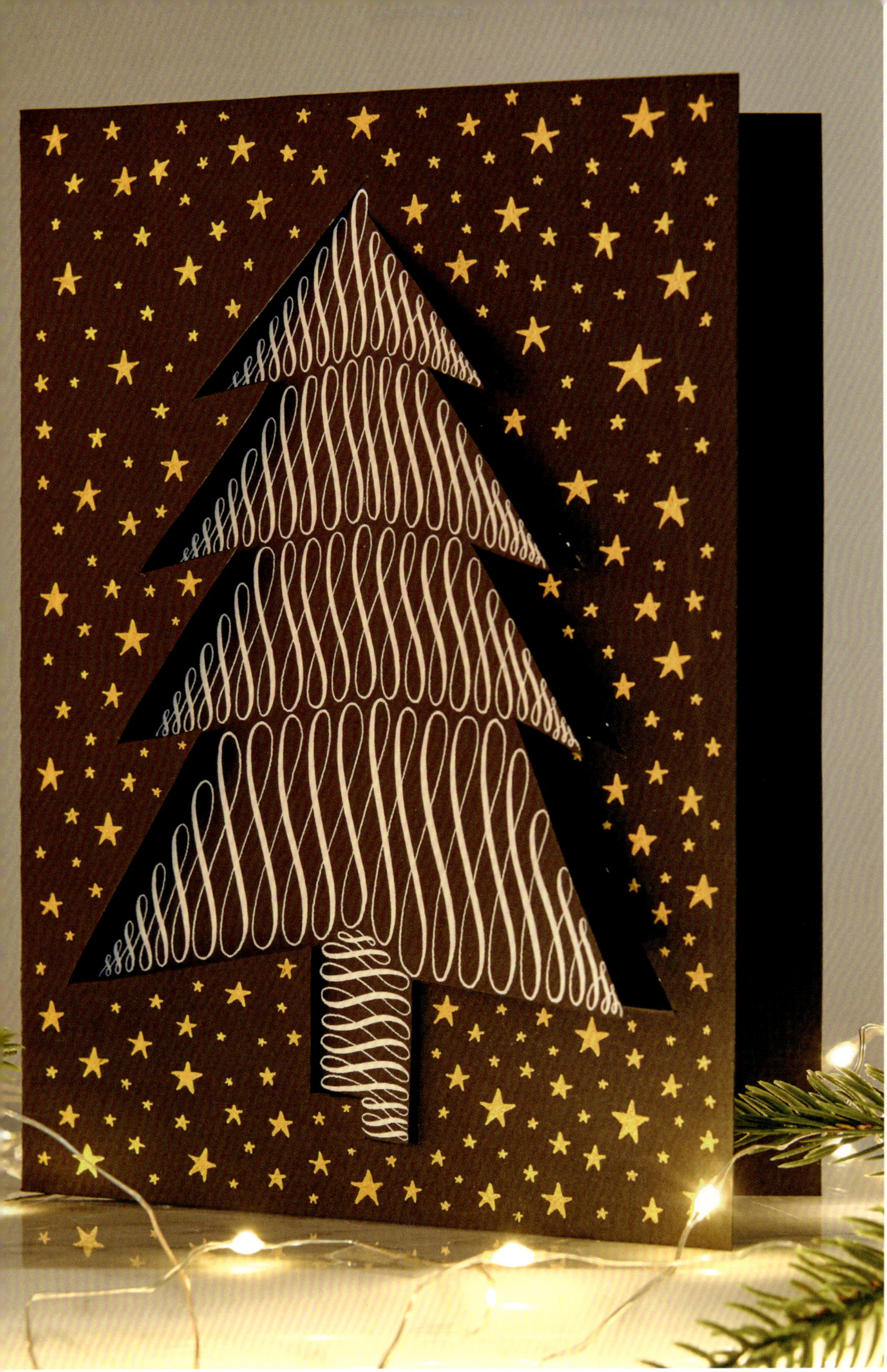

Consider incorporating a holiday greeting into the tree's flourishes or somewhere among the stars. Any calligraphy style looks good alongside intricate loops and swirls.

Tip
Twister

If you're sending this card flat in an envelope, include a note inside encouraging the recipient to retwist the tree for display.

Twist-out tree holiday card

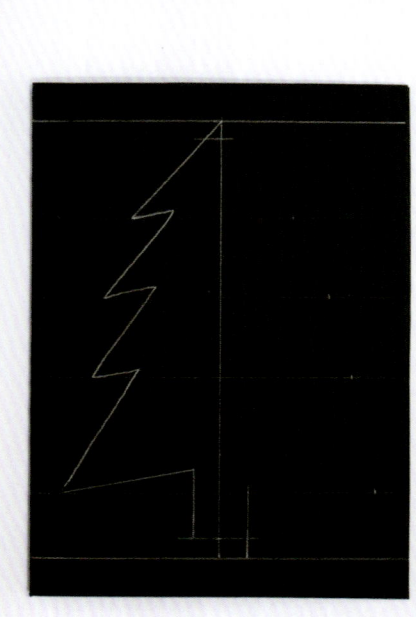

1

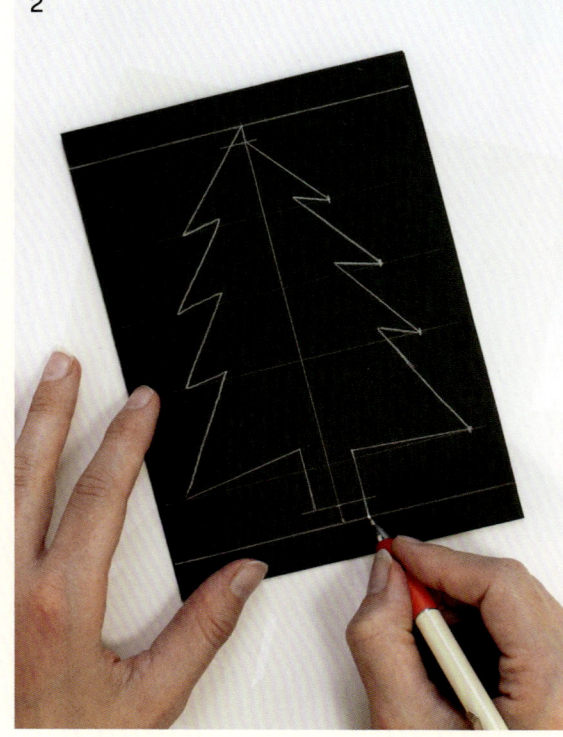

2

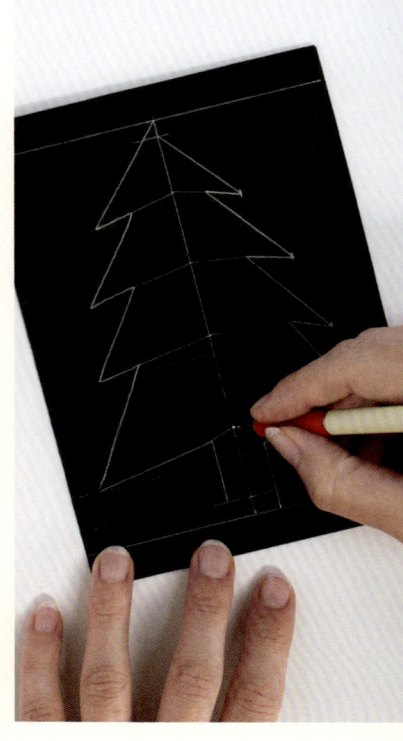

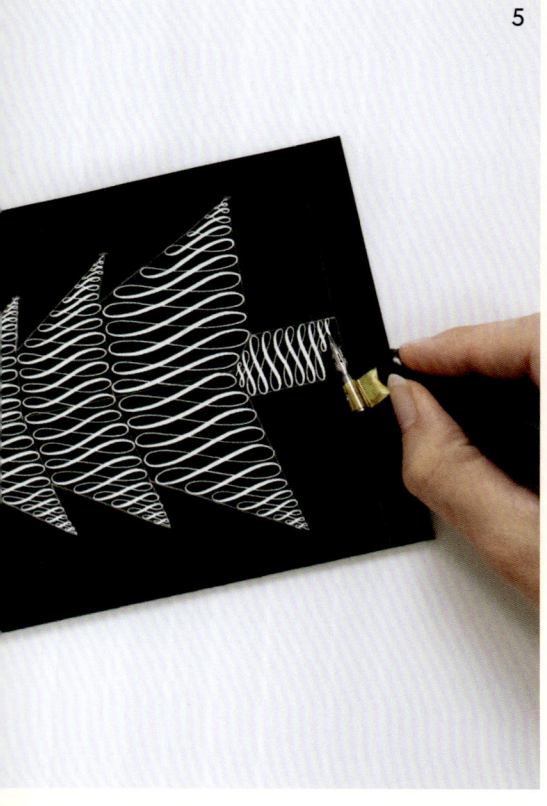

5

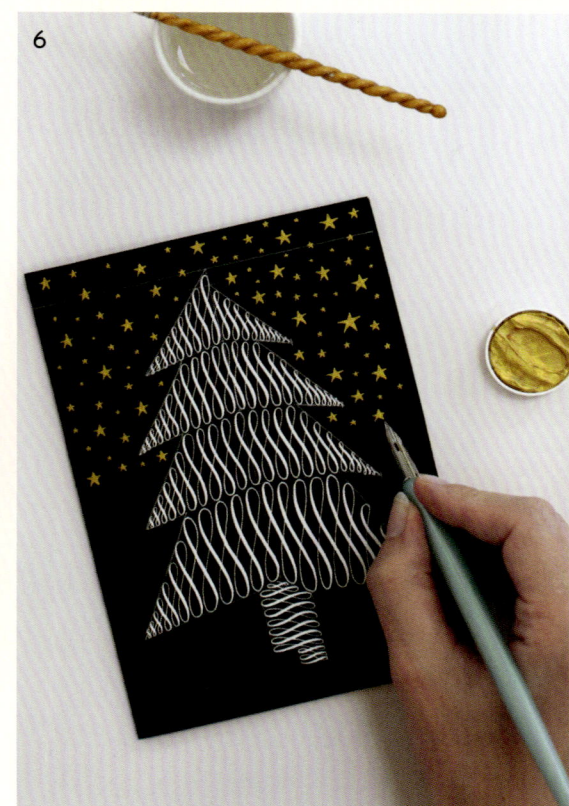

6

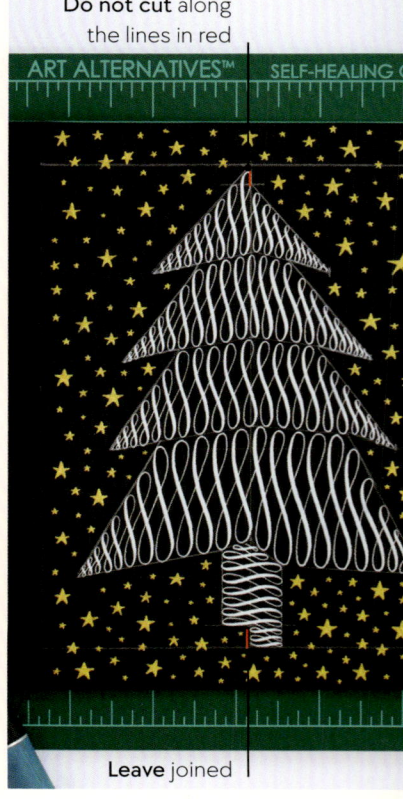

Do not cut along
the lines in red

ART ALTERNATIVES™ | SELF-HEALING C

Leave joined

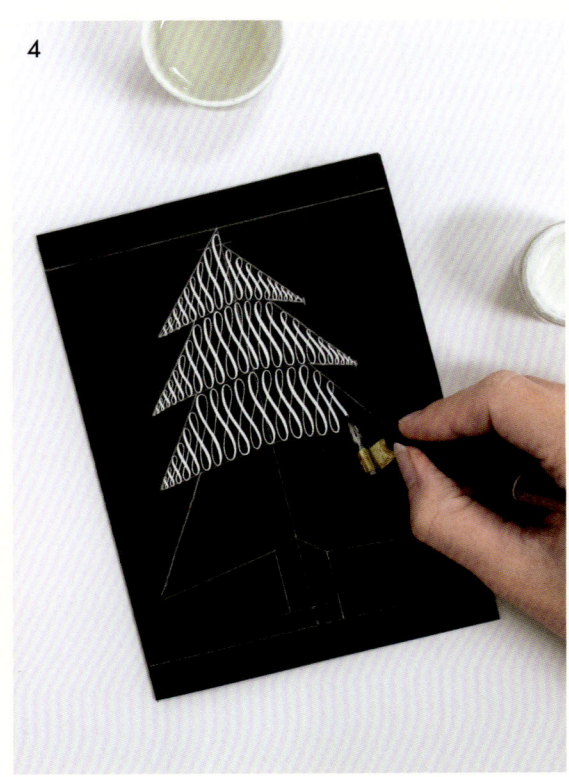

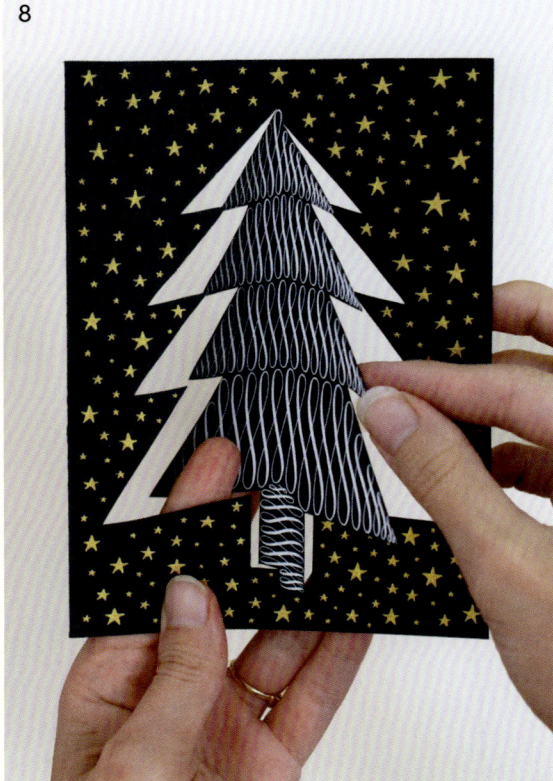

1 Using the white pencil, draw a vertical line down the center of your card. Add two horizontal lines: the first one ¹/₂in (1.25cm) from the top, and the second one ¹/₂in (1.25cm) from the bottom of the card. Draw two marks ¹/₄in (5mm) below the top horizontal line and above the bottom horizontal line. Sketch the left half of a pine tree outline, as shown. The trunk should end at the lower ¹/₄in (5mm) mark. Use a ruler to lightly draw horizontal lines extending from each tier's tip on the left side over to the right side of the card. Mark these distances on the corresponding tier lines on the right side. This will help you sketch the right side of the tree symmetrically.

2 Use the horizontal lines and distances you just marked to complete the right-hand side of the tree. The trunk for this side should go all the way to the bottom horizontal guideline, but the top should go only up to the little mark below the top horizontal guideline.

3 Connect each tier of the tree at the points where they jut furthest inward just above the horizontal guidelines.

4 Use your pointed pen and white ink to fill in each tier of the tree with flourishes that look like a series of connected cursive S's.

5 Rotate your card counterclockwise until it's nearly horizontal, then fill the trunk with additional S flourishes.

6 Once the white ink has dried, use gold watercolor paint (see p.130) to add stars around the tree. To reduce smudging, start at the top and work down.

7 Open your card and lay it flat (tree side up) on a cutting mat or a sturdy piece of cardboard. Then, use a craft knife to cut the tree out along its outline. Do not cut along the guidelines that are highlighted in red. Otherwise, your tree will fall out of the card!

8 Take your black eraser and use a light touch to get rid of your white pencil guidelines. Then, carefully twist the left side of the tree behind the card and the right side of the tree toward you. Twist to the point where the tree has a pleasing dimensional effect while taking care not to rip the flaps that keep the tree connected to its card.

Tip

Which pen and nib?

An oblique pen holder with a nib like the flexible Brause EF66 works well for the white flourishes, while the less flexible Nikko G nib in the holder of your choice is suitable for the gold stars.

Twist-out tree holiday card

Letter from Santa

Stockings and gifts have always been part of Christmas morning, and now you can include this enchanting letter from Santa Claus in your yearly traditions. It's guaranteed to add a touch of joy to your festive celebrations.

SUPPLIES

5½x8½in (14x21.5cm) off-white drawing paper

Ruler

Graphite pencil

Chopstick or stir stick

Red gouache in a small jar

A flexible nib (such as the Brause EF66) and pen holder

A medium-flex nib (such as the Nikko G) and pen holder

Gold watercolor paint

Paintbrush

Eraser

The idea behind this festive and intricate letterhead is that you'll fill it with well-wishes for the little people in your life. The deep red gouache, delicately flourished reindeer, and shimmering stars will make it seem as though the letter has come straight out of Santa's workshop. For the quintessential Santa experience, enclose the letter in an envelope with the child's name written on the front in flourished letters and their location written in print beneath.

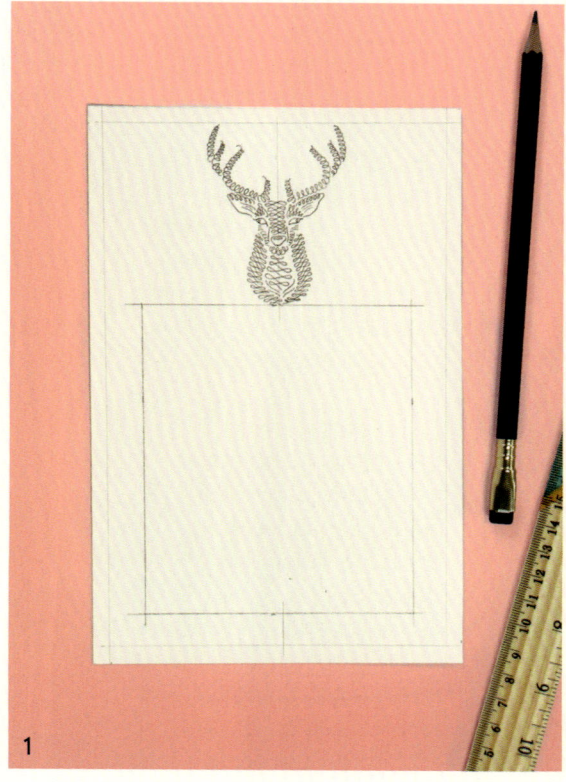

1

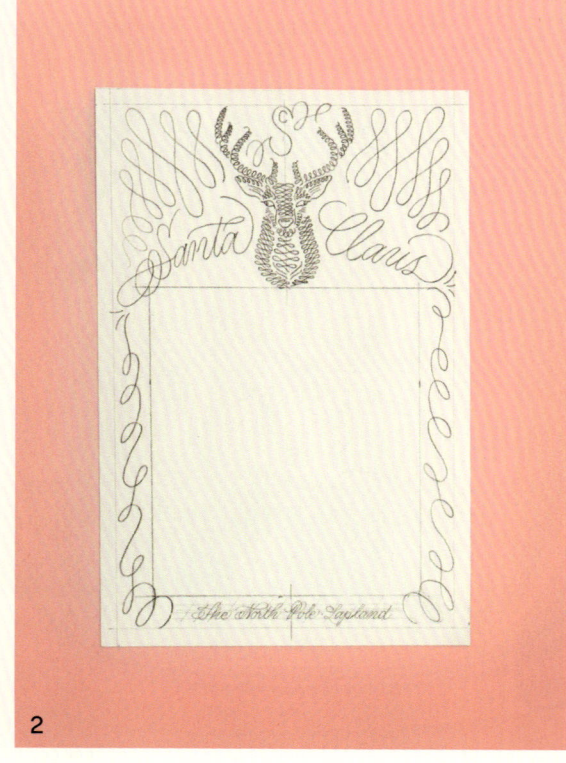

2

1 Use your pencil and ruler to draw a border that's ¼in (5mm) from the edge of your page. Then, draw a square that's ¾in (2cm) from the left and right edges of the page and the bottom of the page. Draw the top of the square 3in (7.5cm) from the top edge of the page. Finish up by marking the vertical center of the page. Then, draw a flourished reindeer in the top center of the letterhead. Use the template on page 199 for the reindeer.

2 Use your pencil to write "Santa" and "Claus" on either side of the reindeer. Then, fill in the rest of the border with loopy flourishes. Finally, center Santa's address at the bottom of the page.

3 Use a chopstick to stir some water into the red gouache. Then, switch

between using a flexible nib and a medium-flex nib to trace over the pencil draft with the gouache. The flexible nib is great for larger flourishes where you want a lot of stroke contrast. The medium-flex nib can be used for making the tiny flourishes required for the reindeer and for writing Santa's address at the bottom.

4 Once you're certain the gouache has dried, gently erase any pencil guidelines. Then, use a paintbrush to apply some gold watercolor paint (see p.130) to the medium-flex nib, and add some gold stars to fill the empty space in the flourished border. When you have finished that, write your own note from Santa in the blank square. This looks best in black ink, echoing the color of the reindeer's eyes.

Use the template on page 199 for the reindeer.

STYLE

Copperplate-esque calligraphy with a bit of flourish is the best choice for "Santa Claus." Don't forget to add flourishes to the hand-lettered "SC" at the top, too!

Tip

Eye details

Be sure to draw the reindeer's eyes with black ink so they stand out.

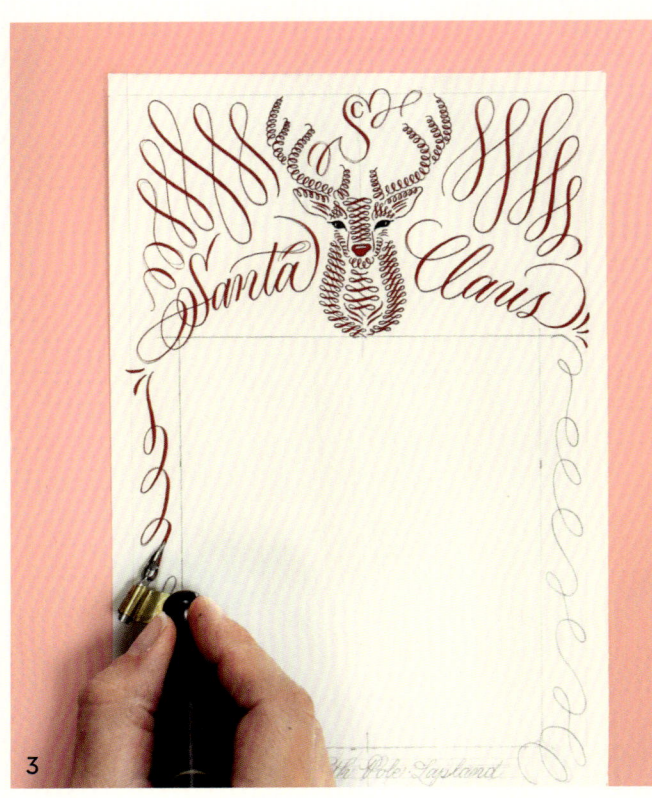

3

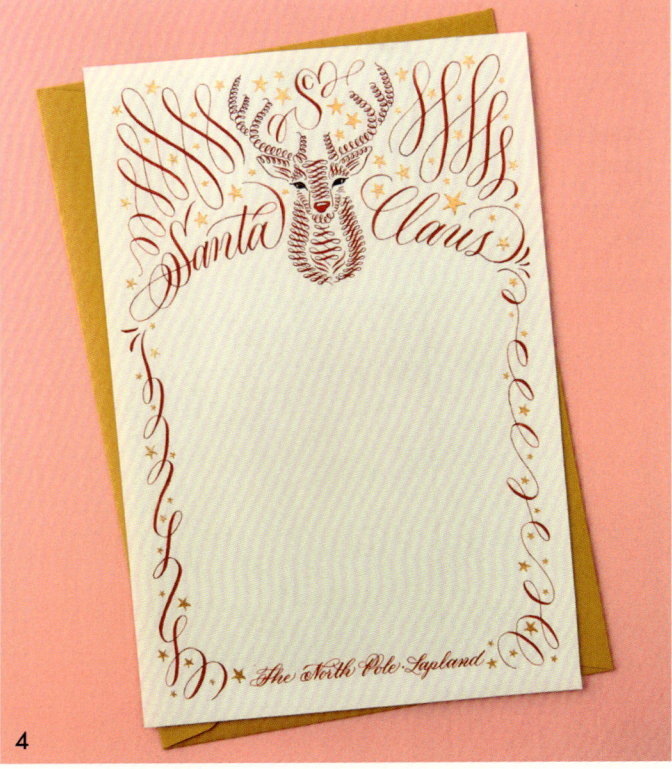

4

Letter from Santa

Paper ornaments

These striking paper holiday ornaments last for years and are the perfect project for beginner calligraphers. Make a few each year to add to your collection of tree baubles or to give away as gifts.

SUPPLIES

Colored cardstock (in your preferred color)

White or graphite pencil, depending on your cardstock color

Eraser

Scissors

Small paintbrush

Silver watercolor paint

Assorted tubes of gouache and/or metallic watercolor paints

Pen holder and nib of your choice

Hole punch

Ribbon or string

Consider turning the creation of your ornaments into a family endeavor. This is a great project to do together with younger members of the family as they can help decorate ornament cutouts to add a personal touch to your tree and make memories. You can decorate these with calligraphy flourishes or words, while children may prefer to add sweeping strokes of metallic watercolor paint and splashes of glitter.

These ornaments offer versatility beyond traditional tree decorating. They make fabulous gift tags, place cards, or wine bottle charms. You can also make several ornaments and string them together to make an artistic garland, or you can scatter them across a holiday dinner table when hosting a special occasion.

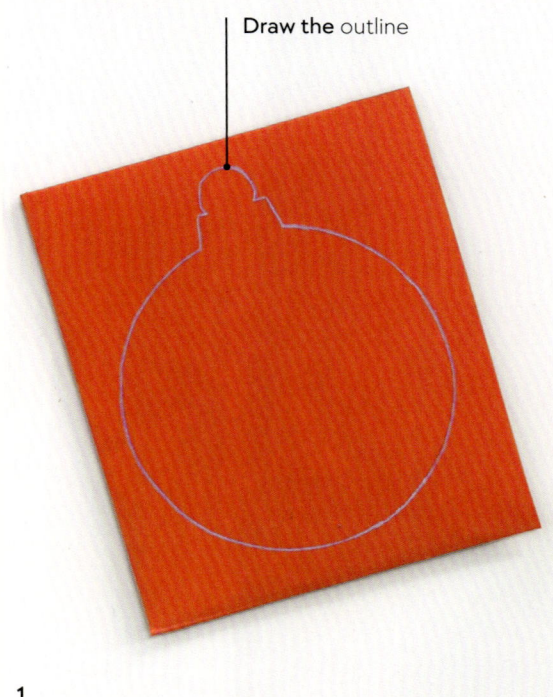

Draw the outline

1

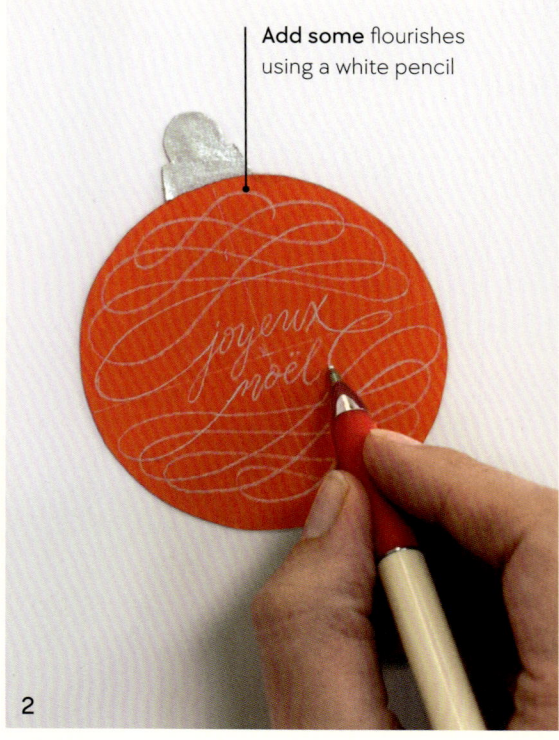

Add some flourishes using a white pencil

2

1 Draw an ornament outline on your cardstock. You can either freehand draw your ornament, cut and trace an outline that you find online, or reference the template on page 199. The ornament shown here is a simple 3in (7.5cm) circle with a tab-shaped top.

2 Cut out the shape and use the paintbrush and silver watercolor paint to brush over the tab. Next, use your pencil to plan out the words and design any flourishes that you want to include on your ornament.

3 Apply the ink, gouache, or metallic watercolor of your choice to your nib. Then, trace over your pencil writing and flourishes. Once you

finish, add embellishments like stars and snowflakes as needed to lend additional holiday cheer to the bauble. Punch a hole at the top of the ornament's tab with a hole punch. Then, thread ribbon or string through the hole and use the ornament as you wish, perhaps on a tree or as part of a garland.

reference the template on page 199.

STYLE

Lowercase Kaitlin-style calligraphy has been used to write "joyeux noël" here, but you can use any style that appeals to you.

Tip

Decorating both sides

It's up to you whether you decorate only one side of the ornament or both. If you intend to hang them on your tree, you can add embellishments to both sides. For place cards, decoration on one side is enough.

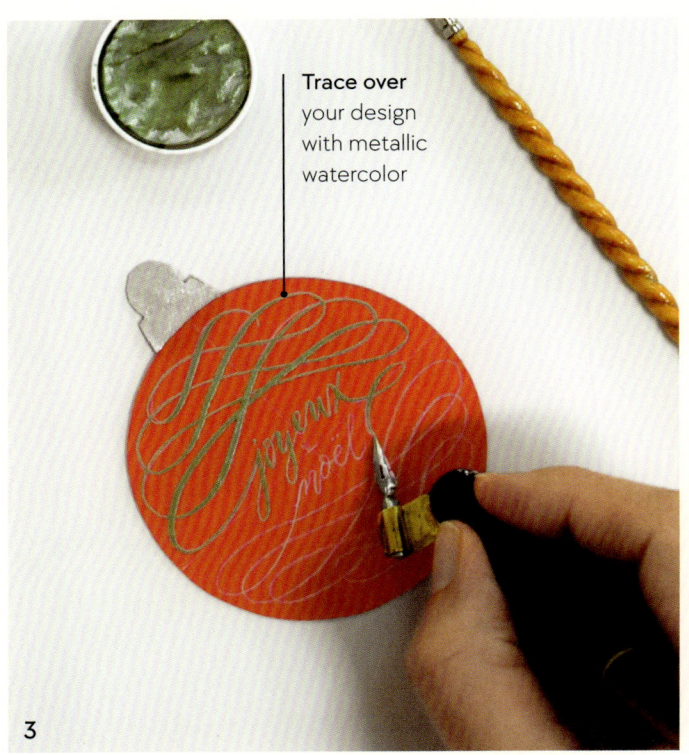

Trace over your design with metallic watercolor

3

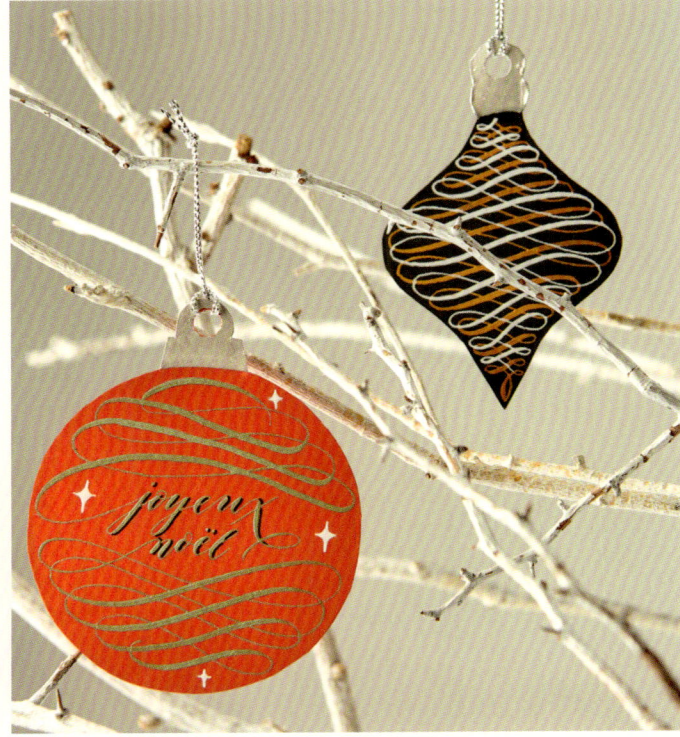

Paper ornaments

Halloween skull

It's important to find the right mix of whimsical and spooky elements when creating Halloween projects. This skull achieves that delicate balance, infusing a sense of playfulness with just the right touch of the eerie.

SUPPLIES

Watercolor paper
(in the size you prefer)

Graphite pencil

Iron gall ink

Nib (such as a Nikko G) in holder of your choice

Crowquill nib in holder of your choice

Eraser

Orange watercolor paint

Paintbrush of any size

Blunt syringe

This Halloween art strikes a mostly playful tone, with just a little bit of spookiness coming from the skull motif. Look closely, and you'll notice that the skull is made entirely of lines from Act 4, Scene 1 from *Macbeth*, including the chilling "By the pricking of my thumbs/something wicked this way comes." Pumpkin-orange spatters add a bit of festive flair and fall warmth to the piece. This artwork is great for displaying as part of your Halloween decor, using as a greeting card concept, or incorporating into a seasonal sketchbook page.

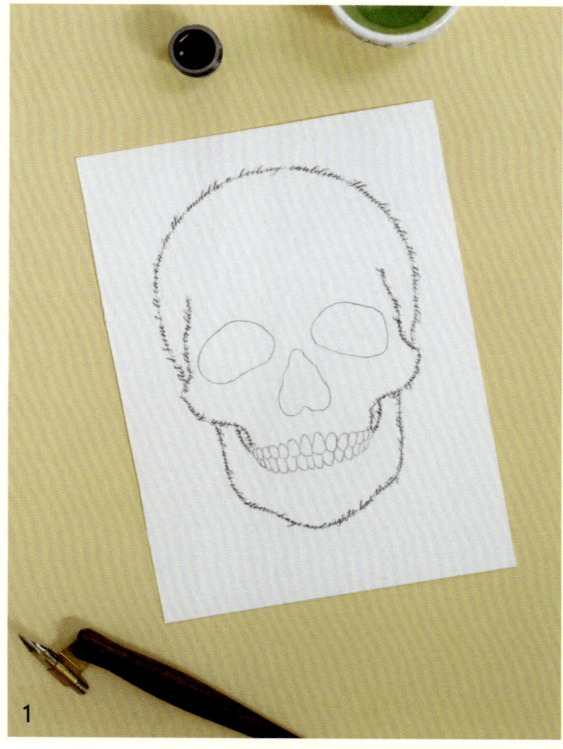

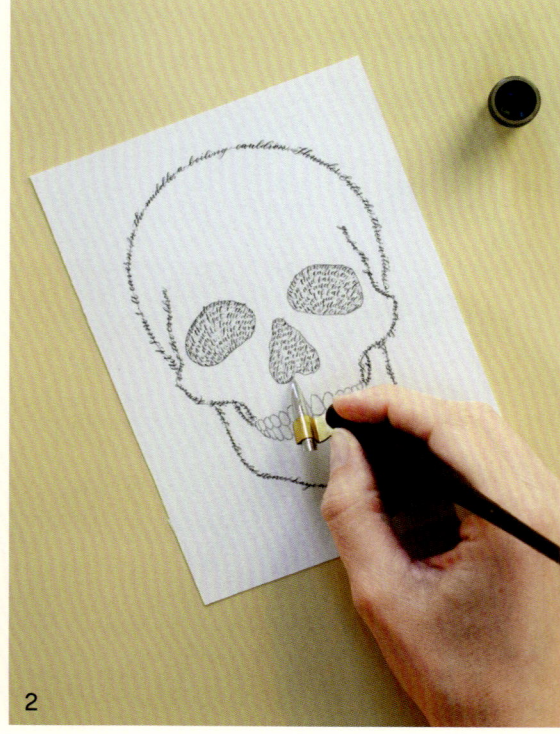

1 With pencil, draw or trace a skull (see page 200). Then, use iron gall ink and your pointed pen to begin writing the lines to Act 4, Scene 1 of *Macbeth* around the outside of the skull. Don't worry too much about what words go where; the aim is to make cohesive artwork, not crystal-clear calligraphy.

2 Continue writing calligraphy lines to fill in the skull's eyes and nose. Try to create lines of text that follow the curve of the skull's eye sockets to give the piece extra interest.

3 Use your crowquill nib to trace over the teeth outlines with teeny-tiny calligraphy. Some calligraphy might not be completely legible. You may also need to cut off words midway through and continue them on another tooth. Once dry, use an eraser to get rid of all the pencil guidelines.

4 Use a paintbrush to mix some water into the paint, then transfer some of the moistened paint to a palette and add a bit more water. Pull a bit of the orange watercolor/water mixture into your blunt syringe, then spatter paint onto a scrap piece of paper (see pp.134–135). Use your syringe to spatter paint on the piece until you're happy with how it looks.

STYLE

Kaitlin-style calligraphy has been used here. However, you shouldn't take legibility or consistent letterforms too seriously when creating this skull. Your first goal is to make art that clearly resembles a skull.

Tip

Making paint spatters with a blunt syringe

Test, test, test: Do not skip testing out your spatters on a scrap piece of paper. You invested a lot of time calligraphing your skull, and you don't want to ruin it with poorly executed paint spatters. Get the hang of making spatters before you add them to your artwork (see pp.134–135).

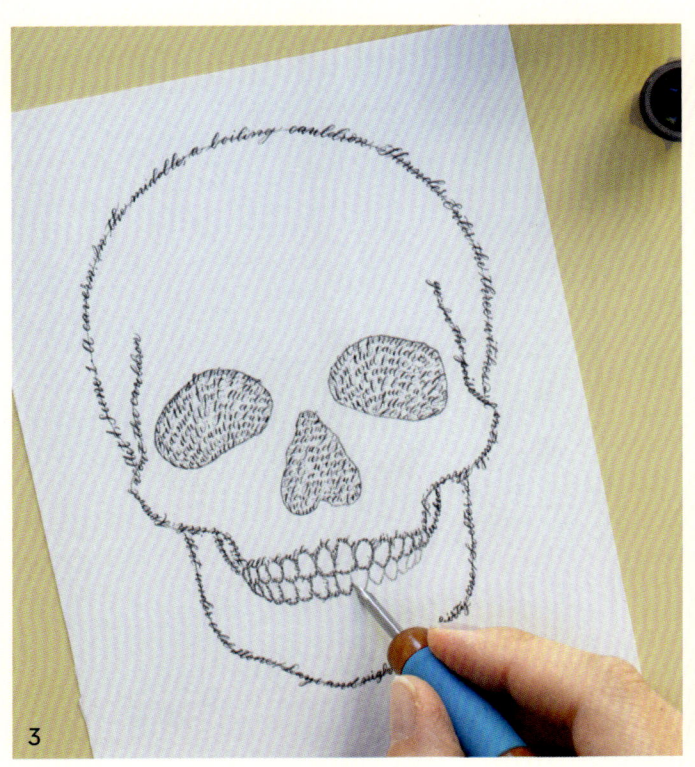

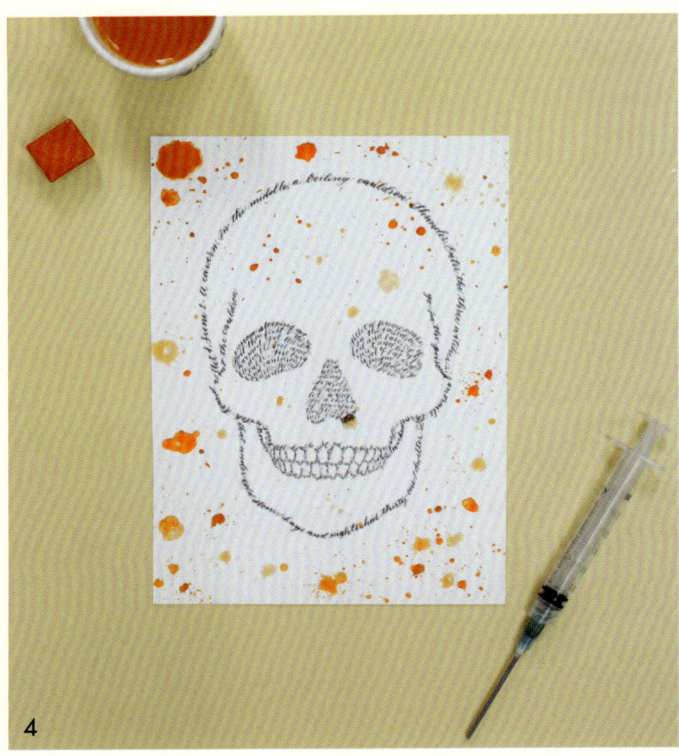

Butterfly Mother's Day card

Any mother will be thrilled to receive this card, which features a joyful butterfly-shaped explosion of flourishes and Mother's Day greetings. Feel free to experiment with the color scheme to create your own unique card.

● **DIFFICULTY**
intermediate

Crafting one of these cards can be a beautiful gesture of recognition to honor the hardworking and nurturing women in your life. I found myself doing just that on a recent Mother's Day, creating a series of these cards for the caring teachers at my children's preschool. If you are thinking about making a batch of these, start by making a master butterfly template to trace (or use the one on page 201 as reference). Complete the first card following this tutorial, then use it as a visual guide to approximate the flourish and calligraphy placement on the rest, blending efficiency with personal touch.

SUPPLIES

5x7in (13x18cm) card (you can make this from a piece of card folded in half)

White pencil

Black eraser

Ruler

White gouache

Red gouache

Pen holder and nib of your choice (such as a Brause EF66 nib in an oblique pen)

STYLE

The calligraphy used is a combination of elements of Flourished style (pp.98–105) and Janet style (pp.90–97). It's a perfect example of how you can mix and match aspects of different styles.

A mixture of Mother's Day greetings in different languages has been used to fill in the butterfly shape on this card.

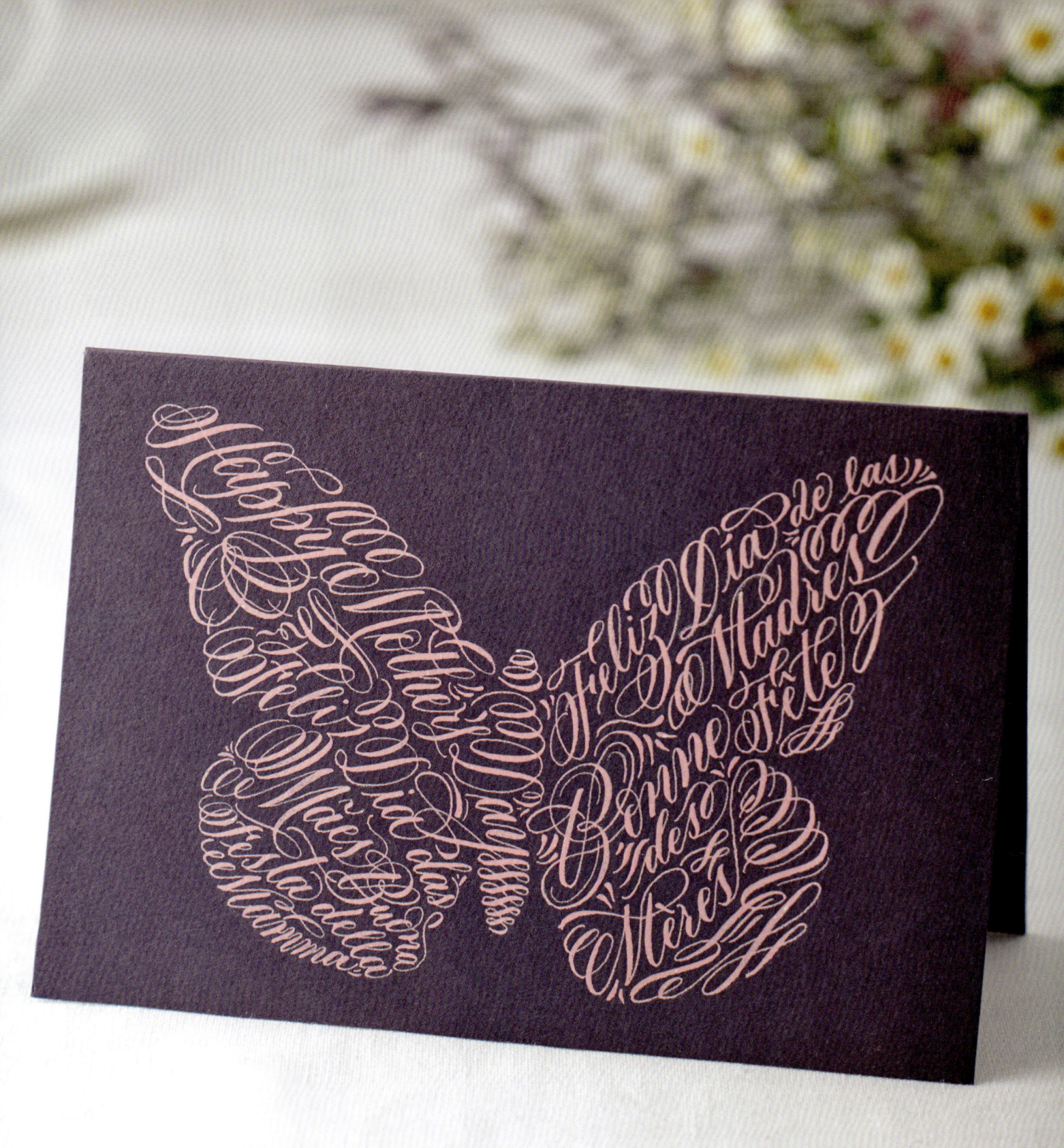

159   Butterfly Mother's Day card

1

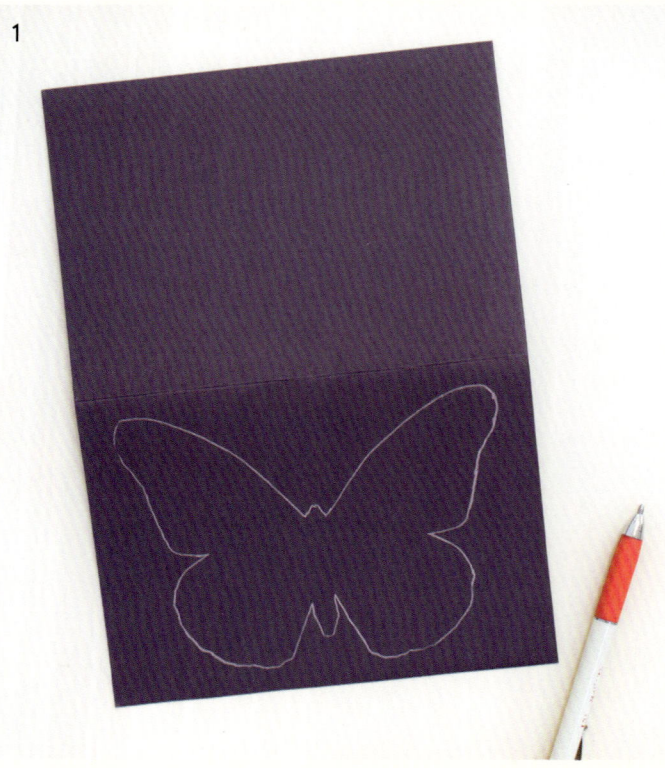

2

Fill the wing with Mother's Day greetings

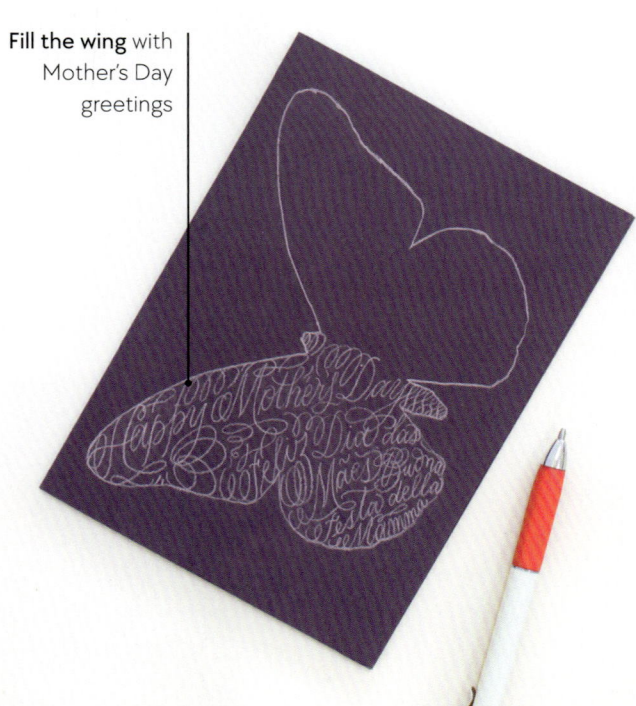

3

Add the flourishes coming from the letters until you have filled both wings

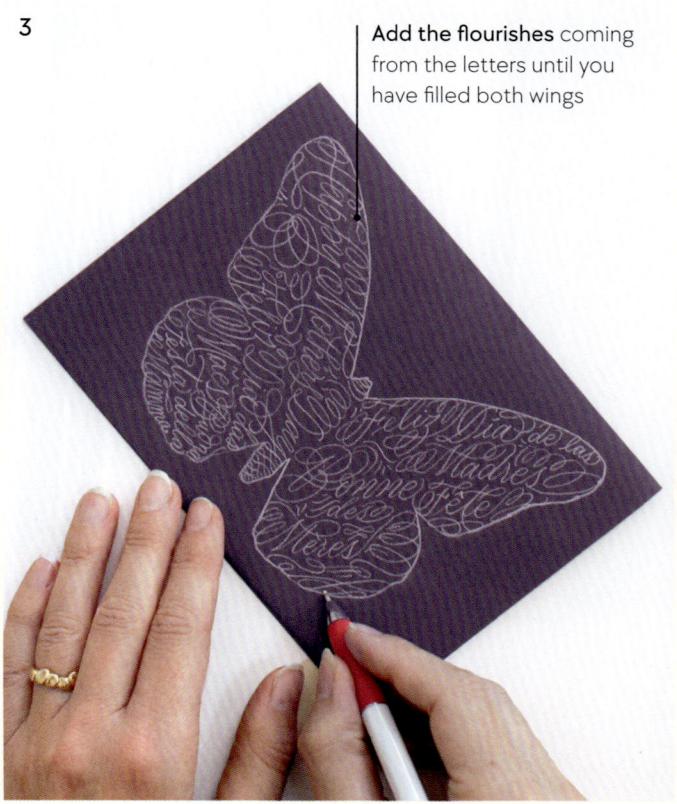

4

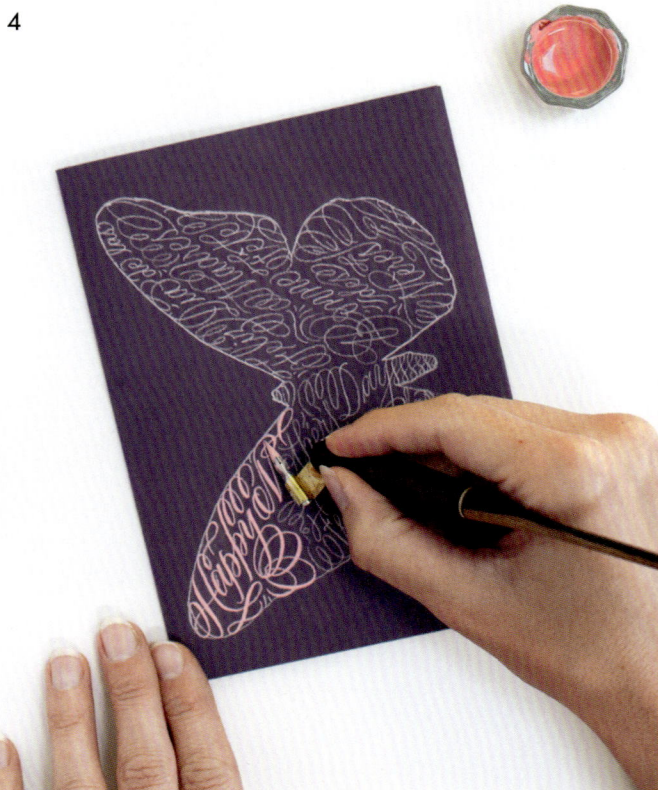

1 Use your white pencil to draw a butterfly outline on the front of the card. If it's easier, you can trace the template on page 201 (you may need to resize it) or look online for a suitable shape and print it out (you can use photo editing or word processing software to modify the outline's size).

2 Fill in the left-hand side of the butterfly's wings with the following greetings: "Happy Mother's Day" (English), "Feliz Dia des Mães" (Portuguese), and "Buona Festa della Mamma" (Italian). The general orientation of the calligraphy should follow the top curve of the butterfly's wing from top to bottom. Fill any spaces with flourishes. Try to use the "D" of "Day" to fill in the top half of the butterfly's thorax, and the "y" in that same word to fill in the bottom half.

3 Move on to the other wing, adding the following greetings: "Feliz Día de las Madres" (Spanish) and "Bonne Fête des Mères" (French). You can also add the message in another language if that will make it more personal to you.

4 Mix the white and red gouache together with some water, then stir the mixture to make a smooth pink "ink." Use that ink to begin tracing over the calligraphy draft. A high-flex nib works well for creating good contrast between the upstrokes and downstrokes of the calligraphy.

5 Allow the gouache to dry. While a few minutes might suffice, letting it set for several hours is ideal. Once the gouache is completely dry, use the black eraser to remove any pencil lines and reveal your beautiful design.

Tip
Adding the words

If you're right-handed, start tracing the calligraphy on the top left first and work your way down. Then, trace the calligraphy on the top right and finish by tracing the calligraphy on the bottom right. Doing so will reduce the risk of smudging wet gouache. If you're left-handed, do the opposite and start at the top right. No matter which hand you write with, remember to rotate the card as needed as you write to ensure smooth and confident strokes.

5

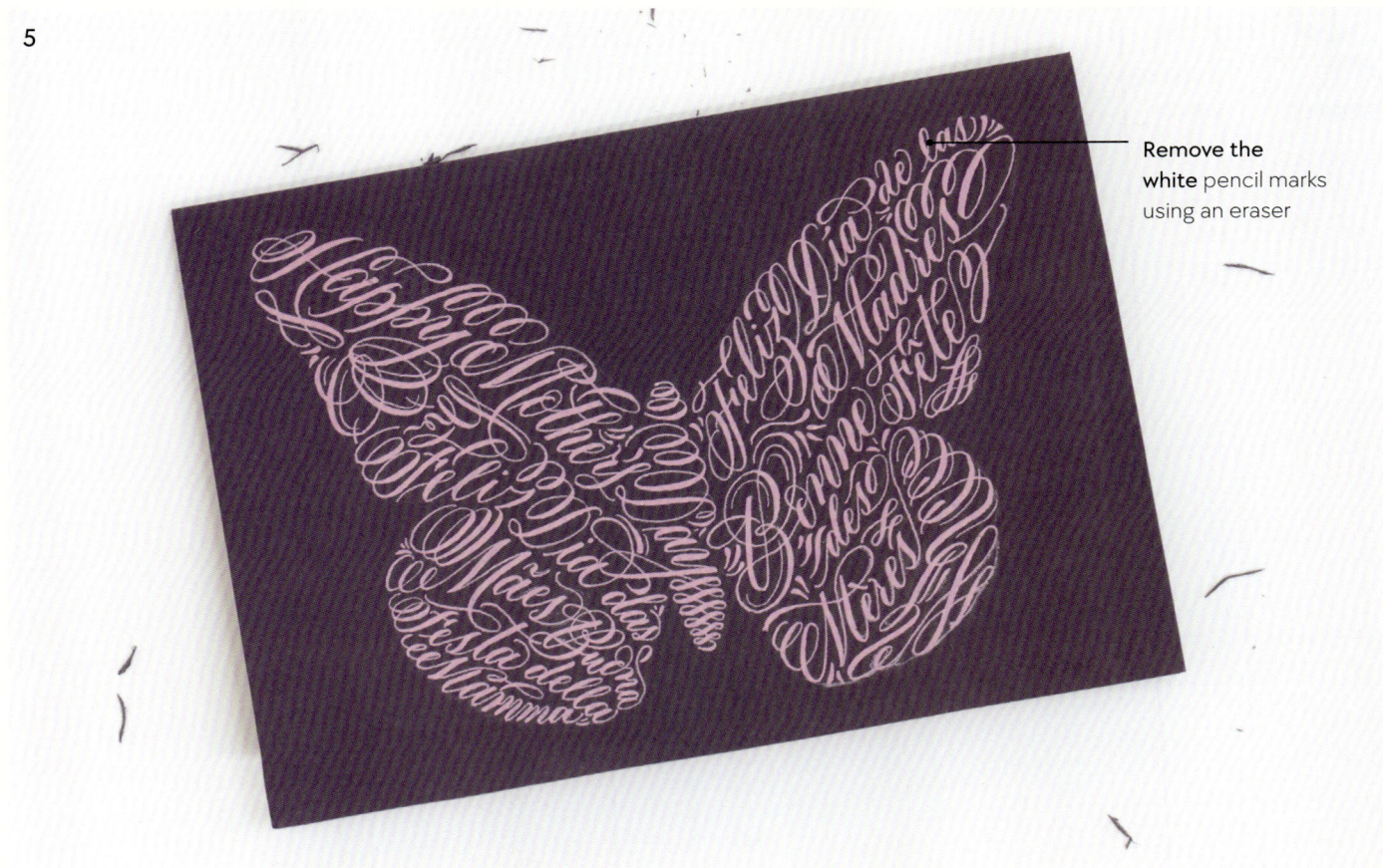

Remove the white pencil marks using an eraser

Personalized wrapping paper

If you want a meditative project that doesn't require perfection, try making your own wrapping paper. You'll be thrilled with how it looks on a gift, and the recipient will adore the paper just as much as the present inside.

● **DIFFICULTY**
beginner

The secret to this project is to not get hung up on perfection. Remember that any spacing errors won't be obvious once the paper is neatly folded around a gift box. For an extra festive look, consider adding gold spatters to the paper at the end. Spatters lend a more celebratory and artistic look, while opting not to include the spatters keeps things clean.

Personalized wrapping paper is endlessly adaptable. It can read "Happy Birthday," "Happy Anniversary," or even "I love you." You can also add your recipient's name, which helps make the wrapping paper a keepsake in its own right.

When planning your wrapping paper, think about the effect you want to achieve and the recipient's personality and preferences. Do they have a favorite color, for example, and would they appreciate a well-placed flourish or two?

This is a fairly quick project, so I recommend using a thin ink such as iron gall, which will flow across the paper. Note that thin inks often have gradation when dry, so you can expect a naturally two-tone look, which further adds to the uniqueness of an already stunning wrapping paper.

SUPPLIES

Off-white drawing paper

Black ink

Green ink

Metallic gold watercolor paint

Nib of your choice in the holder of your choice

STYLE

To keep this project easy and casual, use Kaitlin-style calligraphy. It's quick, forgiving, and can be done without pencil guidelines.

Creating your own wrapping paper will make your gift more memorable.

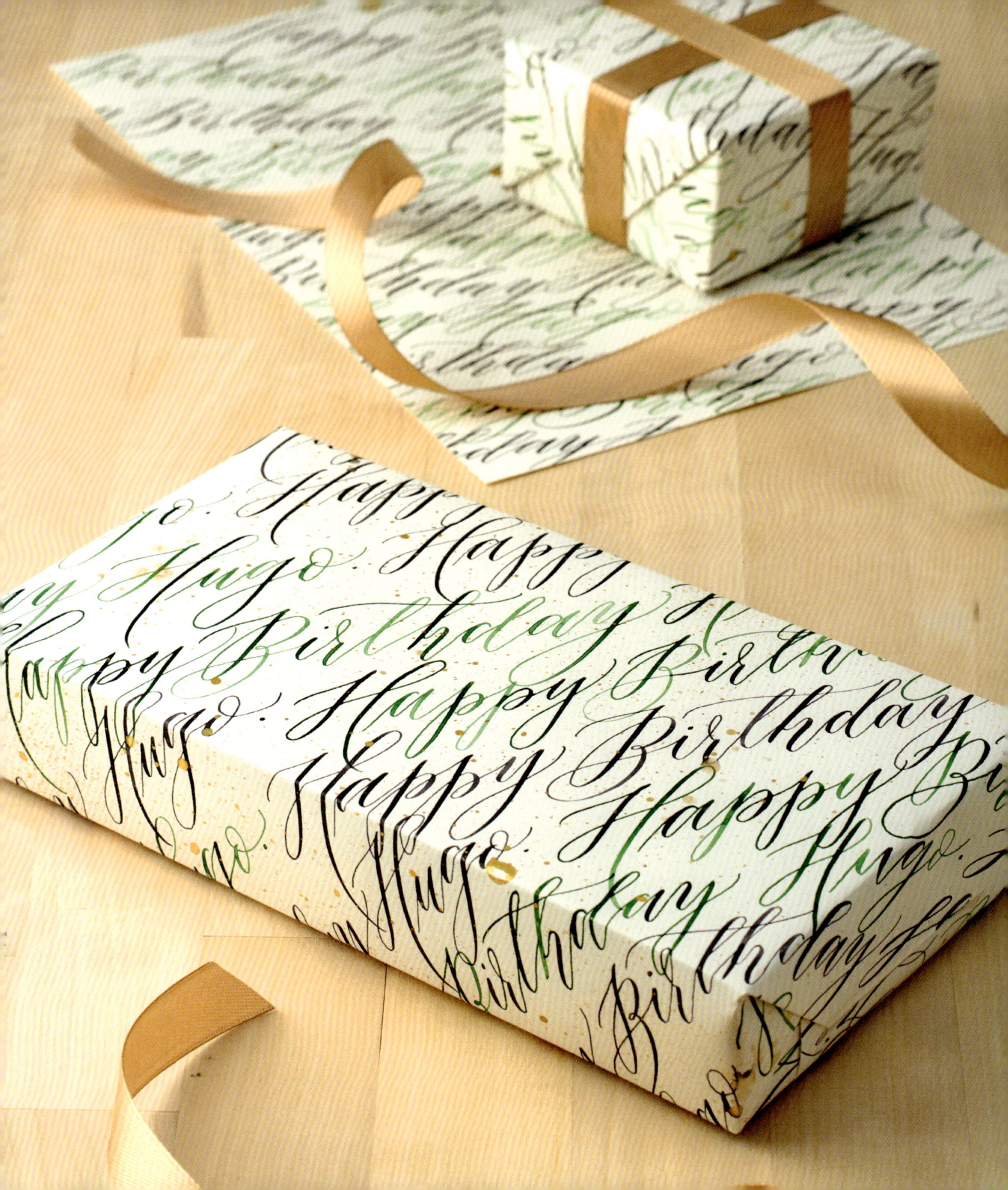

1 Begin writing your greeting and the recipient's name in bouncy, casual calligraphy (see pp.74–81) on a diagonal angle in the top left-hand part of your page. If you are left-handed, you may find it easier to start writing at the top right part of the page. Continue over the next few lines with the same message, ensuring that the words are not repeated directly underneath each other. As you write the message, alternate your inks every time you start the message.

2 Continue to write the greeting and the recipient's name down the page. As you make your way down the paper, it can be easier to maintain consistent spacing between the lines if you start writing closer to the middle than the edge of the page. Experiment to see what works best for you.

3 Once you're finished, you can add some gold spatters. Moisten a pan of metallic gold watercolor. Then, saturate a toothbrush in the watercolor and use your thumb to flick the bristles to make a fine spray of gold. If you want to add a few dramatic spatters of gold, use a blunt art syringe to do so. Let the paper dry fully (ideally an hour or two) before wrapping your gift.

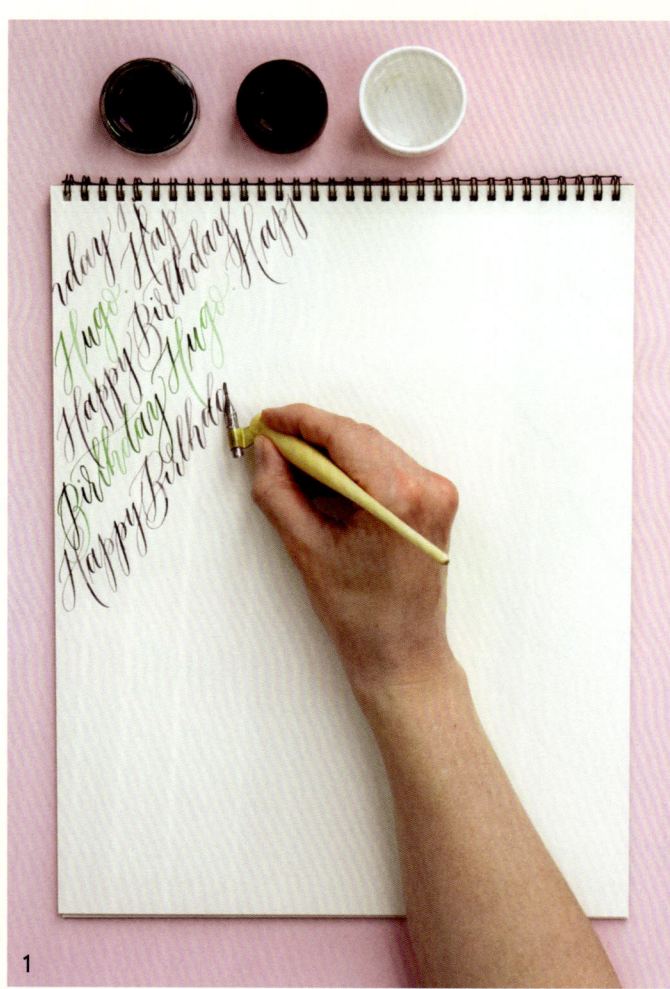

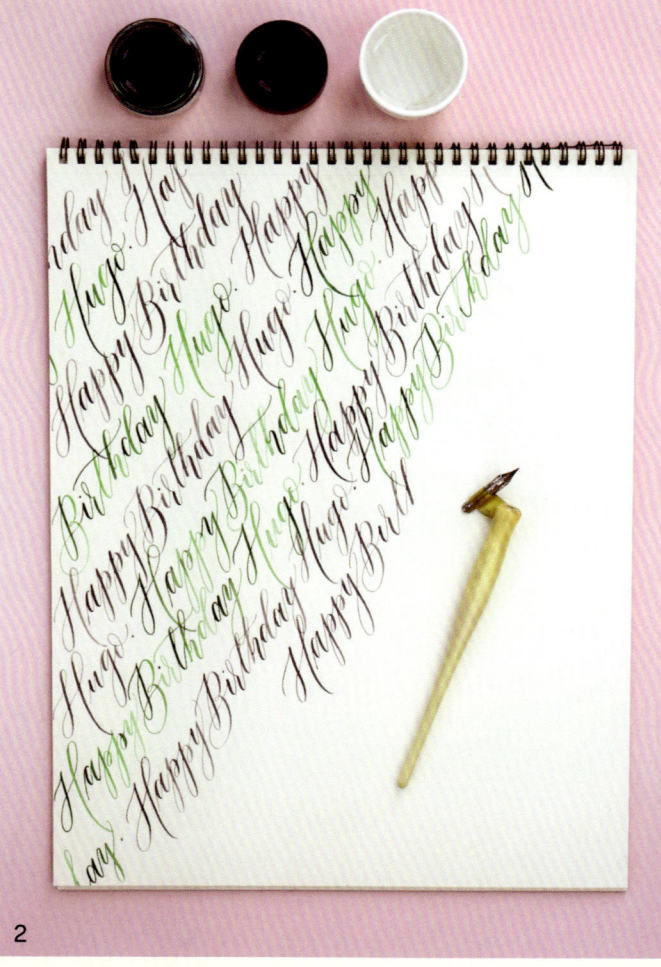

"If you want to add a few dramatic spatters of gold, use a blunt art syringe to do so."

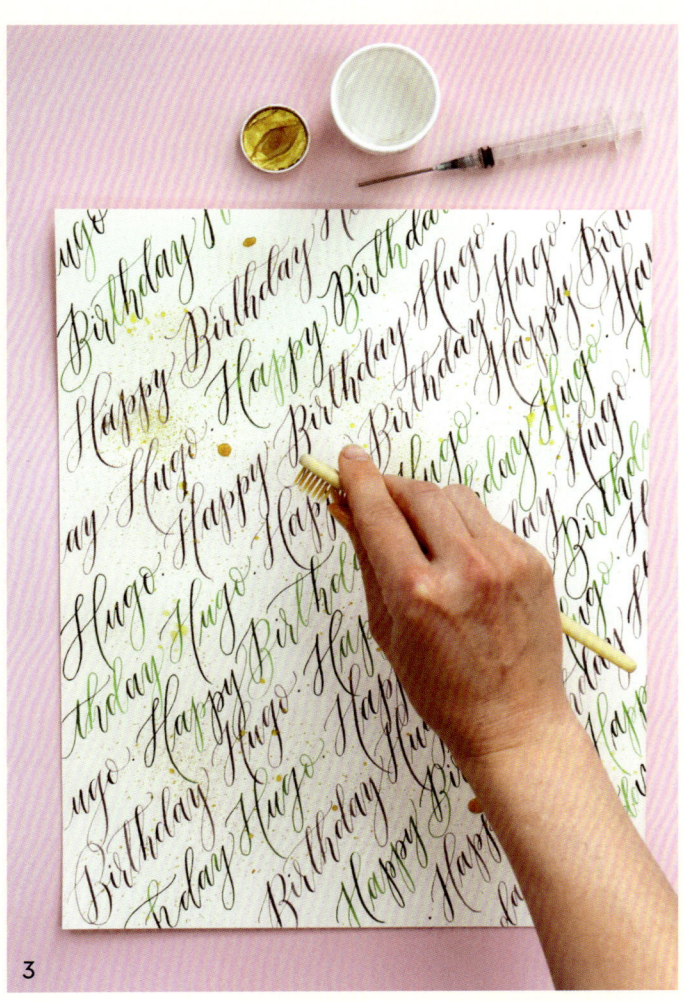

3

Tip

Large paper

Large pads of drawing paper come in handy for this project. Most have a matte texture and a muted white color that elevates the elegance of your DIY wrapping paper.

　　　　Personalized wrapping paper

Wedding invitation

For a wedding invitation that stands out, try this gold and white design. It mixes white ink, gold watercolor paint, calligraphy, block lettering, and plenty of flourishes to create a piece that will become a keepsake.

SUPPLIES

White printer paper

Graphite pencil

White eraser

Photocopier (optional)

Ruler

Yellow pencil or highlighter

Black cardstock cut to 4x9½in (10x24cm)

White pencil

Black eraser

White ink

Metallic gold watercolor paint

Small paintbrush

Nib and pen of your choice

Guests can glean so much from a wedding invitation, including the feel of the event, the personalities of the couple, and the budget. This glitzy black, white, and gold invitation benefits from plenty of flourishes and a unique size that's not often seen in wedding goods. It predicts a fun, elegant, and slightly informal event. As a bonus, it comes together fairly quickly; try to budget around 45 minutes per invitation—you'll need less time as you get a feel for the spacing.

When designing your draft version, think about balancing out more flourished text elements with simpler block text and centering some of the elements. Ultimately, handwritten invitations are a fine balance; they need to be beautiful and personal, but replicable and achievable.

Note that producing handmade wedding invitations is a time-consuming process. If the wedding has a small guest list, it may be possible to handcraft all the invites. However, for a larger event, this won't be possible. In that case, there are a few time-saving hacks you could try. For example, you can digitize your design and use a computer program to enhance and replicate it on screen. There are some printing techniques like letterpress and gold foil that can still make digital invitations feel artisan-made and special. Then you can use some ribbon or a paper sash to tie everything together.

You can also use your calligraphy skills for the envelopes. Don't forget to start early as you'll need to send out the invitations well in advance of the event.

Make an important event feel more special with handwritten invitations.

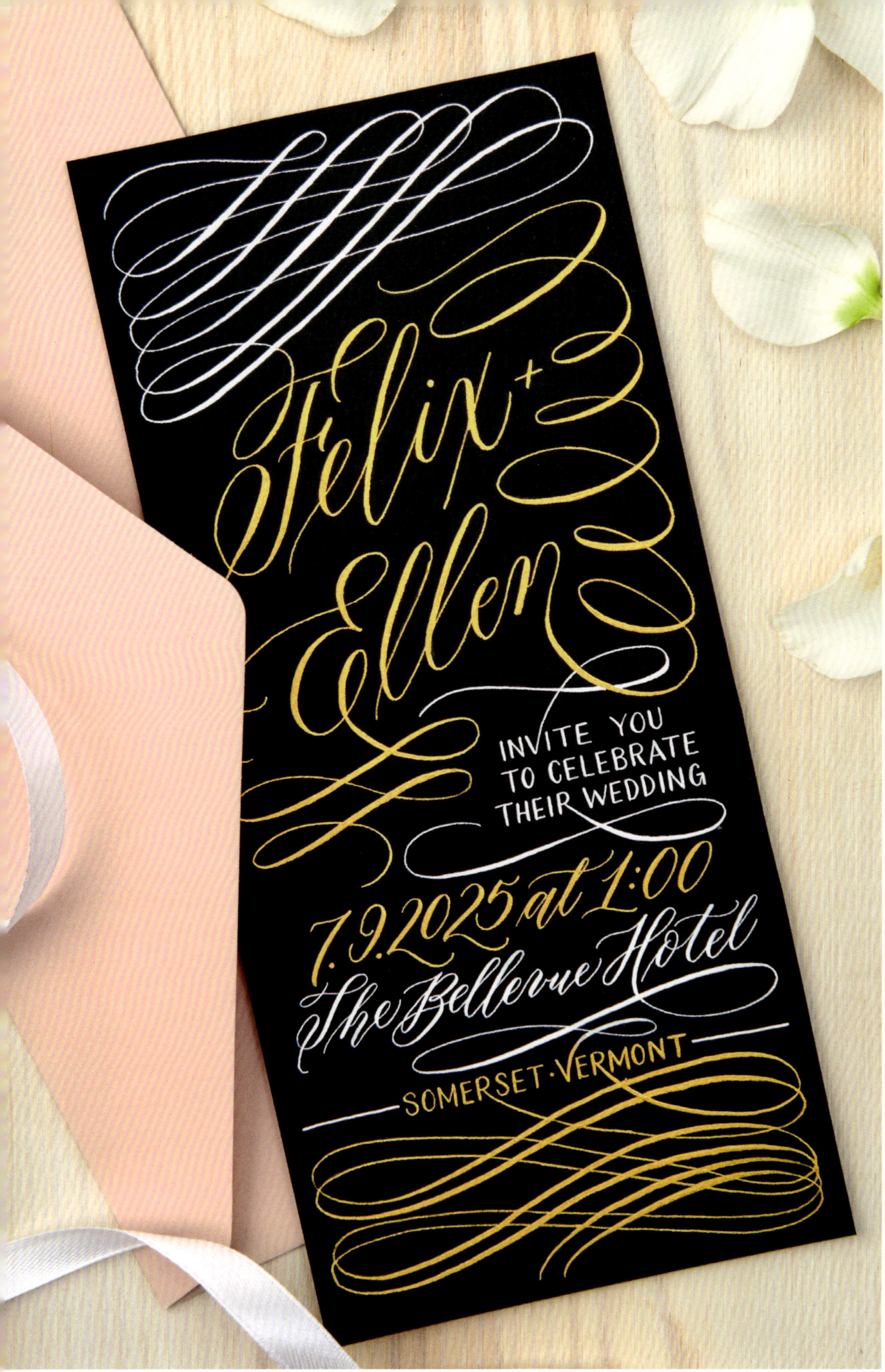

This invitation was created using casual Kaitlin-style calligraphy with plenty of flourishes. Sans serif lettering helps make certain details stand out. The luxe color scheme helps elevate the invitation's glamorous look.

Tip

Inside the border

For a clean look, don't let your flourishes touch the edge of the rectangle. Instead, draw a border about ⅛in (5mm) from the edge of your card and stay inside those lines.

1

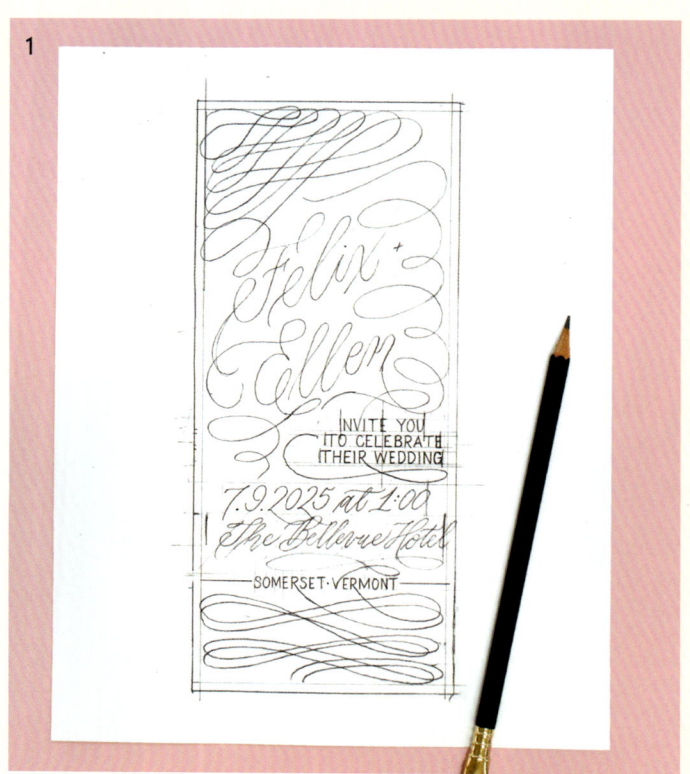

2

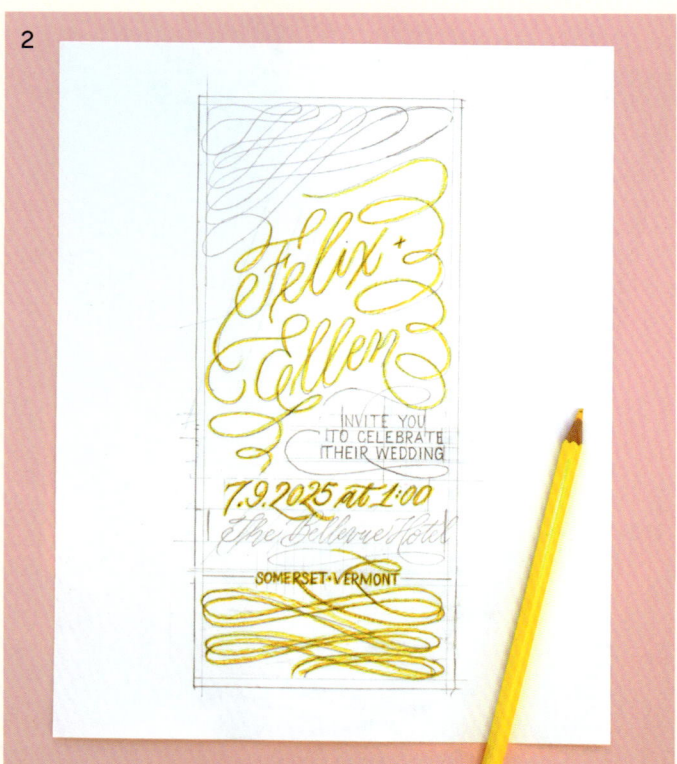

4

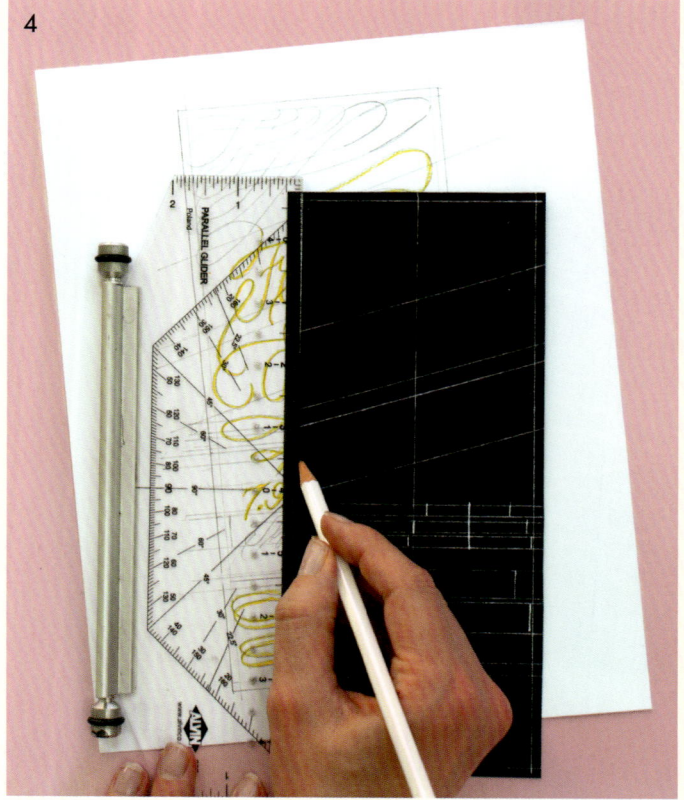

5

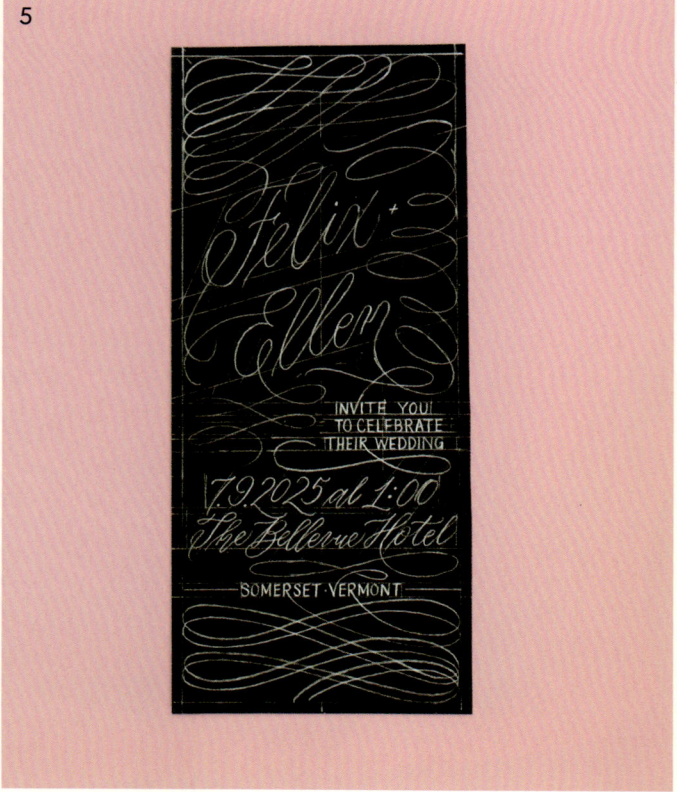

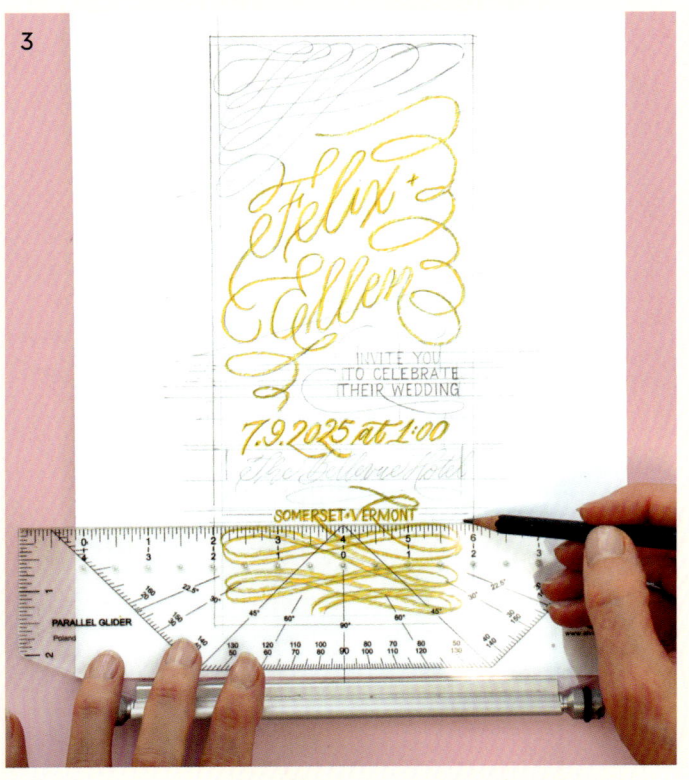

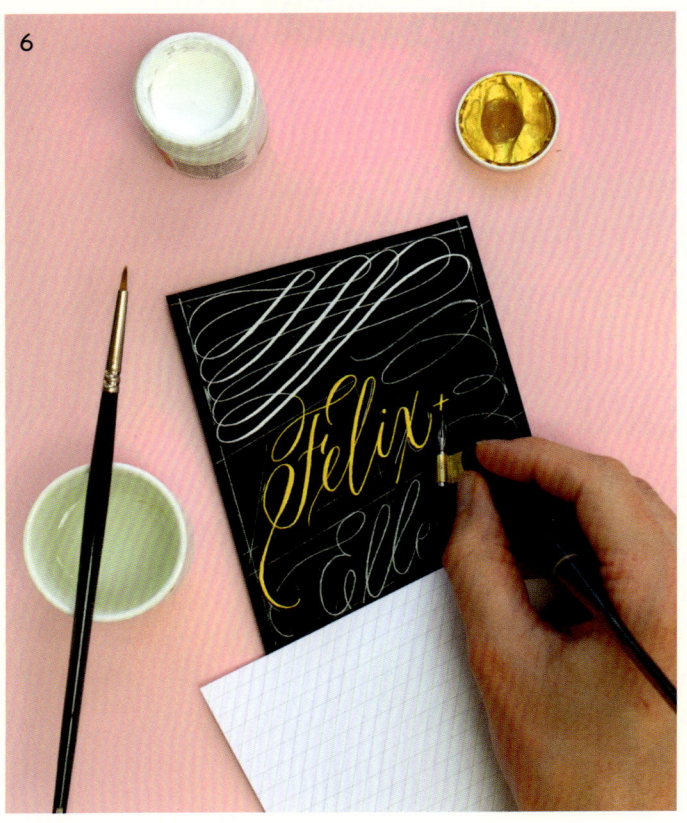

1 Begin by making a pencil draft version of the invitation on white paper. Try out different ways of adding the information about the event, alternating lettering styles to help with legibility. Use a ruler to make guidelines and center the text. When you're happy with the layout for the lettering, connect some flourishes to the letters to fill in the rest of the space.

2 Next, decide which parts of the invitation will be written in gold. If you have a photocopier, you could make a few copies of the draft to see what works best. Use a yellow pencil or highlighter to go over different parts of the writing to see how it looks.

3 Refine the pencil draft, using a ruler to extend the guidelines where needed. Be sure to take measurements so you know where words and flourishes should begin and end on the real invitation.

4 Use your ruler and white mechanical pencil to replicate the guidelines onto the black card. It can be helpful to place the black card directly over the pencil draft, then line up your ruler with the lines that are visible from the sides. You will need to measure other guidelines.

5 Keep your graphite pencil draft close at hand to use as a reference as you make a white pencil draft on the black card.

6 Working from top to bottom with white ink and gold watercolor, add the lettering to the black card. Keep a scrap piece of paper underneath your hand as you write. If you don't protect your white pencil draft, your hand will rub most of it away. Once you're certain your ink and paint have dried (wait overnight if possible), gently use a black eraser to get rid of any pencil guidelines.

Tip
Guidelines

If you're creating several of these wedding invitations, you might not need to make a white pencil draft of the entire piece for every copy. You will probably still need to make white pencil guidelines on each invitation, however.

Wedding invitation

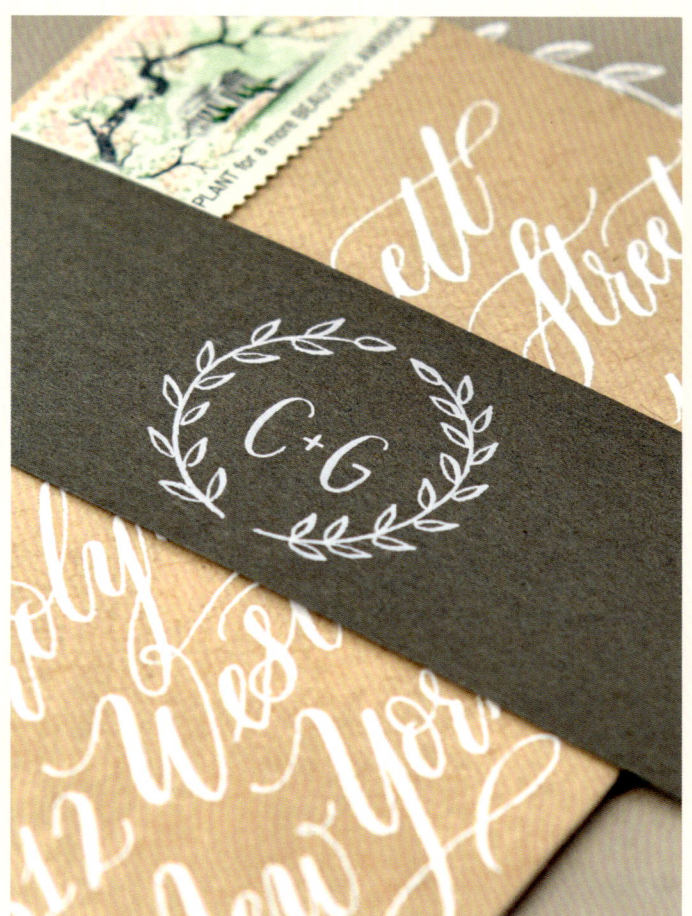

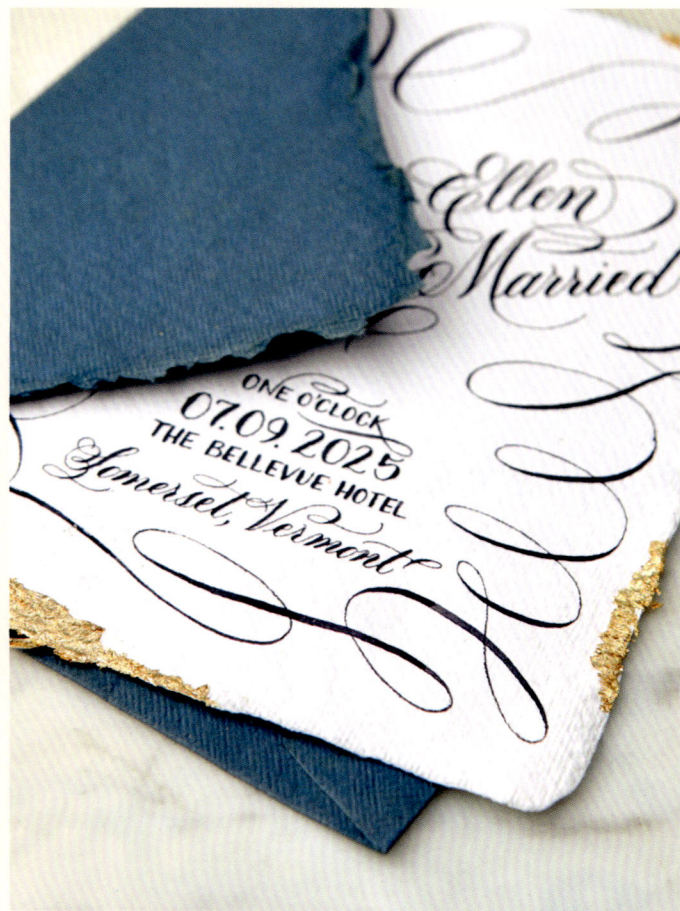

Invitation inspiration

The wedding invitation examples shown here are simple enough to handmake a dozen or so, as long as you give yourself ample time to do so.

Tips for handmade invitations

Handmade invitations are beautiful, but they require a sizable time commitment "and budget considerations. Especially when you're inviting a crowd, the charm of handcrafted invitations needs to be balanced with practicality. Here are a few tips for creating wedding invitations:

- **Start early:** Like making calligraphy itself, the process of creating handmade invitations cannot be rushed. Starting early gives you the luxury of time to experiment, make errors, and find the perfect touches that truly represent you (or the couple you're creating invitations for). Plus, it reduces last-minute stress.
- **Budget wisely:** Set a clear budget from the beginning and remember, "handmade" doesn't automatically mean "cheap." Materials, especially high-quality ones,

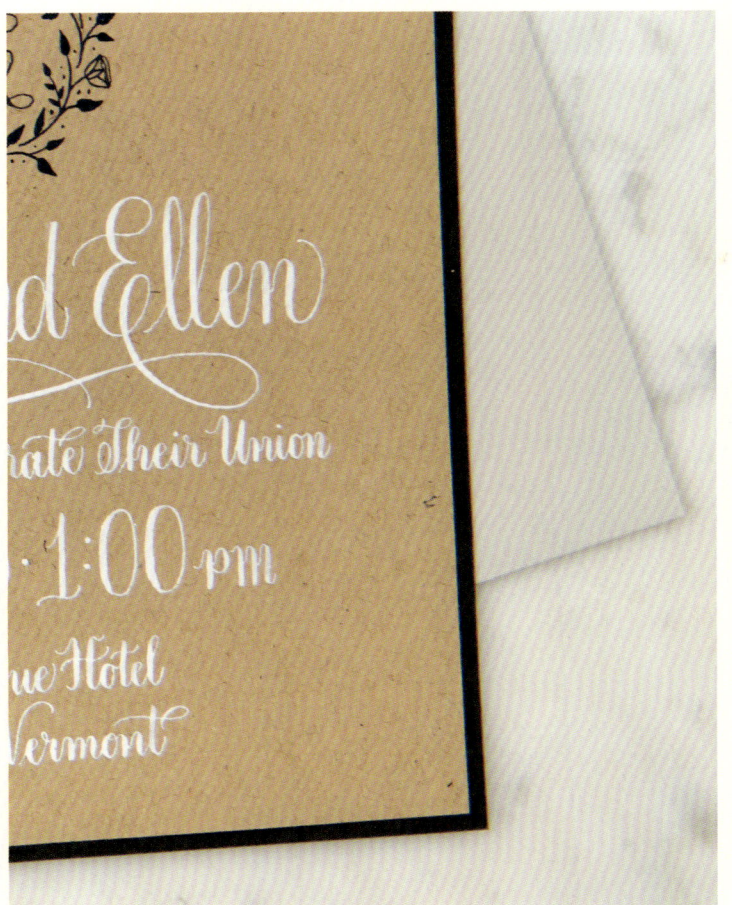

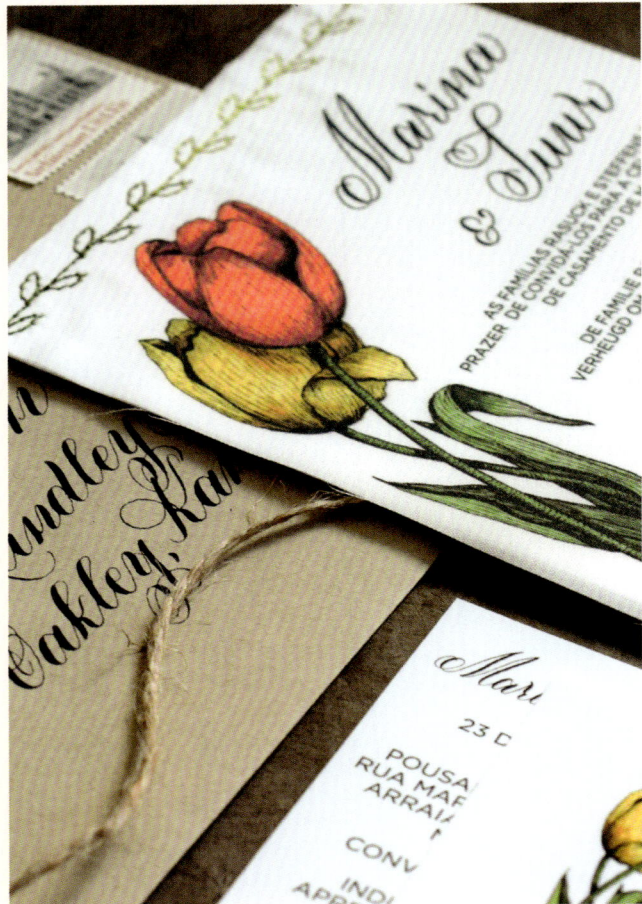

can add up quickly, not to mention the potential need for specialized tools or software. By knowing your limits, you can make informed choices about where to splurge and where to save.

- **Mix and match:** Perhaps the invitations themselves are printed, but you send them in hand-calligraphed envelopes. A hybrid approach can save both time and money, while still offering a personalized touch.
- **DIY smart:** Use resources like online tutorials and the talents of friends and family. If you're not sure how to do something, chances are that someone online can teach you. Recruit helpers to tie

everything together with a paper sash and slip it into an envelope. Incorporating others' talents not only adds a unique touch to your invitations but can also create a sense of community around the event.

- **Prioritize:** Decide which aspects of the invitation are most important. For example, if the budget is tight, you could design a hand-illustrated motif that is added to a digitally printed invitation. It's about finding that perfect balance that reflects your priorities, will appeal to your guests, and aligns with your vision.

Above left: Make your DIY invitations feel more substantial by gluing a piece of cardstock to the back. Cut the card about ¼in (5mm) larger than your invitation, then center the calligraphy piece on top of this.

Above right: Fabric wedding invitations are a unique handmade envelope concept. Use software like Photoshop to make your design, then upload it to a fabric printing website. Cut out the individual fabric invitations and sew them to cardstock.

Wedding invitation

Gallery

Use these examples to spark your inspiration. Typically, an invitation suite includes more than just the invitation, so consider what else you want to add. You could include detail cards, illustrated venue maps, RSVP cards, paper sashes (see p.170), and even ribbon.

1

Despite its flourishes, this design is legible because the flourishes are orderly. Look closely, and you'll notice that there aren't any stand-alone flourishes; they all connect to a letter. This invitation is a great example of why it's a good idea to mix calligraphy and sans serif lettering—the combination makes everything more legible.

2

Handmade paper is a fantastic choice for wedding invitations because of its rustic texture, heavy weight, and deckled edge. It can be tough to write on, so don't forget to use a runny ink and a fairly blunt nib such as the Brause Rose. To produce several hand-written invitations like this one, you can make a master design and use a light box to trace over it onto the handmade paper.

3

An earthy color scheme is always a classy choice. This square invitation was written on text-weight craft paper, which was then glued to a thick dark cardstock backing. I mixed a deep gray gouache to match the color of the backing. The star of this invitation is a floral wedding "logo" featuring the couple's first initials.

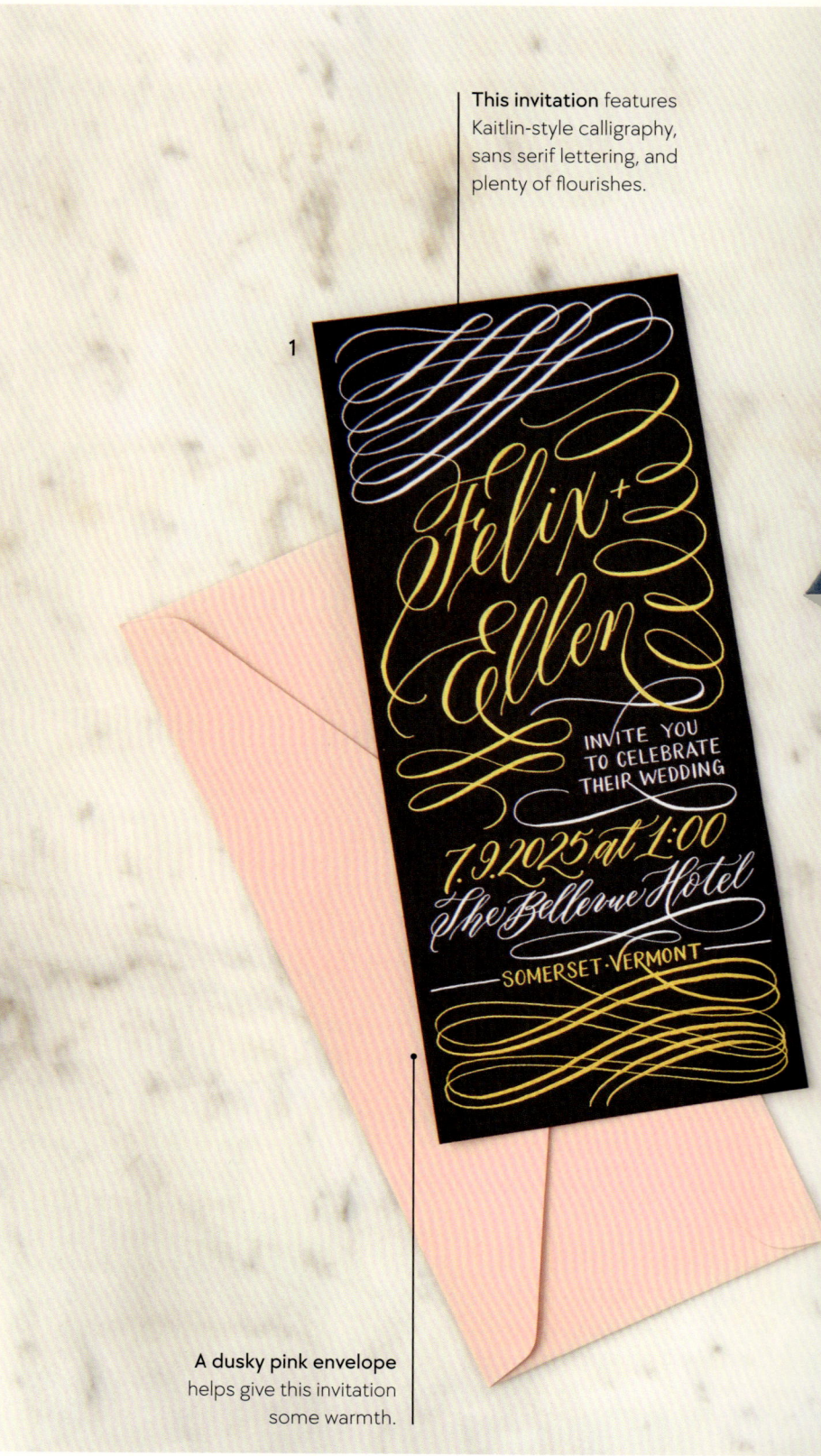

This invitation features Kaitlin-style calligraphy, sans serif lettering, and plenty of flourishes.

A dusky pink envelope helps give this invitation some warmth.

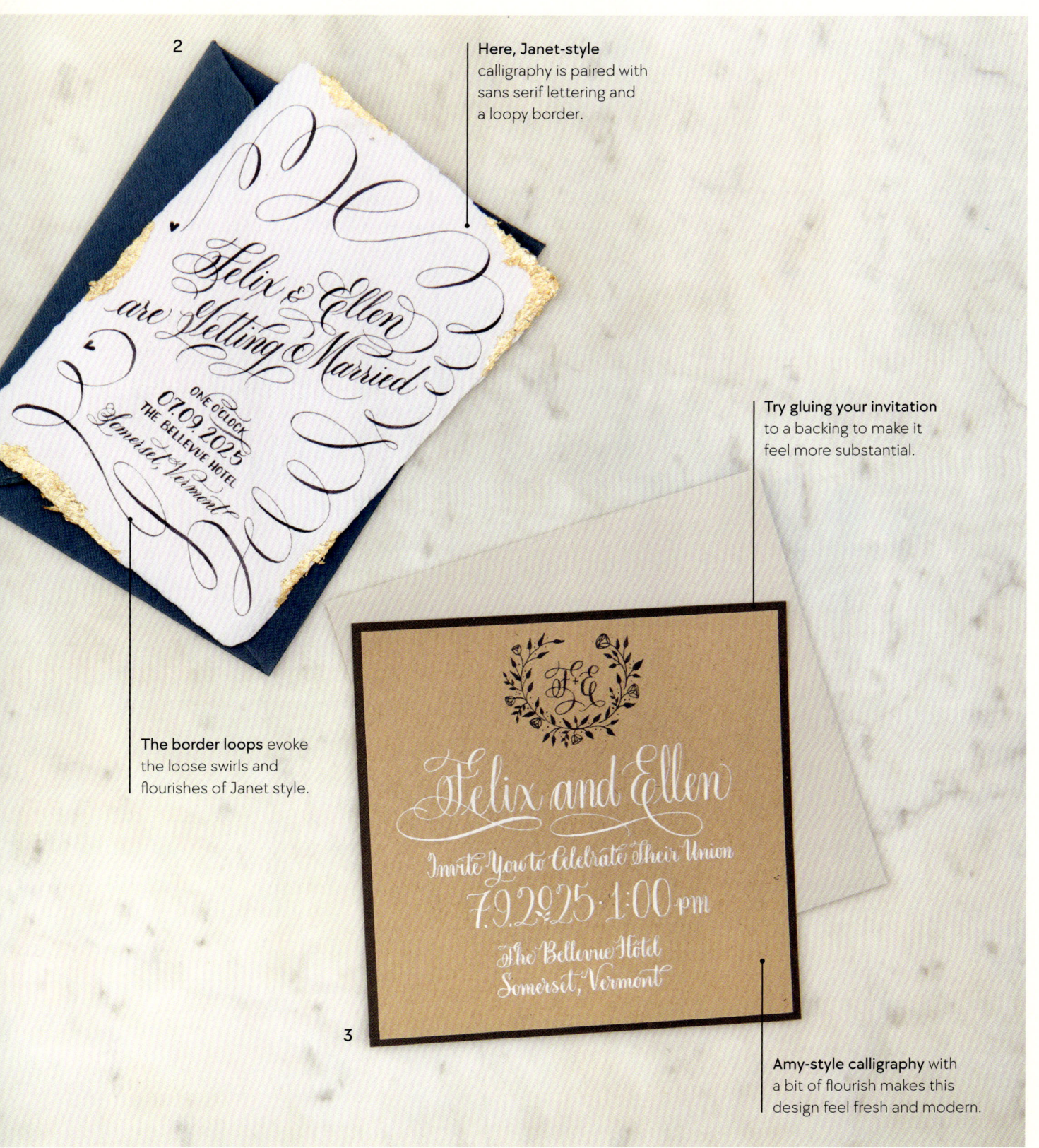

2

Here, Janet-style calligraphy is paired with sans serif lettering and a loopy border.

Felix & Ellen are Getting Married

ONE O'CLOCK
07.09.2025
THE BELLEVUE HOTEL
Somerset, Vermont

Try gluing your invitation to a backing to make it feel more substantial.

The border loops evoke the loose swirls and flourishes of Janet style.

3

Felix and Ellen

Invite You to Celebrate Their Union
7.9.2025 · 1:00 pm

The Bellevue Hotel
Somerset, Vermont

Amy-style calligraphy with a bit of flourish makes this design feel fresh and modern.

Dinner party place cards

These place cards, inspired by travels through Italy, are adorned with abundant loops and swirls. Accents of grape clusters and leaves suggest a bit of Bacchic fun.

● **DIFFICULTY**
advanced

Using an earthy color scheme—warm brown, mossy green, and deep purple—stays true to the Mediterranean theme. Consider making these place cards when you're hosting a truly special meal, and feel free to change the color scheme and the featured fruit or vegetable to suit the occasion. A good choice of paper for this project is handmade watercolor paper with deckled edges. If you cannot source that, use regular watercolor paper.

Drafting flourishes is the most time-consuming part of this project. Have fun with it and experiment with their positions until you get them just right. Making a pencil draft for a flourish-heavy piece like this one is important; otherwise, you might end up with awkward-looking loops and swirls.

SUPPLIES

5x3¼in (13x8.25cm) watercolor or handmade paper

Bone folder (optional)

Ruler

Graphite pencil

Eraser

Walnut ink

Small paintbrush

Light green watercolor paint

Deep violet watercolor paint

White ink

Nib (such as the Brause EF66) in the holder of your choice

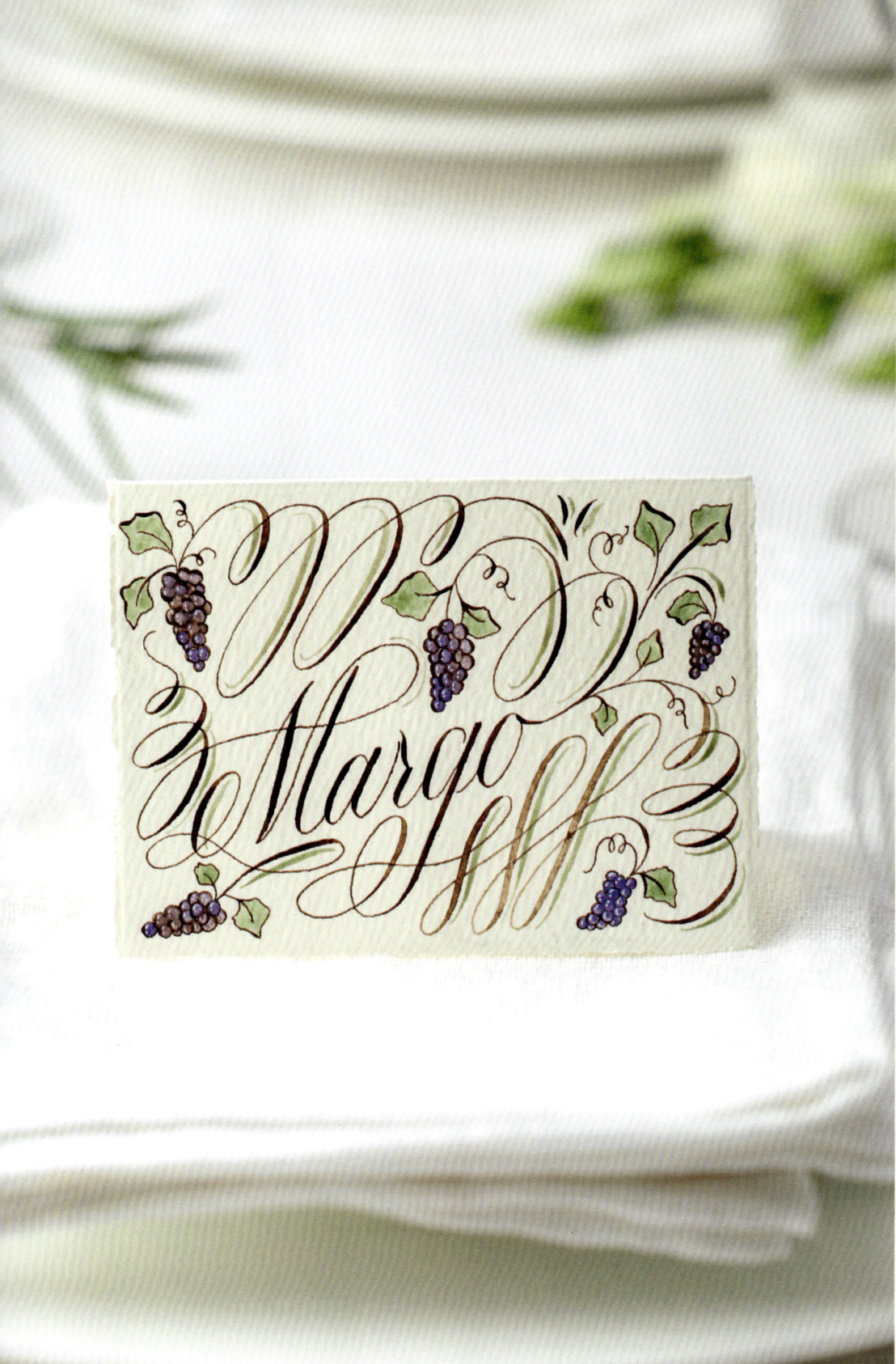

This project uses Flourish calligraphy (see pp.98–105), a very classic-looking style that gives you a lot of freedom to add flourishes. Practice on another piece of paper before going straight to your final version.

Make your guests feel special with a personalized place card.

Dinner party place cards

1

2

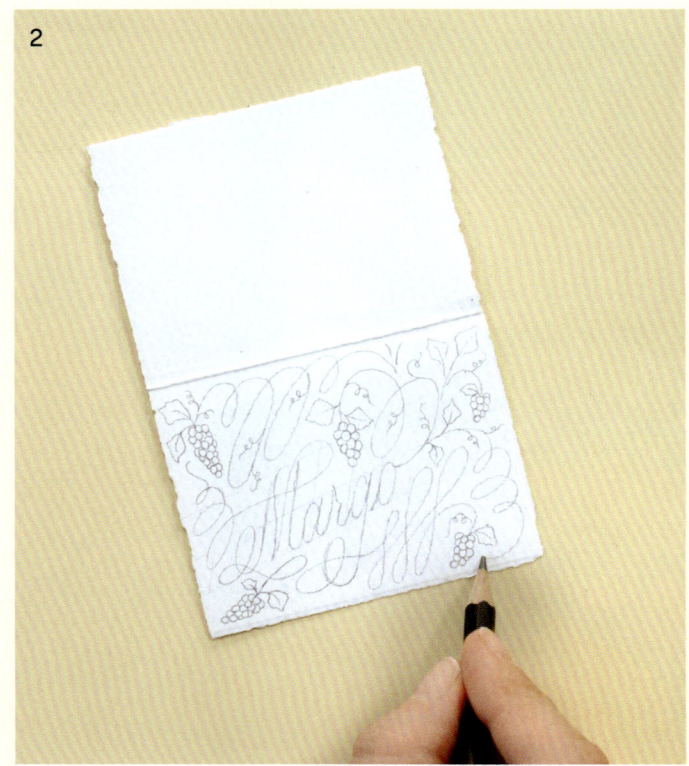

4

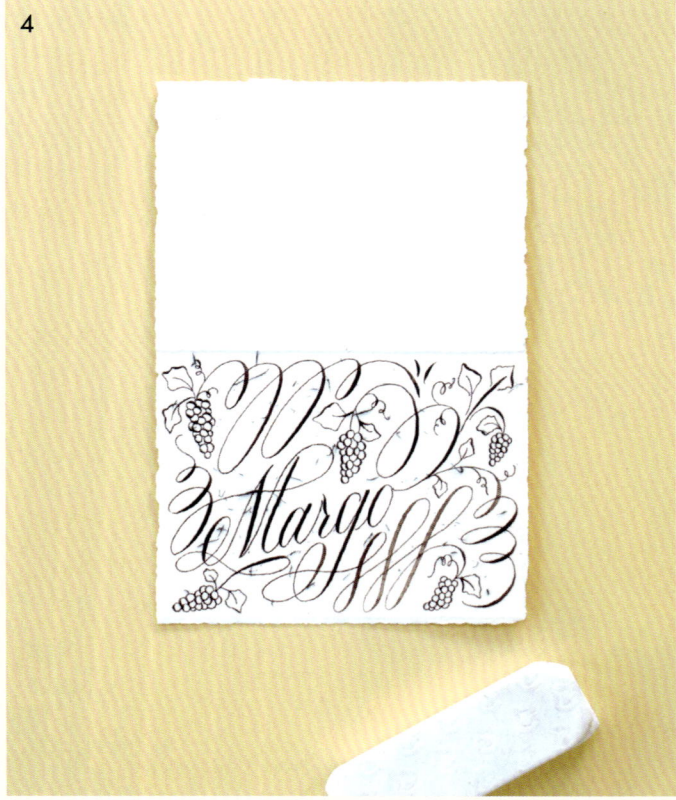

5

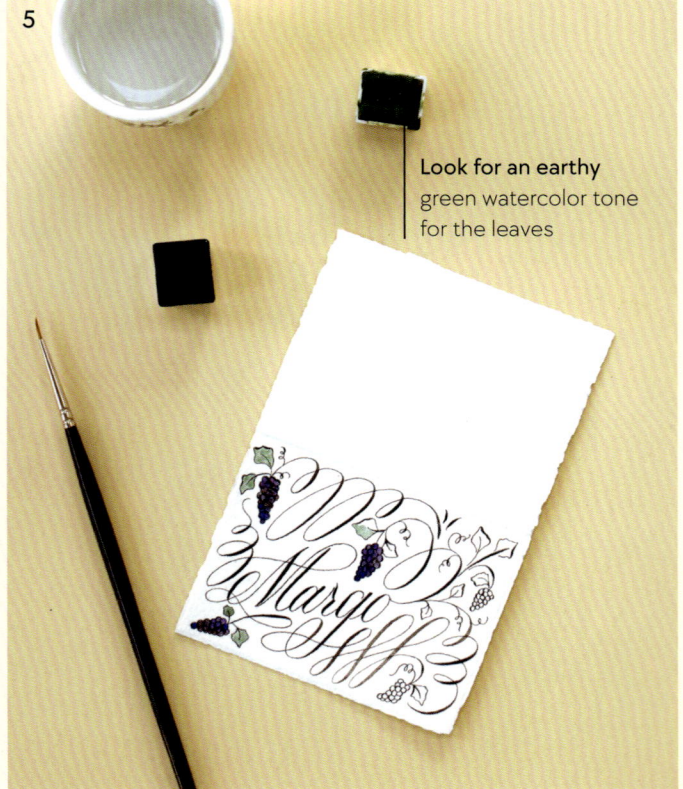

Look for an earthy green watercolor tone for the leaves

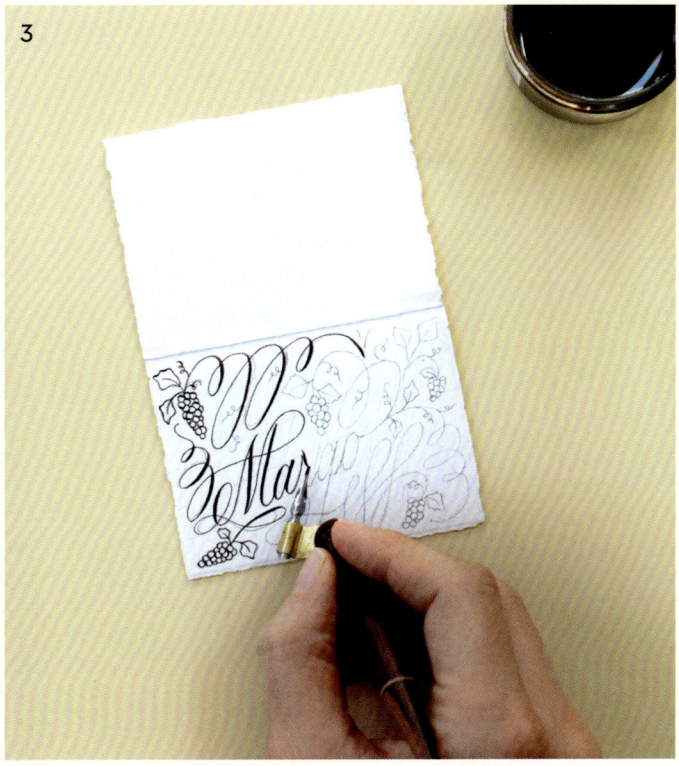

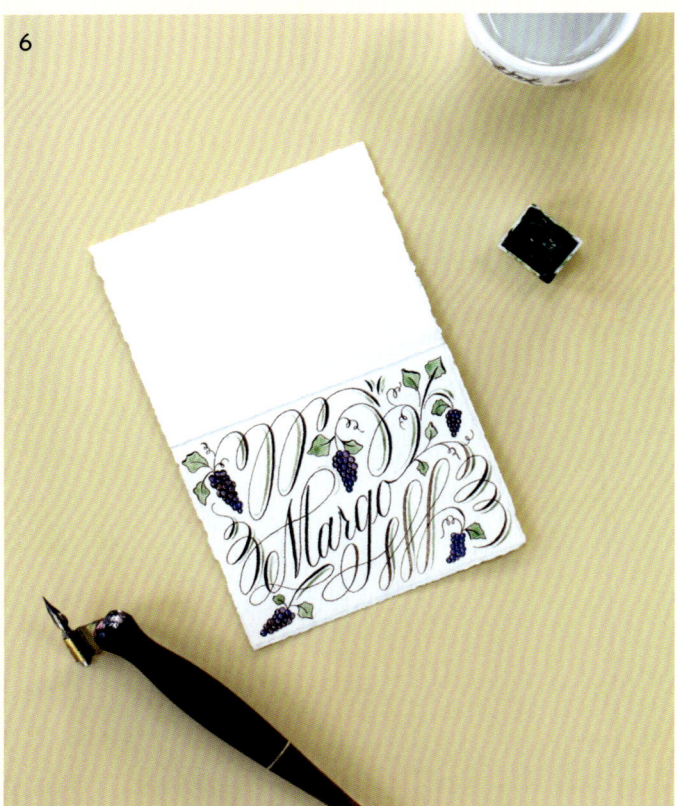

1 Fold your blank place card in half and use a bone folder or the edge of your ruler to make a crisp fold. Then, with a ruler and pencil, make three diagonal parallel guidelines across the front of your place card. If possible, include slant lines at an angle of 55 degrees. Then, in pencil, use Flourish-style calligraphy (see pp.98–105) to write the name of the person attending the party.

2 Use your pencil to flesh out the area around the name with plenty of flourishes and five grape bunches. Be sure to connect some of the flourishes to the recipient's name. Making a draft will ensure that the piece feels cohesive.

3 Dip your pointed pen into walnut ink, then slowly trace over the pencil lines. Work carefully to avoid smudging the ink as you make your way across the card. Don't forget to rotate the place card as needed while making your flourishes. This will allow you to achieve the most effective and comfortable writing position.

4 Once the ink dries (this should take only a couple of minutes), gently erase the pencil lines.

5 Use the green watercolor paint and a small paintbrush to add color to your leaves. Remember that walnut ink is not waterproof, so try not to let your green watercolor-soaked brush rest on the walnut ink outline around the leaf. Then, use the deep violet watercolor paint to fill in the grapes (see tip below.)

6 Apply some of the green paint to your nib, and use it to add green accents to the flourished strokes around the name. Don't flourish the name itself because the omission of flourishes will help it stand out. Finish by using white ink to add a tiny dot or two to the left part of every grape, which will help the fruit look polished and add some contrast.

Tip
Adding highlights

Since the grapes are so dense, your paint will probably interact with the walnut ink. This will muddle the brown and violet color, resulting in a more natural and authentic look. The grapes will stand out more when you add white highlights to them.

Dinner party place cards

Family bonsai

A family bonsai is an innovative take on the traditional family tree. The branches reach out expansively but remain anchored to the trunk, symbolizing the enduring ties among family members. This is especially appropriate for many modern families.

● DIFFICULTY
advanced

SUPPLIES

10 x 12in (25.4 x 30.5cm) off-white drawing paper or watercolor paper

Scrap paper

Graphite pencil

Eraser

Waterproof black ink

A medium-flex nib in a straight pen (such as the Nikko G)

A flexible nib in an oblique pen (such as the Brause EF66)

Gold watercolor paint

Small paintbrush

It's hard not to appreciate the bonsai's clean, organic shape and the fact that its roots end in the pot, symbolizing the foundational strength of the family unit.

Before you take on this project, be aware that it's not a quick endeavor. Your family bonsai is likely to take several days to create. As you work, remember that you're making a family heirloom—something that will be passed down for generations. When preparing your pencil draft, give yourself time to take a step back and double-check that you've got the balance of branches right. Then, trace over your work with ink and add gold to the leaves. Remember that just because you've applied ink to the artwork, that doesn't mean you're finished. Give yourself a break of several hours or days, then prop your drawing up and stand at least 3 feet away. Look at the piece with fresh eyes and consider what it might need. For example, you may decide that your tree could use more contrast in the branches and a darker pot. Once you're happy with how your family bonsai looks both close-up and from farther away, you're finished.

STYLE

Try using Janet-style calligraphy here, adding flourishes as needed to fill in space.

All families are different. Part of the challenge is to create a bonsai to fit your family.

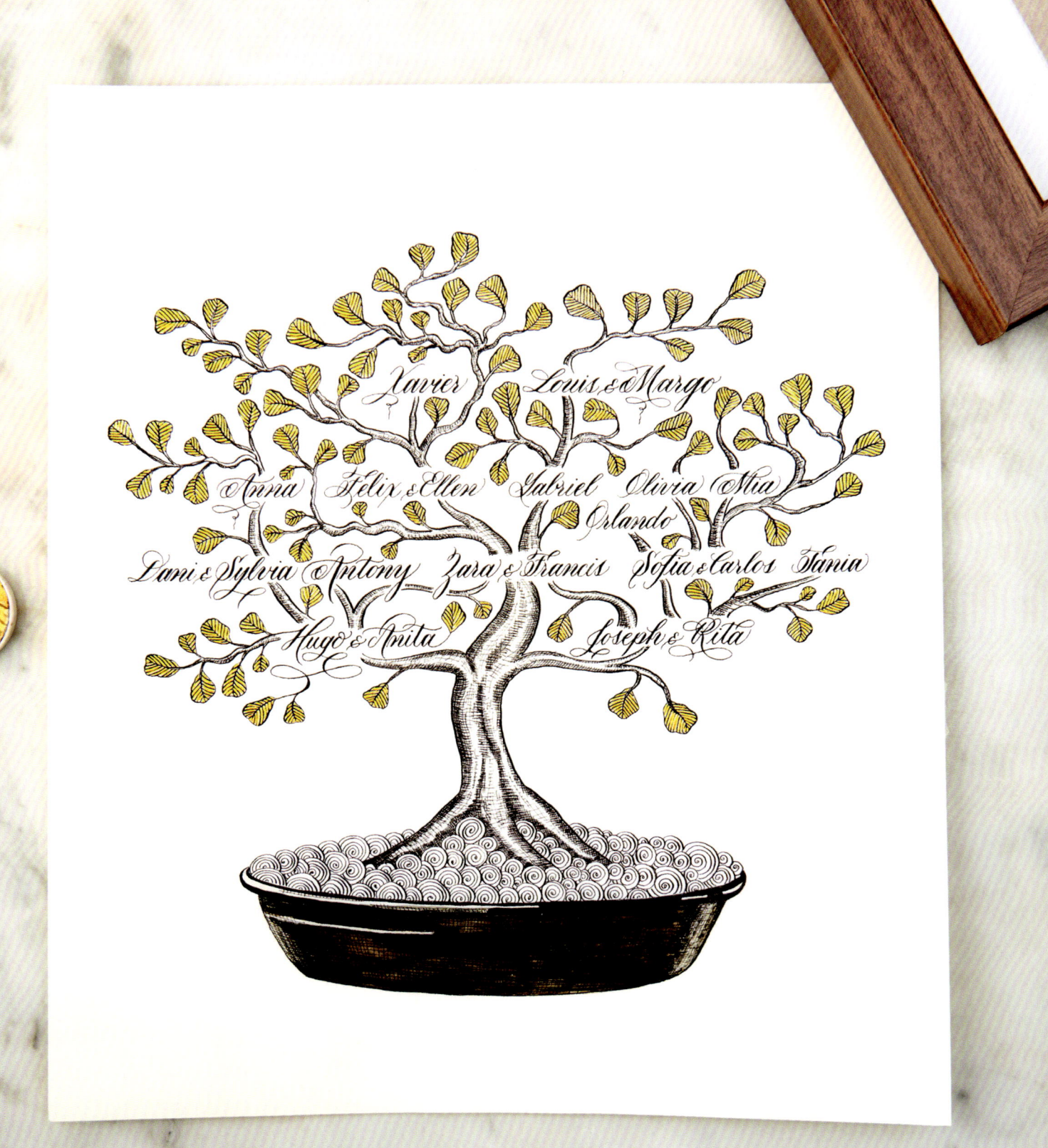

Family bonsai

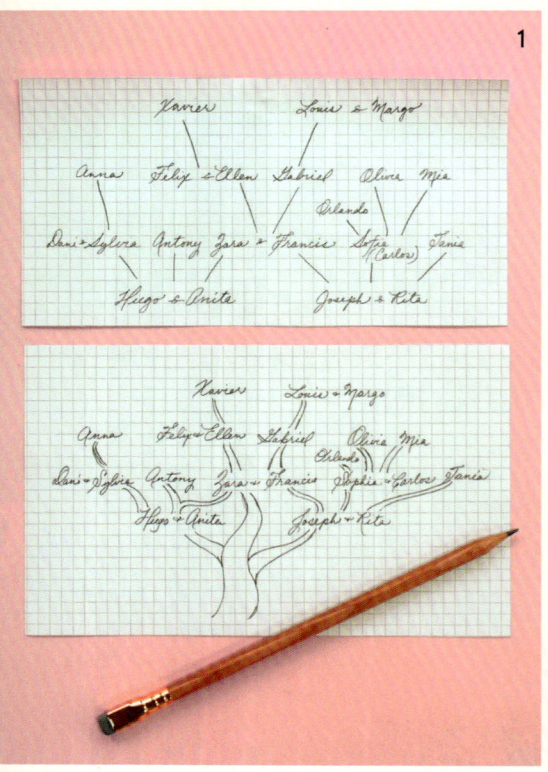

1

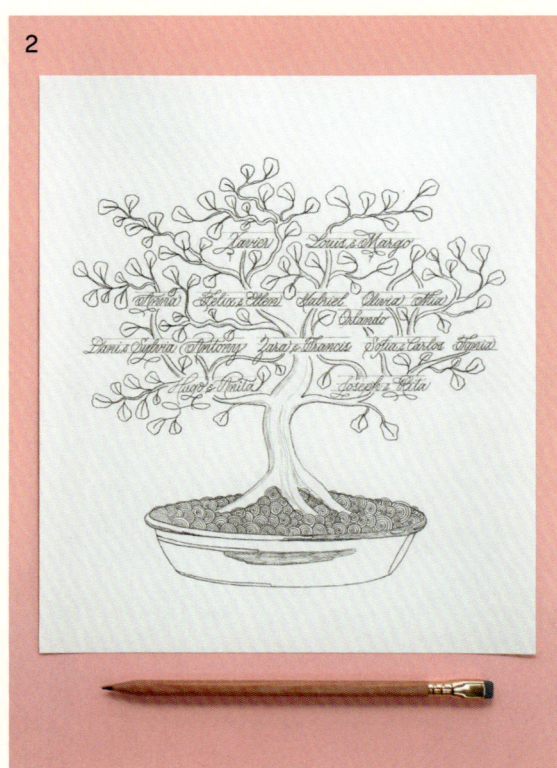

2

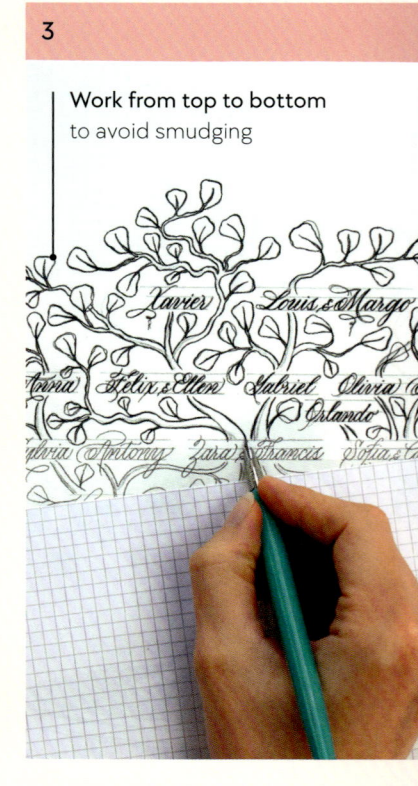

3

Work from top to bottom to avoid smudging

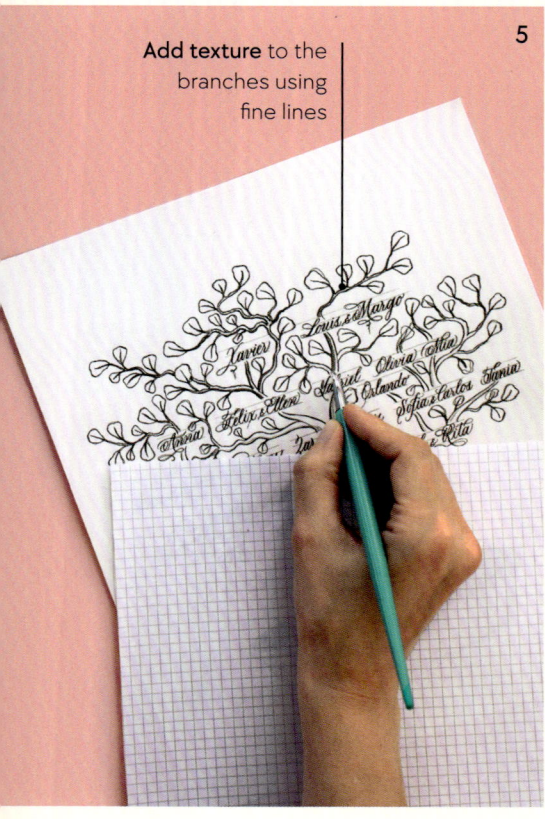

5

Add texture to the branches using fine lines

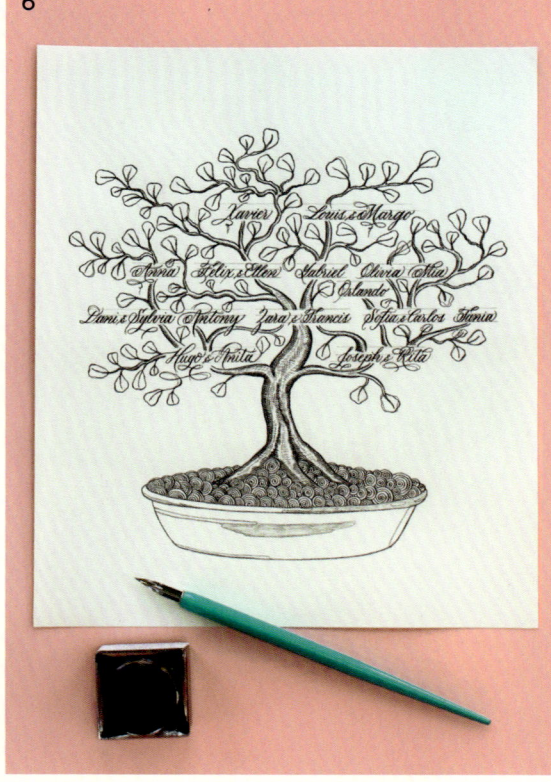

6

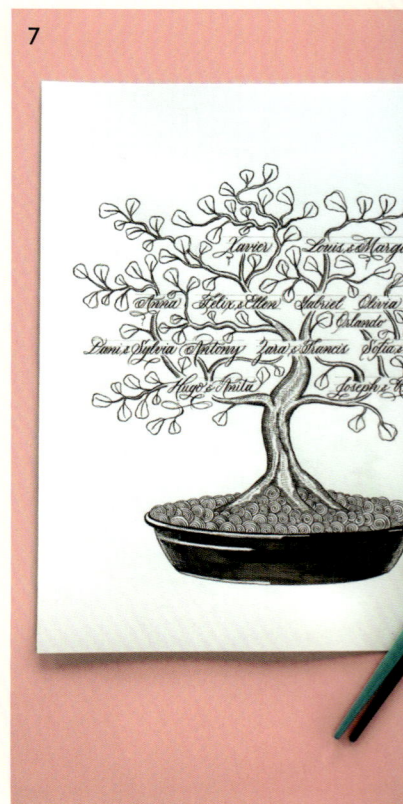

7

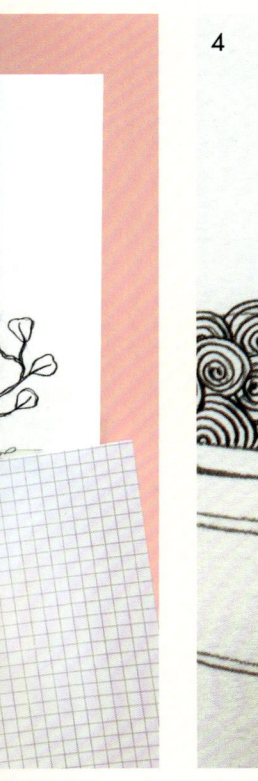

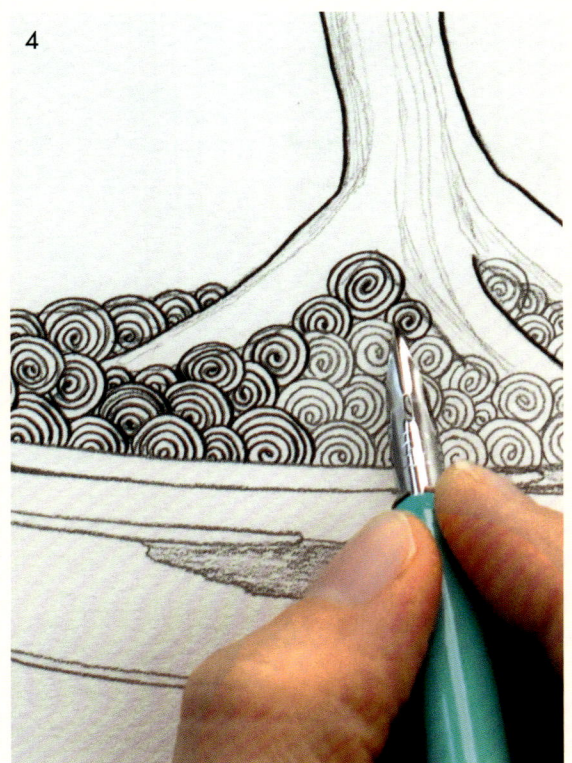

4

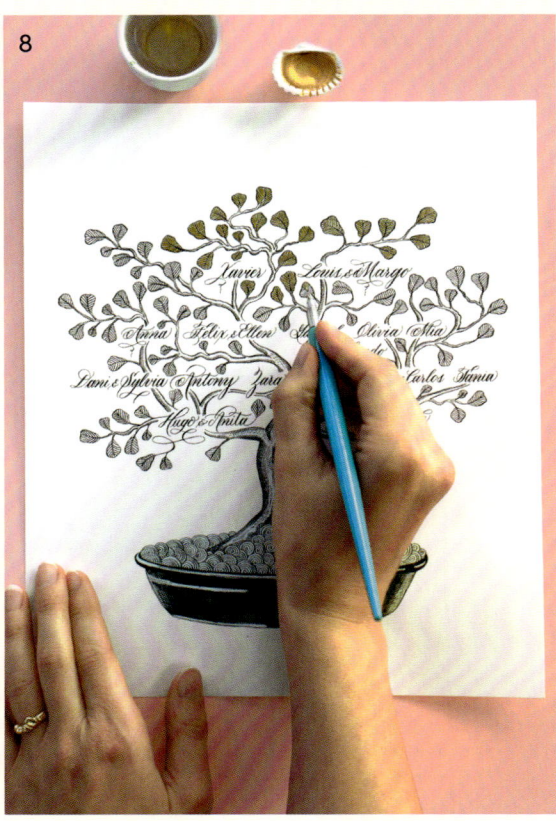

8

1 Write down the names of the people in your family and use lines to signify their relationships to each other. Then, draw a rough sketch of the tree and branch design.

2 Use the sketch to make a pencil draft on your chosen paper. Write the names on the page, then add the branches, trunk, and pot. Draw additional small branches and leaves.

3 Place some scrap paper under your hand to prevent your pencil draft from smudging. Then, work your way down the tree tracing over branches and leaf outlines with your medium-flex nib and black ink. When writing the names, you can switch to a flexible nib in an oblique pen in order to strike a good contrast.

4 Continue to work your way down the tree until you've traced over the entire pencil draft. Add swirls to represent the soil.

5 Now, add dimension to the tree branches and trunk with crosshatching. Begin by drawing small, densely spaced curved lines that hug the horizontal contour of the edge of a branch. Then, draw several densely spaced lines that follow the vertical contour of the branch to cross the lines that you just drew.

6 Continue to crosshatch your way down to the roots of the bonsai. Rotate your page as needed in order to give yourself the best angle, and take plenty of breaks. Crosshatching takes time, but the results are worth it.

7 Dilute some of the black ink with water. Then apply it to your bonsai's pot using a small paintbrush, leaving a few contoured shapes to suggest highlights. Once the ink has dried, you can crosshatch over the pot to give it a little more texture.

8 When the ink is dry, erase any pencil draft lines. Work slowly to avoid creasing the paper. Use black ink to draw several diagonal veins on the inside of each leaf. Then, use gold watercolor paint on your nib to draw diagonal veins between each pair of black diagonal veins.

Tip
Crosshatching

This is a technique where two layers of parallel lines are drawn at right angles to each other to create shading and texture in a drawing. This method creates a range of tonal effects that allows for the depiction of light, shadow, form, and depth.

Family bonsai

keepsake birth certificate

When a baby is born, the parents usually receive an official birth certificate. While this document is important, it isn't usually visually appealing. This project is designed to fix that problem with a keepsake that will be cherished for years to come.

● DIFFICULTY
intermediate

With the help of a couple of strategic flourishes and a sweet gold heart, this informal birth certificate celebrates a baby's birth in a classic and timeless way. The addition of the stamped feet makes each certificate unique to the baby it's created for.

The example shown here includes minimal information, but you can add any details that are important to you. These could include the baby's birth weight, height, head circumference, the parents' names, attendants, and relevant doctors' names.

SUPPLIES

Drawing paper in any size that suits you

Skin-safe stamp pad

Graphite pencil

Eraser

Ruler

A medium-flex nib (such as the Nikko G) and pen holder

A flexible nib (such as the Brause EF66) and pen holder

Sumi ink

Gold watercolor paint

Paintbrush

STYLE

Flourished calligraphy style has been used here as it is highly decorative, and the flourishes can be used to fill the page. Sans serif block letters work well in contrast to provide further details.

Make this heirloom piece for yourself or for a friend or relative to celebrate the birth of a baby.

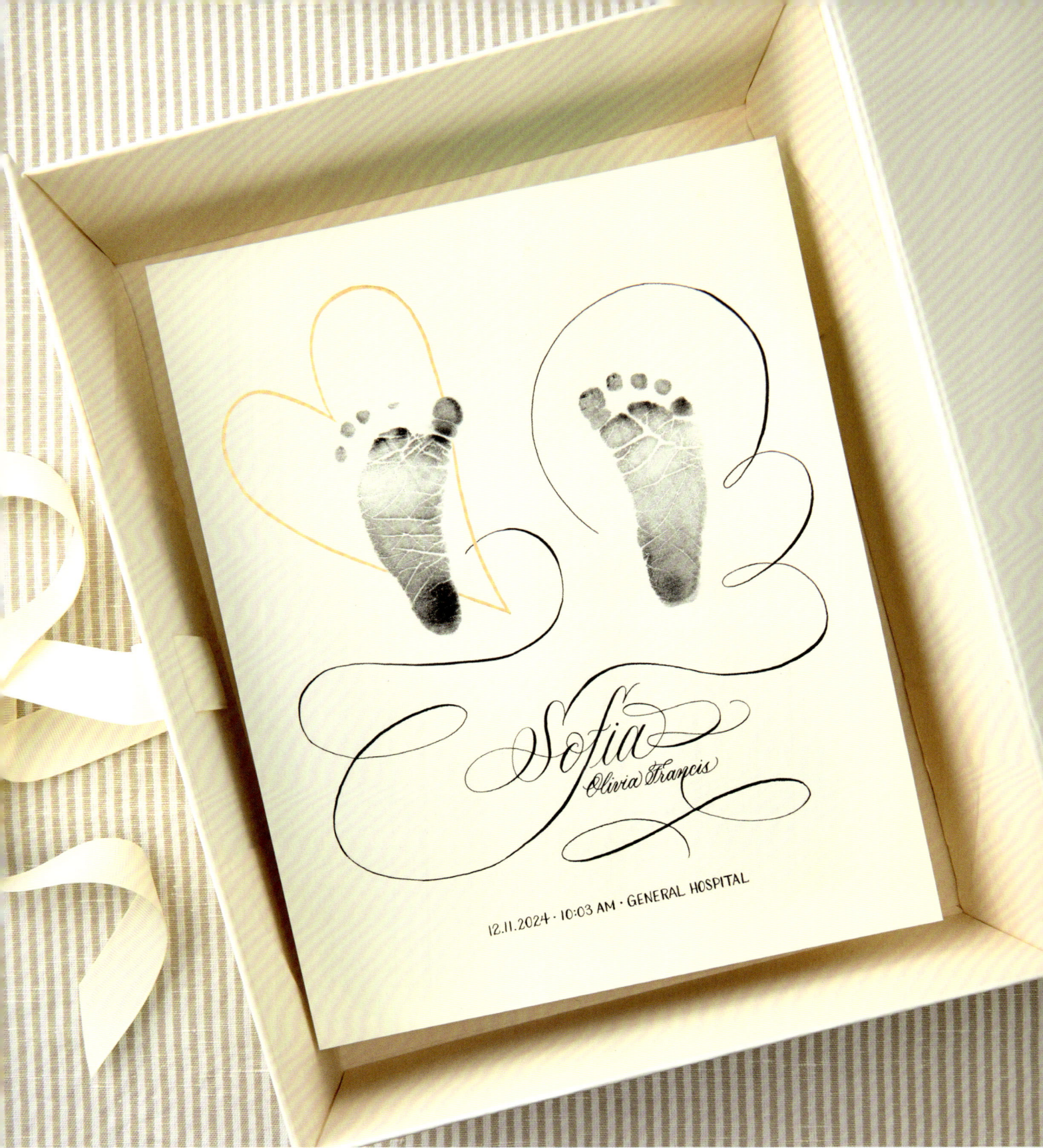

Sofia
Olivia Francis

12.11.2024 · 10:03 AM · GENERAL HOSPITAL

Keepsake birth certificate

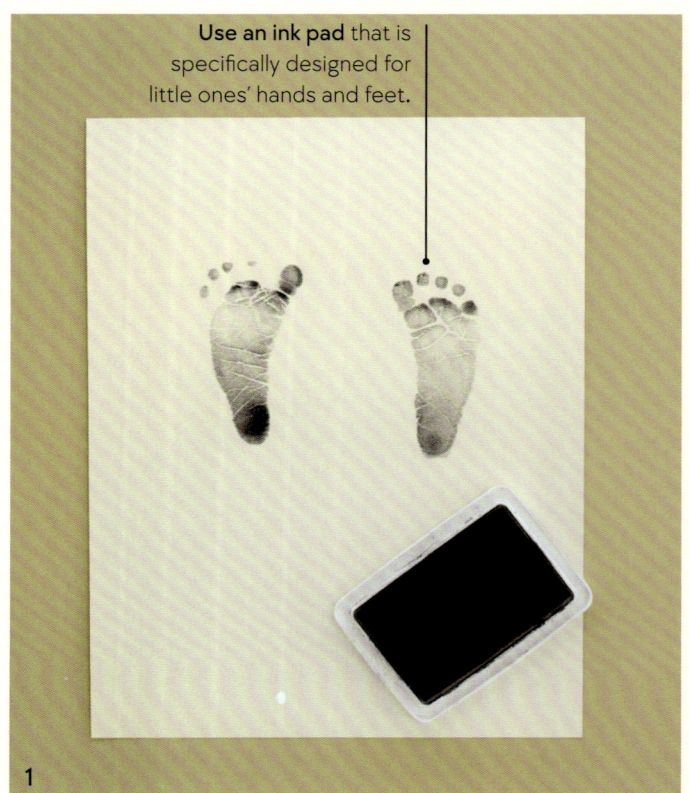

Use an ink pad that is specifically designed for little ones' hands and feet.

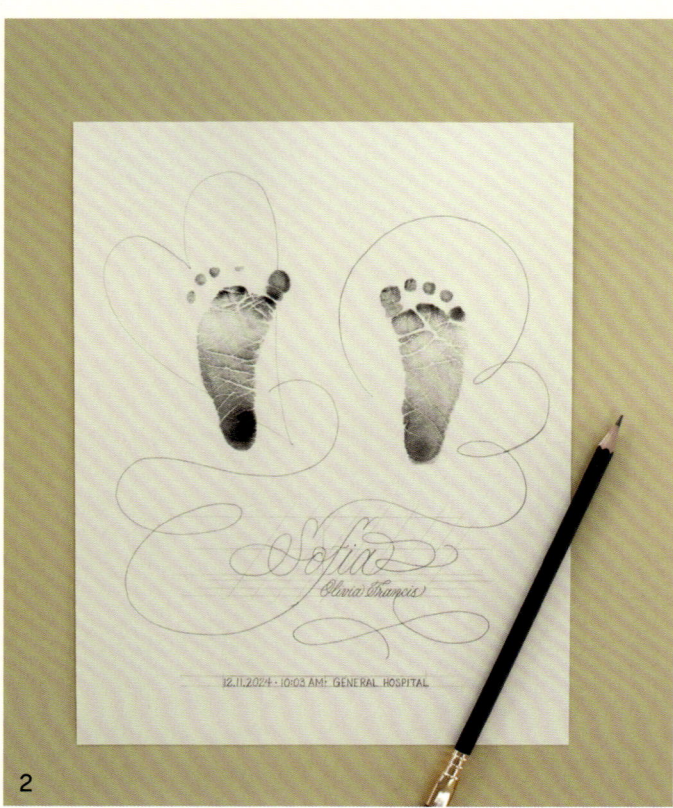

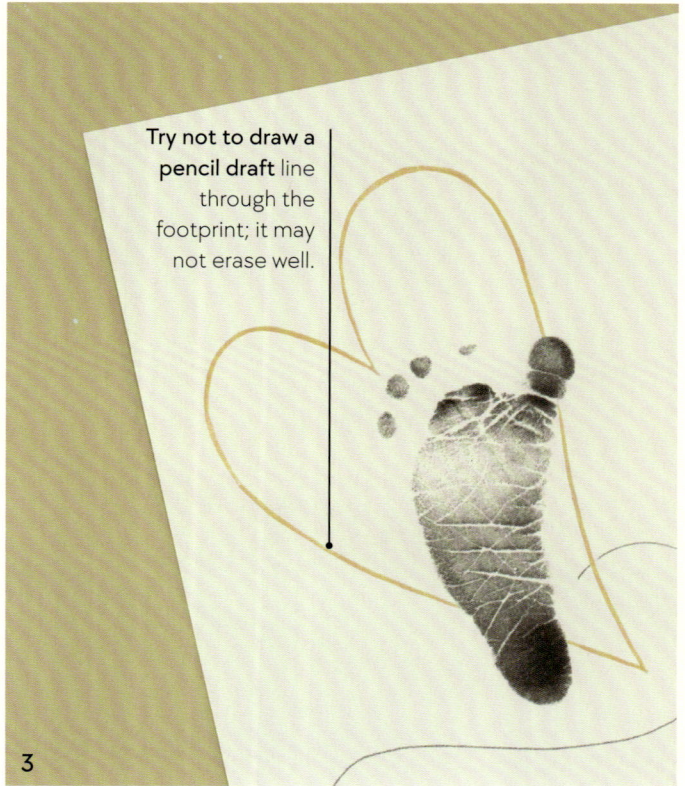

Try not to draw a pencil draft line through the footprint; it may not erase well.

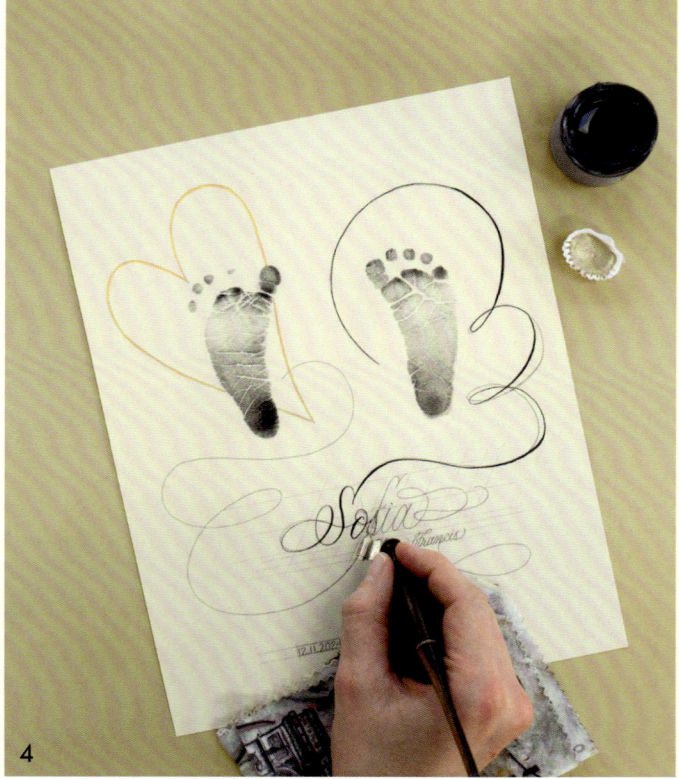

1 Begin by using the stamp pad to put the impressions of the baby's feet on your drawing paper. If possible, make footprint impressions on at least three sheets of paper, in case you need to start again later.

2 Use a ruler and pencil to make guidelines for the baby's first name under the feet. Draw smaller guidelines below for the baby's other names and at the bottom of the page for the baby's birth information. Use your pencil to add a draft version of the calligraphy and lettering. Experiment with different flourishes to unify the piece. Add a long flourish from the first letter of baby's name to "hug" the left footprint. Then, add a flourish from another letter of baby's name to circle around the right footprint.

3 Use the paintbrush to load gold watercolor paint onto the flexible nib, then trace over the heart with it. Clean the nib and leave the paint to dry.

4 Use the flexible nib and sumi ink to trace over the flourishes, then the medium-flex nib for the smaller calligraphy and hand-lettered details.

5 Wait until the ink and paint have dried, then erase the pencil guidelines.

Tip

Flourishes

When drawing the long flourishes, make sure your hand is warmed up and try to wear a long-sleeved shirt, to help your hand glide across the page.

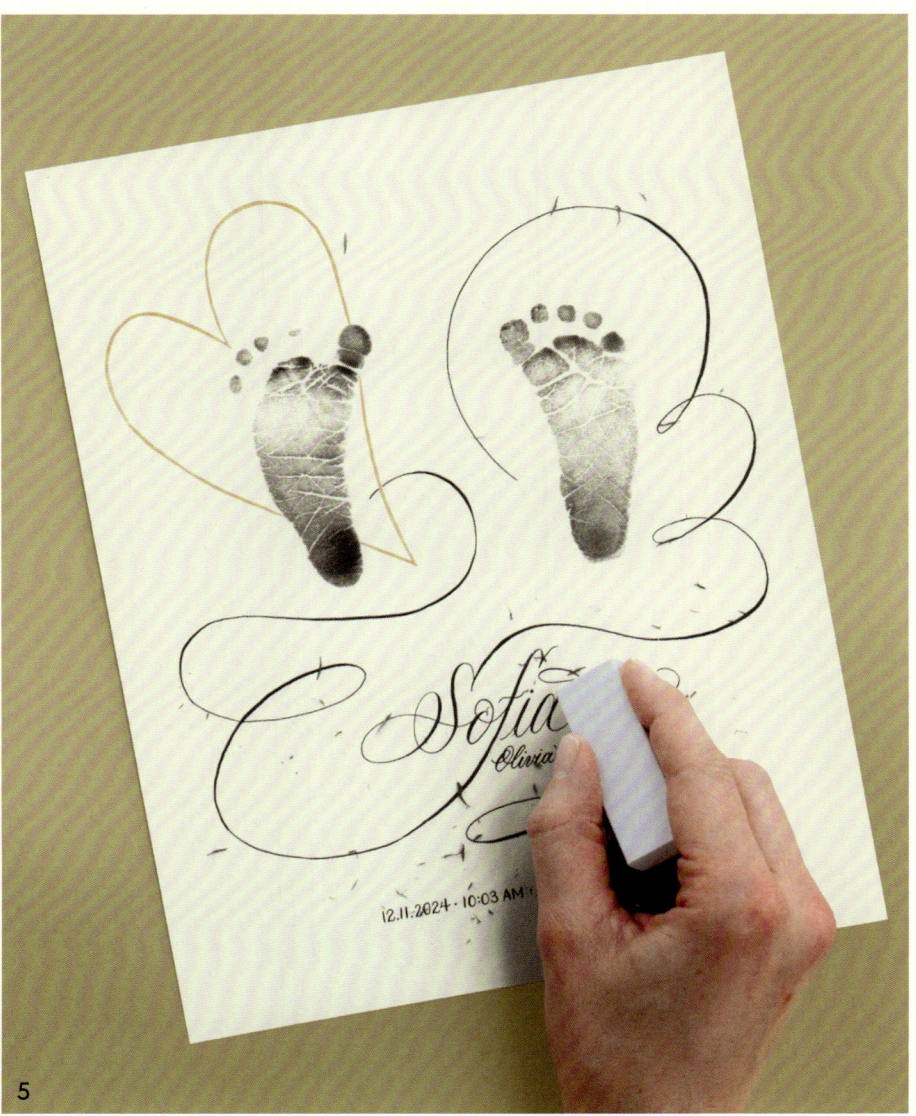

5

Keepsake birth certificate

Nursery art

This nursery artwork celebrates the classic nursery rhyme "Frère Jacques." You could devote one creation session to tracing over the pencil draft. Then, the next day, focus on adding in the crosshatching.

● DIFFICULTY
intermediate

For this project, you can use any paper that suits you, although Ingres paper is ideal. It is a textured drawing paper named after the painter Jean-Auguste-Dominique Ingres. This durable paper is traditionally made from cotton, has a finely ribbed surface that is great for pointed pen calligraphy, and comes in a range of soft colors.

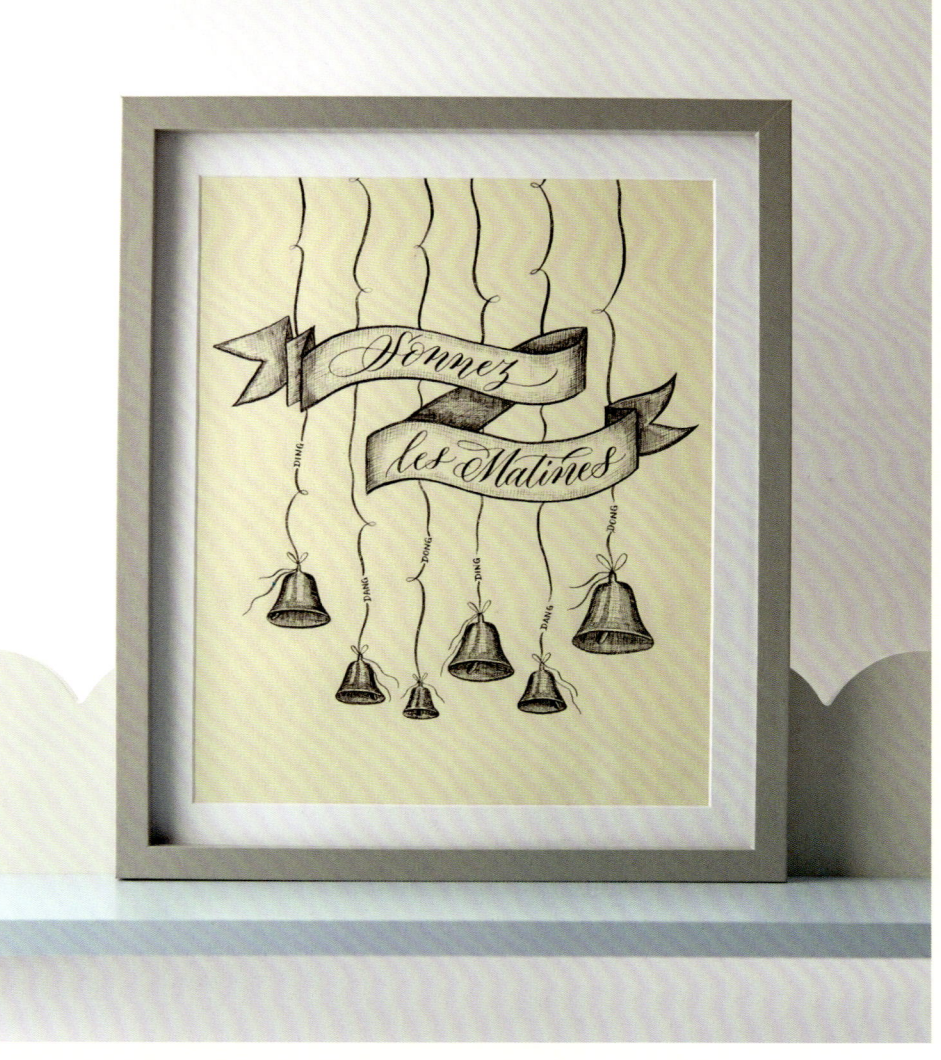

SUPPLIES

8x10in (20x25cm) pastel-colored Ingres paper

Graphite pencil

Ruler

Eraser

Iron gall ink

A very flexible nib (such as the Brause Rose) in the holder of your choice

A medium-flex nib (such as the Nikko G) in a straight pen

1 Divide your paper into four quadrants using a faint pencil line. Then, draw the two-part banner in the upper center of the page. Add six wavy lines, some with a loop or two, behind the banner at regular intervals. Draw assorted sizes of bells to connect to the loops. Then, write "Sonnez" in the top part of the banner and "les Matines" in the bottom part. Finish by writing the nursery rhyme's bell sounds ("Ding, dang, dong, ding, dang, dong") directly into the wavy lines using sans serif print.

2 Next, use a very flexible nib to trace over your pencil lines. Protect your paper from the oils on your palms with a piece of scrap paper.

3 Use your medium-flex nib in a straight pen to add crosshatched detail to your piece. Draw tiny lines closely spaced together, and then overlay additional sets of lines at different angles to build up texture and shading. Start with one direction, then cross over these lines with another set at an angle to create depth. To finish, carefully erase any pencil guidelines.

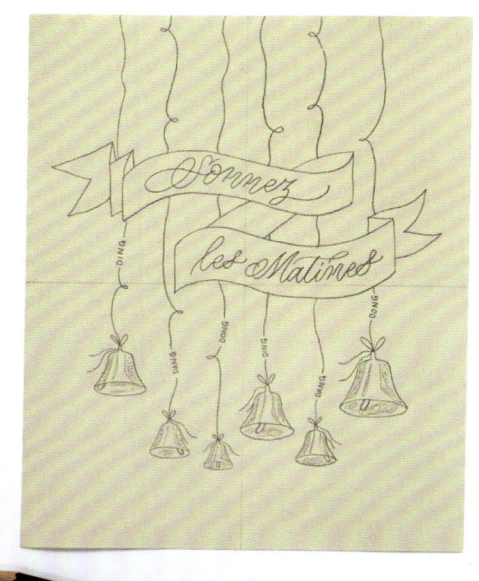

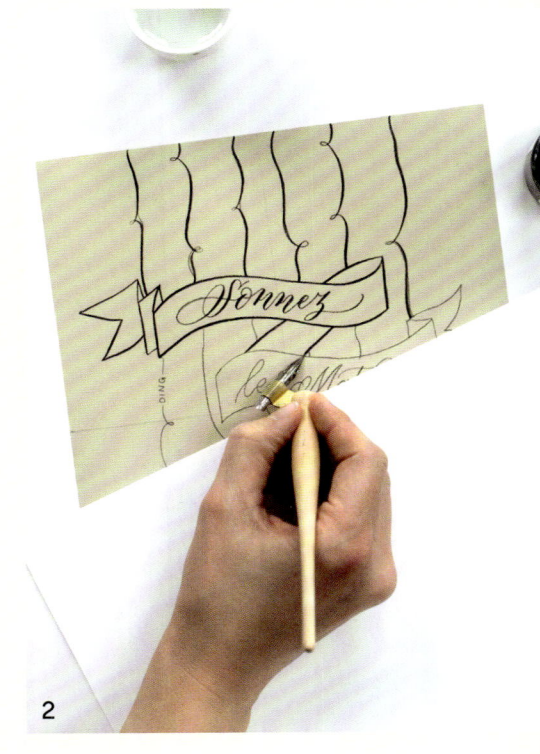

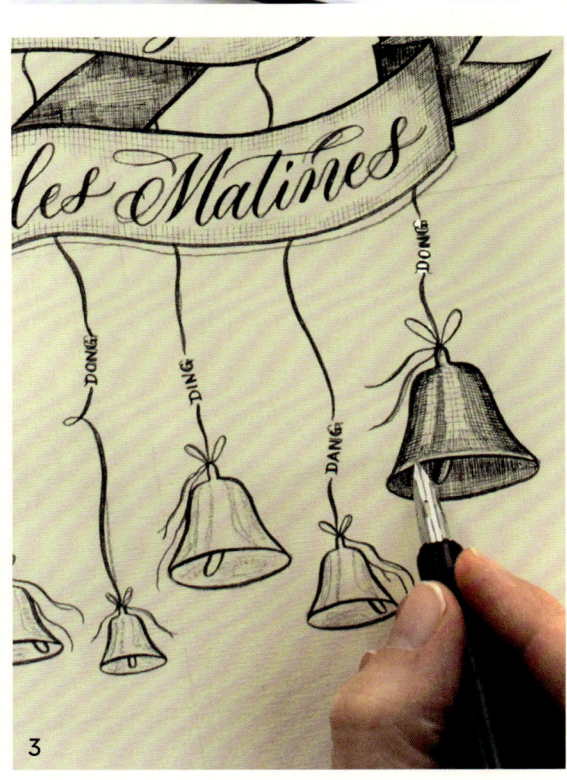

STYLE

The calligraphy for "Sonnez les Matines" is written using Kaitlin-style calligraphy. This is a good choice for writing on a curved baseline.

Nursery art

Ampersand art

This calligraphy ampersand art tutorial stands out for its unique approach to personalizing art with meaningful words, transforming the symbol into a canvas that narrates shared memories and bonds.

● DIFFICULTY
beginner

SUPPLIES

Computer, tablet, and printer (optional)

5x7in (13x18cm) handmade cotton paper

Pencil

Ink, gouache, or watercolor tones of your choice

Pointed pen and nib

Eraser

This project can be endlessly adapted to suit the recipient. It doesn't necessarily need to be an ampersand—for example, if a coworker is moving on, you could create a calligraphy-filled company logo to highlight fun memories from working together. Before you begin, write up a list of 10–15 fond memories or words that remind you of the recipient. This could include cities you have visited, inside jokes, or foods that you both enjoy. You can use any color scheme you prefer for the inks and the paper, as long as your choice maintains a strong contrast between the two. However, it is worth noting that creating this project on light-colored paper will usually be faster, as it allows you to trace the ampersand (or other letter or symbol) from a reference underneath. With a darker card or paper, you will need to draw an outline of your design freehand.

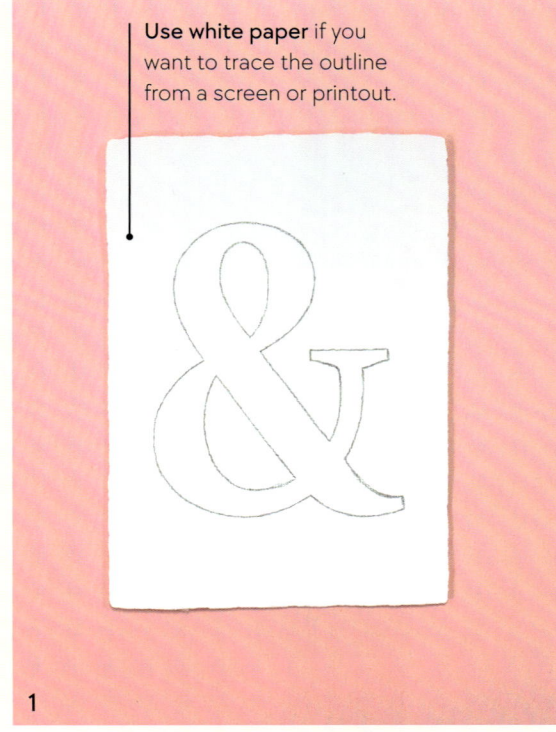

Use white paper if you want to trace the outline from a screen or printout.

1

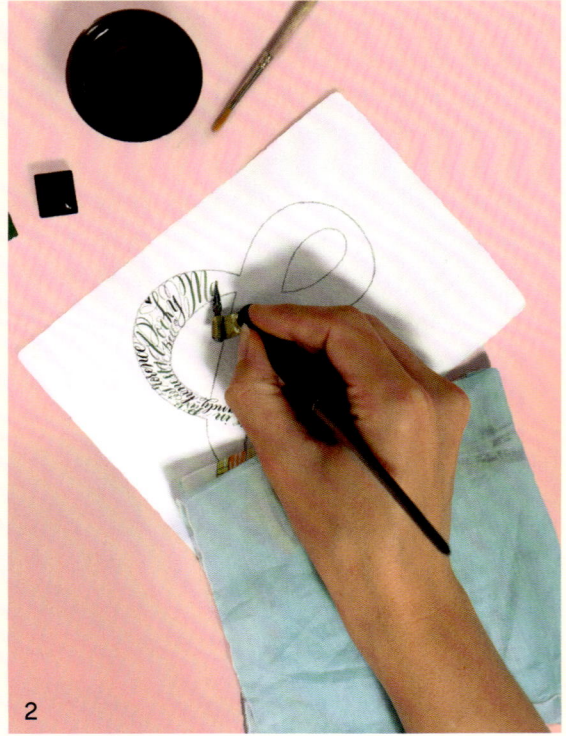

2

1 Type a large serif ampersand using a word processing program, use the template on page 196 as a reference, or sketch the outline freehand. If using light-colored paper, trace the outline in pencil, either from a printout of the reference or using your computer or tablet screen as a light box.

2 With your memory list nearby, begin to fill in the outline. For an ampersand, you may find it easiest to start at the top left of the serif before rotating the paper as you work your way around the curve. Switch between inks as you complete one memory and move on to the next.

3 Continue to follow the outline of the ampersand, following the direction you would follow if you were writing it out normally. Experiment with writing out memories in different sizes to fill the space, or break words and phrases apart in awkward spots. Move carefully across the paper to avoid smudging.

4 Once the outline is filled, allow several hours for the ink to dry fully, then use a clean, reliable eraser to rub off your pencil draft. Finally, mount or frame the piece, ready to present it to the recipient.

STYLE

This project uses Kaitlin-style calligraphy (see pp.74–81), because it can be used without a pencil draft, and it allows for the most freedom for varying the height of the strokes in order to fill space.

Tip

Avoid ink smudges

Place a piece of fabric or paper under your hand to protect your paper from the natural oils in your skin. Oil-coated paper doesn't receive ink very well.

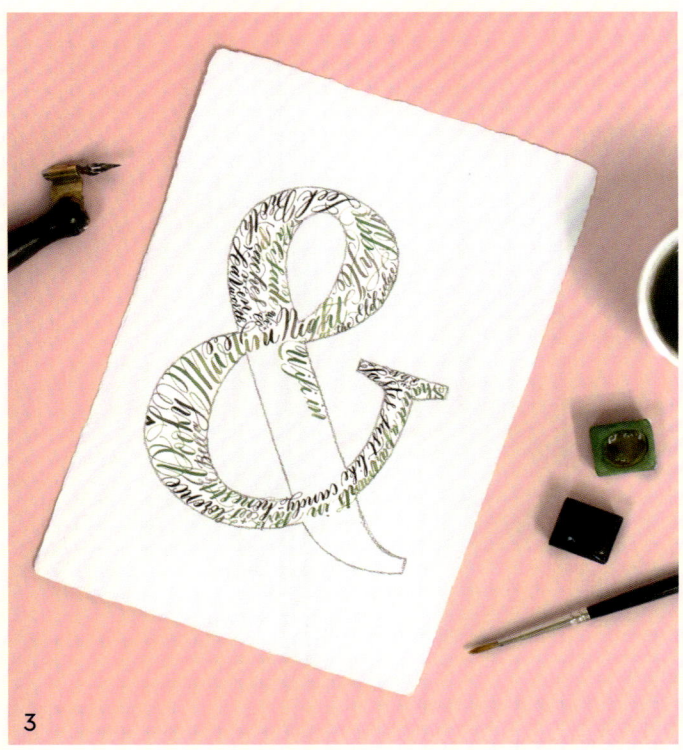

3

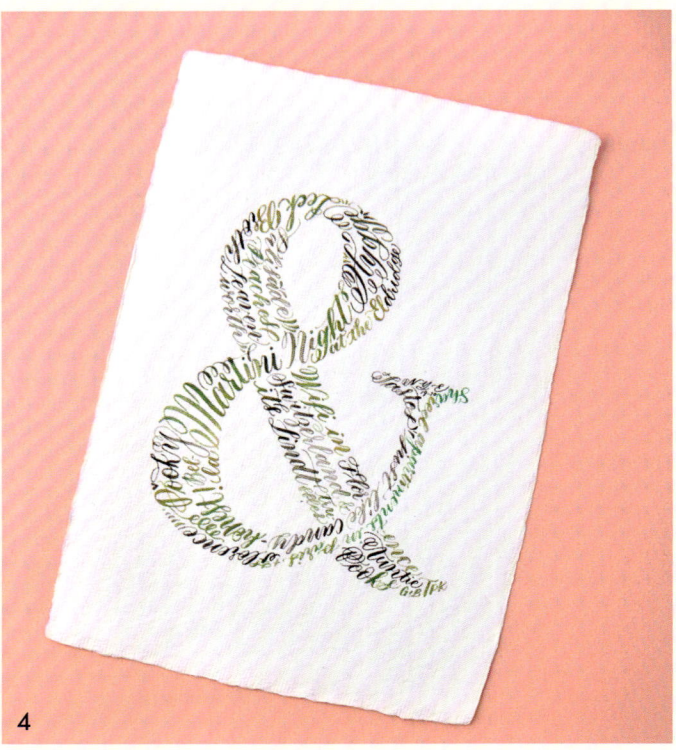

4

Ampersand art

Flourished map

This project goes to show that not all calligraphy has to be rooted in script. Instead, it uses Lasso lettering and copious flourishes to capture a country's colors and regions in a beautiful map.

SUPPLIES

10x12in (25.4x30.5cm) pastel-colored Ingres paper

Graphite pencil

Eraser

Iron gall ink

Red ink

Dark gold watercolor paint

A small very flexible nib (such as the Brause EF66) and pen holder

Don't be fooled by the simple steps that are required to make this project—it's a time investment. Plan to spend a few days creating it.

For this project, you'll need three distinct ink or watercolor paint colors. The colors that you use for this project will depend on the country that you've chosen to create. For the example shown here—Germany—the obvious colors to use were black, yellow, and red. For a country that is associated with two colors, like Australia (green and yellow), you could use light green, dark green, and yellow. If you want to show a region or a state, there may be particular colors that are the obvious choice or you could pick any colors that suit you.

If the map isn't densely packed with flourishes, its shape won't be recognizable. Don't be shy about putting in those loops and swirls!

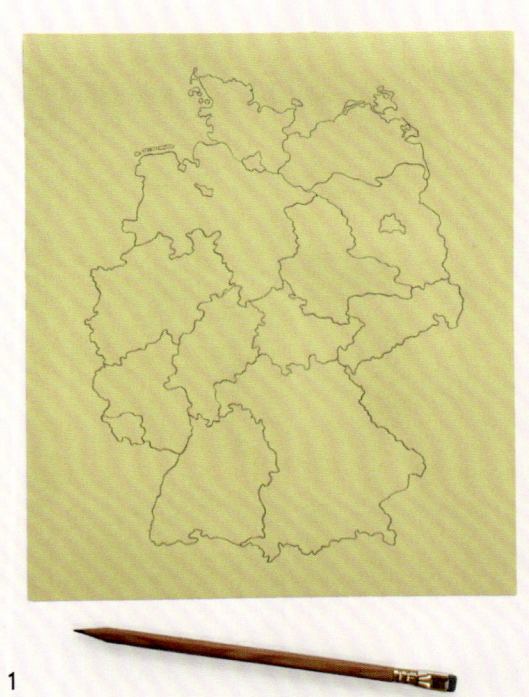

1

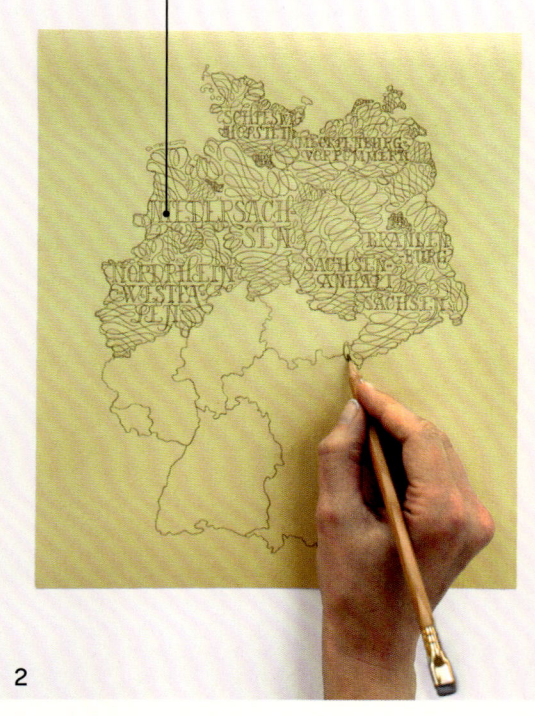

2

1 Print out a map of the country or region that you want to use, making sure that it includes state or region boundaries. Put the map behind the Ingres paper, then place both on top of a light box or against a bright window. Trace over the outlines that you see through the Ingres paper with your pencil.

2 Use your pencil to write the map's region names in flourished serif block letters in the Lasso style (see p.107). Extend flourishes to the perimeters of the state/region boundaries in order to densely fill in the map.

3 Select three different ink colors that represent the country or area. Look over the map you printed and choose a color for each region or state, aiming to distribute the colors so that they're separate, making it easy to see the different areas in the final artwork. Once you've chosen your inks, alternate using them to go over the pencil draft.

4 When the ink is completely dry, carefully erase the pencil guidelines. At this point, you may see gaps that need to be filled. Add any extra flourishes needed, and your map is complete.

STYLE

Lasso lettering is perfect for projects like this because its many flourishes allow you to densely fill in areas.

Rotate your paper freely to achieve optimal writing angles. Don't forget to take breaks and check your posture frequently as you're inking.

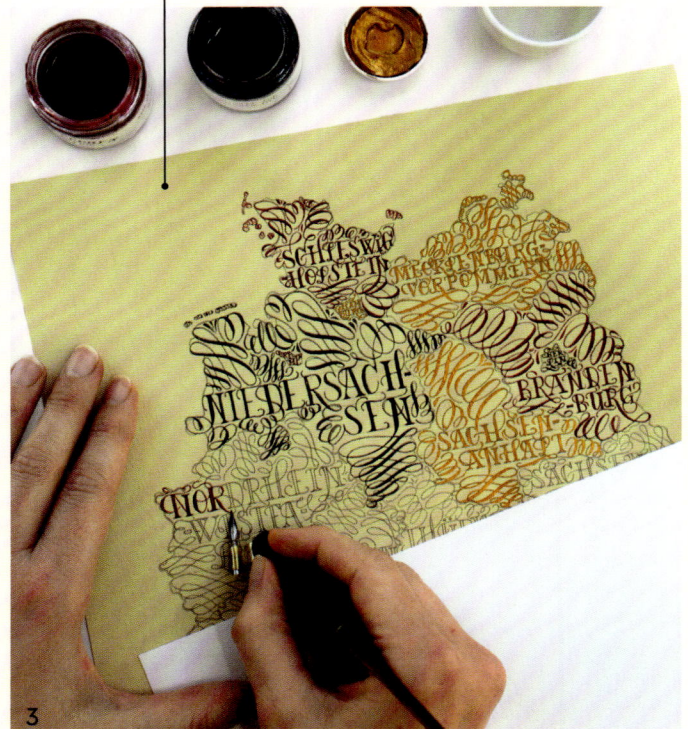

3

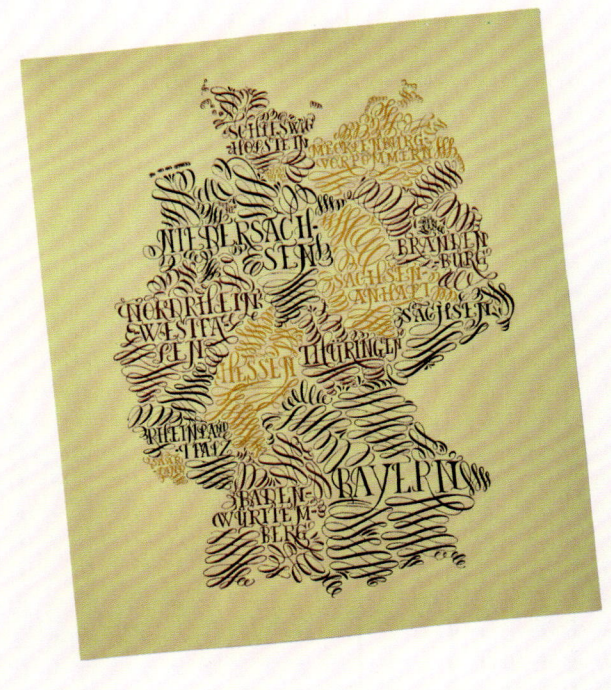

4

Flourished map

Filigree leaf bookmark

This exquisite gold-and-silver bookmark combines intricate natural designs with the timeless elegance of precious metals. Featuring an inspirational quote designed to uplift the reader's spirit, it's an ideal gift for book lovers.

● **DIFFICULTY**
intermediate

With delicate lines, a beautiful shimmer, and a deliberate process, illustrating "filigree" leaves is a therapeutic escape. It's the ideal project for those hectic days when you need a mindful retreat from reality.

What really makes this project stand out is its use of metallic watercolors instead of traditional inks. Mix your paint to a creamy consistency following the instructions on pages 130–131, and brush it onto the back of your nib, reloading as often as needed.

A short quote of 6–8 words is best for a project of this size; any longer and the text will be hard to read. I have chosen a favorite Spanish phrase among bookworms: *Leer es soñar con los ojos abiertos* ("Reading is dreaming with open eyes").

As with any project like this one that will be handled often, I strongly recommend applying a protectant or fixative spray. This will ensure the longevity of your artwork and prevent smudging or fading. Be sure to apply the fixative after the paint has fully dried.

SUPPLIES

Black cardstock

Ruler

White pencil

Gold and silver watercolor paints

Paintbrush

Pen and nib (such as the Nikko G)

Black eraser

Fixative (optional but recommended)

STYLE

This project can be done in any calligraphy style. Here, Janet style (see pp.90–97) complements the timelessness of the gold-and-silver design.

Gold and silver watercolors make this project sing in the light.

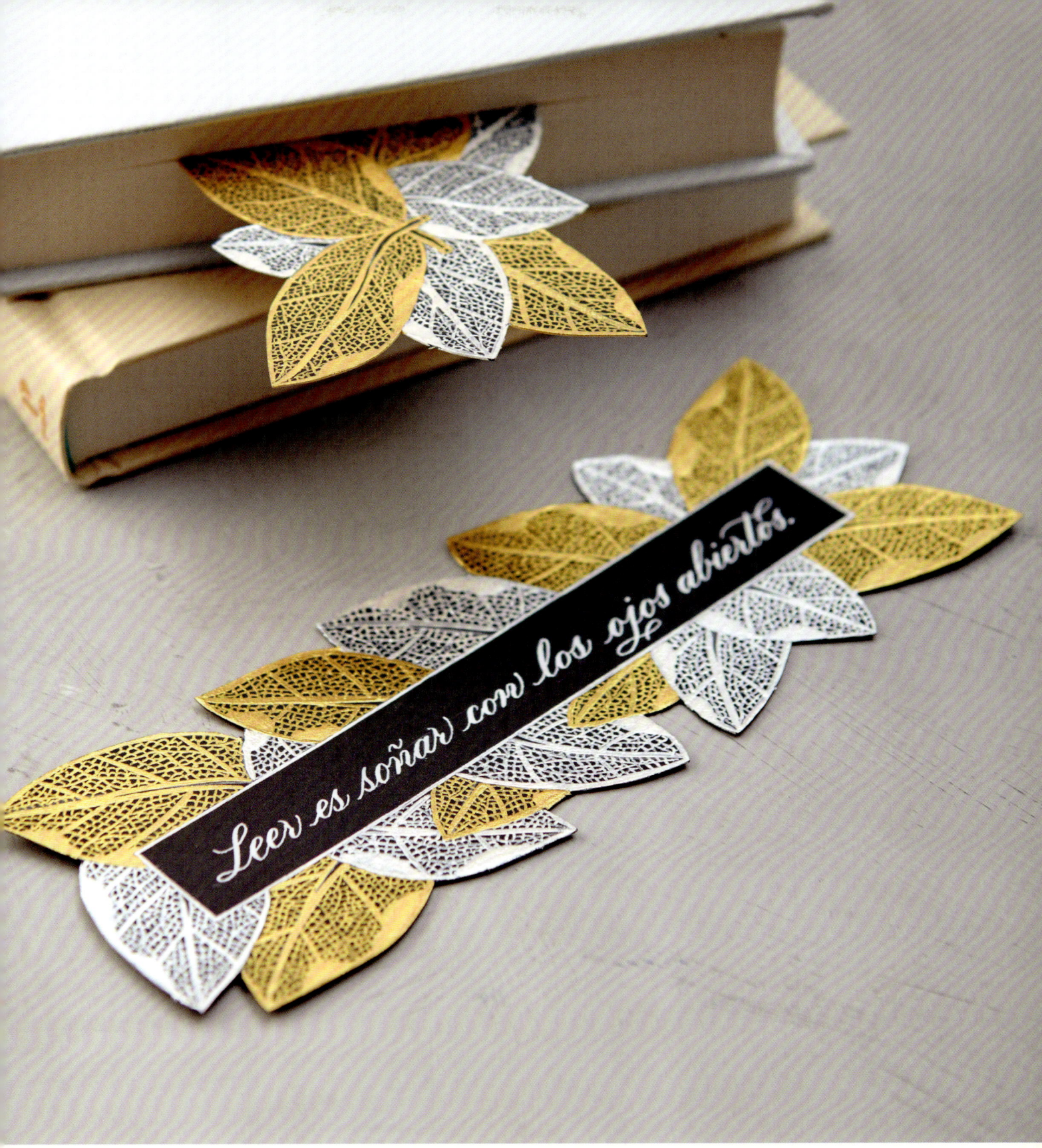

Filigree leaf bookmark

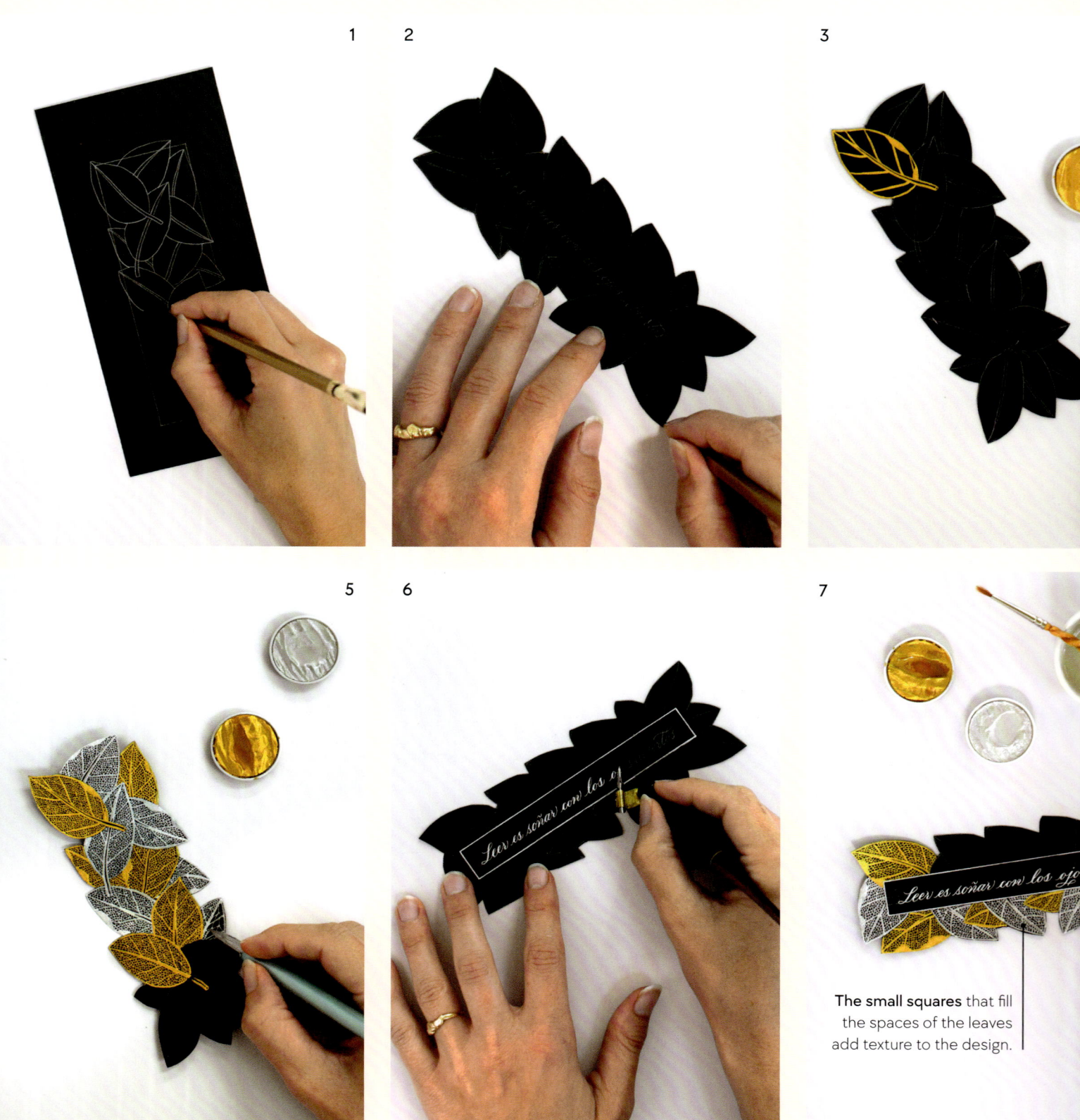

The small squares that fill the spaces of the leaves add texture to the design.

4

Draw irregular lines through the "Y" shapes between the larger veins.

8

Let fully dry before erasing pencil lines

Leer es soñar con los ojos abiertos.

1 Use your ruler and white pencil to draw a 2x6in (5x15cm) rectangle on the cardstock. Add a number of leaf shapes, positioned so that the edges extend slightly beyond the boundary of the rectangle. Include only a few whole leaves in the design, with the rest peeking out from behind them.

2 Cut out the design around the leaf edges, then turn the cardstock over. With your ruler and pencil, draw a ⅞x5in (2x12.5cm) box. Inside, draft a short calligraphic quote; then, using the leaf-shaped edges as guides, draw more leaves around the border of the box.

3 Turn to the leaf-only side. Prepare your watercolor (see p.130), and use it to trace over each leaf's outline with bold, confident strokes. Add 3–4 thick diagonal lines each side of the central vein, followed by two thicker areas on one side of each leaf.

4 With light pressure, draw thin, upside-down "Y" shapes between the diagonal veins, then add uneven lines through the center of the "Y" shapes.

Once this is complete, with even lighter pressure, draw tiny squarelike shapes to fill in the rest of the leaf.

5 Alternate using gold and silver watercolor to repeat the process for all the leaves.

6 Once this side has fully dried, turn it over. Using silver watercolor, trace over the rectangle with a thick, steady line, then trace over the calligraphic quote.

7 Repeat steps 3–4 to add the leaves on this side of the bookmark.

8 Once everything has fully dried, use a black eraser to erase any visible pencil lines. Apply a fixative spray or protectant, if possible.

Tip

Take it slow

This project is simple to make, but it takes a lot of time to draw the veins and fill in each leaf. Enjoy the process; I find that drawing the tiny squares is a mindful, relaxing activity—and the time you take to get the details right will make the final gift so much more rewarding.

Filigree leaf bookmark

Glossary

ascender: the upward part of a letter that goes above the x-height

baseline: the guideline that the letters rest on

bleeding: when ink spreads out across the paper outside the letterforms (also known as "feathering")

block letterforms: letters that are not joined together; typically characterized by simple, straight lines and clear, distinct shapes

descender: the part of a letter that goes below the baseline

draft: a pencil version of your calligraphy that you will later go over with ink

drill: an exercise done repeatedly to practice different elements of calligraphy such as letter formation, stroke consistency, and pen control

exemplar: a reference model or sample of an alphabet that demonstrates the letterforms and stylistic elements of a specific calligraphy style

feathering: similar to bleeding, when ink spreads out across the page outside the letterforms

flex: the ability of a nib to spread its tines under pressure, creating varying line thicknesses

flourish: decorative stroke added to or around letters to enhance their appearance

gouache: a type of opaque watercolor paint that can be used to write calligraphy

GSM: abbreviations used to indicate grams per square meter, used to measure the weight of different papers

lb (pounds): measurement used to indicate how much different papers weigh

lowercase: small letters that are not capital/uppercase letters

nib: the metal part of a writing instrument used to create calligraphy

oblique pen holder: a pen holder with an angled flange that holds the nib at an angle; especially useful for right-handed calligraphers

parallel glider: a ruler that rolls up and down so that you can create parallel or vertical lines; it's especially useful for creating calligraphy guidelines

pen holder: a handle that looks like a pen and is designed to hold a calligraphy nib, allowing for comfortable and controlled writing

pointed pen: a pen with a nib that is used to create calligraphy

sans serif: block letterforms that don't have decorative lines or tails; often used in modern typeface styles

serif: a small decorative line or tail that is part of a letter

stroke contrast: the difference between thick and thin strokes in calligraphy

tines: the two prongs at the tip of a nib that split apart to control ink flow and create varying line thicknesses

top line: the highest line on calligraphy guidelines; capital letters reach up to this line

uppercase: capital letters that are typically larger and often used to begin sentences and proper nouns

upstroke: a stroke made by moving the pen upward, applying less pressure to create a thinner line

x-height: the distance between the baseline and the average height of a lowercase letter

Resources

NIBS

Low-flex nibs: Good options include the Tachikawa T-600 and the Gillott 1158. Most crowquill nibs are also low-flex.

Medium-flex nibs: The two widely known beginner nibs are the Nikko G and the Zebra G. Other excellent medium-flex choices include the Gillott 303, Leonardt Principal, and Leonardt Hiro 41.

High-flex nibs: Look for the Hunt 22, Brause EF66, Brause Rose, or the Hunt 101 Imperial.

Crowquill nibs: Try the Tachikawa T-99 Maru, the Hunt 108, and the Leonardt Hiro 800.

PAPER

Laserjet paper: 80lb (120gsm) HP Premium Laserjet. This paper is great for practicing and printing guidelines and worksheets.

Smooth and high-quality cotton paper: recommended brands include Indian Cotton Paper Co. cotton paper. For classic, sumptuous luxury, try Crane & Co.

Watercolor paper: Try Strathmore cold press and Stonehenge Aqua cold press.

Paper pads: Rhodia, Tomoe River, and Clairefontaine all make quality papers that are suitable for both practice and projects.

OBLIQUE PEN HOLDERS

If you're looking for an oblique pen that will securely hold several different kinds of nibs, get a Nikko G oblique. The Nikko G nib has a fairly standard shank size, so oblique pens fitted for the Nikko G can also accommodate nibs that have a similar shank size. Examples include the Brause Steno, the Hunt 22, and the Hiro 41. Some nibs, like the Brause EF66, require a brass flange.

STRAIGHT PEN HOLDERS

A Tachikawa T-40 pen works for using most standard nibs plus several crowquill nibs.

PAINTS AND INKS

Gouache: Note that not all gouache is suitable for calligraphy use. When it comes to gouache, quality matters, and you'll need to source a gouache with very finely ground pigment particles that flow off your pen. My favorite gouache is Schmincke Calligraphy Gouache.

Watercolor: Some jarred watercolors, like Ecoline Liquid Watercolors and Dr. Ph. Martin's Hydrus Fine Art Watercolors, have a runny viscosity. You can use them as inks by dipping your pen directly into the paint. For a metallic ink, try Finetec watercolor and use a paintbrush to apply to your nib. For gorgeous portable artist-grade watercolors, try Greenleaf & Blueberry.

Sumi ink: Yasutomo makes velvety ink with a matte finish.

India ink: Dr. Ph. Martin's makes user-friendly India inks in a variety of vibrant colors.

Iron gall ink: Rousy iron gall ink is a favorite; Walker's Copperplate is also an excellent choice.

Walnut ink: Daniel Smith ink is a modern, synthetic ink designed to mimic the rich, warm brown tones of traditional walnut ink. It's my favorite walnut-like ink. To make your own walnut ink, look for walnut ink crystals.

Waterproof ink: Ziller ink is the perfect waterproof ink. Ziller Soot Black ink is totally smudge-proof and waterproof, and can be diluted with water when needed to improve ink flow.

White ink: Dr. Ph. Martin's Bleedproof White is a great white calligraphy ink. Dr. Ph. Martin's "Pen White Ink" was formulated specifically for calligraphy, although the dipper bottle can be cumbersome to use.

Metallic ink: Dr. Ph. Martin's Iridescent inks are dippable metallic inks. Another option is Lumiere by Jacquard, an acrylic paint that needs to be diluted with water to make it suitable for writing.

Mica powder: Look for PearlEx, a powdered pigment that can be used to add shimmer to your ink.

MISCELLANEOUS

Gum arabic: Winsor and Newton makes a high-quality liquid gum arabic, while Jacquard makes a good powdered gum arabic.

Protectant: MicroGlaze is a good product to use when you want to protect your work from fingermarks and other marks.

Paintbrushes: Look for something with a bristle head that's about $\frac{1}{16}$in (2mm) wide like a size 3 Winsor & Newton Sceptre Gold brush.

Templates

Elaborate mail art
(pp.140–143)

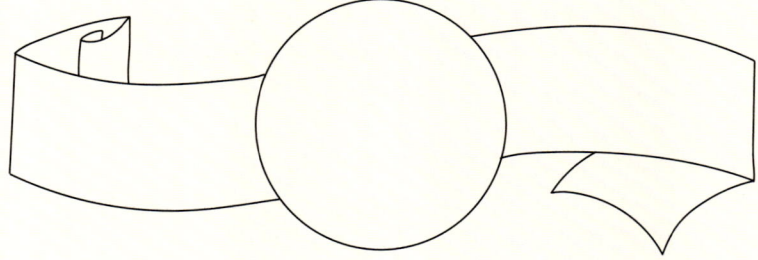

Twist-out tree holiday card
(pp.148–151)

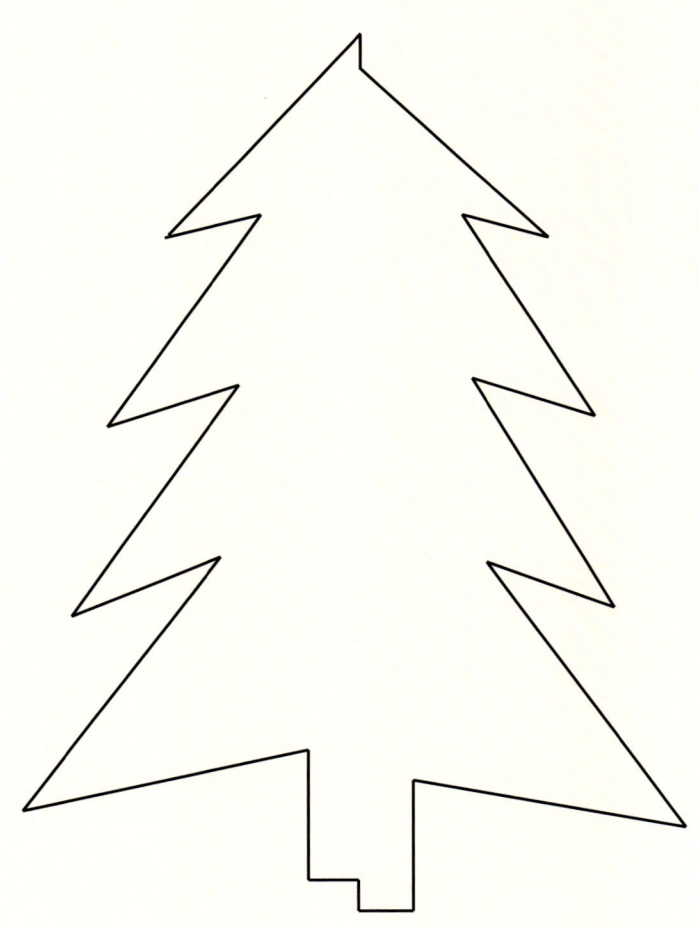

Letter from Santa
(pp.152-153)

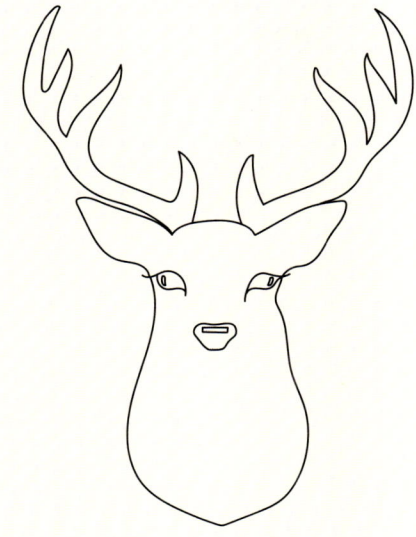

Paper ornaments
(pp.154–155)

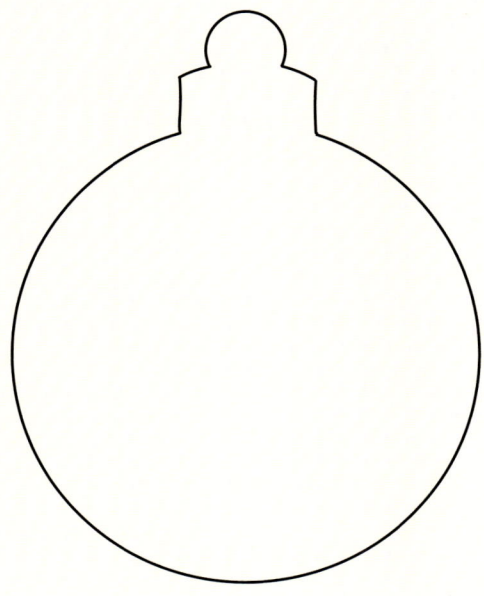

Templates

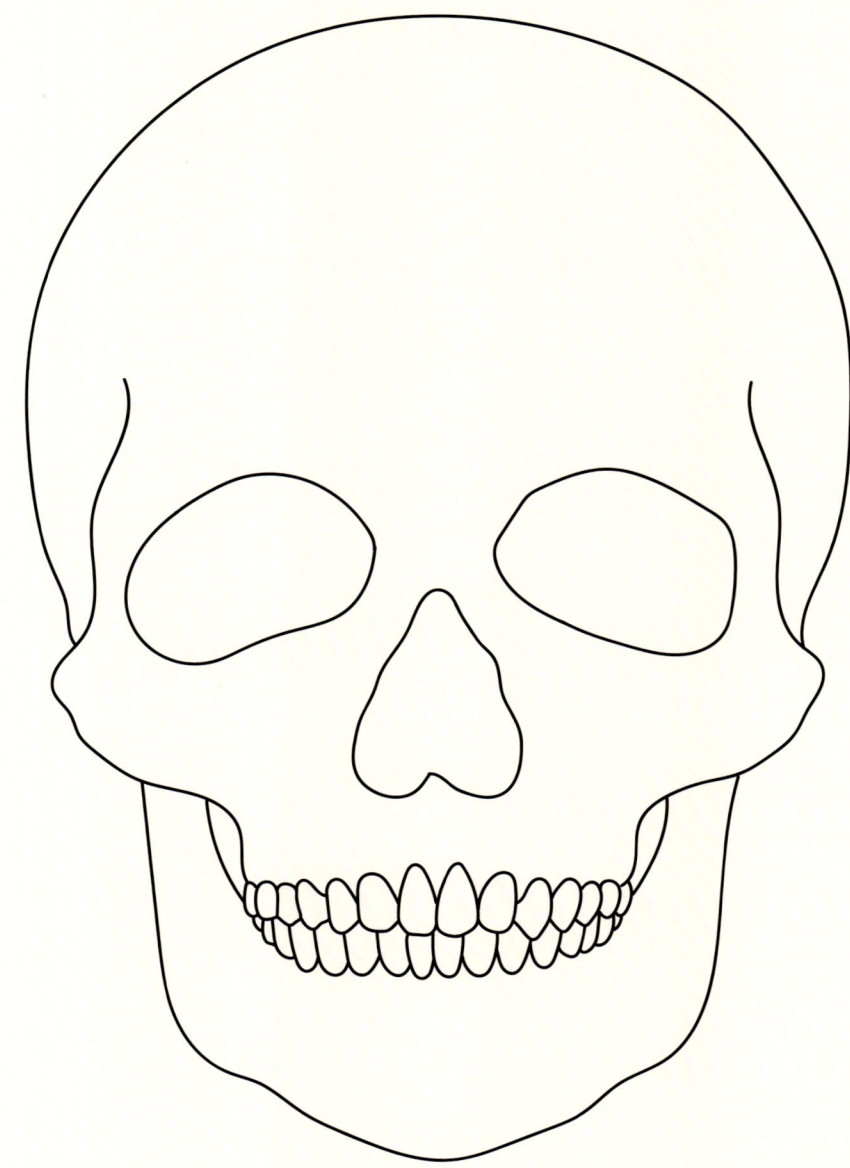

Butterfly Mother's Day card
(pp.158–161)

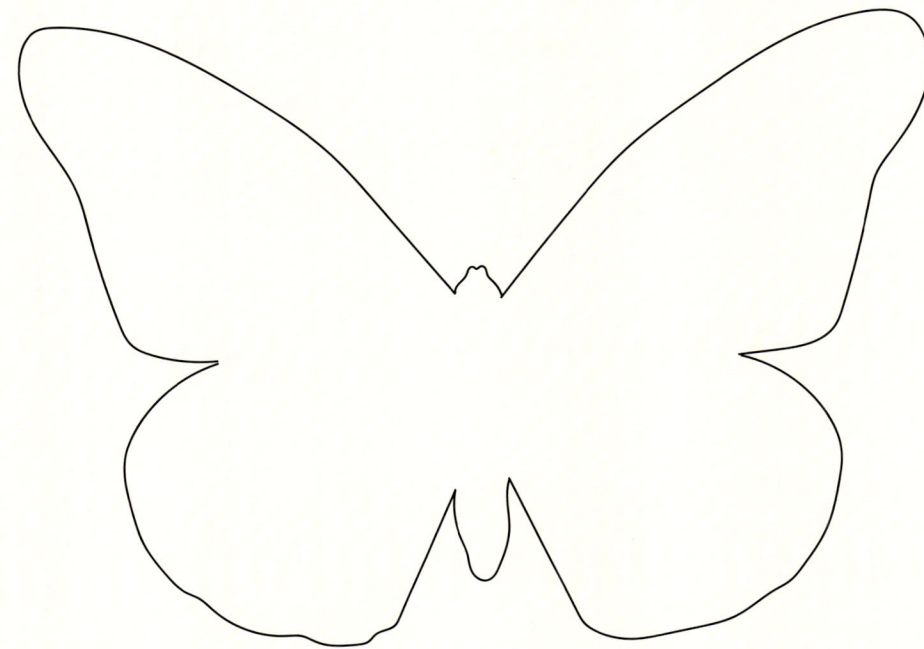

Nursery art
(pp.186–187)

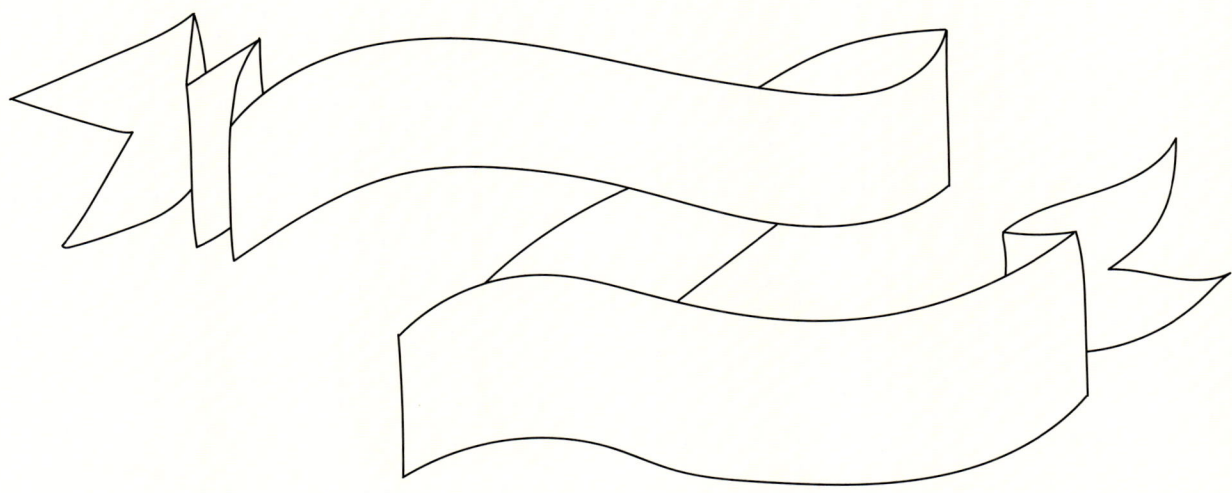

Index

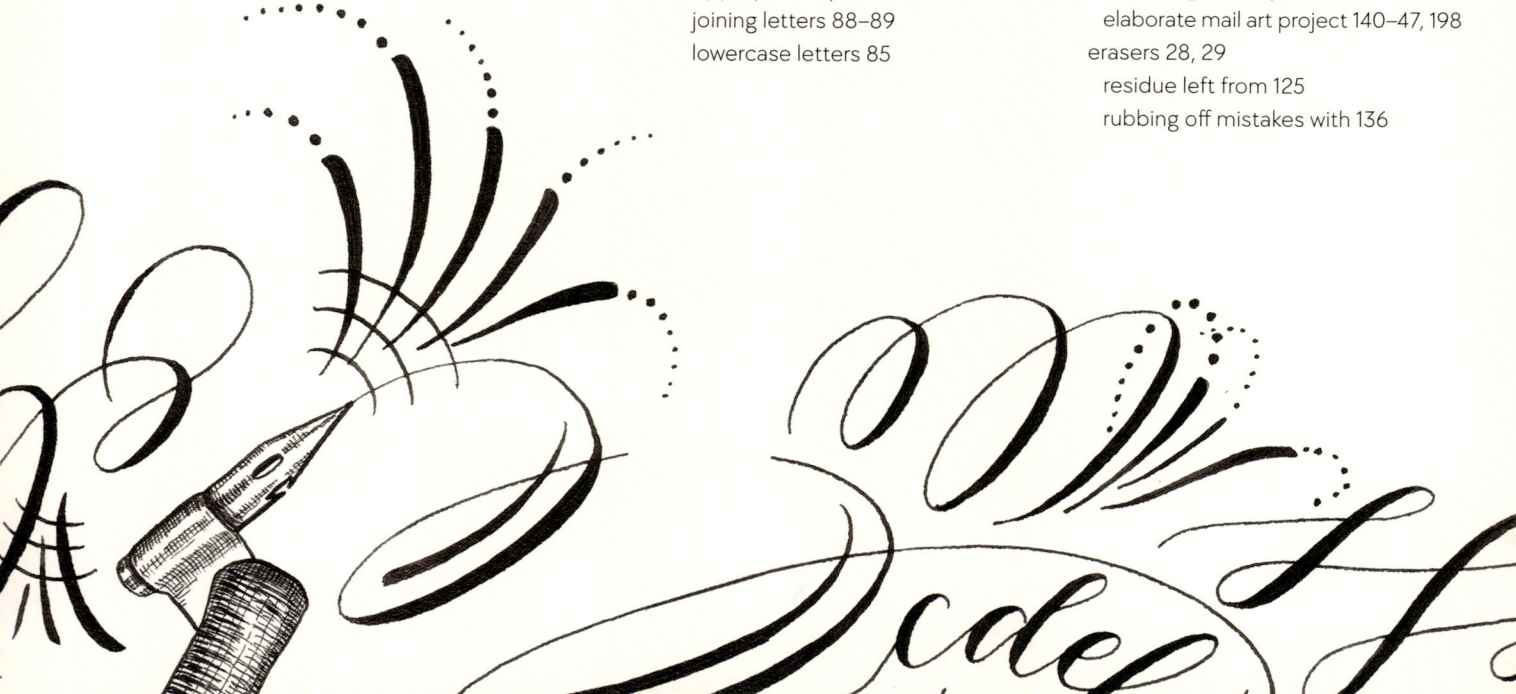

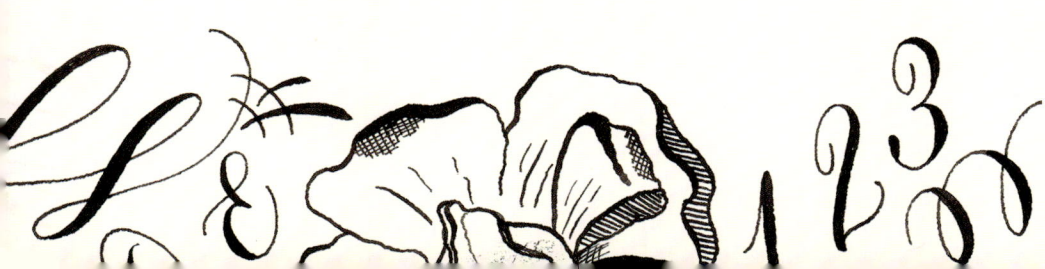

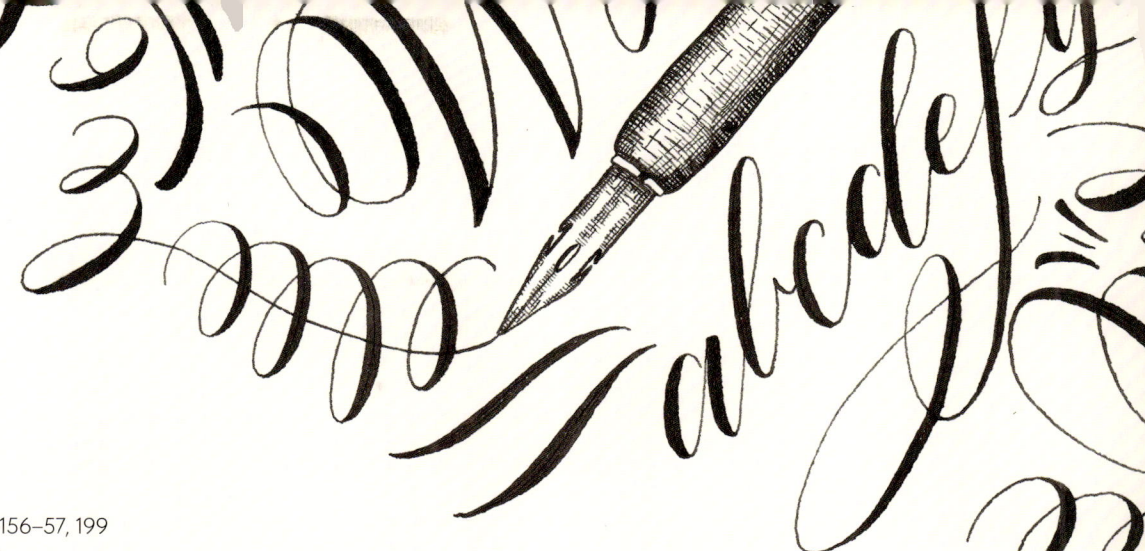

Acknowledgments

Author's acknowledgments

First, I want to thank you for picking up this book. I hope that you feel excited about your own capabilities after reading it. Remember—everyone starts somewhere, and I truly believe that anyone who feels excited about pointed pen calligraphy can master it.

It's important to say that a book like this isn't just the work of one person. On a micro level, it mainly came about as the result of the hard work of four creative women: myself, Jordan Lambley, Amy Slack, and Nicola Hodgson. We collaborated on a deeply effective level, and, while I'm so happy that this book is out in the world, you can be assured that I'm missing my "coworkers" at DK.

More broadly speaking, I am grateful to so many people—this space can't accommodate them all. First and foremost, I have my readers at The Postman's Knock (TPK) to thank for all the encouragement, support, and feedback that I've received over the years. My husband, Hernán, never wavers in supporting my goals. When I come up with an idea that seems too big, he always helps me make it happen. Jess Greenleaf is the sister I never had, and she keeps me well supplied with ideas and artist-grade Greenleaf & Blueberry watercolors. My dear friend Rodger Mayeda has supported TPK in every conceivable way, and he made many of the oblique pens you see in this book. My longtime art teacher, Donna Roberts, planted the seed for all of this with her gentle encouragement to always see the bigger picture, both literally and figuratively. My family has also played a huge part in my artistic development. My mother has influenced my aesthetic enormously, and my father, brothers, nieces, and nephew are among my biggest cheerleaders. Though my children are too young to understand what I do, they give me so much inspiration. When I became a mother, I entered a new chapter in my creativity, allowing my work to mature and gain more meaning and depth. Thanks, too, to my friends in Colorado and beyond who helped me stay grounded and motivated throughout the year that I worked to create this book. I feel so lucky to have all of you in my life.

Publisher's acknowledgments

DK would like to thank Dan Crisp for additional illustrations, Steve Crozier, Pankaj Sharma, and Jagtar Singh for repro work, Francesco Piscitelli for proofreading, and Vanessa Bird for indexing.

Image credits

The publisher would like to thank the following for their kind permission to reproduce their photographs:
(Key: a-above; b-below/bottom; c-centre; f-far; l-left; r-right; t-top)

135 Getty Images / iStock: bruce7 (b)
All other images © Dorling Kindersley Limited

About the author

Lindsey Bugbee is a renowned calligrapher and artist whose passion for lettering and design has captivated a global audience. With a meticulous eye for detail and a love for creativity, Lindsey has established herself as a leading figure in the world of modern calligraphy, handwriting, and artistic expression.

Lindsey has always been interested in creating and sharing art in a variety of mediums. Throughout her secondary school years, she earned national awards for her illustration and batik work. While at university, she immersed herself in the art of language, studying English and French literature. As part of her academic journey, she took a semester abroad to include living, traveling, and studying art history in Florence and Paris.

Lindsey is the founder of The Postman's Knock, where she shares her expertise, tutorials, and inspiration with a community of aspiring calligraphers and artists. Through her blog, she has inspired thousands to pick up a pen and explore the art of beautiful writing. Lindsey's work is characterized by its elegance and versatility, seamlessly blending traditional techniques with contemporary styles. Her calligraphy and illustrations have been featured in numerous publications and have adorned everything from wedding invitations to personal keepsakes. Her approachable teaching style and comprehensive guides make her a beloved mentor to many who are new to the art form.

In addition to her blog, Lindsey offers online courses and worksheets, where she breaks down complex techniques into easy-to-follow steps, ensuring that students of all skill levels can achieve stunning results. Her dedication to her craft and her ability to connect with her audience have made her a respected and cherished figure in the calligraphy community. Lindsey resides in Boulder, Colorado, with her husband, Hernán, and their two children, Remy and Pia. When she's not creating art or teaching, she enjoys cozy days with friends filled with good conversation, enhancing her home's hygge factor, and experimenting with new recipes from her growing collection of cookbooks. You might also find her at the farmers' market, tending to her garden, honing her Spanish skills, exploring the Boulder trails with her son, or planning her family's next travel adventure.

Discover Lindsey's work online at:
Website: www.thepostmansknock.com
Instagram: thepostmansknock
Youtube: LindseyBugbeeTPK
Facebook: thepostmansknock
Pinterest: thepostmansknock

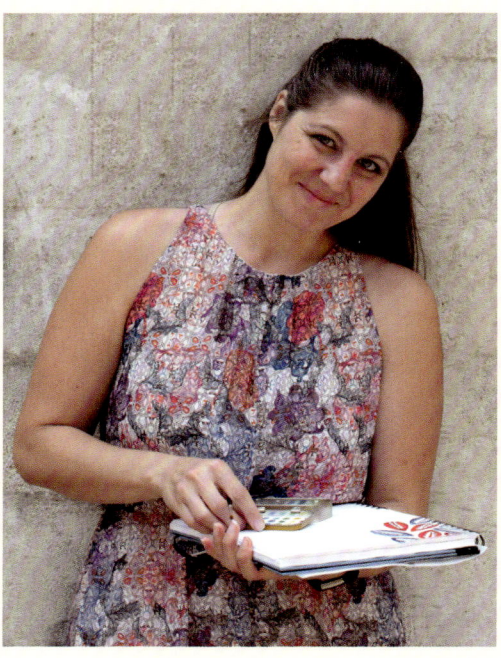

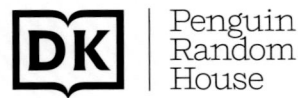

Acquisitions Editor Amy Slack
Senior Acquisitions Editor Zara Anvari, Becky Alexander
US Senior Editor Jennette ElNaggar
Project Art Editor Jordan Lambley
Production Editor David Almond
Production Controller Luca Bazzoli
Jacket Designer Jordan Lambley
Sales Material & Jackets Coordinator Emily Cannings
Editorial Manager Clare Double
Art Director Maxine Pedliham
Publishing Director Katie Cowan

Editorial Nicola Hodgson
Design Emma Forge, Tom Forge
Photography Lindsey Bugbee, Nigel Wright

First American Edition, 2024
Published in the United States by DK Publishing,
a division of Penguin Random House LLC
1745 Broadway, 20th Floor, New York, NY 10019

A catalog record for this book
is available from the Library of Congress.
ISBN 978-0-5938-4154-9

DK books are available at special discounts when purchased in bulk
for sales promotions, premiums, fund-raising, or educational use.
For details, contact: DK Publishing Special Markets,
1745 Broadway, 20th Floor, New York, NY 10019
SpecialSales@dk.com

Printed and bound in China

www.dk.com

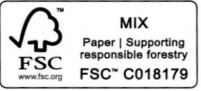

This book was made with Forest
Stewardship Council™ certified
paper—one small step in DK's
commitment to a sustainable future.
Learn more at www.dk.com/uk/
information/sustainability